AF837901

Palgrave Studies in the History of Economic Thought

Series Editors
Avi J. Cohen
Department of Economics
York University & University of Toronto
Toronto, ON, Canada

G. C. Harcourt
School of Economics
University of New South Wales
Sydney, NSW, Australia

Peter Kriesler
School of Economics
University of New South Wales
Sydney, NSW, Australia

Jan Toporowski
Economics Department
School of Oriental & African Studies
University of London
London, UK

Palgrave Studies in the History of Economic Thought publishes contributions by leading scholars, illuminating key events, theories and individuals that have had a lasting impact on the development of modern-day economics. The topics covered include the development of economies, institutions and theories.

More information about this series at
http://www.palgrave.com/gp/series/14585

Alexandre M. Cunha ·
Carlos Eduardo Suprinyak
Editors

Political Economy and International Order in Interwar Europe

palgrave
macmillan

Editors
Alexandre M. Cunha
Cedeplar
Universidade Federal de Minas Gerais
Belo Horizonte, Minas Gerais, Brazil

Carlos Eduardo Suprinyak
Cedeplar
Universidade Federal de Minas Gerais
Belo Horizonte, Minas Gerais, Brazil

ISSN 2662-6578 ISSN 2662-6586 (electronic)
Palgrave Studies in the History of Economic Thought
ISBN 978-3-030-47104-0 ISBN 978-3-030-47102-6 (eBook)
https://doi.org/10.1007/978-3-030-47102-6

© The Editor(s) (if applicable) and The Author(s), under exclusive license to Springer Nature Switzerland AG 2021
This work is subject to copyright. All rights are solely and exclusively licensed by the Publisher, whether the whole or part of the material is concerned, specifically the rights of translation, reprinting, reuse of illustrations, recitation, broadcasting, reproduction on microfilms or in any other physical way, and transmission or information storage and retrieval, electronic adaptation, computer software, or by similar or dissimilar methodology now known or hereafter developed.
The use of general descriptive names, registered names, trademarks, service marks, etc. in this publication does not imply, even in the absence of a specific statement, that such names are exempt from the relevant protective laws and regulations and therefore free for general use.
The publisher, the authors and the editors are safe to assume that the advice and information in this book are believed to be true and accurate at the date of publication. Neither the publisher nor the authors or the editors give a warranty, expressed or implied, with respect to the material contained herein or for any errors or omissions that may have been made. The publisher remains neutral with regard to jurisdictional claims in published maps and institutional affiliations.

Cover illustration: © Chrissie

This Palgrave Macmillan imprint is published by the registered company Springer Nature Switzerland AG
The registered company address is: Gewerbestrasse 11, 6330 Cham, Switzerland

Preface

We all seem to have aged faster than usual in the past few weeks, if not for the worries and anguish of a moment of profound uncertainty, simply because time appears to move quicker before our eyes. Streets, public spaces, and tourist sites in the world's major cities all suddenly empty due to the collective effort to fight the COVID-19 pandemic reflect the seriousness of the moment we are living and the deep transformations that are taking place, whose results are still difficult to foresee at present.

An intriguing and fascinating aspect of historical analyses is their capacity to reveal that the time of history is not the same as the time of physics. Historical time can sometimes move much faster than the ticking of the clock or stretch itself to the point of appearing almost motionless. Periods of substantive transformations tend to amplify this perception of acceleration in historical time. While trying to interpret the meaning of these transformations as they occur tends to be an innocuous effort, at least from the historian's point of view, history can help us gauge the scope and depth of the rising challenges. The many apparent parallels between our own time and the interwar period provided one of motivations for the present volume. At first, these similarities referred mostly to the rise of populist nationalistic political regimes and the economic ideologies underpinning them, which strained the fabric of the established international order. The outbreak of a global pandemic in 2020—whose closest parallel is the 1918 influenza pandemic, the "Spanish Flu"—only further convinced us that the interwar period can bring new layers of meaning to the analysis of our current predicaments.

This book originated as part of a research project developed within the scope of the Jean Monnet Chair "Economics, Political Economy and the Building of the European Integration Project" (co-funded by the Erasmus+ program of the European Union), based at the School of Economics of the Federal University of Minas Gerais (UFMG), Brazil. When we wrote the application for this grant in late 2016, stressing the importance of the interwar period for understanding the European integration process, we did not anticipate the extent to which current political and economic dilemmas would come to mirror the problems that plagued the interwar period, especially the favorable ambiance to the growth of political extremism and the coming to power of governments with a strong authoritarian bent in large and important democracies around the world. In other words, flirting with fascism was not yet on the horizon when the project was written. Nevertheless, this question was very much present in February 2019, when we gathered at the Institute of Social Sciences, University of Lisbon, to present and discuss the first drafts of the chapters contained in this book during the workshop "Interwar Economics and the Intellectual Origins of European Integration", jointly hosted by UFMG's Jean Monnet Chair and the Research Group *Power, Society and Globalization* of the Institute of Social Sciences. Besides giving the contributors ample feedback on how to improve the arguments developed in their individual chapters, the workshop also reinforced our sense of the overlapping themes and concerns that connected our different research interests and perspectives.

As we now write this preface, in May 2020, the world has witnessed with perplexity the unsettling effects of a pandemic on health systems, economic activity, and social order more generally, and we still do not know how much longer the crisis will persist. Most prognostics indicate the world will face its worst economic recession since the Great Depression of the 1930s; coming to grips with the situation and planning for the near future will be a daunting task. All of a sudden, we can see in a different light the attention given to the notion of uncertainty by interwar economists such as John Maynard Keynes and Frank Knight—just one evident example of how ideas developed then can shed new light on the challenges we face now.

The historian's craft does not involve futurology. Nevertheless, given this game of truncated reenactments of the past we sometimes seem to be playing, one might do well to consider that we may be experiencing a decisive shift in history. For this very reason, it seems instructive to remember that the Spanish flu was followed by the Roaring Twenties, but also by the 1930s depression and the dark events that led to the Second World War. May we know how to avoid at least the tragedies that are in our control.

We wish to express our gratitude to several institutions and individuals who have contributed decisively to making this volume possible. First of all, we thank the European Union's Erasmus+ Program for supporting the research that originated this volume, funded through a Jean Monnet Chair grant (Project number 587558-EPP-1-2017-1-BR-EPPJMO-CHAIR).

Other funding agencies have also contributed to support different parts of this project. We thank the Brazilian National Research Council (CNPq) and the Coordination for the Improvement of Higher Education Personnel (CAPES) for their support to our individual research activities. We also thank the Institute of Social Sciences at the University of Lisbon for the warm welcome and logistical support extended to the workshop "Interwar Economics and the Intellectual Origins of European Integration." We are especially grateful to Prof. José Luis Cardoso, who co-organized the event with us, and to Maria Margarida Bernardo for her assistance with many practical issues.

Our own university, UFMG, has been providing privileged conditions for the development of research and teaching activities in the field of European integration studies over the past few years, even in the face of drastic reductions in resources for scientific research in Brazil. Special thanks are due to the Center for European Studies and to UFMG's International Office—notably to Prof. Fabio Alves, who served as Dean of International Affairs when this project began—as well as to the Economics Department and the Center for Development and Regional Planning, which provided an institutional base for the Jean Monnet Chair.

We wish to thank Palgrave Macmillan for their careful editorial work and assistance, and especially our commissioning editor, Elizabeth Graber, for her interest and confidence in this project since our first meeting in Bogotá in 2017, during the 6th Conference of the Latin American Society for the History of Economic Thought (ALAHPE).

The chapters contained in this book went through an extensive peer review process that contributed much to improving the original drafts.

We thank the anonymous referees who helped us for their availability and competence in carrying out this task.

We also wish to thank a group of colleagues who contributed their criticism and comments at different stages of this project, namely Guilherme Sampaio, Nicolas Brisset, Marcel Boumans, Quinn Slobodian, Mauro Boianovsky, Susan Howson, Michael Ambrosi, Anthony Howe, Dieter Plehwe, Scott Scheall, Joseph Love, Fabio Masini, Joseph Persky, Liane Hewitt, and Luiz Felipe Bruzzi Curi.

Finally, our special thanks go to all the colleagues who contributed the fruits of their research to this book, thus enriching our project with such diverse and insightful perspectives on interwar history and its aftermath.

Alexandre M. Cunha, in a personal note, would also like to thank the constant support and love of his wife, Tarsila. She, our almost three-year-old son Caio, and our soon-to-be daughter, always bring light to my cloudy days and, simply, make me happy.

Belo Horizonte, Brazil
May 2020

Alexandre M. Cunha
Carlos Eduardo Suprinyak

Contents

Notes on Contributors

Katia Caldari is Associate Professor of Economics in the Department of Economics and Management at the University of Padova, Italy. She received her Ph.D. in History of Economic Thought from the University of Florence. She collaborated with the Marshall Library of Economics for the Marshall's Archive, and with several universities including the University of Rome and Osaka University. Caldari has been an invited guest for the Associate Research Directors Program at the Fondation Maison des Sciences de l'Homme and has collaborated with the Université Côte d'Azur. She has been a member of the Executive Committee and Secretary General of the Italian Association for the History of Political Economy (STOREP), European Association for the History of Economic Thought (ESHET) Council, and the ESHET Executive Committee. Her main interests are the contributions of Alfred Marshall, François Perroux, and Robert Marjolin, and French economic planning. She has published several articles on these topics.

José Luís Cardoso is Research Professor at the Institute of Social Sciences of the University of Lisbon, Portugal. He is author and editor of several books on the Portuguese history of economic thought from a comparative perspective, with special emphasis on the study of the processes of diffusion and assimilation of economic ideas. He has published articles in the main international journals on the history of economic thought. His research topics also include political, economic, and financial history of the eighteenth to twentieth centuries. He is the general editor of the series Classics of Portuguese Economic Thought (30 vols.), co-founder of *The European Journal of the History of Economic Thought* and co-editor of the e-journal of Portuguese History. He was President of the European Society for the History of Economic Thought in 2014–2016.

Alexandre M. Cunha is Associate Professor of Economics at the Federal University of Minas Gerais (UFMG), Brazil. He specializes in the history of economic thought and intellectual history, studying the international diffusion of economic ideas in different historical contexts, with emphasis on eighteenth century Enlightenment studies and Europe in the interwar and immediate postwar periods. He was the head of the university's Centre for European Studies (2014–2018), the Academic Coordinator of a Jean Monnet Module (2015–2018) and currently the holder of a Jean Monnet Chair (2017–2020), granted by the Erasmus+ Programme of the European Union. Since 2016, he has also served as a member of the Council of the European Society for the History of Economic Thought (ESHET).

Erwin Dekker is Assistant Professor of Cultural Economics at the Erasmus University Rotterdam, The Netherlands. He is also post-doctoral fellow at the Mercatus Center at George Mason University. He is working on an intellectual biography of Jan Tinbergen, the first Nobel Prize winner in Economics, which will be published in 2020. He published the book *The Viennese Students of Civilization* (2016) on the cultural context of the Austrian School of Economics. His research focuses on the intersection of art, culture, and economics. He has published in articles in the fields of Cultural Economics, Austrian economics, Economic Methodology, and Intellectual History, and he is also working on an edited volume with the working title *Governing Markets as Knowledge Commons*.

Raphaël Fèvre is Post-doctoral Researcher at the Centre Walras Pareto of the University of Lausanne, Switerland. Fèvre works on topics in history of economic thought and methodology of the twentieth century. He is particularly interested in understanding how the dual trend of fascination and repulsion vis-à-vis the rise of authoritarian European regimes contributed to shape some of the central intellectual debates of the interwar period.

Harald Hagemann is Professor Emeritus of Economic Theory at the University of Hohenheim, Germany. He is also a Life Member of Clare

Hall, University of Cambridge and an Honorary Fellow of the Brazilian Association of Graduate Schools in Economics ANPEC. In the academic year 1999/2000 he was Theodor Heuss Professor at the Graduate Faculty of Political and Social Sciences at the New School for Social Research in New York. His main research covers Growth and Structural Change, Technological Change and Employment, Business Cycle Theory, History of Economic Thought, and the emigration of German-speaking economists in the Nazi period. He is Honorary Past President of the European Society for the History of Economic Thought ESHET of which he had been President 2010–2012. From 2013 to 2019 he was Chairman of the Keynes-Gesellschaft. Currently he is the German coordinator of the trilateral VIGONI project "Fabricating Modern Economics (FAME): Italy, Germany, and France, and the Process of Transnationalization and Internationalization of Economics from the Interwar Period until 1989."

Roberto Lampa is First Grade Researcher at the National Scientific and Technical Research Council (CONICET), Argentina. He is also an Assistant Professor at the Institute of Higher Social Studies, Universidad Nacional de San Martin. He holds an International Ph.D. in History of Political Economy from the University of Macerata and a post-doc from the University of Salento. He has been a visiting scholar at the Université Paris 1 Pantheon-Sorbonne, New School for Social Research, University of Macerata, and Universidad de Buenos Aires. His current research issues at CONICET draw on over three years of case studies related to the global crisis from a historical, theoretical, and empirical angle. He is a member of the Executive Board of the Latin American Society for the History of Political Economy (ALAHPE) and a member of the Editorial Board of *Forum for Social Economics* journal.

Oksana Levkovych is Ph.D. Candidate in the Department of International Relations at The London School of Economics and Political Science, UK. She holds a Master's degree in Political Economy from King's College London and a Master's degree in English Culture from the University of Lisbon. Levkovych specializes in international political economy and the history of economic thought. She studies radical changes in the UK foreign trade policy and the break-up of international economic cooperation during the interwar period. Drawing on archival policy records, she offers an international political economy analysis from a historical, local data perspective. Her findings provide novel insights into protectionism and liberalism, explaining the interwar collapse of the international trade regime through the role of leading individuals and domestic-level policy decisions.

Antonio Masala is Senior Researcher of Political Philosophy at University of Pisa, Italy. Previously he was researcher at IMT Advanced Studies Lucca, Visiting Research Fellow at Queen Mary University of London and at Yildiz Technical University of Istanbul. Among his main research interests are classical liberalism, neoliberalism, biopolitics, populism. His latest book is *Stato, società e libertà. Da liberalismo al neoliberalismo*, Rubbettino 2017. He recently edited, with Lorenzo Viviani, the volume *L'età dei populismi. Un'analisi politica e sociale*, Carocci 2020.

Timo Miettinen is University Researcher in the Centre for European Studies at the University of Helsinki, Finland. He is also the Team Leader of the Academy of Finland funded Centre for Excellence in Law, Identity, and the European Narrative. Miettinen specializes in modern philosophy, German thought in particular, and has published widely on the topics of history, social ontology, universalism, and liberalism. His latest book Husserl and the Idea of Europe was published in 2020.

Alberto Mingardi is Associate Professor of the History of Political Thought at IULM University, Italy. He is also a presidential scholar in political theory at Chapman University, director General of the Istituto Bruno Leoni, a think tank in Milan, and an adjunct Fellow at the Cato Institute.

James Ashley Morrison is Assistant Professor in the Department of International Relations at the London School of Economics & Political Science, UK. He specializes in International Political Economy, where he has a particular interest in the influence of ideas and intellectuals on foreign economic policy. He has published on topics in economic history and the history of economic thought in the Anglophone tradition. His first book (to be published in 2021) is on JM Keynes, Winston Churchill, and the interwar gold standard.

António Costa Pinto is Research Professor in the Institute of Social Sciences at the University of Lisbon, Portugal. He has been a visiting professor at Stanford University, Georgetown University, a senior associate member at St Antony's College, Oxford, and a senior visiting fellow at Princeton University, the University of California, Berkeley and New York

University. He was president of the Portuguese Political Science Association (2006–2010) and his research interests include corporatism and authoritarianism, political elites, democratization, and transitional justice in new democracies, and the European Union. He recently published, Co-Ed., *Authoritarianism and Corporatism in Europe and Latin America* (2019).

Pierre-Hernan Rojas is Assistant Professor at the Catholic University of Paris, France. He is also associate researcher at EconomiX, a research center operated by the University of Paris-Nanterre and the CNRS. He earned his Ph.D. in economics in 2016 at the University of Paris-Dauphine, PSL Research University. His main academic interests are the history of the international monetary system and international monetary economics. He is particularly interested in the historical and theoretical background of national and international monetary reforms. His works on the interwar debates in France and Great Britain related to the restoration of the international gold standard were published in *The European Journal of the History of Economic Thought*. He is currently working on the role of money doctors in the development of modern monetary systems.

Carlos Eduardo Suprinyak is Associate Professor of Economics at the Federal University of Minas Gerais (UFMG), Brazil. He specializes in the history and methodology of economics, studying the interplay of social, political, and economic ideas in early modern England, the institutionalization of economics in Brazil during the postwar era, and the history of economics and international politics in interwar Europe. In 2017, he received the Craufurd Goodwin Best Article in the History of Economics Prize, awarded by the History of Economics Society, and in 2019, he received the ESHET Young Researcher Award. He is also co-editor of *Research in the History of Economic Thought and Methodology* and a co-host of Smith and Marx Walk into a Bar: A History of Economics Podcast.

Valerio Torreggiani is Research Fellow in the Institute of Social Sciences at the University of Lisbon, Portugal. He received his Ph.D. in the History of Europe (nineteenth- twentieth centuries) from the Tuscia University of Viterbo. He has been post-doctoral fellow in Economic History at Roma Tre University, visiting fellow at the University of Lisbon, and post-doctoral fellow in Political Economy and the History of Economic Thought at the Accademia dei Lincei of Rome. He is a member of the Network for the Analysis of Corporatism and Organized Interests (NETCOR), European Society for the History of Economic Thought (ESHET), History of International Organization Network (HION), International Association for Comparative Fascist Studies (COMFAS), Società Italiana per la Storia del Lavoro (SISLav), Società Italiana per lo Studio della Storia Contemporanea (SISSCO), and Laboratorio Italiano di Storia Economica (LISE). His main research interests include the transnational diffusion of corporatist ideas, analyzed under an interdisciplinary political, economic, juridical, and cultural perspective, with a specific attention to the British world in the first half of the twentieth Century; the history of trade unions and employers' federations; and the history of contemporary financial systems. On these topics he has authored several articles and book chapters, published in national and international peer-reviewed journals and volumes, as well as a monograph, *Stato e culture corporative nel Regno Unito* (2018), and one co-authored volume, *Istituzioni, capitali e moneta. Storia dei sistemi finanziari contemporanei* (2017).

List of Tables

CHAPTER 1

Introduction

Alexandre M. Cunha and Carlos Eduardo Suprinyak

This book discusses arguments about international order that took shape in interwar Europe, using the history of economic ideas as a privileged analytical perspective. Many of the disputes examined in the following pages, however, also touched upon another underlying topic: the history of European integration. The book itself is the result of a research project that articulates the history of economic ideas with the history of European integration, as detailed in the preface.[1] Directly or indirectly, the European integration process is thus one of the important questions

[1] This research project was developed within the scope of the Jean Monnet Chair "Economics, Political Economy and the Building of the European Integration Project" (co-funded by the Erasmus + program of the European Union), based at the School of Economics of the Federal University of Minas Gerais (UFMG), Brazil.

A. M. Cunha (✉)
Cedeplar, Universidade Federal de Minas Gerais, Belo Horizonte, Minas Gerais, Brazil
e-mail: amc@cedeplar.ufmg.br

C. E. Suprinyak
Federal University of Minas Gerais, Belo Horizonte, Brazil
e-mail: suprinyak@cedeplar.ufmg.br

© The Author(s) 2021

A. M. Cunha and C. E. Suprinyak (eds.), *Political Economy and International Order in Interwar Europe*, Palgrave Studies in the History of Economic Thought,
https://doi.org/10.1007/978-3-030-47102-6_1

motivating this volume, even if the circumstances prevailing during the interwar period meant we could only capture these longer-term trends by placing them within a broader framework. More concretely, we could say our analysis concerns the conditions of possibility underlying the process that resulted in the progressive integration of a subset of European countries in the post-World War II era.

Critical readings on the historiography of European integration have pointed to the difficulties associated with works, still rather limited in number, which trace the subject back to the interwar years, especially the 1930s. Studies often refer to the period but usually without moving beyond the same basic topics, such as Aristide Briand's proposals for a "European Union" in the League of Nations or the federalist schemes advocated by Count Richard von Coudenhove-Kalergi's Pan-Europa Movement. The interwar era, however, offers a much broader palette of relevant issues for scholarly inquiry. Developments in the history of economic ideas and political economy, for instance, can illuminate some of the key issues that sustained arguments about the reconstruction of international order, which in turn point to the more specific subject of regional integration in the European continent.

The 1920s and 1930s saw the gestation of fruitful ideas about international order, broadly considered, and the possibilities of cooperation between European nations, more specifically, without which the institutions of European integration could hardly have emerged in the immediate postwar period. To say this, however, is not to postulate the existence of a direct line of descent connecting certain visionary ideas and future institutional designs. A well-contextualized analysis of the interwar era helps us envision the multiplicity of perspectives in dispute at the time. Moreover, it illustrates how certain intellectual trends can be variously appropriated for different political and ideological purposes, serving both conservative and progressive agendas depending on the prevailing circumstances. Such questions provide the raw material for the chapters collected in this book.

1 International Order and European Integration

An important new trend in the historiography of European integration proposes a change in denomination for the field, to avoid the teleological implications—the notion of a manifest destiny—which the term "integration" carries. As sustained by Laurent Warlouzet (2014, xviii), it would be preferable to describe the field as the history of European cooperation, since "this expression refers to all interactions between European states and non-state actors since 1919, by giving value to both their diversity and intensity." "It would also make it possible," Warlouzet continues, "to restore their specificity in an overall comparison between various types of regional cooperation, or with cooperation at a global level." At least for the interwar period, the idea of cooperation certainly seems much more suited to capture the issues at stake than the alternative concept of integration.

Mark Gilbert (2008, 642) was one of the scholars responsible for motivating a debate on historiographical trends in the field of European integration studies, criticizing the pervasive notion of a progressive history, which imparts to much of the literature a belief that "integration represents a trend from which there will be no receding."[2] In an argument echoing points previously raised by Timothy Garton Ash (1996), Gilbert shows how the European Commission used its institutional weight to influence the dissemination of a history of European integration that tended to reinforce orthodox readings of this process, thus producing a "Whig history in its purest form" (Gilbert 2008, 646; see also Gilbert 2003). In this meta-narrative, the past is understood almost exclusively in terms of direct connections to present events. The current form of European integration—featuring a democratic structure of voluntary membership, the rule of law, and economic liberalism—thus becomes the primary focus of analysis, and the past is filtered through this specific and restricted set of questions.

Gilbert also identifies another problematic historiographical trend, to which political scientists contributed directly: a tendency to excessively theorize the integration process. In the hands of historians, such theoretical frameworks resulted in detailed accounts that reinforced the perception of European integration as a progressive history. Using the "institutionalist" and "structuralist" frameworks identified by Craig Parsons (2002) as an example, Gilbert (2008, 653) shows how "such interpretations are commonplace in historiography and, insofar as they provoke debate and reassessment are useful scholarly tools, but they should not be confused with comprehensive interpretations."

[2] See also, among others, Kaiser and Varsori (2010).

This serves as an important warning. The very nature of a book like this one, which aims to encourage diversity in methods, approaches, and themes, can create some expectation for a more comprehensive and unifying approach in the opening and closing chapters. This is not our ambition, however. What draws together the different analyses and results contained in each of the chapters is their attention to historical detail and context, moving away from broad theoretical frameworks that could indirectly reinforce the narrative of progressive history. Both in this introduction and in the postscript, our goal is to reinforce precisely the diversity, the various open questions, the inconsistencies found in the objects of analysis themselves and, fundamentally, the multiple paths that link past to present, including the still untrodden routes of many possible futures.

An illustration of how the interwar period offers abundant elements for tracing these untrodden routes is the proliferation of references to various ideas of Europe, declarations of common Europeanness, and multiple schemes for unification or cooperation that differed from the liberal platform that would guide the integration process after 1945. Conflicting ideas of Europe and experiences of Europeanization based on non-liberal or anti-liberal perspectives, which have only recently begun to receive their due attention, are the subject of a collective volume edited by Dieter Gosewinkel, *Anti-Liberal Europe: A Neglected Story of Europeanization* (2015). In his introduction, Gosewinkel (2015, 6) develops an argument that closely resembles our own concerns with the need for careful treatment of terms within their proper historical context: "any synchronous comparison that assumes the usage of the terms 'liberal', 'anti-liberal' and 'Europe' is semantically equivalent or even largely similar in the various European countries in, say, 1940 must fail due to profound national particularities and diversity of political semantics in intellectual history."

The very origins of neoliberalism in the interwar period offer a case in point, with direct implications for arguments about international order at the time. Investigating the dawn of the movement in France, François Denord (2001, 24–25; see also 2007) shows how many principles that contrasted with traditional liberalism informed the discussions held during the Walter Lippmann Colloquium, which converged toward a consensus recognizing several aspects in which state intervention was required to ensure the well-functioning of society. More explicitly, Quinn Slobodian opens his recent book *Globalists: The End of Empire and the Birth of*

Neoliberalism (2018) with the following clarification: "self-described neoliberals did not believe in self-regulating markets as autonomous entities. They did not see democracy and capitalism as synonymous. They did not see humans as motivated only by economic rationality. (…) In fact, the foundational neoliberal insight is comparable to that of John Maynard Keynes and Karl Polanyi: the market does not and cannot take care of itself" (Slobodian 2018, 2).

Another point that deserves attention is the remarkable coincidence of narratives about the history of European integration. As Gilbert (2008, 654) insists, "it happens only rarely that major historical developments (…) generate a broad interpretative consensus among historians in the short term." At stake here are the dramas of a relatively new discipline, whose first major works date back to the 1960s, with strong institutional and political aspects working to reinforce an orthodox story. Nevertheless, as pointed out by Kiran Patel (2019, 328), the last ten years have witnessed the emergence of a significant body of scholarship attentive to these and other pitfalls, which have contributed decisively for the field to reach a new level of maturity. One of the challenges facing this renewal is to escape the trend, identified by Warlouzet (2014), which portrays the transformations in the political dynamics and institutional design of European integration—from the establishment of the European Coal and Steel Community (ECSC) in 1951, through the European Economic Community (EEC) created by the Treaty of Rome of 1957, all the way to the European Union (EU) in 1992—as an alternating pattern of "crises" and "relaunches." Such a pattern fits well with the type of progressive history identified by Gilbert, describing a linear progression in which a crisis that threatens to disrupt the integration process elicits instead a set of reactions and institutional responses that revitalize it, thus configuring a step forward in the construction of a communitarian Europe.

These features of historical scholarship tended to produce a deliberate optimism regarding the prospects for continuous development of the European integration process. In 2008, Gilbert felt the need to close his article clarifying that the criticism he directed to this exaggerated confidence was not "Euroscepticism," but simply "common sense." The different circumstances that have recently emerged, from the 2008 crisis to the Brexit process, indicate that these rosy interpretations of the EU's historical significance must be largely requalified. The interwar period offers a privileged space where we can distance ourselves from the biases inherent in progressive histories of European integration, extending our gaze to the broad set of alternative perspectives on international order elaborated at the time. The renewed internationalism that gained momentum in Europe during the 1920s would eventually be wrecked by the economic and social crisis of the early 1930s and the escalation of tensions that finally led to a new war. Even though a different set of arguments about international order also developed during the 1930s, the image we retain from the interwar era evokes a Europe that was unable to conciliate its conflicting interests and construct a lasting peace. Economic crises, political and social tensions, aggressive conservative and nationalist rhetoric, and even authoritarian solutions are some of the defining elements of the 1930s that can cast some light on the challenges currently afflicting not only Europe but also the world.

Nevertheless, much of the diverse and prolific scholarship on interwar history—diplomatic, social, economic, political—often incorporates "progressive" narratives not unlike those found in the historiography of European integration. The temptation to think of World War II as a point of destination strongly affects historical accounts of the period, especially the 1930s. In this volume, we wish to stress that the years following World War I can be fruitfully thought of as a veritable postwar era, defined by the vivid memories of recent experience, while the term "interwar" should be understood as simply delimitating a scope, rather than postulating the existence of a continuum between the two World Wars. Likewise, our analysis of the economic and political crisis that opened the 1930s on the European continent cannot be conditioned by the escalation of tensions leading to a new military conflict at the end of the decade.

Crisis is an inescapable theme in studies of the interwar era. The analysis offered by Robert Boyce in *The Great Interwar Crisis and the Collapse of Globalization* (2009) offers interesting elements for understanding the different dynamics of economic and political trends between the 1920s and 1930s, in a thoroughly contextualized narrative that interprets the interwar experience without having World War II as the ultimate point of reference. Insisting that the 1929 crisis "remains the most thoroughly misunderstood episode of the interwar years," he explains the breaking down of the international economic and political systems not as two discrete events, but rather as causally connected developments. Boyce insists that the two systemic collapses were intimately bound up together, mutually feeding into each other in what effectively amounted to a *dual* crisis. This argument offers interesting points of contact with the studies collected in this volume, reconnecting the problems of international order and political economy that defined the period (Boyce 2009, 3–8).

The volume of scholarship tracing back the history of European integration to the interwar years remains limited, but the topic has attracted increasing attention in the wake of the critical historiographical trends discussed above. Analyzing Willy Buschak's (2014) book on the attitudes toward European integration adopted by the labor movement during the interwar period, Patel (2019, 344) describes it as "a reminder of how little we still know about such pro-European movements and activities before 1945," reinforcing the importance of this and other interwar debates for understanding the history of European integration and cooperation. Among the extensive literature discussed by Patel in his survey of recent advances in the history of European integration, he mentions two studies that resonate strongly with discussions proposed in this volume. The first is Antonin Cohen's *De Vichy à la Communauté européenne* (2012), which points to substantive continuities between third-way arguments in interwar France, some of which gained space within the institutions of the Vichy regime, and the design of the regional integration scheme enshrined by the Schuman Plan in 1950. The second work is Peo Hansen and Stefan Jonsson's *Eurafrica: The Untold History of European Integration and Colonialism* (2015), in which Africa appears as part of alternative blueprints for European integration developed during the interwar period, a vision that survived into the early stages of the post-WWII integration process, still strongly imbued with late-colonial thinking. Hansen and Jonsson's book thus brings an important dimension introduced by the so-called "global turn" in many fields of historical scholarship to the study of European integration.[3]

Even though collective works naturally give rise to asymmetries in terms of emphases, coverage, and analytical frameworks, they make up for this by presenting a plurality of voices and perspectives. The interesting volume edited by Peter M. R. Stirk, *European Unity in Context: The Interwar Period* (1989), corresponds in many ways to our own project. The treatment dispensed to the subject is guided by the conflict between pan-Europeanism and nationalism that gained strength when the failure of the League of Nations to fulfill its initial promise became apparent. In his introductory essay, Stirk already emphasized how the interwar period

[3] See Hunt (2014) and Conrad (2017).

remained heavily neglected by historical scholarship, despite its relevance for understanding the obstacles and persistent challenges facing the European integration process. Two other collections of essays published in recent years have also explored the multiple dimensions of the interwar crisis and their implications for the history of Europe since then.

The chapters contained in the volume *Ideas of Europe Since 1914: The Legacy of the First World War* (2002), edited by Menno Spiering and Michael Wintle, move beyond the economic and political crises to investigate a crisis of identity (and conscience). They stress how Europe's self-identity after World War I alternated between moments of crisis and renewal. As the editors explain in their introductory chapter, "one undeniable effect of the First World War was that many were forced actually to think for the first time about the very concept of Europe." Whereas notions such as "'Europeanness', European civilization and European superiority were taken for granted around 1900, they never would be again in the same way after the First World War," as "doubt and doom descended on Europeans when thinking about their civilization" (Spiering and Wintle 2002, 4). The book also shows, however, how the 1920s brought back aspects of Eurocentric triumphalism. Coudenhove-Kalergi's Pan-European movement, for instance, embodied just this attitude, displaying a flag with a golden sun that represented a European civilization illuminating the world. In one of the book's essays, Michael Wintle points out how this renewal of triumphalism in the 1920s would provide the fascist movements of the following decade with elements for representation of European superiority: "this partial return to the bombast and arrogance of the 1890s New Imperialism shows that the Great War had not quite changed things for ever: it had dealt a mortal blow to Eurocentric arrogance, but there was more than a flicker of life left. The quasi-fascist regimes of the later 1930s could certainly empathize with that self-importance *vis-à-vis* the other continents" (Wintle 2002, 115).

Finally, the insightful collective work *Europe in Crisis: Intellectuals and the European Idea, 1917–1957* (2012), edited by Mark Hewitson and Matthew D'Auria, jointly analyzes the interwar period and the early stages of European integration in the immediate aftermath of World War II. From the vantage point of intellectual history, the book offers interesting perspectives on the process of institutionalization that culminated in the Treaty of Rome in 1957, while avoiding the notion that 1945 somehow represented a "zero hour," a historical shift that suddenly made Europe's integration projects feasible (Hewitson and D'Auria 2012, 11). In this respect, the work averts certain traits often found in the historiography of European integration, such as the opposition between the roles played by intellectuals and politicians, or the distinction between the prevalence of "ideas" during the interwar period and political and diplomatic "actions" after World War II, showing instead the rich interplay between ideas and policy-making that characterized the process.

In all these attempts to untangle the crisis of the interwar era, we find different perspectives traversing the ideas and actions of people in history, sometimes working in harmony, others in conflict. As political economy held one of the keys to any successful resolution of crisis, the articulation between European plans of international order and the history of economic ideas creates a rich field for scholarly inquiry.

2 Political Economy and the Search for Order

The appeal to order is a standard conservative trope. When the established currents of social life are threatened, the push to "restore order" typically resorts to an ideal past when certain values and norms could guarantee harmony and stability. The discourse of order thus often coincides with moments of profound social dislocation, when crisis and revolution lead many to long for an idyllic, conflict-free world that was left behind. Historical analysis of such episodes tends to focus, quite understandably, on those elements that pushed the limits of the established order. We recount the early twentieth century as a story of war, depression, and radical political movements, rather than moderate coalitions attempting piecemeal reform to preserve the liberal-democratic capitalist establishment. We recall the raucous 1930s or the labor agitation immediately following World War I, while leaving aside the appeasement and economic recovery of the late 1920s. Within this framework, the politics of order becomes entangled with authoritarian ideologies that thrived on the opportunistic support of those who stood to benefit from a restored status quo.

Any successful revolution, however, needs to create its own viable order. Comparing the history of Europe in the aftermath of both World Wars, Charles Maier (1987, 154) argued that "stabilization is as challenging a historical problem as revolution." Moreover, even if such stabilization will often involve some form of compromise with vested interests and entrenched social hierarchies, this does not mean we ought to interpret it as a conservative movement. "Stabilization," Maier continued, “does not preclude significant social and political change but often requires it.” This lesson was not lost on those who tried to find solutions to the challenges facing interwar Europe. Some of the immediate responses to the threats of bolshevism, cartelization, and aggressive imperialism may have involved an unduly nostalgic throwback to the tenets of nineteenth-century liberalism. Woodrow Wilson, for instance, has long been chastised for applying obsolete political concepts to a changed international reality. As the interwar era advanced, however, it became increasingly clear to most observers that successful stabilization—the creation of a new, stable order—would require a fair amount of creative solutions that departed significantly from the canons of social, political and economic thought and practice.

The rise and dissemination of a political discourse on “international order”—in parallel to related concepts such as “world” and “global” order—itself testifies to the Janus-faced nature of the stabilization strategies employed in interwar Europe. On one hand, the search for a broad, ecumenical international order reflected the need to fill the political void left by the disintegration of imperial spaces after World War I, especially in Eastern Europe and the Middle East. Quinn Slobodian (2018, 27–54), for instance, has posited a direct connection between the collapse of the Austro-Hungarian Empire and the rise of what he terms “neoliberal globalism.” As an ideology geared to securing an integrated world economy, globalism held the promise that political fragmentation—a conspicuous result of the principle of national self-determination sponsored by Woodrow Wilson—would not irrevocably sever the ties between former imperial powers and their dominions. At stake, therefore, was the preservation of the conditions guaranteeing economic prosperity and political stability that had been enjoyed by the traditional European powers during the late nineteenth century.

On the other hand, arguments about a new “global order” became increasingly infused with progressive elements that departed from established political wisdom. Daniel Gorman (2012) has chronicled the emergence of “international society” during the 1920s, understood as a network of institutional spaces for the promotion of internationalism that transcended, by and large, the domain of the sovereign nation-state. Even if the movement drew part of its energy from the typically transnational categories of imperial politics, internationalism also “proved corrosive for European empires,” especially by embracing a “language of universality” that fed into claims for human rights and colonial autonomy (3).

Gorman called attention to the proliferation, after World War I, of civil society organizations that took the world, not the nation, as the appropriate space for their activism, covering a wide range of fields—economics, politics, culture, religion, etc. Internationalist rhetoric, nonetheless, often aimed at the reform of traditional politics itself. The platforms embraced by such high-profile figures as Aristide Briand, Gustav Stresemann and Frank Kellogg are only the most evident instances of this trend. Gorman highlighted the League of Nation's role as a pioneering "international civil service" (11–12), but despite its flawed record as an instrument of peace, the League did militate in favor a reinvented system of international politics where self-determination could translate into diversity and pluralism.

By the end of the interwar period, projects for reconstructing the world order had not only multiplied in number, but also incorporated many unorthodox ideas. The British federalist movement, to name only one example, channeled frustration with traditional power politics and imperial rivalries into the refinement of an institutional blueprint that departed significantly from established political practice. In the new language of global order that emerged at the time, Or Rosenboim (2017) sees an alternative to imperial politics that reflected "a growing ambivalence about the cultural and political legacy of empire" (7). The concept of democracy, in particular, stood in need of reconsideration to make room for "regional, transnational, federal, or global institutions," rather than relying solely "on the basic unit of the territorial state" (8). Likewise, a stable global framework should be flexible enough to accommodate the different values and practices encountered in a diverse world. Transnational forms of association could create bonds and loyalties that transcended the nation-state, thus turning pluralism into a source of order, rather than chaos. There were tensions, of course, between the "universal" values sponsored by advocates of a liberal-democratic world order and the cultural substratum found in many of the new nations now emerging into the political scene. Even if the legacy of empire proved hard to shake off in some cases, these tensions often provided yet another impetus for creative thinking and institutional innovation. "Although visions of world order in the 1940s oscillated between ambitious schemes and minimalist reforms," Rosenboim summarized, "they shared a common perception of the unique opportunity warranted by the world-changing war to refashion world order" (19).

Underlying many of these interwar schemes for restoring order was a deep-rooted belief that scientific knowledge held the key to social, political, and economic stabilization. The experience of World War I is often credited for making it plain and visible how the state could take the reins of the socioeconomic machinery into its own hands, and with this came the realization that governments now needed certain types of expertise to adequately fulfill their new functions. The interwar era thus saw the birth of the concept of technocracy. Charles Maier, once again, described how North American notions of scientific management had already become widespread in Europe by the 1920s, a process of intellectual appropriation that "extended the original approaches of Taylorism into all areas of labour productivity, technological efficiency, and even corporate organization" (1987, 22). The new social gospel of engineering "suggested a self-image of impartial technical arbitration, a dedication to scientific standards and objectivity above the clash of interests in the factory" (25). As with other interwar trends, this could serve both conservative and progressive aims. If a reformed Taylorism helped give some concreteness to projects for industrial self-management and worker's control that proliferated immediately after the war, it also supported the logic of interest group representation, headed by experts in the various fields, that lay behind different forms of corporatist political organization, including fascism.

Even economic planning, that most symbolic of interwar appeals to technocracy, offered a platform where the boundaries between left and right were easily blurred. Taylorism had traveled as far as the Soviet Union, where economic planning became an instrument for operating the socialized means of production with greater efficiency. For left-wing governments that had fallen short of a socialist revolution, however, planning posed the threat of merely substituting capitalist rule with expert rule as yet another form of working-class alienation—a rationalized capitalism that was all the more oppressive precisely because it functioned more smoothly. At bottom, this reflected the uneasy relationship between scientific expertise and democratic *ethos* that often constrained political arguments during the interwar era and beyond. Technocracy offered the promise of order at the cost of a reduced space for effective political engagement and mobilization. The democratic aspirations of the early twentieth century aimed for a broad devolution of power, while carrying the burden of antiquated forms of representative politics and the volatility of public opinion in the dawning age of mass communication. This tension naturally carried over to discussions about a reconstructed international order, conceived by some as a potential source of new, broader spaces for political deliberation, while others regarded it as another layer of technical decision-making by experts operating at a distance from social turmoil.

In fact, many of the supranational institutions created during the interwar years already incorporated a strong technocratic dimension. Patricia Clavin (2013) shows how, despite its loose organization and political shortcomings, the League of Nations managed to set up networks of expertise around specific areas of policy analysis, whose participants "privileged technocratic cooperation" and preferred to speak in a technical language that "frequently attempted to conceal the political signification of issues" (6, 16). Clavin's study focuses on the League's Economic and Financial Organization (EFO), one of such networks dedicated to assist in the task of economic reconstruction and stabilization after the war. In line with the principles that animated the creation of the League, the EFO originally worked to restore the liberal economic framework that had prevailed in the late nineteenth century, promoting policies that facilitated a reduction of tariffs and the reestablishment of the international gold standard. Nevertheless, the upheavals of the 1920s and 1930s, especially after the onset of the Great Depression, led the organization to move increasingly toward novel paradigms of political economy. The EFO's history was thus profoundly entangled with the broader transformations taking place in economic science at the time. The roster of economists who worked for the organization included many of the profession's luminaries by mid-century: Bertil Ohlin, Jacob Viner, Gottfried Haberler, Jan Tinbergen, James Meade, Gustav Cassel, Tjalling Koopmans, Ragnar Nurkse, Oskar Morgenstern, Gunnar Myrdal, Kenneth Boulding, and still others. To Clavin, however, the usual labels derived from the history of economic ideas can be misleading when applied to the practical work they produced for the League, marked by far greater convergence than the theoretical feuds between "Keynesians," "Austrians" and others would imply (37).

The example offered by the League of Nation's Economic and Financial Organization puts into relief the centrality of political economy to interwar projects of order and stabilization. The tone was set early on, with the publication of John Maynard Keynes' *The Economic Consequences of the Peace* (1920), which framed the question of a restored European order strictly in terms of the economic settlement arising from Versailles. Keynes built his argument on the premise of a deeply interconnected international economic machinery, whose adequate functioning required a swift and thorough reincorporation of Germany. A similar argument had been elaborated not long before in Norman Angell's *The Great Illusion* (1910), a landmark tract on the liberal internationalist tradition. In his highly influential *The Great Society* (1914), Graham Wallas likewise reflected on the contrast between the extension of "social scale" brought about by modern industry and technology, on one hand, and the deep-rooted values and institutions that militated against cohesion and cooperation, on the other. Interwar disputes about the political economy of the "great society" covered a wide range of alternatives, from the Wilsonian combined platform of free trade and self-determination, through Keynes' later argument in favor of national self-sufficiency, all the way to the Bolshevik model inaugurated with the Russian Revolution.

The Soviet experiment is often credited for casting a long shadow on interwar arguments about political economy, either as aspiration or repugnance. Adam Tooze (2014), however, has offered a welcome corrective to the overemphasis on Bolshevik communism as a disruptive force during the 1920s. In his reading, political economy was indeed the defining issue beneath the tribulations that followed World War I, but the threat came instead from the perceived overwhelming dominance of a capitalist democratic order centered around a new superpower, the United States. In contrast with the situation prevailing in the aftermath of World War II, when a new bipolar world order had clearly emerged, the geopolitical balance after 1918 was grossly uneven. For Tooze, the First World War culminated in "a crusading victory for a coalition that proclaimed itself the champion of a new world order." In his classic study of the post-WWI settlement, Maier (1975) also called attention to the success of "bourgeois" stabilization in Europe during the 1920s. The labor activism of 1919 was invigorated by the Wilsonian promise of international peace and democracy; roughly a decade later, this had given room to the politics of accommodation along corporatist lines (136–38). The limits to this stabilization, however, soon became clear.

Tooze highlights how the new Anglo-American supremacy was anchored on political and economic premises that led to a "moralization and politicization of international affairs," complete with assignment of blame and guilt to the defeated. The outlawry of war as an immoral practice served, among other things, to consecrate a status quo that mostly benefitted the victors. Tooze's argument resembles the words of an illustrious contemporary observer, E. H. Carr (1939), who condemned the "idealist" platform embraced by Wilson and his followers as a simple rationalization of privilege in international politics. For those on the weaker side of the bargain, not surprisingly, such moral grandstanding did not carry much weight. Tooze speaks of a "dialectic of order and insurgency" to explain how the successful stabilization of the 1920s brought on its heels the upheavals of the 1930s. "The spectacular escalation of violence unleashed in the 1930s and the 1940s," he argues, "was a testament to the kind of force that the insurgents believed themselves to be up against." The United States hoped to bypass militarism and imperial rivalries to exercise their influence "at arm's length through the means of soft power – economics and ideology." Economics and international security, however, could no longer be disentangled in the quest for a viable world order. So long as the new hegemon remained committed to "a conservative vision of its own future," based on isolationism and a weak federal government, the collapse was inevitable.

As the march of events made clear, the epochal challenges of the interwar era demanded new, radical solutions. Some of the alternative models of political economy explored at the time, like fascism and Nazism, were violent and destructive; others were hopelessly utopian, like guild socialism or plans for a democratic world federation; but many ideas outlined during those tumultuous decades later came to fruition, in different ways. Patricia Clavin (2013, 344) notes how "economic and financial issues were first when it came to imagining and building the peace" after World War II, a lesson learned from the failed settlement of the 1920s. The functioning of post-WWII supranational institutions such as the IMF and the European Commission likewise mirrored the work of the League of Nations' technical agencies—including the appeal to a socially detached, technocratic *ethos* that led to concerns with democratic deficits. Attempts during the mid-1920s to establish Franco-German cooperation in the iron and steel industries foreshadowed the Treaty of Paris negotiations many years later (Maier 1975, 516–19). The experience of economic nationalism in the 1930s motivated schemes to insulate the world economy from the vagaries of domestic politics, especially through laws and institutions that created a stable market order (Slobodian 2018, 4–10).

Examples could be multiplied. The interwar legacy comprises a host of creative blueprints that have informed arguments about political economy ever since. This book is an attempt to pick up some of these threads and show how the multiple crisis of the period—moral, political, economic, diplomatic—were all deeply entangled and resist analytical fragmentation. Any successful new order would have to stabilize all of them at once. As we deal with our own unstable orders today, we have much to gain from reconnecting the different disciplinary strands of interwar history into a more comprehensive picture, where political economy appears at times as a creative driving force, at others as a casualty of circumstances.

3 The Structure of the Book

The essays collected in this book all contribute, in different ways, to recovering the wealth of ideas and debates about the reconstruction of the world order that proliferated in interwar Europe, underscoring their relevance to evolving twentieth-century paradigms of political economy. The volume thus builds upon and contributes to scholarship on several fields: though anchored on the history of economics, it also explores topics on politics, philosophy, international relations, and European studies. Moreover, even if most chapters could be naturally framed as studies in intellectual history, our emphasis on the concept of political economy is meant to call attention to the practical dimension of ideas: the ways in which abstract formulations about economics have been made to serve specific causes, either as part of larger political and ideological arguments, or as instruments for direct intervention on reality. In other words, we have tried to avoid the mere search for intellectual ancestors or the quest for ideas that were unjustly "forgotten" by history, and focus instead on how the myriad concepts and theories produced during the interwar years became enmeshed in political platforms, institutions, and habits that have shaped, in one way or another, the history of Europe since then.

Even if this is a book about interwar Europe, we did not intend to offer an exhaustive and perfectly balanced coverage when selecting contributors and topics. Some periods and areas thus received more attention than others. Overall, however, the themes explored in the several chapters touch on common threads uniting different interwar experiences, and their resonance with parallel developments outside of the specific cases under study should be clear. We believe the subjects covered in the volume are diverse enough to capture most of the intersections between arguments on political economy and international order that proliferated in Europe at the time.

The book is divided into three parts, each focusing on a different set of issues where economics and politics interacted to further certain agendas of international stabilization. Part I, "Economics and Order," explores how different understandings of the powerful notion of order permeated interwar discourse on political economy, finding its way into the works of many prominent economists from that era. In Chapter 2, Raphaël Fèvre shows how John Maynard Keynes and Walter Eucken had much more in common than the strict post-WWII opposition between Keynesianism and ordoliberalism would lead us to believe. Crucially, both offered competing paradigms of political economy that took a pragmatic stance toward the role of the state as a guarantor of economic order, domestically and internationally. Alexandre M. Cunha, in Chapter 3, addresses the French third-way "non-conformist" debate of the 1930s, tracing the influence of so-called communitarian personalism on different fronts, such as the federalist approaches to international order or the idea of community in François Perroux's political economy of corporatism. Also dwelling on the multifaceted territory of third-way platforms in interwar France, Katia Caldari uncovers, in Chapter 4, the origins of the peculiar combination of corporatism-planning-neoliberalism that became a central inspiration for Jean Monnet's design of the European integration process after World War II, later replaced by an ordoliberal-influenced institutional architecture. In Chapter 5, Erwin Dekker inquires into the reasons for Dutch economist Jan Tinbergen's initial suspicions regarding the European integration process, which he considered a poor substitute for an international order and an obstacle to global economic integration. Dekker finds clues to understand Tinbergen's position in his experiences in the Netherlands and his work for the League of Nations during the interwar years. Concluding Part I, Pierre-Hernan Rojas explores debates on European monetary order, highlighting how the contributions of Robert Triffin were influenced by his analyses of the monetary problems of Belgium in the 1930s and of different Latin American countries in the early 1940s. Rojas thus examines the origins of the design adopted by the European Payments Union in 1950, as well as Triffin's insistence on deeper regional monetary integration as an instrument to cope with the inconsistencies of the Bretton Woods system.

Part II, "Democracy and Technocracy," shifts the focus to the tension between new ideas of government by expertise—which were especially cogent in the economic domain—and the democratic aspirations inherent in schemes for a reconstructed international order. In Chapter 7, António

Costa Pinto explores different cases of corporatist institutional reform in interwar Europe, under both democracy and dictatorship, as well as their channels of ideological legitimation. He argues that corporatism and "economic parliaments" were then at the forefront of a cross-national diffusion process, both as a new form of organized interest representation and as an authoritarian alternative to parliamentary democracy. In Chapter 8, Valerio Torreggiani tackles one of the quintessential transnational institutions of the interwar era—the International Labour Organization—to show how tripartism was advanced as a device for promoting democratic engagement in a world of expert government and representation. Building on the legacy of the British pluralist movement but neutralizing its more radical overtones, the ILO's tripartite model of conflict resolution eventually became an instrument of conservative stabilization during the 1920s, along corporatist lines. Chapter 9, by Carlos Eduardo Suprinyak, highlights the work of G. D. H. Cole, one of the British pluralists discussed by Torreggiani, who spearheaded a campaign to abolish state sovereignty in the name of horizontal, participatory politics. The emergence of central planning as a compelling paradigm of political economy, however, forced Cole to reconsider the role of state authority in a democratic socialist commonwealth. Finally, in Chapter 10, Timo Miettinen offers a philosophical take on the interwar origins of ordoliberalism, reconstructing the movement as a response to the early-twentieth-century crisis of scientific reason. Ordoliberal thinkers thus looked for new ontological and epistemological foundations that could turn liberalism into "a scientific theory with normative implications," strongly relying on economics for intellectual legitimacy.

The book's third and final part, "The Power of Ideas," comprises a set of essays that illustrate how certain concepts and notions, when embedded in concrete institutional structures, can exert a powerful influence on the course of history. In Chapter 11, Antonio Masala and Alberto Mingardi reflect on the legacy bequeathed by classical liberal thinkers to the European unification project. Considering the works of Luigi Einaudi, Friedrich A. Hayek, and Wilhelm Röpke, Masala and Mingardi assess the extent to which the nineteenth-century pacifist tradition of classical liberalism came back to life in the contributions of these authors. In Chapter 12, Oksana Levkovych discusses how Philip Snowden, Chancellor of the Exchequer to the British Labour Government of Ramsay MacDonald (1929–1931), played a pivotal role in arguments about commercial policy, effectively postponing the British abandonment of its long-standing free trade policy in the face of a growing protectionist tide. As the case shows, even if they cannot resist the vigorous currents of history indefinitely, powerful agents imbued with deep-seated convictions can affect the timing of political decisions, thus narrowing the range of possible outcomes. Chapter 13, by Harald Hagemann, describes how the scientific diaspora occasioned by interwar dislocations led to some "involuntary internationalization" in economic studies of the business cycle. The proliferation of research institutes dedicated to the subject across Europe, increasingly staffed by emigrant scholars, produced convergence and homogenization of the standards guiding the collection and analysis of economic data, which reinforced their potential as instruments at the service of supranational governance. Business cycle research is also the focus of Chapter 14, by Roberto Lampa, which explores the role played by the Oxford Institute of Statistics as the institutional base for an alternative to both Marshallian and Keynesian economics in interwar Britain. Offering yet another shelter for expatriate scholars, the OIS gave expression to growing Continental concerns with securing a stable international order that guaranteed peace in Europe. Finally, closing the volume, we have a postscript by James Ashley Morrison and José Luis Cardoso, who connect some of the threads uncovered in the various chapters and explore their broader implications for the history of Europe during the twentieth century and beyond.

References

Ash, Timothy Garton. 1996. 'Is Europe Becoming Europe?' *Sanford S. Elberg Lecture in International Studies*, Institute of International Studies, Berkeley, University of California, 3 April 1996. Available at: http://globetrotter.berkeley.edu/conversations/Elberg/GartonAsh/ga-elb01.html.

Boyce, Robert. 2009. *The Great Interwar Crisis and the Collapse of Globalization*. New York: Palgrave Macmillan.

Buschak, Willy. 2014. *Die Vereinigten Staaten von Europa sind unser Ziel: Arbeiterbewegung und Europa im frühen 20. Jahrhundert*. Essen: Klartext.

Carr, Edward H. 1939. *The Twenty Years' Crisis, 1919–1939: An Introduction to the Study of International Relations*. London: Macmillan.

Clavin, Patricia. 2013. *Securing the World Economy: The Reinvention of the League of Nations, 1920–1946*. Oxford: Oxford University Press.

Cohen, Antonin. 2012. *De Vichy à la Communauté européenne*. Paris: Presses universitaires de France.

Conrad, Sebastian. 2017. *What Is Global History?* Princeton: Princeton University Press, 2017.

Denord, François. 2001. "Aux origines du néo-libéralisme en France: Louis Rougier et le Colloque Walter Lippmann de 1938." *Le Mouvement Social* 195 (2): 9–34.

———. 2007. *Néo-libéralisme, version française: Histoire d'une idéologie politique.* Paris: Demopolis.

Gilbert, Mark. 2003. *Surpassing Realism: The Politics of European Integration Since 1945.* Lanham, MD: Rowman & Littlefield.

———. 2008. "Narrating the Process: Questioning the Progressive Story of European Integration." *Journal of Common Market Studies* 46 (3): 641–62.

Gorman, Daniel. 2012. *The Emergence of International Society in the 1920s.* Cambridge: Cambridge University Press.

Gosewinkel, Dieter. 2015. *Anti-Liberal Europe: A Neglected Story of Europeanization.* New York: Berghahn Books.

Hansen, Peo, and Stefan Jonsson. 2015. *Eurafrica: The Untold History of European Integration and Colonialism.* London: Bloomsbury Academic.

Hewitson, Mark, and Matthew D'Auria, eds. 2012. *Europe in Crisis: Intellectuals and the European Idea, 1917–1957.* New York: Berghahn Books.

Hunt, Lynn. 2014. *Writing History in the Global Era.* New York: Norton.

Kaiser, Wolfram, and Antonio Varsori, eds. 2010. *European Union History: Themes and Debates.* New York: Palgrave Macmillan.

Maier, Charles. 1988 [1975]. *Recasting Bourgeois Europe: Stabilization in France, Germany, and Italy in the Decade After World War I.* Princeton: Princeton University Press.

———. 1987. *In Search of Stability: Explorations in Historical Political Economy.* Cambridge: Cambridge University Press.

Parsons, Craig. 2002. "Showing Ideas as Causes: The Origins of the European Union." *International Organization* 56 (1): 47–84.

Patel, Kiran Klaus. 2019. "Widening and Deepening? Recent Advances in European Integration History." *Neue Politische Literatur: Berichte aus Geschichts- und Politikwissenschaft* 64 (2): 327–57.

Rosenboim, Or. 2017. *The Emergence of Globalism: Visions of World Order in Britain and the United States, 1939–1950.* Princeton and Oxford: Princeton University Press.

Slobodian, Quinn. 2018. *Globalists: The End of Empire and the Birth of Neoliberalism.* Cambridge: Harvard University Press, 2018.

Spiering, Menno, and Michael Wintle, eds. 2002. *Ideas of Europe Since 1914: The Legacy of the First World War.* New York: Palgrave Macmillan.

Stirk, Peter M. R., ed. 1989. *European Unity in Context: The Interwar Period.* London: Pinter.

Tooze, Adam. 2014. *The Deluge: The Great War and the Remaking of the Global Order, 1916–1931*. London: Allen Lane.

Warlouzet, Laurent. 2014. "European Integration History: Beyond the Crisis." *Politique Européenne* 44 (2): 98–122.

Wintle, Michael. 2002. "Europe on Parade: The First World War and the Changing Visual Representations of the Continent in the Twentieth Century." In *Ideas of Europe Since 1914: The Legacy of the First World War*, edited by Menno Spiering and Michael Wintle. New York: Palgrave Macmillan.

PART I

Economics and Order

CHAPTER 2

Eucken's Competition with Keynes: Beyond the Ordoliberal Allergy to the Keynesian Medicine

Raphaël Fèvre

"Keynes [was] indeed a typical modern, ambivalent phenomenon. A participant in the destruction of orders (*Mit-Zerstörer von Ordnungen*); a man who was just recklessly playing with fire and actually contributed to the general collapse" (Walter Eucken, letter to Wilhelm Röpke, May 29, 1946).[1] These harsh words from Walter Eucken in his private correspondence, nearly a month after Lord Keynes's death, reflect the well-known ordoliberal allergy to the Keynesian medicine. Eucken was commenting to his friend Wilhelm Röpke, who had just written a critical piece entitled "Keynes and his time" (*Keynes und unsere Zeit*) published in the liberal Swiss journal *Neue Zürcher Zeitung* (May the 5th, 1946). Yet over and

[1] My translation from the original German. I am grateful to Jean Solchany for sending me a reproduction of this letter, which he quotes in his intellectual biography of Wilhelm Röpke (Solchany 2015, 310).

R. Fèvre (✉)
Centre Walras Pareto, University of Lausanne, Lausanne, Switzerland

© The Author(s) 2021

A. M. Cunha and C. E. Suprinyak (eds.), *Political Economy and International Order in Interwar Europe*, Palgrave Studies in the History of Economic Thought,
https://doi.org/10.1007/978-3-030-47102-6_2

above the political and ideological opposition to Keynes's thought stated by Eucken (and substantiated in the secondary literature), I intend to reconsider this issue from a different angle. This chapter suggests that Eucken adopted the position of Keynes's challenger, since the former was indeed an attentive commentator of the latter's work, often starting from rather similar premises or concerns.

Son of the neo-Kantian philosopher and Nobel-prize winner Rudolf Eucken, Walter Eucken (1891–1950) was the head of the *Freiburg School of law and economics* (Vanberg 1998, 2004), and a key figure of German ordoliberalism.[2] Though Eucken died suddenly at the age of 59, the shadow of his thought weighed on the economic reforms of West Germany's early years, the true formative period of the *Social Market Economy* (Rieter and Schmolz 1993; Goldschmidt and Wohlgemuth 2008; Muresan 2014). Both Keynes and Eucken wanted to refashion the liberal ideal from the inside, but proved highly antithetical in their conception of the role of the state in a market economy, an antithesis embodied by the opposition between discretionary policy, on the one hand, and rules-based policy on the other (Kolev 2010; Feld et al. 2018). The factors that lead British and German liberalism onto such conflicting paths are to be found by at the same time considering theoretical conceptions and national and international contextual aspects related to the question of power in modern capitalist society (Fèvre 2018b). Eucken, and thus ordoliberal ideas, were mainly responsible for keeping Germany Keynesian-proof on a political level.[3]

However, my contention is that Eucken considered himself not so much a *critic* of Keynes, as one of his *competitors*. Though subtle, such a distinction is nonetheless crucial in fully grasping Eucken's political economy, in addition to understanding some of the reasons why they both reached such a symmetrical approach to post-WWII programmes.

The first part of this chapter sheds light on the ordoliberal reluctance towards Keynesianism by contextualising the reception of Keynes's masterpiece—the *General Theory* (1936b)—in the German area. From

[2] Recent years have witnessed the rise of the copious literature on ordoliberalism, with an emphasis on the place of this tradition in the history of political ideas on the one hand (Ptak 2004; Bonefeld 2017; Biebricher 2019), and in the history of economic thought on the other (Kolev 2013; Fèvre 2017a).

[3] On the tortuous path of Keynesian ideas in Germany, see articles by Jürgen Backhaus (1985), Jan-Otmar Hesse (2012) and Harald Hagemann (2013).

the mid-1930s on, the misleading association of Keynes with *Third Reich* economic policies stalled the ordoliberal reading of Keynes, making even the beginning of a reasonable dialogue almost impossible. However, ordoliberal thinkers did endorse different strategies regarding Keynes. On the one hand, Röpke waged a staunch crusade against Keynesian economics while, on the other hand, Eucken paid careful attention at Keynes's claims. Proof of this attitude can be found in the fact that Keynes and Eucken urged Hayek to appreciate the urgency of the post-war situation, calling for the need to find a practical means of State action.[4] Eventually though, Keynes and Eucken did endorse different perspectives on the international order required for reconstruction. Eucken in particular rejected Keynes's Plan, arguing that its new institution for managing foreign trade would favour concentration of power on an international scale.

The second part of this chapter deals with Eucken's reception of Keynes's work in order to outline Eucken's competitive attitude. In his *Grundlagen der Nationalökonomie*, Eucken (1940) gave a twofold treatment of Keynes, both supportive and critical. Ten years later in the English preface of the translated version of his *Foundations* (1950), Eucken endorsed a more nuanced position regarding Keynes's ideas by stressing the complementary aspects of their works. Finally, the Chapter draws a parallel between Keynes and Eucken's ways of reinterpreting some of the core elements of the two diverse national traditions of economic thought they had grown up with: Marshallian economics in Britain and Historicism in Germany. All of these—mainly methodological—points have to do with the manner in which both achieved a fruitful balance between economic theory, political discourse (or activities), and social goals.

[4] In the following pages, I will elaborate on Keynes and Eucken's letters to Hayek in response of *The Road to Serfdom* (1944), using them as a heuristic tool for further investigation. Nils Goldschmidt and Jan-Otmar Hesse (2013) published and commented on a translated version of Eucken's letter. The original (German) version of this letter can be found in Friedrich Hayek's Papers at Stanford University [HIA FAH Papers, Box 18, Fo. 40].

1 Shaping the Economic Order: From Interwar National Experiences to the Post-war International Order

1.1 The General Theory's Reception in Interwar Germany

The German version of the *General Theory* (henceforth *GT*) was published in the same year (1936b) as the original text. Keynes was already known in the German-speaking countries since he had earned an international reputation with his insider's view of the *Versailles* negotiations recounted in lively detail in *The Economic Consequences of the Peace* (1919). By comparison, the German translation of the *GT* found a rather cooler—if not frankly negative (see Hudson 1985, 49)—reception.[5] In particular, brief passages of the German preface were particularly incriminated. There, Keynes supposedly wrote that his theory was "much more easily adapted to the conditions of a totalitarian state (*Totaler Staat*)", and while he had above all "Anglo-Saxon countries in view—where a great deal of laissez-faire still prevails—it remains applicable to situations in which national leadership (*stattliche Führung*) is more pronounced".[6]

Keynes's preface as well as the apparent similarities of his policy proposals with the practical policies and objectives pursued by the Nazis, did in fact tarnish his reputation for some German contemporaries, as indeed it confused some later commentators of Keynes's thought, like Donald E. Moggridge or Robert Skidelsky (see Hagemann 2014, 162). When Joan Robinson (1972, 8) later observed that "Hitler had already found how to cure unemployment before Keynes had finished explaining why it occurred", she was in practice adding fuel to this groundless fire. The fire was kept alive by anti-Keynesians like Röpke (1963, 221), for instance, stressing that Keynes turned out to be nothing less than "the intellectual authority for economic policy in National Socialist Germany".

Yet as a matter of fact, "Hitler's economic policies were not really Hitler's" (Backhaus 1985, 167). Indeed, by the beginning of 1932, the

[5] Translated by Fritz Waeger, the German version was entitled *Allgemeine Theorie der Beschäftigung, des Zinses und des Geldes* (1936), and printed by *Duncker & Humblot* (Berlin).

[6] Here I rely on Bertram Schefold (1980, 175), who corrected (and translated) the omission of *The Collected Writings*.

Brüning government was seriously considering fighting recession, deflation and unemployment by means of public works and job creation. However, this programme did not get underway until Hitler finally reoriented it towards "massive rearmament" when he came to power (Garvy 1975, 403). Hence prior to the publication of Keynes's *GT* of 1936, Germany already had its own "anticipators" or "proto-Keynesians", which accounts for the similarities between the German economic policies of the thirties, and the general spirit of the Keynesian programme (Klausinger 1999). Wilhelm Lautenbach, "a scholar and a policy-maker simultaneously" (Backhaus 1985, 177), was the main architect of this German version of Keynesianism. He supported "a radical plan for credit-financed government spending" (Tooze 2001, 170), that found its way through the Brauns Commission, created to find an answer to the unemployment crisis coming with the Great Depression.

Both Eucken and Röpke were part of these expert circles and were among the scholars who called for an immediate short-run expansionist programme in Weimar Germany (Commun 2018; Feld et al. 2018). Röpke in particular drew a distinction between "primary" and "secondary" depression and stressed that Germany was entering the latter kind of depression. In this case, the state had to drastically lower taxes, raise expenditure and finance public works in order to provide a strong "initial spark" (*Initialzündung*) that would eventually boost the economy.[7] Eucken shared Röpke's concerns and solutions, by contrast to Hayek for instance, who tried to dissuade Röpke from advocating an expansionist policy (see Magliulo 2018). In retrospect, Eucken (1951, 65) confirmed that when "there are millions of unemployed, any government will have to pursue a policy of full employment [...] social conscience forbids us to tolerate mass unemployment, and so does reason of state". Eucken (1951, 59) went so far as to claim that if at that time the government had accepted the plan designed by Lautenbach—"deservedly known as the German Keynes"—, then "there might perhaps never have been a National Socialist revolution".

From the 1930s to the early 1950s, Eucken maintained a similar perspective on the need for a Keynesian-like policy to overcome severe crises. But then, how can one understand the ordoliberal rejection of the full-employment goal? The short answer is that, according to ordoliberals,

[7] At that time, Röpke (1932, 1936a) was aiming to conciliate Hayek's and Keynes's approach to business cycles (see Fèvre 2018c).

there is room for a Keynesian *moment*, nothing more and nothing less. What pushed the ordoliberals to a harsh dismissal of the "full employment" philosophy of Keynesian interventionism was its installation as a perennial guide in the management of the day-to-day economic life. As a policy on the economic process (*Prozesspolitik*), Eucken (1948c, 179) associated it with a form of centrally planned economy like that of the National-socialist state, eventually leading towards protectionism and nationalism. Therefore, the apparent similarities between the Keynesian agenda and the economic policies of the *Reich* made this connection appear all too plausible.[8]

Retrospectively, linking Keynes's message to the *community over individuals* formula promoted by the Nazi "welfare state" appears sheer nonsense, as Bertram Schefold (1980) and Harald Hagemann (2014) convincingly argued.[9] In the "*Concluding notes on the social philosophy towards which the General Theory might lead*," Keynes (1936b, 381) left no room for ambiguity regarding his contempt for national socialism, stressing that "the authoritarian state systems of to-day seem to solve the problem of unemployment at the expense of efficiency and of freedom".[10]

Clearly, Eucken's and Röpke's reception of Keynes's *GT* did not occur in a neutral context. The ordoliberal allergy to the Keynesian medicine probably had to do with this unhappy reception. Turning away from his early proximity with Keynesian-like ideas, Röpke (1944, 196) associated "the practice of German National Socialism and Anglo-Saxon theory (Keynes)" when discussing the full employment policy, thereby

[8] 'Within a broader perspective, the study directed by Peter E. Hall (1989) on *The Political Power of Economic Ideas: Keynesianism across Nations* showed how western countries' counter-cyclical fiscal policies against unemployment came about primarily without any reference to Keynes. Theodor Roosevelt's *New Deal* is an obvious example, but other examples can also be seen in Sweden, France or Italy (see also Bateman 2006, 283–86).

[9] On the characterisation of the Nazi *Sozialstaat*, see Hong (1998) and Kurlander (2011).

[10] Further arguments and proof of Keynes' anti-Nazism were condensed in Mark Pernecky and Thomas Richter (2009, 259–60). Interestingly enough, some ordoliberals too—but neither Röpke (exile) nor Eucken (half-exile) (see Johnson 1989)—had been accused of sympathy with the authoritarian Nazi State (Tribe 1995; Ptak 2004; Goldschmidt 2005; Köhler and Nientiedt 2017).

discrediting the latter. Röpke vehemently manifested this visceral rejection in his private correspondence with Lionel Robbins.[11] There, Röpke denounced the "spirit of irresponsibility" which Keynes's writing supposedly revealed, stressing that he found the *GT* "little short of satanic" (Röpke 1935, 1936b). Was Röpke's gut reaction to Keynes motivated by the general theory itself, by the policy prescriptions that came with it, or by the German preface mentioned above—or even by all at once? In these exchanges, Röpke did not offer arguments that would answer these questions. From this period on, Röpke waged a crusade against Keynes's heritage in numerous books and articles. However, my contention is that Walter Eucken did endorse an alternative strategy.

1.2 Letters to Hayek: Plea for a Positive Programme

As will be documented by the letters Keynes (1944) and Eucken (1946a) wrote to Hayek in reaction to their reading of *The Road to Serfdom* (henceforth *RS*), both Keynes and Eucken proved to share a pragmatic view of political action in contrast with the long-run perspective contemplated by Hayek's "Olympian economics".[12] Keynes read *the RS* in the Summer of 1944, on his way to the Bretton Woods' conference. He wrote a letter to Hayek famously expressing that "morally and philosophically" he found himself "in a deeply moved agreement" with the central message of this "grand book" (Keynes 1944, 335). By the beginning of 1946 Eucken too, after having read the German edition of *the RS*,[13] expressed—in his own restrained way—his agreement

[11] From this perspective, post-war Lionel Robbins turned out to be decidedly the *anti*-Röpke, as he stressed: "I find myself in the reverse position to Professor Roepke, who was Keynesian, and is so no longer. There was a time when I thought Keynesian stabilisation schemes utterly reprehensible, but I have gradually been forced to believe that these ideas were not so wrong" (Robbins quoted in Howson 2011, 663).

[12] Here, I have borrowed Skidelsky's metaphor (2006, 84). Challenging Hayek's viewpoint, Skidelsky referred to Hayek's so-called value-free economic theory. I use "Olympian" here in line with Hayek's way of reading his work as utopian, claiming the indispensability of "an ideal picture of a society which may not be wholly achievable, or a guiding conception of the overall order" (Hayek 1982, 62).

[13] The book (Hayek 1945) was edited and introduced by Wilhelm Röpke, translated by his wife Eva Röpke. For the same publishing house (*Eugen Rentsch Verlag*), two years earlier Wilhelm Röpke had published *The Social Crisis of our Time* (1942), a book in many ways comparable to the *RS*.

(Eucken 1946b, 139). He was then working hard to defend and impose ordoliberal views upon the occupation powers of the French zone, while he was still professor at the University of *Freiburg im Breisgau.*

Indeed, Eucken participated in scientific committees, produced reports (1946a, c) and wrote numerous articles for the general public designed to steer the economic (in particular industrial and banking) policy of the German administration and the Allies. As pointed out above, it was not the first time Eucken had been active in the experts' discussions on public policy proposals, yet he remained silent on that level during the whole national-socialist period. With the collapse of the *Reich* and the rise of a new post-war era, the ordoliberals as a whole, and Eucken in particular, went on a campaign for the denazification of the West German economic order (Fèvre 2018a). This meant the abandonment of the previous system of planification plagued with defects to the benefit of a consciously designed competitive order.

Hence, Eucken and Keynes (even more so[14]) were actively contributing to the shaping of the new economic order both as civil servants and public intellectuals. By contrast, Hayek's "war effort" remained on the purely intellectual level, notwithstanding his willingness to participate (see Caldwell 2007, 9–15).

Over and above Keynes and Eucken's shared misgivings about the collectivist (Soviet-like)[15] tendencies that were making vigorous headway in the post-war period, they actually put their finger on the same weakness in Hayek's message: he offered no practical directions to set the European economies on their future path. Actually, neither a liberal like Aaron Director (1945) nor a moderate like Arthur C. Pigou (1944)—or indeed numerous others[16]—had made any such remark in their published book reviews. Schumpeter (1946, 269) even justified Hayek's lack of an

[14] The many political implications of Keynes's work have been meticulously documented (Skidelsky 2005).

[15] In fact, in the post-war period an ambiguous use of terms like planning, collectivism, socialism and the like prevailed among economists and social reformers, sometimes used as synonymous, sometimes with different meanings. Focusing on Hayek's case, the paper by David M. Levy et al. (2005) provides a stimulating analysis of this issue.

[16] For instance, see reviews in leading journals (Branch 1945; Friedrich 1945; Greene 1945; Guillebaud 1944; Mayer 1945; Nourse 1945; Roll 1945; Smith 1945).

"alternative policy of his own" arguing that "such criticism would be unjustified" for he had never promised anything of the sort.[17]

Advancing his "only serious criticism of the book", Keynes insisted on two points. First, Hayek's thesis would be too idealistic and too Manichean, therefore of no use for practical action. Secondly, Keynes claimed that some activities could indeed be safely planned, as long as they remained "rightly orientated" towards liberal ends (in a sense of personal liberties and freedom of choice):

> You agree that the line has to be drawn somewhere, and that the logical extreme is not possible. But you give us no guidance whatever as to where to draw the line. In a sense this is shirking the practical issue [...]. I should guess that according to my ideas you greatly under-estimate the practicability of the middle course. [...] I should say that what we want is not no planning, or even less planning, indeed I should say that we almost certainly want more. [...] Moderate planning will be safe if those carrying it out are rightly orientated in their own minds and hearts to the moral issue. (Keynes 1944, 386–87)

In the end of this passage, Keynes followed a somewhat *Crocean* path: moral and practical issues can be separated and still be in line with the ideal principles of liberalism.[18] Here we come to a sharp distinction between Keynes's liberalism, on the one hand, and that of Röpke, Eucken or Hayek on the other: "I accuse you [Hayek] of perhaps confusing a little bit the moral and the material issues" (Keynes 1944, 387). In Keynes's mind, complete planning could be more efficient than a market economy. And yet one cannot accept "the superfluous sacrifice of liberties" involved with "extreme planners", for the economic problem could be solved in a more reasonable way. Here we have the *General Theory* message all over

[17] As Caldwell (2003, 289) noted, Hayek would (much) later address Keynes's (and also Eucken's) comments in *The Constitution of Liberty* (1960) and in *Law, Legislation and Liberty* (1982). But Keynes's seminal criticism of Hayek, outlined by Skidelsky (2006, 82) as "lacking a short-period theory of statesmanship", remains unanswered.

[18] The Italian historian and philosopher Benedetto Croce (1866–1952) was a Hegelian liberal, famous for his distinction between *liberalismo* and *liberismo* (see Soliani 2011, 145–49). Broadly speaking, he made a sharp separation between the ideal ends of liberalism, as a philosophical category (*liberalismo*), and the practical means that can be used in order to fulfil this purpose, which lie in the field of political economy (*liberismo*).

again, in line with the *Concluding notes* referred to above. Ultimately, Keynes rejected collectivism on moral—not economic—grounds.[19]

Clearly, Eucken was far warier of planning than Keynes, and yet the former did not insist that much on the issue in writing to Hayek. Indeed, Eucken especially warned Hayek against a return to old-fashioned *laissez-faire* liberalism. Looking at the post-war context and taking the particular case of Germany as a valuable lesson, Eucken argued that a mere return to *laissez-faire* would be a disaster, as it would ultimately amount to the confiscation of power by private interest groups. According to him, the new liberal order should be worked through "from the beginning", i.e. by State intervention—a type of planning—on the *forms* of the economic order (*Wirtschaftsordnung*): roughly the market structures and the monetary system. He then addressed Hayek as follows:

> You underscore the difference between a competition-based order [*Wettbewerbsordnung*] and laissez faire. Wouldn't it be appropriate, however, to mark this difference more strongly [...]. It is therefore critical, from the beginning, to push for a real competition-based order. Even though the purpose of your book is not to examine in detail the necessary measures to achieve this, one could perhaps nonetheless outline the most fundamental elements in a few pages. Indeed, the right way is a third [*dritter Weg*], new way. (Eucken 1946b, 139–40)

A few years later, Eucken (1948a, b) specified the connection of his own (normative) conception of the economic order and his social philosophy: a redefining of a classic inquiry of German policy on the Social Question (Fèvre 2017b). This path led Eucken to a composite conception of social justice, "which consists of a mixture of commutative and distributive justice" (Wörsdörfer 2013, 294), parting company with Hayek's relentless effort to describe distributive justice as one step on the slippery slope leading unavoidably to complete planning of the economy.

[19] The evaluation of Capitalism in "moral terms" was one of the components that "helped carry his economic message both inward to the most elite policy circles and outward to the larger public" (Backhouse and Bateman 2009, 669; 2013, 86).

1.3 Rebuilding the (International) Economic Order

Clearly, both Keynes and Eucken felt at odds with Hayek's upgraded version of classical liberalism in general, and with his concept of spontaneous order in particular (Hayek 1944, 69–71). The concept of "order" (*Ordnung*) was nonetheless pivotal to Eucken and his fellow *ordo*-liberals. Broadly speaking, order referred to different spheres of social life, such as the political, economic or cultural; although distinct from each other, these are unified by similar internal principles of cohesion and necessity. Hence order was a way of thinking about reality that goes beyond disciplinary frameworks (see Böhm 1950).

Eucken (1940, 227) focused in particular on the "economic order" (*Wirtschaftsordnung*) defined as "the totality of the forms through which the running of the daily economic process—here and there, yesterday and today—took place in practice". However, this does not imply that the actual economic order realised in any country would satisfactorily achieve efficiency and justice. Indeed, in many cases the economic order "can be inhuman" (1940, 239), yet the scientific world has to do deals with the (positive) economic order people are living in. According to Eucken (1940, 238), order had yet another (normative) meaning, for order also corresponded to "the nature of man ... being based on the notion of moderation and balance". Thus, this "order of the economy", or *Ordo*, is also *Naturordnung*—Eucken referred to it as "*ordre de nature*" in French, with an implicit reference to François Quesnay—in the sense that it would be faithful to the nature of man. *Ordo* was, therefore, an imperative necessity according to which the economic system must be organised. In that respect, Eucken (1940, 314) argued that the economic order had to be "consciously shaped" in all its aspects—taking extra care with interrelationships of all these dimensions—with a special emphasis on the rules of the economic game nationally as well as internationally.

From Eucken's viewpoint (1940, 84), Hayek's dichotomy opposing "emerging" (or spontaneous) and "constructed" orders undermined the real issue, since neither of these two types of orders actually ensures the best of systems. The spontaneous economic order cannot be a desirable order de facto. Even subject to the existence of impersonal, general and abstract rules, as Hayek later stressed, ordoliberals considered his approach insufficient as it would renew the defects of classical liberalism. In short, Hayek outlined a far more restricted area for state action in a market economy than ordoliberals did (Bönker and Wagener 2001; Kolev 2013).

Keynes was obviously disconnected from the German-speaking discussion on order, even though he was also paying attention to the wider moral and cultural implications of economic systems. The notion of order occupied neither a central nor a systematic place in his writings. However, Keynes used the notion of order in relation to the international context, in particular during the pre-Bretton Woods discussions. In the early 1940s, Keynes drew up several versions of his "Plan" to build the new world order for the post-war period. He crucially aimed at giving stabilising (fixed) rules on the international monetary order while maintaining discretion on the domestic conduct of the interest rate or investment policies. In this respect, international monetary measures should be compatible with a sophisticated management of foreign trade, where any country could freely engage in its own *New Deal* for reconstruction (Newton 2000).

The international order was not absent from Eucken's consideration, though he rather neglected it in comparison to Röpke (1945).[20] However, Eucken provided a brief discussion of the "Plan for an International Clearing Union" that Keynes published in preparation for the Bretton Woods Conference (the second version of April 1943). In his "Remarks on Keynes's Monetary Plan", Eucken aimed at outlining the consequences that institutional features of the Keynes Plan would have on the economic order governing international trade.[21] As just noted, Keynes designed a new monetary system with the fundamental goal of stabilising exchange rates and restoring appropriate conditions for international trade. Eucken briefly went through the technical details of the Plan without any particularly critical comment. He even concluded positively on the monetary part, yet without showing any real understanding of the revolutionary stakes involved in the Bancor proposal.[22]

[20] Quinn Slobodian (2018) insisted especially on the rise of the international outlook among neoliberals, what he at times referred to as "ordoglobalism".

[21] The text entitled "*Bemerkungen zum Währungplan von Keynes*" (1943) was discussed at the end of November 1943 in private seminars within the Freiburg resistance circle. In April 1944, Eucken made some additional comments (Eucken 1944).

[22] With the Bancor, Keynes sought to deprive the international currency of its function as a store of value and, through negative interest rates applied to both debtors and creditors, to promote balanced accounts of each country in the Union (Amato and

However, and in contrast to an international system that would serve "as a tool for the anonymous functioning of world economic relations", as it should, Eucken (1943, 274) saw the Keynes Plan as an "instrument of authority" exercising deleterious effects upon international trade. Indeed, Eucken condemned sections (8) and (9) of the Plan on the functions of the Union in organising the trade policy of the member countries. From that perspective, Keynes sought to establish a Union that would be "a support for international policies" and that would then become "a pivot of the future economic government of the world" (1943, [§39]) though with a view to "maintaining price stability and controlling the business cycle" (ibid., [§39.5]). Eucken interpreted the creation of international institutions such as the *International Investment Board* and the *International Economic Board* as purposely paving the way towards controlled prices and stocks of basic commodities.

In Eucken's view, with the establishment of these supranational institutions, which would not be directly linked to the mechanisms of exchange rate adjustment or the functioning of currency reserves, the Keynes Plan would involve...

> a new order of the world economy, and a continuous control and regulation of the economic process by the central economic policy (...). This reorganisation of the world can be seen as an economic order dominated by elements of the exchange economy, but the fact that the most important commodity markets are monopolised and that these monopolies must be under central supervision indicates an economic system in which certain elements of the planned economy prevail. (Eucken, 1943, 272)

Ultimately for Eucken (1943, 273), Keynes organised the "concentration of power" on an international scale. Eucken's former student Friedrich Lutz (1943, 21), in a comparative report of the two plans (Keynes and White) drafted for the *International Finance Section of Princeton University*, came to similar conclusions to Eucken's regarding the place of pressure groups at the international level. Hence paradoxically for Eucken (1943, 273), the Keynes Plan outlined international monetary policy and balance-of-payments measures that indeed represented a "serious attempt

Fantacci 2014, 93–94). Money is obviously the great absentee in the present article. While analysing the contradiction between Keynesian and ordoliberal monetary policy, and the links with contemporary Euro policies, Jörg Bibow (2013) gives some hints on the Keynes/Eucken comparison on this issue.

to promote equilibrium tendencies". And yet by assuming certain prerogatives related to the direction of the investment and trade in goods on the global scale, the Keynes Plan encouraged at the same time "the general imbalance in world commodity markets". Eucken (1944, 277) adopted a more nuanced position in his second commentary on the Keynes Plan. He then recognised that in some particular cases, controlling already existing international cartels may be a lesser evil, rather than constant state intervention in these markets. In particular, certain technological shocks may indeed render inoperative the market process for raw materials such as rubber or cotton.

2 Eucken: Keynes's Obvious Challenger

Just like his friend and colleague Röpke, Eucken staunchly rejected a full employment policy, and yet he did not fall into a facile comparison or an overhasty rejection of Keynes's thought (at least in his public writings). Apart from the obvious difference of style between a born-polemicist like Röpke, and Eucken's more balanced and reserved posture, in practice what mattered to Eucken was not so much to play the role of the virulent critic of the British economist, but rather, to embody the true alternative himself. Eucken indeed understood that Keynes—and by extension Keynesian ideas—was the major competitor to confront in the post-war era.

2.1 Eucken's Twofold Reception of Keynes

In Eucken's *magnum opus* on the foundations of political economy, *Die Grundlagen der Nationalökonomie* (1940), Keynes was one of the few non-German-speaking economists mentioned, and the one Eucken dedicated most space to, as much for instance as Böhm-Bawerk and Hayek. Of Eucken's seven citations of Keynes, three are mere anodyne references to the *Memorials of Alfred Marshall* edited by Pigou (1925), and to Chapter 12 of the *GT*, on expectations. The remaining four are of particular interest, as they reflect Eucken's twofold treatment of Keynes's thought.

First of all, Eucken (1940, 326, [n°12]) underlined that Keynes offered a good example of a theoretical study seeking to build on the real economic situation. According to Eucken (1940, 58), Keynes was one of the few contemporary economists who still thought starting from "the stimulus of concrete problems and the force of historical facts"; arriving where his teacher Alfred Marshall meant to get, without actually succeeding. At the same time, however, the two remaining references outlined the main points of disagreement, namely the place of the consumer in economics/the economy on the one hand, and the method of dynamic analysis, on the other hand.

In a subchapter entitled "Economic Development" (*Wirtschaftliche Entwicklung*), Eucken addressed the issue of the consumer's place at both the empirical (the actual economic process) and theoretical (political economy) levels. In his mind, consumer sovereignty[23] tends to increasingly give way to the predominance of the corporations' supremacy. For Eucken, Keynes played a central role in this historical shift:

> In recent decades the influence of consumers on the economic process has diminished, a characteristic fact of the greatest importance in contemporary economic development. Since Carl Menger, economic theory has been demonstrating how the needs of households backed by purchasing power, that is, consumer demand, control the production process even in its most distant recesses. Perhaps this theory is now obsolete and incorrect and a new one must be worked out? This is what Keynes attempted when he sought to explain, among other things, how and why the entrepreneur and not the consumer occupied the key position in the modern economic process. (Eucken 1940, 259)

Eucken's remark prompts two observations. First, was Keynes really an "entrepreneur-side" theorist *à la* Schumpeter? For Keynes (1936b, 104), it goes without saying that "consumption—to repeat the obvious—is the sole end and object of all economic activity. Opportunities for employment are necessarily limited by the extent of aggregate demand. Aggregate demand can be derived only from present consumption or from present provision for future consumption". In this respect, Eucken's assessment appears misleading. However, a closer reading of the *GT* does give Eucken some grounds to stress that "the entrepreneur and not the consumer occupied the central position in the modern economic process" (Eucken 1940, 259). Indeed, for Keynes, the crucial economic

[23] The concept of consumer sovereignty was shaped by the early neoliberals of the interwar period (Olsen 2018).

problem, namely the determination of the level of employment, depended essentially on the behaviour of entrepreneurs rather than of consumers.

The very structure of the *GT* supports this reading: whereas the propensity to consume (Book III) was explained in (just) three chapters, the argument on the inducement to invest (Book IV) occupied eleven chapters. Keynes underlined quite explicitly the crucial role played by the entrepreneur in determining the level of employment from the very beginning of chapter 3 on *The principle of effective demand*, where he summarised what can be read as the main theoretical argument of the *GT*: "the amount of employment, both in each individual firm and industry and in the aggregate, depends on the amount of the proceeds which the entrepreneurs expect to receive from the corresponding output" (Keynes 1936b, 24). To reconcile both Keynes's statements, consumption decisions appeared more trivial, and so deserved less consideration, for full employment ultimately lay in investment decisions.[24]

Second, Eucken's reading favoured a theory/practice dichotomy over a positive/normative dichotomy, suggesting a somewhat materialistic understanding of history. Eucken, a fervent advocate of the consumer's sovereignty, concentrated on a normative set of economic policies with this end in view. His later dictum that "economic thought is a political force" (Eucken 1951, 83) shows all its relevance here. In short, according to Eucken, Keynes both acknowledged the entrepreneur's rising power, and contributed to it. In a sense, Eucken once again saw Keynes as an acute observer of actual economic tendencies, but would rather have seen this particular trend restrained.

Along with this first objection, Eucken stressed a second distinction with Keynes. While complaining about Walras's static conception of the general economic equilibrium, Eucken (1940, 27) was not ready "to abandon the notion of the static state" as a technique, because it would mean "giving up all understanding of economic development". Indeed, he had words of praise for the Schumpeterian "method of variations" (or comparative statics), and thus opposed Keynes's standpoint:

> There is no tenable economic basis for the view expressed by, among others, Keynes and Pigou that after a static state has been disturbed a new static state *cannot* again be reached [...]. It is true that in real economic

[24] I am very grateful to Luca Fantacci for drawing my attention to this aspect of Keynes's work, as well as to the last quotation.

> life the movement to a new static state is regularly interrupted by fresh changes in data. But this is not an objection against this method. For only with its aid can it be known in what direction a variation in data will take effect. The statement that a new static position is reached in the long run must not be misunderstood in the way it is so often. That the new static position is never actually reached does not mean that it is not of interest. Rather it answers the question of the direction of the movement which follows immediately on the change in data. (Eucken 1940, 254)

Crucial here is that Eucken was faced with the very fact that Keynes, like Marshall, was "analysing systems in motion: equilibrium was but a point attractor in such a process" (Backhouse and Bateman 2006, 12). Eucken proved to be more in line with the *Walrasian* viewpoint, therefore with the early Hayek of "economics as equilibrium theory" against the Cambridge tradition, on the one hand, and against the "Economics and Knowledge" Hayek (1937) of the late thirties, on the other. The concept of *Equilibrium* was one of the conflicting (and controversial[25]) issues between our protagonists that are beyond the scope of this article.

Over and above these two criticisms that Eucken expressed—which are crucial in grasping the Keynes/Eucken antagonism about their conception of economic policies—the paper then investigates Eucken's understanding of his role as a competitor.

2.2 *Informing the Economic Policy*

Drawing again on the letter Eucken wrote to Hayek, it offers eloquent evidence of Eucken's budding opposition to Keynes and to the infant Welfare State,[26] which seemed to be taking over in the United Kingdom. Several months before Keynes's death, Eucken wrote:

[25] By contrast to Bruce Caldwell's authoritative—and widely accepted—reading of *Hayek's transformation* (1988), Richard Arena (2003) suggested a contradictory interpretation by pointing out that, first, Hayek's work never implied the use of a Walrasian, or neo-Walrasian, general economic equilibrium; second, Hayek had already shown, before 1936, keen attention to the question of knowledge; and third, the concept of equilibrium he actually used from the beginning was still prevalent after 1936.

[26] In the political perspective, it was Clement Attlee's Labour government that set about founding the British Welfare State. For questioning of Keynes's parentage of the British welfare state, see the article by Backhouse and Bateman (2012, 17), which concludes that "the greatest role that Keynes played in the rise of the welfare state was the authority his name lent to the political economy that underpinned the rise of the welfare state". In

> Voices apparently coming from the liberal side also sounded worrying. For instance, the fact that the Beveridge Plan was included by the Liberal Party in its platform. Or the position of the Economist on the issue of full employment, for example. All this, as well as Keynes's influence, shows a certain ignorance with respect to the formidable risks posed by this development, risks that we [Germans] experienced first-hand in their entirety. (Eucken 1946b, 138–39)

Eucken showed his hand a few years later in the English preface (1950) to the *Foundation of Economics* (*FE*), translated from *Die Grundlagen der Nationalökonomie* (1940) by Terence W. Hutchison as requested by Hayek. Although it was certainly not the original purpose of the book, Eucken's English preface reoriented the message of his book to pitch it as an alternative to the Keynesian hegemony, but tactfully, with a touch of modesty (in comparison with the tone of his private correspondence): "we are not concerned here to criticise; we only want to emphasise that the theory of full employment too is aiming at a better understanding of the real economic world. This book [*FE*] is in the service of the same cause" (Eucken 1950, 10).

Indeed, more than one parallel can be drawn between Eucken's English preface to the *FE* and Keynes's German preface to the *GT*. Eucken seemed to react, and respond, to some of Keynes's statements at least on two accounts. Apart from Eucken's treatment of Marshall's legacy, which he borrowed directly from Keynes,[27] the way the former addressed the place of "theory" in German economics, and his straight reply to his macroeconomics programme at the level of policy, appear to support this hypothesis.

Keynes, revealing a glowing self-confidence, emphasized the interest the *GT* would hold for German scholars, seeing his contribution as a way to fill a serious gap over there:

the same spirit, see *Whose Welfare State? Beveridge versus Keynes* by Maria C. Marcuzzo (2010).

[27] Interestingly enough, this is not Eucken's only borrowing from Keynes. For instance, Eucken referred to Lenin's words about the fundamental relationship of currency stability with the overall social order, like Keynes, showing a positive response: "Lenin was certainly right" (Keynes 1919, 149), or there would be a "considerable element of truth in this remark" (Eucken 1951, 82). As a matter of fact, Keynes would be responsible for giving circulation to this quotation (White and Schuler 2009, 213–14).

> Can I persuade German economists that methods of formal analysis have something important to contribute to the interpretation of contemporary events and to the *moulding of contemporary policy*? After all, it is German to like a theory. How hungry and thirsty German economists must feel after having lived all these years without one. [...] And if I can contribute some stray morsels towards the *preparation by German economists of a full repast of theory designed to meet specifically German conditions*, I shall be content. (Keynes 1936a, xxvi, italics added)

Eucken did not fundamentally call Keynes's theory into question, yet he did not recognise its full relevance in addressing economic policy issues. In a nutshell, Eucken urged contemporary theorists to consider the seminal importance of considering the kind of system—or order—in which economic forces were set into motion. Eucken called it "thinking in economic orders" (*Denken in Wirtschaftsordnungen*). From Eucken's viewpoint, it is only after having clearly specified this system (from "pure exchange" to "centrally administrated" economy), that one can consider theories as appropriate (or not) to cast light on matters of economic policy[28]:

> As we penetrate into the actual conditions of economic life it becomes clear that a precise grasp of the real economic world demands an understanding of the different forms in which economic activity takes place, and therefore that *a morphological analysis must precede a theoretical analysis*. So I believe that it is just the morphological suggestions in this book which may be of interest to English and American readers, particularly *from the point of view of the fundamentals of economic policy*. (Eucken 1950, 11, italics added)

In a sense, Eucken emphasised an *ante*-theoretical level, which stood for him as *another* kind of theory. This morphological theory would be complementary to—and condition the case-by-case relevance of—"usual" economic theory. It is precisely for this reason that the Keynes/Eucken comparison at such a level appears problematic, because they do not cover exactly the same ground. Eucken sought to express this idea during his last lecture at the *LSE*:

[28] Eucken devoted a specific study to economic policy, posthumously published as *Grundsätze der Wirtschaftspolitik* (1952).

> "Less," say the advocates of laissez-faire; "more," cry the central planners. Friends of a compromise solution seek a middle way. They would like the state to plan and, at the same time, to give scope for private planning and initiative. *But the problem needs to be stated differently if it is to be solved.* (Eucken 1951, 95, italics added)

2.3 Keynes and Eucken: Inside-Out National Traditions

Eucken did praise Keynes's scientific method. He saw it as an example of a proper theoretical study starting from direct experience and real questions, like his own methodological standpoint. In truth, the two authors endorsed very distinctive methodological outlooks, so how to explain Eucken's praise?

In his preface to the German edition of the *GT* (as in the Japanese and French ones), Keynes levelled his critical fire at Ricardo's heritage. Indeed according to Keynes, "[t]he Manchester School and Marxism both derive ultimately from Ricardo" (Keynes 1936a, xxv). Therefore, Keynes rejected Ricardian theoretical principles (as interpreted by the head of the *orthodoxy*, Marshall) as well as its political conclusions leading to an antagonistic conception—individualistic *versus* socialist—of state action.

As far as economics is concerned, Eucken's methodology arose from "a schism" (1951, 83) between Menger and Schmoller. It is well known that Eucken's *Grundlagen* proved to be a systematic attempt to overcome the German controversy over methods (in their own ways, Max Weber or Arthur Spiethoff were pursuing the same aim).[29] Unlike his father John Neville Keynes, Maynard did not express his interest in economic methodology by dedicating an essay to it, but significant parts of his works can be read as contributions to this field (see Carabelli 1988). Keynes also had close contact with philosophers of his time, like Ludwig Wittgenstein. In the field of Ethics, Keynes, together with his Bloomsbury companions, remained committed to G. E. Moore's quest for "absolute truth, (…) for friendship and beauty" (Backhouse and Bateman 2006, 1). Similarly, Eucken's neo-Kantian father and the phenomenology of Edmund Husserl

[29] In particular, Eucken aimed at overcoming what he called the "great antinomy" (*Die Große Antinomie*) between History and Theory (Herrmann-Pillath 1994; Weisz 2001; Goldschmidt 2013).

played a crucial role in Eucken's formation (Campagnolo 2003; Klump and Wörsdörfer 2011).

Furthermore, both Keynes and Eucken rose to prominence overshadowed by two figures, hegemonic at the turn of the twentieth century: Alfred Marshall in England, Gustav Schmoller in Germany. While Keynes, with his *GT*, launched his strongest attack on Marshallian orthodoxy and classical economics, Eucken—together with the Freiburg School—marked his divorce from a purely Historical School perspective. In the brief text henceforth known as *The Ordo Manifesto of 1936*, but originally entitled *Our Task* (Böhm et al. 1936), the authors came up with a severe condemnation of fatalism (induced by historical materialism), of unrealistic doctrines plus lack of abstract thinking, and of ideological permeability. They judged these to be the major drawbacks of the Historicist approach, especially under the tutelage of Schmoller.

From the mid-twenties to the early thirties, Eucken was close to the informal "German Ricardians" group led by Alexander Rüstow, and to which Eucken, Röpke, as well as Friedrich Lutz, Adolf Löwe or Adolf Weber belonged (Janssen 2009). The aim of these young thinkers was to set up a faction more interested in theoretical considerations within the *Verein für Sozialpolitik* (Vanberg 2013, 1–5). Their discussion chiefly concerned general equilibrium theory, monetary theory or business cycle theory. Therefore, special attention was paid to the German works by Joseph A. Schumpeter, Ludwig *von* Mises, Gustav Cassel and Knut Wicksell, as well as the Anglo-Saxon contributions by Irving Fisher and by the Keynes of *A Tract on Monetary Reform* (1923) and *A Treatise on Money* (1930). Yet the group of young Ricardians failed to find an institutional identity of its own vis-à-vis Historical orthodoxy, and was eventually plagued by irreconcilable political divisions among its members regarding the best way to address the social and political ills Germany was struggling with.

Despite ordoliberals' opposition to the German tradition, there were still ample *continuities* between ordoliberals like Eucken and the Historical Schools (young and neo), especially on methodological grounds (Schefold 1995, 2003; Tribe 1995). Because thinking *against* is also thinking *from*, the same consideration also applied to Keynes in relation to his teacher Alfred Marshall. Keynes's "ideas were rooted entirely in Marshallian economics" according to Hayek, who underlined this bond in his *Personal Recollections of Keynes* (1995, 241). And indeed Hayek's general, but incisive, consideration was later pinpointed in more detail by the secondary literature (Groenewegen 1995; Hodgson 2005; Hoover 2006).

The bond between Marshall and Keynes is of particular relevance to this paper if we consider that Marshall (1890, 634), who made no secret of his admiration for the German (and British) Historical School, appeared to share certain views with this school of thought: he, too, appreciated the importance of the causal explanation of facts, and, (for instance) expressed scepticism about the use of mathematics to grasp economic realities. Keynes offered a clear demonstration of his closeness to this view by praising Robert Malthus' scientific method. With the accurate and fruitful articulation of an "a priori method of the political philosopher" with "historical induction and filling his mind with a mass of the material of experience", Malthus would have approached, "as the first of the Cambridge economists, [...] the central problems of economic theory by the best of all routes" (Keynes 1972, 107). Keynes never fitted into the "unworldly logician" type of economists for he "synthesized the complex materials at his disposal to convey the essence of the situation" (Maas 2011, 222–23), even if this was not done by placing great emphasis on statistical elements. In some respects, the controversy Keynes conducted about econometrics—notoriously with Jan Tinbergen—on "the problem of measurement, model specification, and the application of statistics" (Bateman 1990, 360) can also be read in that light. Incidentally, Eucken endorsed exactly the same approach: "*The economist who wants to understand the interdependence of economic life with theoretical analysis must also pursue to the fullest extent his observation of actual economic events*" (1940, 299, original emphasis). And just like Keynes, the ordoliberals never felt easy with either the mathematical or statistical approach to economics.

From Marshall to Robinson, Kaldor and Keynes, a core aspect of the Cambridge tradition can be found in the combination of economic history and genuine concerns with the actual economic situation (Arena 1991; for an adverse interpretation see Hodgson 2001, 213–19). All this adds up to what may be described as Keynes's "historical", "pluralist" or "institutional" method,[30] in opposition to the neoclassical pattern that

[30]The American institutionalist John R. Commons also exerted a strong influence on Keynes' conception of Capitalism (Atkinson and Oleson 1998).

rose prominently in US institutions of the second half of the twentieth century.[31]

The point is that this methodological background—Keynes the theorist sensitive to historical-institutionalist inspirations, and Eucken, born and raised in the area of Historicism, trying to address theoretical issues—constitutes a promising area for discussion: possibly casting light on the reason why Keynes and Eucken left such an indelible mark on economic policy conceptions and practices.

3 Concluding Remarks

Although their definitions may be contested, Keynesianism and ordoliberalism are terms that current observers still find useful in approaching contemporary Eurozone policies (Allen 2005; Esch 2014). The opposition between *rule-oriented* (austerity) and *discretionary* (expansionist) policies remains a formidable bone of contention between Eucken and Keynes, and indeed between ordoliberalism and Keynesianism. However, while these broad "-ism" labels have blurred a significant part of the Keynes/Eucken disagreement, they have also obscured the fact that they shared, on some issues, more similarities than immediate impressions might suggest.

In considering Eucken's treatment of Keynes in his *Grundlagen*, this unrecognised affinity leads us to three comments. First, as both authors sought to put a distance between themselves and methodological/theoretical traditions they were trained in (historical-institutionalist), Keynes and Eucken increased their relative proximity. Secondly, Eucken decidedly saw his theory as a counterpart to Keynes's, and adopted the position of a challenger, as is attested by various elements, and especially by Eucken's English preface to the *FE*, with the *proviso* that, in some ways, reference to Keynes was virtually inevitable within the area of discussion that Eucken, too, was addressing. Third, real experience and observation of actual economic problems (albeit with different scenarios and interpretive frameworks) played a primary role in Eucken and Keynes's respective theoretical elaboration. In their conception of the role of the—not merely armchair—economist, political factors or external challenges

[31] Institutions like the Cowls Commission, M.I.T. or the University of Chicago stated the—albeit competing—main lines for what is usually labelled the "Americanisation" of post-war economics (Backhouse 2003, 320; Mirowski 2006, 352–56).

to economics were key. To shape the economic order, both knew they had to convince governments and public opinion. In doing so, the economist had to master the theoretical aspect of economics without which the complex, interrelated process of the economy would remain silent to him. However, technical knowledge alone would undermine the overall message they had to convey; hence, these public intellectuals fighting for reform also had to picture a desirable new path for industrial societies. Philosophy, Ethics, Morals and Politics fuelled their ideas on economics and society.

In the final analysis, Keynes and Eucken show antagonistic but symmetrical positions in the way they integrate politics with their economic ideas, giving a new twist to the opposition between Anglo-Saxon (British) liberalism, on the one hand, and continental (Germanic) liberalism, on the other. Keynes and Eucken, each in his own way, found the right form of words to reach the ear of the government, but their strategies diverged. Keynes, building on a long established tradition of economic and political liberalism, promoted some reforms that were indeed revolutionary, but reforms that in his view could be carried out by "a slow series of experiments" (1933, 190), and "introduced gradually and without a break in the general traditions of the society" (1936b, 378). For his part, Eucken was confronted with a political environment marked by a strong socialist—non-Marxist—tendency generally favourable to state interference in the social and economic spheres. He personally witnessed totalitarianism and felt close to German liberals who, though they were unorganised, were actually there but "forced into the catacombs" (1946b, 143). In a space of public policies fraught with ideological antagonisms, Eucken and the ordoliberals saw the shift to a market economy as the only way to break with a German path largely resilient to liberal ideas.

Acknowledgements For comments on earlier drafts of this chapter, I am particularly indebted to the participants of the "Historical and Philosophical Perspectives on Economics Seminar" of the London School of Economics (London, December 2015), the 20th ESHET Annual Conference (Paris, May 2016), as well as the Jean Monnet Workshop on "Interwar Economics and the Intellectual Origins of European Integration" (Lisbon, February 2019). My gratitude also goes to my fellow colleagues of the Centre Walras Pareto for their remarks and suggestions. Finally, I would like to extend warm thanks to Alexandre M. Cunha and Carlos Eduardo Suprinyak as well as the anonymous referee for insights on how to improve the paper in order to fit into the wider context of this collective volume. All remaining errors and inaccuracies are obviously mine.

References

Allen, Christopher S. 2005. "Ordo-Liberalism Trumps Keynesianism: Economic Policy in the Federal Republic of Germany." In *Monetary Union in Crisis: The European Union as a Neo-Liberal Construction*, edited by Bernard H. Moss, 199–221. London: Palgrave.

Amato, Massimo, and Luca Fantacci. 2014. *Saving the Market from Capitalism: Ideas for an Alternative Finance*. Cambridge: Polity.

Arena, Richard. 1991. "De l'usage de l'histoire dans la formulation des hypothèses de la théorie économique." *Revue Économique* 42 (2): 395–409.

———. 2003. "Beliefs, Knowledge and Equilibrium." In *Cognitive Developments in Economics*, edited by Salvatore Rizzello, 316–37. London and New York: Routledge.

Atkinson, Glen, and Theodore Oleson. 1998. "Commons and Keynes: Their Assault on Laissez Faire." *Journal of Economic Issues* 32 (4): 1019–30.

Backhaus, Jürgen G. 1985. "Keynesianism in Germany." In *Keynes' Economics, Methodological Lssues*, edited by Tony Lawson and Hashem Pesaran, 209–53. London and Sydney: Routledge, 2009.

Backhouse, Roger E. 2003. "The Stabilization of Price Theory, 1920–55." In *Blackwell Companion to the History of Economic Thought*, edited by Jeff Biddle, John B. Davis and Warren J. Samuels, 308–24. Oxford: Blackwell.

Backhouse, Roger E., and Bradley W. Bateman. 2006. "A Cunning Purchase: The Life and Work of Mayard Keynes." In *The Cambridge Companion to Keynes*, edited by Roger E. Backhouse and Bradley W. Bateman, 1–18. Oxford: Cambridge University Press.

———. 2009. "Keynes and Capitalism." *History of Political Economy* 41 (4): 645–71.

———. 2012. "Keynes and the Welfare State." *History of Economic Thought and Policy* 1 (1): 7–20.

———. 2013. "Inside Out: Keynes's Use of the Public Sphere." *History of Political Economy* 45 (suppl 1): 68–91.

Bateman, Bradley W. 1990. "Keynes, Induction, and Econometrics." *History of Political Economy* 22 (2): 359–79.

———. 2006. "Keynes and Keynesianism." In *The Cambridge Companion to Keynes*, edited by Roger E. Backhouse and Bradley W. Bateman, 271–90. Cambridge, UK: Cambridge University Press.

Bibow, Jörg. 2013. "At the Crossroads: The Euro and Its Central Bank Guardian (and Saviour?)." *Cambridge Journal of Economics* 37 (3): 609–26.

Biebricher, Thomas. 2019. *The Political Theory of Neoliberalism*. Stanford: Stanford University Press.

Böhm, Franz. 1950. "Die Idee Des Ordo Im Denken Walter Euckens: Dem Freunde Und Mitherausgeber Zum Gedächtnis." *ORDO: Jahrbuch Für Die Ordnung von Wirtschaft Und Gesellschaft* 3: XV–LXIV.

Böhm, Franz, Walter Eucken, and Hans Großmann-Doerth. 1936. "Unsere Aufgabe / The Ordo Manifesto of 1936." In *Germany's Social Market Economy: Origins and Evolution*, edited by Alan Peacock and Hans Willgerodt, 15–26. London: Macmillan for the Trade Policy Research Centre, 1989.

Bonefeld, Werner. 2017. *The Strong State and the Free Economy*. London: Rowman & Littlefield International.

Bönker, Frank, and Hans-Jürgen Wagener. 2001. "Hayek and Eucken on State and Market Economy." In *Institutional Economics in France and Germany: German Ordoliberalism Versus the French Regulation School*, edited by Agnès Labrousse and Jean-Daniel Weisz, 183–99. Heidelberg: Springer.

Branch, Mary Sydney. 1945. "The Road to Serfdom by Frtedrich A. Hayek." *Social Service Review* 19 (1): 146–48.

Caldwell, Bruce. 1988. "Hayek's Transformation." *History of Political Economy* 20 (4): 513–41.

———. 2003. *Hayek's Challenge*. Chicago: The University of Chicago Press.

———. 2007. "Introduction." In *The Road to Serfdom [The Collected Works of Hayek—II]*, by Friedrich A. Hayek, edited by Bruce Caldwell, 1–36. London: Routledge.

Campagnolo, Gilles. 2003. "Les trois sources philosophiques de la réflexion ordolibérale." In *L'ordolibéralisme allemand : aux sources de l'économie sociale de marché*, edited by Patricia Commun, 133–48. Travaux et documents du C.I.R.A.C. Cergy-Pontoise: CIRAC/CICC.

Carabelli, Anna M. 1988. *On Keynes's Method*. Basingstoke, England: Macmillan.

Commun, Patricia. 2018. "Wilhelm Röpke's Report on the Brauns Commission: Advocating a Pragmatic Business Cycle Policy." In *Wilhelm Röpke (1899–1966): A Liberal Political Economist and Conservative Social Philosopher*, edited by Patricia Commun and Stefan Kolev, 121–32. The European Heritage in Economics and the Social Sciences. Cham: Springer International Publishing. https://doi.org/10.1007/978-3-319-68357-7_7.

Director, Aaron. 1945. "Review of The Road to Serfdom by Friedrich A. Hayek." *The American Economic Review* 35 (1): 173–75.

Esch, Femke A. 2014. "Exploring the Keynesian–Ordoliberal Divide. Flexibility and Convergence in French and German Leaders' Economic Ideas During the Euro-Crisis." *Journal of Contemporary European Studies* 22 (3): 288–302.

Eucken, Walter. 1940. *The Foundations of Economics*. Translated by Terence W. Hutchison. London, Edinburgh, and Glasgow: W. Hodge, 1950.

———. 1943. "Bemerkungen Zum Währungplan von Keynes." In *Der Weg in Die Soziale Marktwirtschaft: Referate, Protokolle, Gutachten Der Arbeitsgemeinschaft Erwin von Beckerath, 1943–1947*, edited by Christine Blumenberg-Lampe, 268–74. Stuttgart: Klett-Cotta, 1986.

———. 1944. "Einige Weitere Bemerkungen Zur Internationalen Währungsfrage." In *Der Weg in Die Soziale Marktwirtschaft: Referate, Protokolle, Gutachten Der Arbeitsgemeinschaft Erwin von Beckerath, 1943–1947*, edited by Christine Blumenberg-Lampe, 275–78. Stuttgart: Klett-Cotta, 1986.

———. 1946a. "Industrielle Konzentration / Concentration industrielle." In *Ordnungspolitik*, edited by Walter Oswalt, 25–37. Comité d'Etudes Economiques Walter Eucken Freiburg im Breisgau. Münster, Allemagne: LIT Verlag, 1999.

———. 1946b. "Letter to Professor F. A. Hayek, March 12 - HIA FAH Papers, Box 18, Fo. 40. (Reproduced and Translated from Original German)." In *Hayek: A Collaborative Biography: Part 1 Influences from Mises to Bartley*, edited by Robert Leeson, translated by Sigrid Saou, 138–43. Hampshire: Palgrave Macmillan, 2013.

———. 1946c. "Über die Gesamtrichtung der Wirtschaftspolitik / Propos sur l'orientation générale de la politique économique." In *Ordnungspolitik*, edited by Walter Oswalt, 1–24. Comité d'Etudes Economiques Walter Eucken Freiburg im Breisgau. Münster, Allemagne: LIT Verlag, 1999.

———. 1948a. "Das Ordnungspolitische Problem/What Kind of Economic and Social System ?" In *Germany's Social Market Economy: Origins and Evolution [1989]*, edited by Alan Peacock and Hans Willgerodt, 27–45. London: Macmillan for the Trade Policy Research Centre.

———. 1948b. "Die Soziale Frage/The Social Question." In *Standard Texts on the Social Market Economy: Two Centuries of Discussion*, edited by Horst Friedrich Wünsche, translated by Derek Rutter, 267–76. Stuttgart: Gustav Fischer Verlag, 1982.

———. 1948c. "On the Theory of the Centrally Administered Economy: An Analysis of the German Experiment. (Part I & II)." Translated by Terence W. Hutchison. *Economica*, New Series, 15 (58, 59): 79–100, 173–93.

———. 1950. "Preface [to the English Edition]." In *The Foundations of Economics*, translated by Terence W. Hutchison, 9–11. London, Edinburgh, and Glasgow: W. Hodge.

———. 1951. *This Unsuccessful Age: Or the Pains of Economic Progress*. London, Edinburgh, and Glasgow: W. Hodge.

———. 1952. *Grundsätze der Wirtschaftspolitik*. Edited by Edith Eucken and K. Paul Hensel. 7th ed. Tübingen: Mohr Siebeck, 2004.

Feld, Lars P., Ekkehard A. Köhler, and Daniel Nientiedt. 2018. "The German Anti-Keynes? On Walter Eucken's Macroeconomics." Working Paper 18/11. Freiburger Diskussionspapiere zur Ordnungsökonomik. https://www.econstor.eu/handle/10419/181495.

Fèvre, Raphaël. 2017a. "L'ordolibéralisme (1932–1950): Une Économie Politique Du Pouvoir." Thèse de doctorat, Lausanne, Suisse: Université de Lausanne & Université Paris 1 Panthéon-Sorbonne. https://tel.archives-ouvertes.fr/tel-01800112/document.

———. 2017b. "Walter Eucken et Wilhelm Röpke face à la 'nouvelle' Question Sociale." *Revue d'histoire de la pensée économique* 3 (1): 209–40.

———. 2018a. "Denazifying the Economy: Ordoliberals on the Economic Policy Battlefield (1946–50)." *History of Political Economy* 50 (4): 679–707.

———. 2018b. "Keynes and Eucken on Power and Capitalism." In *Power in Economic Thought*, edited by Manuela Mosca, 321–48. London and New York: Palgrave Macmillan.

———. 2018c. "Was Wilhelm Röpke Really a Proto-Keynesian?" In *Wilhelm Röpke (1899–1966): A Liberal Political Economist and Conservative Social Philosopher*, edited by Patricia Commun and Stefan Kolev, 109–20. The European Heritage in Economics and the Social Sciences. Cham: Springer International Publishing. https://doi.org/10.1007/978-3-319-68357-7_7.

Friedrich, Carl J. 1945. "The Road to Serfdom by Friedrich A. Hayek." *The American Political Science Review* 39 (3): 575–79.

Garvy, George. 1975. "Keynes and the Economic Activists of Pre-Hitler Germany." *Journal of Political Economy* 83 (2): 391–405.

Goldschmidt, Nils, ed. 2005. *Wirtschaft, Politik und Freiheit: Freiburger Wirtschaftswissenschaftler und der Widerstand*. Tübingen: Mohr Siebeck.

———. 2013. "Walter Eucken's Place in the History of Ideas." *The Review of Austrian Economics* 26 (2): 127–47.

Goldschmidt, Nils, and Jan-Otmar Hesse. 2013. "Eucken, Hayek, and the Road to Serfdom." In *Hayek: A Collaborative Biography: Part 1 Influences from Mises to Bartley*, edited by Robert Leeson, 123–46. Hampshire: Palgrave Macmillan.

Goldschmidt, Nils, and Michael Wohlgemuth. 2008. "Social Market Economy: Origins, Meanings and Interpretations." *Constitutional Political Economy* 19 (3): 261–76.

Greene, Lancaster M. 1945. "The Road to Confusion." *American Journal of Economics and Sociology* 5 (1): 134–35.

Groenewegen, Peter. 1995. "Keynes and Marshall: Methodology, Society, and Politics." *History of Political Economy* 27 (Supplement): 129–155.

Guillebaud, C. W. 1944. "The Road to Serfdom by F. A. Hayek." *Economica* 11 (44): 215.

Hagemann, Harald. 2013. "Germany after World War II: Ordoliberalism, the Social Market Economy and Keynesianism." *History of Economic Thought and Policy* 1 (1): 37–51.

———. 2014. "The German Edition of Keynes's General Theory: Controversies on the Preface." *Research in the History of Economic Thought and Methodology* 32: 159–166.

Hall, Peter A., ed. 1989. *The Political Power of Economic Ideas: Keynesianism across Nations*. Princeton, NJ: Etats-Unis d'Amérique, Princeton University Press.

Hayek, Friedrich A. 1937. "Economics and Knowledge." *Economica* 4 (13): 33–54.

———. 1944. *The Road to Serfdom*. Edited by Bruce J. Caldwell. The Collected Works of F. A. Hayek, Vol. 2. Chicago: The University of Chicago Press, 2007.

———. 1945. *Der Weg zur Knechtschaft*. Edited by Wilhelm Röpke. Translated by Eva Röpke. Erlenbach-Zürich: E. Rentsch.

———. 1960. *The Constitution of Liberty* [*The Collected Works of Hayek—XVII*]. Edited by Bruce J. Caldwell. London: Routledge, 2011.

———. 1982. *Law, Legislation, and Liberty: A New Statement of the Liberal Principles of Justice and Political Economy*. 3 vols. London: Routledge.

———. 1995. *Contra Keynes and Cambridge* [*The Collected Works of Hayek - IX*]. Edited by Bruce J. Caldwell. London: Routledge.

Herrmann-Pillath, Carsten. 1994. "Methodological Aspects of Eucken's Work." *Journal of Economic Studies* 21 (4): 46–60.

Hesse, Jan-Otmar. 2012. "The 'Americanisation' of West German Economics after the Second World War: Success, Failure, or Something Completely Different?" *The European Journal of the History of Economic Thought* 19 (1): 67–98.

Hodgson, Geoffrey M. 2001. *How Economics Forgot History: The Problem of Historical Specificity in Social Science*. London, New York: Psychology Press.

———. 2005. "Alfred Marshall versus the Historical School?" *Journal of Economic Studies* 32 (4): 331–48.

Hong, Young-Sun. 1998. *Welfare, Modernity, and the Weimar State, 1919–1933*. Princeton, NJ: Etats-Unis d'Amérique, Princeton University Press.

Hoover, Kevin D. 2006. "Doctor Keynes." In *The Cambridge Companion to Keynes*, edited by Roger E. Backhouse and Bradley W. Bateman, 78–97. Cambridge, UK: Cambridge University Press.

Howson, Susan. 2011. *Lionel Robbins*. New York: Cambridge University Press.

Hudson, Michael. 1985. "German Economists and the Depression of 1929–1933." *History of Political Economy* 17 (1): 35–50.

Janssen, Hauke. 2009. "Zwischen Historismus Und Neoklassik: Alexander Rüstow Und Die Krise in Der Deutschen Volkswirtschaftslehre." *ORDO. Jahrbuch Für Die Ordnung von Wirtschaft Und Gesellschaft* 60 (1): 101–18.

Johnson, Daniel. 1989. "Exiles and Half-Exiles: Wilhelm Röpke, Alexander Rüstow and Walter Eucken." In *German Neo-Liberals and the Social Market Economy*, edited by Alan Peacock and Hans Willgerodt, 40–68. Trade Policy Research Centre. London: Palgrave Macmillan.

Keynes, John Maynard. 1919. *The Economic Consequences of the Peace* [*The Collected Writings of John Maynard Keynes-II*]. Edited by D. E. Moggridge. London and Basingstoke: Macmillan, 1971.

———. 1923. *A Tract on Monetary Reform* [*The Collected Writings of John Maynard Keynes-IV*]. Edited by Elizabeth Johnson and Donald E. Moggridge. London and Basingstoke: Macmillan, 1973.

———. 1930. *A Treatise on Money: The Applied Theory of Money* [*The Collected Writings of John Maynard Keynes-VI*]. Edited by Elizabeth Johnson and Donald E. Moggridge. London and Basingstoke: Macmillan, 1973.

———. 1933. "National Self-Sufficiency." *Studies: An Irish Quarterly Review* 22, 177–193.

———. 1936a. "Preface to the German Edition." In *The General Theory* [*The Collected Writings of John Maynard Keynes-VII*], edited by D. E Moggridge, xxv–xxvii. London and Basingstoke: Macmillan, 1973.

———. 1936b. *The General Theory* [*The Collected Writings of John Maynard Keynes-VII*]. London and Basingstoke: Macmillan, 1973.

———. 1943. "The Keynes Plan—Proposals for an International Clearing Union (April 1943)." In *The International Monetary Fund: 1945–1965: Twenty Years of International Monetary Cooperation*, edited by J. Keith Horsefield. Vol. III. Washington: International Monetary Fund, 1969.

———. 1944. "Letter to Professor F. A. Hayek, June 28." In *Activities 1940–1946* [*The Collected Writings of John Maynard Keynes-XXVII*], edited by D. E Moggridge, 385–88. London and Basingstoke: Macmillan, 1980.

———. 1972. *Essays in Biography* [*The Collected Writings of John Maynard Keynes-X*]. London and Basingstoke: Macmillan.

Klausinger, Hansjörg. 1999. "German Anticipations of the Keynesian Revolution? The Case of Lautenbach, Neisser and Röpke." *The European Journal of the History of Economic Thought* 6 (3): 378–403.

Klump, Rainer, and Manuel Wörsdörfer. 2011. "On the Affiliation of Phenomenology and Ordoliberalism: Links between Edmund Husserl, Rudolf and Walter Eucken." *European Journal of the History of Economic Thought* 18 (4): 551–78.

Köhler, Ekkehard A., and Daniel Nientiedt. 2017. "The Muthesius Controversy: A Tale of Two Liberalisms." *History of Political Economy* 49 (4): 607–30.

Kolev, Stefan. 2010. "Hayek as an Ordo-Liberal." *HWWI Research Paper*, nos. 5–11: 1–22.

———. 2013. *Neoliberale Staatsverständnisse im Vergleich*. Stuttgart, Allemagne: Lucius & Lucius.

Kurlander, Eric. 2011. "'Between Detroit and Moscow': A Left Liberal 'Third Way' in the Third Reich." *Central European History* 44 (2): 279–307.

Levy, David M., Sandra J. Peart, and Andrew Farrant. 2005. "The Spatial Politics of F.A. Hayek's Road to Serfdom." *European Journal of Political Economy* 21 (4): 982–99.

Maas, Harro. 2011. "Sorting Things Out: The Economist as an Armchair Observer." In *Histories of Scientific Observation*, edited by Lorraine Daston and Elizabeth Lunbeck, 206–29. Chicago and London: University of Chicago Press.

Magliulo, Antonio. 2018. "Before Hitler: The Expansionary Programme of the Brauns Commission." In *Hayek: A Collaborative Biography: Part XIII: "Fascism" and Liberalism in the (Austrian) Classical Tradition*, edited by Robert Leeson, 129–59. Archival Insights into the Evolution of Economics. Cham: Springer International Publishing. https://doi.org/10.1007/978-3-319-91358-2_3.

Marcuzzo, Maria C. 2010. "Whose Welfare State? Beveridge versus Keynes." In *No Wealth But Life: Welfare Economics and the Welfare State in Britain, 1880–1945*, edited by Roger E. Backhouse and Tamotsu Nishizawa, 189–206. Cambridge: Cambridge University Press.

Marshall, Alfred. 1890. *Principles of Economics*. 8th ed. Basingstoke and London: Macmillan, 1964.

Mayer, Joseph. 1945. "The Road to Serfdom by Friedrich A. Hayek." *Annals of the American Academy of Political and Social Science* 239 (May): 202–3.

Mirowski, Philip. 2006. "Twelve Theses Concerning the History of Postwar Neoclassical Price Theory." In *Agreement on Demand: Consumer Theory in the Twentieth Century*, edited by Philip Mirowski and D. Wade Hands, 38:343–79. History of Political Economy (Annual Supplement). Durham and London: Duke University Press.

Muresan, Stefan Sorin. 2014. *Social Market Economy*. Bonn: Springer.

Newton, Scott. 2000. "A 'Visionary Hope'Frustrated: JM Keynes and the Origins of the Postwar International Monetary Order." *Diplomacy and Statecraft* 11 (1): 189–210.

Nourse, Edwin G. 1945. "The Road to Serfdom by Friedrich A. Hayek." *Journal of Farm Economics* 27 (2): 484–88.

Olsen, Niklas. 2018. *The Sovereign Consumer: A New Intellectual History of Neoliberalism*. Cham: Springer.

Pernecky, Mark, and Thomas Richter. 2009. "Keynes' Preface to the German Edition of the General Theory: Nazi Sympathies or Methodological Empathies?" *Forum for Social Economics* 40 (2): 253–64.
Pigou, Arthur C., ed. 1925. *Memorials of Alfred Marshall*. London: MacMillan.
———. 1944. "The Road to Serfdom by F. A. Hayek." *The Economic Journal* 54 (214): 217–19.
Ptak, Ralf. 2004. *Vom Ordoliberalismus Zur Sozialen Marktwirtschaft: Stationen Des Neoliberalismus in Deutschland*. Opladen: Leske + budrich.
Rieter, Heinz, and Matthias Schmolz. 1993. "The Ideas of German Ordoliberalism 1938–45: Pointing the Way to a New Economic Order." *European Journal of the History of Economic Thought* 1 (1): 87–114.
Robinson, Joan. 1972. "The Second Crisis of Economic Theory." *The American Economic Review* 62 (1/2): 1–10.
Roll, Eric. 1945. "The Road to Serfdom by Friedrich A. Hayek." *The American Economic Review* 35 (1): 176–80.
Röpke, Wilhelm. 1932. *Krise Und Konjunktur*. Wissenschaft Und Bildung 300. Leipzig: Quelle und Meyer.
———. 1935. "Letter to L. Robbins, December 22. [LSE Archive: ROBBINS/3/1/2]." ROBBINS/3/1/2. [LSE Archive].
———. 1936a. *Crises and Cycles*. Edinburgh, London, and Glasgow: W. Hodge.
———. 1936b. "Letter to L. Robbins, May 6. [LSE Archive: ROBBINS/3/1/2]." ROBBINS/3/1/2. [LSE Archive].
———. 1942. *Die Gesellschaftskrisis Der Gegenwart* [*The Social Crisis of Our Time*]. Chicago: University of Chicago Press, 1950.
———. 1944. *The Moral Foundations of Civil Society* [*Civitas Humana*]. 2nd Revised edition. New Brunswick (U.S.A): Transaction Publishers, 2002.
———. 1945. *Internationale Ordnung – Heute* [*International Order and Economic Integration*]. Dordrecht: Springer, 1959.
———. 1963. *Economics of the Free Society*. Based on the 9th German edition. Chicago: H. Regnery.
Schefold, Bertram. 1980. "The General Theory for a Totalitarian State? A Note on Keynes's Preface to the German Edition of 1936." *Cambridge Journal of Economics* 4 (2): 175–76.
———. 1995. "Theoretical Approaches to a Comparison of Economic Systems from a Historical Perspective." In *The Theory of Ethical Economy in the Historical School*, edited by Professor Dr Peter Koslowski, 221–49. Studies in Economic Ethics and Philosophy. Berlin Heidelberg: Springer.
———. 2003. "Die Deutsche Historische Schule als Quelle des Ordoliberalismus." In *L'ordolibéralisme allemand : aux sources de l'économie sociale de marché*, edited by Patricia Commun, 101–18. Travaux et documents du C.I.R.A.C. Cergy-Pontoise: CIRAC/CICC.

Schumpeter, Joseph A. 1946. "The Road to Serfdom by Friedrick A. Hayek." *Journal of Political Economy* 54 (3): 269–70.

Skidelsky, Robert J. A. 2005. *John Maynard Keynes, 1883–1946: Economist, Philosopher, Statesman*. New York: Penguin Books.

———. 2006. "Hayek versus Keynes: The Road to Reconciliation." In *The Cambridge Companion to Hayek*, edited by Edward Feser, 82–110. Oxford: Cambridge University Press.

Slobodian, Quinn. 2018. *Globalists: The End of Empire and the Birth of Neoliberalism*. Cambridge, MA: Harvard University Press.

Smith, T. V. 1945. "The Road to Serfdom by Friedrich A. Hayek." *Ethics* 55 (3): 224–26.

Solchany, Jean. 2015. *Wilhelm Röpke, l'autre Hayek: aux origines du néolibéralisme*. Paris: Publications de la Sorbonne.

Soliani, Riccardo. 2011. "Some Notes about Croce and Einaudi on 'liberismo' and 'liberalismo.'" In *Freedom and Happiness in Economic Thought and Philosophy: from Clash to Reconciliation*, edited by Ragip Ege and Herrade Igersheim, 144–60. London: Routledge.

Tooze, J. Adam. 2001. *Statistics and the German State, 1900–1945: The Making of Modern Economic Knowledge*. Cambridge Studies in Modern Economic History 9. Cambridge [etc.]: Cambridge University Press.

Tribe, Keith. 1995. *Strategies of Economic Order: German Economic Discourse, 1750–1950*. Ideas in Context 33. Cambridge and New York [etc.]: Cambridge University Press.

Vanberg, Viktor. 1998. "Freiburg School of Law and Economics." In *The New Palgrave Dictionary of Economics and the Law*, edited by Peter Newman, 2:172–79. London: Macmillan.

———. 2004. "The Freiburg School: Walter Eucken and Ordoliberalism." *Walter Eucken Institute: Freiburg Discussion Papers on Constitutional Economics* 4 (11).

———. 2013. "Hayek in Freiburg." In *Hayek: A Collaborative Biography: Part 1. Influences from Mises to Bartley*, edited by Robert Leeson, 93–122. Hampshire: Palgrave Macmillan.

Weisz, Jean-Daniel. 2001. "A Systemic Perception of Eucken's Foundations of Economics." In *Institutional Economics in France and Germany: German Ordoliberalism versus the French Regulation School*, edited by Agnès Labrousse and Jean-Daniel Weisz, 129–56. Heidelberg: Springer.

White, Michael V., and Kurt Schuler. 2009. "Retrospectives: Who Said 'Debauch the Currency': Keynes or Lenin?" *The Journal of Economic Perspectives* 23 (2): 213–222.

Wörsdörfer, Manuel. 2013. "Von Hayek and Ordoliberalism on Justice." *Journal of the History of Economic Thought* 35 (3): 291–317.

CHAPTER 3

Third-Way Perspectives on Order in Interwar France: Personalism and the Political Economy of François Perroux

Alexandre M. Cunha

The French context of the 1930s is particularly representative of the intricacy of the interwar period. The effects of the economic crisis that

This chapter is a partial result of the research activities of a Jean Monnet Chair (co-funded by the Erasmus + program of the European Union) at the Universidade Federal de Minas Gerais (Grant number 587558-EPP-1-2017-1-BR-EPPJMO-CHAIR). Financial support from CNPq (the Brazilian National Research Council) is also gratefully acknowledged. Like for the other chapters in this volume, a preliminary version of the text was presented at the workshop "Interwar economics and the intellectual origins of European integration," held on February 11–12, 2019 in Lisbon, Portugal. I would like to thank participants of the workshop, as well as the anonymous reviewer of the chapter, for their comments and suggestions.

A. M. Cunha (✉)
Cedeplar, Universidade Federal de Minas Gerais, Belo Horizonte, Minas Gerais, Brazil
e-mail: amc@cedeplar.ufmg.br

© The Author(s) 2021

A. M. Cunha and C. E. Suprinyak (eds.), *Political Economy and International Order in Interwar Europe*, Palgrave Studies in the History of Economic Thought,
https://doi.org/10.1007/978-3-030-47102-6_3

hit that country in particular from 1932 on were some one of the main ingredients that motivated the search for alternatives between liberal capitalism and communism, giving form to a wide range of third-way sources for discourse and movements, some with particular sensitivity to the international question.

It is exactly among these third-way movements, challenging the political and economic order of the period, that the influence of a personalist perspective spread, aiming to find a third "communitarian" alternative and offering multiple connections and philosophical bases to different movements, such as federalist groups.

The influence of communitarian personalism in the French debates of the 1930s is the guiding thread here, connecting personalism with federalist ideas and also with corporatist perspectives. The chapter will therefore focus on "personalism," "federalism" and "corporatism," with attention to the framework of influences that Catholic philosophy and a Catholic-based social and political ideas offer to that debate. Nevertheless, it is necessary to have in mind that these three concepts operate in very different levels and fields, personalism more at the philosophical level, federalism more as a proposal for political organization, and corporatism more as an economic-social doctrine. But it is precisely because of these differences that the points of contact and articulations between these perspectives in the French debate of the 1930s are of particular interest. Based on an original reflection on the relationship between individuals and communities, both personalist perspectives become part of the (conceptual) content of federalist propositions, as well as federalist ideas become an element present in certain personalist platforms. Additionally, several individuals were involved in both debates at the same time, including some of the most preeminent names for both debates, as is the case of Alexandre Marc (for the federalism) and Emmanuel Mounier (for the personalism). Young nonconformist intellectuals in the period also connected these perspectives with a third-way criticism that chooses corporatism as a central issue, being the work of François Perroux in the interwar period the key illustration of these overlays. These concepts, therefore, even operating at different levels, were directly linked to corporatism through a communitarian angle and incorporated in the third-way perspectives defended by Perroux in the period.

As will be explained below, personalism promotes a vision of the human person that goes beyond the idea of the individual in liberalism and highlights person's multiple simultaneous links with different communities. At the same time anti-liberal and non-nationalist, the emphasis on the idea of community given by personalism was a key to different perspectives on the economic and political order in the period, which can be explored both at the international level (at the level of the community of nations) as well as at the sub-national level, in terms of the different communities within nations. This influence of communitarian personalism on these visions of order will be explored here on two fronts, first in the criticism of the abstract internationalism represented by the League of Nations and of the international disorder that takes shape in the federalist discourse, and then in highlighting the importance of intermediate groups (as the family, communities or professional groups), rejecting both individualism and statism, which is the basis of Perroux's third-way conception of corporatism.

This chapter starts defining personalism and locating it among the so-called nonconformist groups within this map of various third-way discourses in the French debate of the 1930s, and then, in the second section, explores particular points of criticism from these groups on the international order. Finally, in the third section, these different questions converge into the analysis of François Perroux's ideas, reflecting interesting dimensions of the connections between communitarian personalism (as well as integral federalism) and corporatism in France third-way interwar debates. Perroux's case offers, thus, a very interesting illustration of how personalist philosophy penetrated the political economy of corporatism.

1 Personalism and Nonconformist Third-Way Discourses

Personalism is not a simple word. It is not the purpose here to make a broad recovery of the origin of the term and all its philosophical inflections in different parts of the European continent, since the goal here is the development of this current from the specific context of the French debates in the 1930s. However, we can start by qualifying that this is, naturally, a concept created from a reframing of the term "person" with the explicit intention of preserving the idea of the "individual" but opposing the idea of "individualism." It is important to highlight right from the start that the concept of personalism as analyzed here has no direct relation to the idea of personalist regimes proper to authoritarian governments, or to processes of the personalization of the leadership. This idea of "person," or more precisely of "human person," thus makes reference to a collective being, focusing precisely on the broader "organic" relationships that connect the individual with collective instances such as the family, "*commune*," and groups of professional activity.

Based on the perspective that humans are not atomic individuals but communitarian creatures, each with an absolute individual value, personalist philosophy is dedicated to promoting an integral vision of human individuals in society. Personalism also includes a kind of pedagogy of community life, and it offers a political thought about the relationship between the individual and society within Catholic philosophy (but not exclusively restricted to it). Even if we exclusively consider the French debate of the period, it would be more accurate, as Dries Deweer (2013, 109) insists, to speak of "personalisms," since, despite the common project, the movement assumes several stages, including, for example, the line of Jacques Maritain's "neo-thomist personalism" or the more "existentialist personalism" of Emmanuel Mounier, combining a certain phenomenological mark with the spiritualism of Henri Bergson. Mounier's perspective is undoubtedly the one that would be most influential in terms of third-way discourses in France at the time.

The interest in the influence of debates in the field of Catholic philosophy for third-way discourses in the period goes beyond the specific question of personalism and includes a whole set of themes linked to Catholic-based social and political ideas and, broadly, to "spiritual humanism." The connection of these ideas with the promotion of corporatism, for example, which is another important source of third-way discourses in the interwar period, is also an important topic here and will be highlighted below in the analysis of the ideas of François Perroux.

Catholicism (via the papal encyclicals *Rerum Novarum*, 1891, and *Quadragesimo Anno*, 1931) was, in fact, one of the fundamental sources in promoting a third-way discourse associated with corporatism, and it is not surprising that doctrinal transformations in social Catholicism have also shaped an important part of these debates in the midst of wars. Actually, some of the main protagonists of this interwar third-way debate were exactly a group of young Christians, Catholics in particular, who did not fight in World War I and who began to engage in political debate in the late 1920s.[1]

[1] Debates in the field of corporatism would be basically banned in the postwar period, given their easy association with fascist regimes, but it is possible to speak of a certain

Communitarian personalism, as developed, for example, in the work of Mounier, presents a dual opposition to both individualism and collectivism and seeks to promote the idea of the "human person," full of articulations with different community bodies. It is, therefore, an original source of the third-way discourse since it reflects an attempt to escape both the monological conception of the individual in liberalism and the tendencies to reject human autonomy in communitarianism. It took shape in the debates of the 1930s in France and can be directly associated (albeit not exclusively) with young, Catholic intellectuals from nonconformist groups and ended up providing important elements of the third-way discourse that influenced, though with new colors, the concrete actions that would shape the integration process years later.

The sources of third-way discourse in interwar France are, nevertheless, complex and polysemic and include not only personalist discourse within nonconformist movements but also other groups, such as neo-socialists, former revolutionary syndicalists, and (neo)corporatists in broader terms (Bastow 2001, 173). Even though there were some connections between several of these third-way anti-liberal sources,[2] the emphasis here is on nonconformism, since it can be directly associated with a set of particularly interesting perspectives on international order in the period and visions about the future of Europe. This includes some ideas that would be promoted in the European integration process from the immediate postwar period, connecting, for example, planning, corporatism and communitarian personalism. It is also important to include here the direct connections between the nonconformist movement and the activism on Franco-German rapprochement from young intellectuals organized, for

level of the recombination of elements coinciding in the plan of this "spiritual humanism." In a sense, it is possible to understand that the third-way aspirations of a personalistic basis are grounded in a much broader Europeanist discourse of a philosophical nature. The ties to phenomenology and existentialism are clear in personalism; however, as a diffused and eclectic movement, without a clear universal reference point, the personalist perspective acquires different configurations in the work of different philosophers. The configuration of the personalist movement within the French debate of the period has, in this sense, correlations, for example, with ideas previously developed by other names in different parts of the continent, such as Rudolf Hermann Lotze, Rudolf Eucken (father of the central name of Ordoliberalism, Walter Eucken), and Charles Renouvier or, more particularly, Max Scheler, Nikolai Berdiaev, and Heinrich Pesch (Pasture 2018, 31).

[2] On anti-liberal discourse in interwar Europe, see Gosewinkel (2015).

example, in the *Circle du Sohlberg* or in the *Club du Moulin Vert* (Cohen 2006, 131; Hellman 2002, 31). Since the rapprochement between France and Germany was one of the central problems of the interwar period and, at the same time, a key dimension in the promotion of European integration in the postwar period, it is particularly interesting to notice its connection in the early 1930s with the third-way perspectives of personalist and federalist groups.

To understand the nature of the 1930s debate in France, and in particular the position of the nonconformists, some basic issues must be addressed. The combination of the economic crisis that began in the United States in 1929 and touched Europe in the early 1930s, with the political problems that were increasing and contributing to the growth of anti-parliamentary currents and dissatisfaction with the political and economic directions both in the domestic and international spheres, contributed to a general climate of growing uneasiness about the destiny of Western civilization itself and of disillusionment with the adopted trajectories. It is in this intersection that one notices an intellectual effervescence, which includes the arrival of young people (who did not fight in World War I) in the political debate, mixing pessimism and the will of transformation at the same time. The nonconformists, specifically, as highlighted by Ory and Sirinelli (2004, 140), were born mostly in the first decade of the twentieth century, and are part of that partially orphan generation, quickly propelled into public debate with the premature death of many of their intellectual fathers.[3]

A key issue that qualifies the importance of the nonconformist movement and "the spirit of the 1930s" in French thought is that it was gradually becoming clear that political views prior to the First World War were no longer sufficient to think about a world in crisis (Ory and Sirinelli 2004, 139). Thus, even though the ideas produced by these groups did

[3]This component of disillusionment and pessimism ran throughout the whole interwar period, but it gained strength essentially in the 1930s. To a large extent this pessimism can be read as the opposite reaction to the euphoric attitude of living the moment intensely, typical of the 1920s ("*les années folles*"). This same combination of disillusionment and pessimism was present in different parts of Europe, translating an important aspect of the spirit of the time when expressing criticisms and questions about the cultural development of modern civilization. This critical attitude guided much of the creative energy of an entire generation that came into public debate in the 1930s. The answers offered were the most diverse, nevertheless the unrest and uneasiness about the course of the civilization was largely coincidental.

not have an immediate impact, the repertoire of themes and perspectives raised, whose central values were anti-capitalism, anti-liberalism and anti-nationalism, ended up guiding important developments in the debate of political ideas.

The historiography of political ideas in France, particularly along the lines pointed out by Jean Touchard (1960), would insist that the 1930s offer, in spite of the substantial diversity of intellectual origins of those involved, a convergence of perspectives and dreams of these young intellectuals who, using a common language and vocabulary, aspired to overcome traditional forces and renew French politics. It is in this line of interpretation that the influential work of Jean-Louis Loubet del Bayle (1969) is inserted, seeking to discern within the multiplicity of groups that professed "non-conformist" perspectives after the end of the 1920s in France three main groups that could be highlighted as marked by the philosophical influence of personalism: *Jeune Droite*, *Ordre Nouveau*, and *Esprit*. The first one, and least original of the three, corresponded essentially to the young, Catholic intellectuals somehow close but not aligned with the *Action Française*[4]; the second group (easily associated with the name of Alexandre Marc) originally professed their perspectives in the "*Manifeste pour un ordre nouveau*" from 1930 and was crucial in the development of a federalist/personalist critique on the international order; and finally the third group, which ended up being the best known of the three, gathered around journal *Esprit*, founded and directed by Emmanuel Mounier (Loubet del Bayle 1998, 21–4).

In response to what was read as a crisis of civilization, the third-way discourse of these nonconformist groups was guided by a search for alternatives between liberal capitalism and communism, as well as, at the level of the political-institutional arrangement, for a solution between the supposed softness/weakness of democracies (particularly stimulated by the criticism of the French Third Republic) and the totalitarian

[4] *Action Française*'s reactionary nationalism, under the leadership of Charles Maurras, exerted a great attraction on the French Catholic elite early twentieth century. Maurras actively sought to came close to Catholicism after the First World War, with the aim of achieving a nationalist and monarchist alliance, both of believers and non-believers. However, a Vatican doctrinal condemnation of Maurras and the *Action Française* in 1926 had a major impact among French Catholic intellectuals, most of whom sympathized with *Action Française*. This opened space for several re-elaborations of perspectives and worked as an important component of the development of French personalism in the 1930s (Deweer 2013, 109).

mechanism of emerging dictatorships (Ory and Sirinelli 2004, 139). An inevitable dimension of this discourse, which permeated several of the groups involved, was that it was not a matter of looking for an intermediate point between liberalism and communism as a kind of reconciliation between different perspectives or a moderate mediation.[5] On the contrary, the third-way discourse in France in the 1930s was markedly radical; it was about the search for a new way, for a rupture. It was not without reason that the term "revolution" was insistently used by these groups in various resignifications.

Of the three nonconformist groups influenced by personalism that Bayle (1969) analyzed, those who pointed out original perspectives of criticism of this crisis of civilization—which would somehow last throughout the debate, even if it had little influence on the political debate at that time—were the group centered on the *Esprit* review, who most directly identified with personalism and whose main leader was Emmanuel Mounier, and those centered on the *Ordre Nouveau* review, founded by Arnaud Dandieu and Robert Aron, who most identified with federalism. Both groups, however, professed coincident perspectives, and there was also some overlap between their members, the most important example being Alexandre Marc, who was directly interested in unifying sympathetic movements to the federalist cause. Even with their different trends, it is possible to read these two groups, at least in the early 1930s, as part of the same personalist/federalist movement. What particularly unified them at that time, despite their different emphases, was a defense of a decentralized federalist political system and a coincident rejection of both capitalism and the liberal democratic nation-state, as well as the state of communist regimes (Loughlin 1989, 192). The fundamental connection between these groups in the beginning, even though they later moved more or less distinctly within the political spectrum, was nevertheless anchored in personalism. It was precisely the belief that the center of all political, economic and social structures was, in the human person, understood as the spiritual individual rooted in a rich, concrete reality

[5] The third-way perspective of the French interwar debate, therefore, is not related to an intermediate point of bargaining and compromise, as in the perspective analyzed by Aurelian Craiutu (2017) in *Faces of Moderation*, discussing the importance of virtue of moderation in the success of representative governments and its institutions in contemporary democratic regimes.

that formed the basis of the political philosophy of French federalism (Loughlin 1989, 195).

By emphasizing the concept of community as a bridge between the individual and society and rejecting nationalism as well as statism, an important trait of the identity that personalism would assume in the French context would be precisely its articulation with the federalist perspectives. This would have a clear expression in Alexandre Marc's ideas. A federalism that was seen as a process that brought together both decentralization (from the state to levels such as the region or community) and a bottom-up approach in which the lower instances were delegated competences of a higher level in the spatial hierarchy. By withdrawing importance from the state and privileging the links that articulate the shared belonging of the individual to multiple communities to start the family, the personalist discourse favors a non-nationalist vision and is attentive to a renewed perception of the European space. This is one of the important points of articulation between personalist ideas and federalist perspectives in the work of Alexandre Marc. There is also, broadly speaking, a strong perception of the potential role to be played by religion in the federalist discourse about European cooperation, with a conception of Europe marked by the idea of a Christian project[6] in which different denominational ideas would serve as the basis for establishing a lasting peace (Pasture 2018, 31).

The Christian Democratic perspective, in a broad sense, had a substantive impact on the debate on international order and, in particular, on the European integration process in the postwar period, which is widely recognized in the historiography. The same is true in terms of the repercussions on the formation of some of the founding fathers of the European Union, including Konrad Adenauer, Alcide de Gasperi, and, specifically in the French context, Robert Schuman or Jean Monnet (Pasture 2018, 25). In particular, the echoes of the communitarian personalism of the 1930s in the Christian democratic perspective of

[6]The idea of a Christian Europe was equally important in one of the most famous movements of the interwar period, the Pan European Union proposed by Richard Coudenhove-Kalergi. Nevertheless, the idea of Europe as a Christian project were equally part of other author's perspectives in the past and an emblematic example is the fragment "Christendom or Europe" ("*Die Christenheit oder Europa*") written in 1799 by Novalis [Friedrich Philipp von Hardenberg], calling for a universal Christian church to restore a Europe whose unity had been destroyed by the Reformation and the Enlightenment.

some of these key individuals linked to the postwar European integration process were substantive, further increasing the interest in properly understanding the main articulations of ideas promoted in the mix of political currents in the interwar period.

A common attitude of these personalist/federalist groups is the reaction to what *Esprit* called a "rupture with established disorder," a disorder that was expressed on several levels and that possessed a clear component of criticism of the international order, which was diagnosed as part of a more general and profound crisis than the economic and political crisis and which concerned a "crisis of civilization" that was perceived with a privileged focus on the human condition and the perception that this established a reductionism in social relations that was marked by a kind of ideology of material progress and an inner and spiritual crisis that hit modern humans. The motto of the *Ordre Nouveau* group translated this spiritualist perspective well: "The spiritual first, then economics, politics at their service."

The marked attitude of these three nonconformist groups, defined at the beginning of the decade, thus translated into a series of denials and negative positions: anti-parliamentarism, anti-capitalism, anti-liberalism, anti-rationalism, and anti-materialism, among others. In this way, these groups end up anticipating a general feeling of the deterioration of the economic and political climate that would worsen over the course of the decade (Loubet del Bayle 1998, 25–6). In the proper terms of the 1931 manifesto drawn up by Alexander Marc and Gabriel Marcel for an *Ordre Nouveau*: "Traditionalists, yet not conservative, realists, yet not opportunists, revolutionaries, yet not rebels, constructive, not destructive, neither war-mongers nor pacifists, patriots, yet not nationalists, socialists, yet not materialists, personalists, yet not anarchists, human, yet not humanitarian" (apud Hellman 2002, 31).

The primary focus of these young intellectuals' criticisms of the "established disorder" at the international level is the type of internationalism represented by the League of Nations, understood as artificial, ineffective, and decorative. It was precisely a reaction to the kind of internationalist militancy of the 1920s that was concerned with ensuring peace in Europe but equally committed to an ideal of maximum respect for national sovereignties that was translated into a deliberately moderate discourse. Heinrich Mann spoke of Europe as a "supreme state," demanding a supra-nationalist allegiance, Émile Borel of the "United States of Europe," and Richard Coudenhove-Kalergi of "Pan-Europe"; there was a certain convergence toward a kind of ideal or hope that it would be possible to promote peace through the law so that different European nations, united in a common legal perspective, would be able to build an order that would respect national specificities and guarantee peace. The most direct expression of this, which promoted the mobilizing myth of a European federation while promising not to touch the sovereignty of nations, was undoubtedly the project of the European Union that was launched by Aristide Briand in the League of Nations in 1929 (Guieu 2010, 3).

As advocated René Dupuis and Alexandre Marc in*Jeune Europe* (1933, 150–75), the aim was to find a middle ground between imperialist nationalism and abstract internationalism, exactly where the fundamental critique of these nonconformist young people lay with the internationalism of the 1920s. For them, the European community should not be a cosmopolitan and international result (which was the weakness of other proposals, such as Richard Coudenhove-Kalergi's Pan-Europe) but rather a supranational and decentralized entity (Pasture 2018, 31–2).

2 Personalist and Federalist Views on the "International (Dis)Order"

It is not necessary to fully subscribe to Zeev Sternhell's (1984) influential, but also controversial, argumentative line to recognize that in these nonconformist personalist/federalist groups of the early 1930s, there are elements closer to a fascist perspective in terms of its anti-parliamentarism and anti-liberal democracy discourse. We can also easily agree with Sternhell in arguing that the works of Touchard (1960) and Bayle (1969), and much of the historiography inspired by these works, tended to analyze the "spirit of the 1930s" in France with an almost exclusive focus on the first half of the decade. Few works have been concerned with the second half of the decade, particularly with the relationship of these groups and individuals with the Vichy regime. Even though it is not our objective here to offer an answer to this line of historiographical questions, it seems to us important to insist that it was only gradually that the debate of ideas throughout the 1930s incorporated a binary opposition between fascism and anti-fascism, and this was definitely not a fundamental cut in the French debate in the early 1930s, which allows us to see just how different perspectives were intermingled at that time (dangerously intermingled, it is possible to add).

It is not productive to reread this period of French thought with eyes set on the immediate postwar period, when there was room only for the absolute denial of fascism and when several characters with openly favorable or at least ambiguous attitudes toward the Vichy regime eagerly sought to redefine or reframe their trajectories (as François Perroux, for example, quickly and skillfully did). What seem most interesting to us are precisely the persistence of an ambiguous attitude toward fascism in the third-way discourse in France in the 1930s and of the elements of this communitarian and personalist nonconformism that took shape in the early 1930s and had a persistent duration throughout the 1930s and even during the Vichy period, until became part of the federalist discourse of some key personalities in the European integration process in the postwar period.

The reflection on the international disorder on the part of these personalist and federalist groups started from a criticism of the disorder established at the domestic level, specifically in relation to the growing incredulity of the French Third Republic. The attack on liberal democracy, particularly on the parliamentary representation system, is thus a recurring point in French third-way discourses in the 1930s as part of a broad criticism of the Third Republic that was then in the process of progressive erosion. The effects of the economic crisis that were felt directly in metropolitan France in particular since 1932 in combination with a succession of political and financial scandals strongly shook the regime. Disbelief in political elites on both the right and the left favored radicalization. On the left, the French communist party lived through its most sectarian period, refusing to work with other left-wing parties and preparing for insurrection; on the right, the fascist leagues were spreading, forming militias and preparing for armed conflict (Loughlin 1989, 181; Bernard and Dubief 1985). This context, in which the economic crisis made room for a political crisis, was the fundamental stage for another radicalization space that was equally anti-parliamentary and based on the position of these young nonconformist groups and their third-way movements.

In 1932, Alexandre Marc qualified this radical criticism of the established order:

> The ascertainment of the liberal failure, of the current sterile and inhuman disorder, of the instinctive disgust that parliamentary and pseudo-democratic illusions are now arousing in every well-born soul. — The

> refusal of all conformism, by the very individuals who cover themselves with revolutionary garb, whose bravado and provocation are now an integral part of the established regime. The intransigent will of breaking with a world where everything conspires against the dignity of man and the revolutionary audacity in the search for truly new solutions. — The taste for construction and order that creates an abyss between us and those who come to the Revolution due to an ambiguous desire for 'upheaval' and bloody adventures. (Marc 1932, 332)

Undoubtedly, the ferment for all this critical movement was fundamentally given by the internal context of the country, but the alignments at the level of the international order are equally important for the understanding of the process. In this sense, another component that aggravated the crisis at that time and in that context was the disagreement of France with the positions of the USA and United Kingdom in relation to the topic of war reparations and in the criticism of the League of Nations' inability to offer answers to a context of the progressive radicalization of nationalisms, which would be one of the privileged focuses of personalist and federalist criticism.

Following some of Bayle's (1969, 185–91) conclusions on the nonconformist groups' views on international disorder, we can highlight the critical attitude of these groups toward the Versailles settlement that was breaking down and, in particular, toward the League of Nations and the specific perspectives on internationalism that it represented at that time. That critical attitude, even if possessing different degrees of radicalism, was professed by different nonconformist groups. The *Ordre Nouveau* group in 1933 even applauded Hitler for breaking with the League of Nations:

> Allow us, Mr. Chancellor, to congratulate you. The gesture you have just made, by administering a resounding blow to the hypocritical cheek of the League, is salutary. The monster of Geneva, born of a coupling between the democratic phraseology, puritanical hypocrisy and pacifist stupidity, on the one hand, and, on the other hand, the interests of the gigantic trusts, international banks and economic statism, is a challenge to the most basic intelligence and honesty. By withdrawing from these learned assemblies, which are all the more harmful because they are more stupid and useless, you have accomplished an act of public health; you have served the truth. (Ordre Nouveau 1933, 23)

A compliment to Hitler's attitude, even if in 1933, was definitely significant, but it may not be the main point to be underlined here. In fact, it is noteworthy the open hostility to the League of Nations by the *Ordre Nouveau* group as well as how the inclusion of that reference to the collusion of interests between states and international financial capital can be clearly associated to the anti-capitalist and anti-liberal elements in the group's discourse (Bayle 1969, 187).

One year before the publication of the above quoted excerpt, the same criticism of the League of Nations by two of the main names of the *Ordre Nouveau* group was published in the *Esprit* review, including however an expression of disapproval on the connection between the maintenance of modern nation-states and the authoritarian government model:

> The League of Nations has not only failed for contingent reasons. Their very principle is struck with absolute sterility because modern nation-states are only maintained by the insidious police dictatorship; serve, under high pretexts, only basely material interests; and cannot come into contact with each other only to oppose, fight and destroy themselves. (Marc and Dupuis 1932, 317)

In fact, *Esprit*'s criticisms of the League of Nations were not so explicit and did not so openly show their hostility, particularly because *Esprit* agreed with the supranational perspective of the institution (and also so as not to run the risk of approaching the kind of nationalistic prejudice that *Esprit* condemned and that was closer to *Jeune Droite*'s positions). Nevertheless, *Esprit* clearly criticized the League for not being able to overcome the simple administration of the Treaty of Versailles, remaining exclusively concerned with safeguarding the arrangement reached in the treaty. *Jeune Droite*'s position about the League of Nations was, in fact, not far from *Action française*'s orthodoxy on the subject, which reinforced nationalistic tendencies in this regard. *Esprit*, on the other hand, even with the coincident hostility of the *Jeune Droite* members (in particular Thierry Maulnier) toward the Treaty of Versailles, was more concerned with matters of justice (Bayle 1969, 188).

The diagnosis of the failure of postwar Europe was, nevertheless, a common point for these different groups and reinforced the perspective presented by Robert Francis, Thierry Maulnier and Jean-Pierre Maxence in *Demain la France* (1934): "Europe divided, Europe constituted by exacerbated nationalisms, by a helpless bureaucracy of Geneva, by a

France considered by the leaders themselves as a secondary nation"—in short, "the Europe of Geneva has failed. The Treaty of Versailles is no more than a convention repeatedly violated, solicited, adulterated" (Francis et al. 1934, 72–86; Bayle 1969, 188–89).

France's foreign policy (based on the Treaty of Versailles and the League of Nations since 1918) was a convergent target of criticism from these nonconformist groups. Raymond Poincaré and Aristide Briand, even if located in very different fields, were the central representatives of this policy and were equally responsible for insisting on attitudes detrimental to France and international peace. The criticism was applicable both to the Poincaré nationalist positions and to Briand, with what they understood as a non-effective international pacifism, but Briand was the most frequent target of the critics. It was again the *Ordre Nouveau* that offered the harshest criticism (in the same "*Lettre à Hitler*" 1933, mentioned above), highlighting both the bankruptcy of the diplomatic paths followed (which, while followed in the name of peace, could easily result in war) and their collusion of interests with international finance. The letter talks of a "sleepy and tearful" France that "would be able, in the name of peace, to make war on you [Hitler]" (Ordre Nouveau 1933, 25–26; Bayle 1969, 189–90).

Mounier was also eloquent on this point some years after in his *Manifeste au service du personnalisme* from 1936, insisting that pacifism can work against peace: this "cosmopolitan and juridical pacifism is the international doctrine of bourgeois idealism as nationalism is the one of an aggressive individualism. Both are two complementary products of the liberal disorder, grafted on two different phases of its decomposition. These are two ways to degrade and oppress the person" (Mounier 1936 [2003], 129).[7]

[7] It is interesting to note how the personalist perspective is capable of promoting certain interesting convergence spaces, even among very different groups in the political spectrum. An interesting example of this is the proximity in certain aspects of Mounier's discourse in his *Manifeste au service du personnalisme* (1936), in particular in the session that opens the Chapter 6, titled "*Le nationalisme contre la nation*," and the ideas of the Marxist philosopher and sociologist Henri Lefebvre, at that time one of the most prominent intellectuals of the French Communist Party, in his 1937 book, *Le nationalisme contre les nations*. Although Lefebvre's book makes no mention of Mounier, there are several personalist references in the text. In the February 1938 edition of Esprit, the book would be praised in a review by Roger Labrousse, who insisted precisely on the point that it was not possible to ignore in this book "a series of references, even loans, to personalism," and that these references would serve to facilitate Esprit's readers' agreement

Esprit and *Ordre Nouveau*, as well as *Jeune Droite*, were, above all, preoccupied with denouncing the errors of nationalism and pacifist internationalism and reflecting on the basis on which a new European political order could be developed, which should necessarily include a critical reflection on the principles that led Europe on the verge of chaos.

Broadly speaking, we can also emphasize the importance of the communitarian perspective in the visions of the future about Europe that were being processed by these nonconformist groups. For Mounier, this question should be understood in terms of an actual revolution, a communitarian revolution, that was taking shape at that very moment. In an article published in January 1935, Mounier wrote about this as a broad process of a spiritual nature, permeating different political systems and pointing in the direction of a profound transformation:

> Finally, today, a new revolt, in reaction against the consequences of the first. Fascism and Communism converge from this point of view. They are the first jolts of the immense communitarian wave, which begins to sweep over Europe. Let there be no mistaking that this second Renaissance is as profound as it may be, perhaps even more far-reaching than the first. Individualism, certainly, is not at its last jolt: do we not know feudalities still surviving in the twentieth century? But history has given a little help. A great commotion begins. Men, weary of their psychological complications and their vain solitude, will try the most desperate, perhaps the craziest, outings to find their way back to the community. All their efforts will be spiritual to some degree. (Mounier 1935, 548)

What must be highlighted here and what seems to us to be the core of the personalist perspective in relation to his vision of the future of Europe is precisely the progressive weight given to the communitarian question. Even if immersed in a discourse of a strongly spiritualistic nature, it seems to us that the theme, progressively decanted, would end up being a fundamental legacy of the group that, in different ways, would have repercussions on French thought about the international order of the period and would ultimately influence the debates on integration in the immediate aftermath of World War II.

Nevertheless, between the 1930s and the post-World War II era, there was the Vichy period, and it was precisely through a new reflection, in

with Lefebvre's background arguments, even if not necessarily "about the tactic" proposed by him (Labrousse 1938, 789).

communitarian terms and connected to the idea of national revolution, that personalist perspectives remained important in the discourse of the period, with François Perroux being a central character in this process.

3 Corporatism, Community and the Science of Man in François Perroux's Works

The work of François Perroux represents not only a point of convergence from different perspectives highlighted here but also a source of original developments on these issues that help to perceive some specific colors of the third-way ideas in the period, as well as the growing ambiguities of some of these characters in the dark years of Vichy France.

In order just to offer a very short overview of Perroux's trajectory, we can begin by saying that he was one of the most creative and prominent French economists of the twentieth century. Working with a broad set of themes along his trajectory, he progressively sought to move toward a new theoretical scope for the treatment of asymmetric relations between agents and economic units, which became the basis of his theory of domination and his ambition to renew the "theory of general interdependence and to make of it something quite other than a new kind of equilibrium," as noted by Bernis (2000, 498). With contributions ranging from the 1930s to his death in the 1980s, Perroux produced studies throughout his life in very different subjects, such as corporatism, national accounts, planning, the dynamics of the disparities and inequalities among nations (with important implications for the field of international political economy), and several other developments of his theory of the dominant economy, particularly in the field of spatial economics. One of his important contributions is related to the definition of a structuralist approach to the studies in the field of economic development, marked by his characteristic humanistic perspective of the Catholic base. However, Perroux became internationally known and is still remembered in the economic literature, almost exclusively with regard to his contributions to the growth and development poles approach, with significant implications for industrial planning in different parts of the world between the 1950s and the 1970s (see Higgins and Savoie 1988; Meardon 2000).

This extensive intellectual trajectory also combines a path that includes prestigious positions in the French academic system and the organization of large and very specialized work teams, particularly in the 1940s and the 1950s, that would project his influence onto different fields of economic and political action. Nevertheless, his trajectory is also marked by many ambiguities (see Chavagneux 2003), particularly associated with his institutional involvement and influence in the Vichy regime. Moreover, his diverse connections with the regime offered an important platform for the projection of his name and the dissemination of his ideas about the community to a large audience.

The question of the community is, to some extent, a point of arrival for Perroux's reflections in the interwar period. It was effectively under the sign of corporatism that Perroux developed his main ideas throughout the 1930s. He expressively exemplified the multiplicity of perspectives that overlapped in the economic debate in the interwar period, and his name stands out as an interesting and complex case of the analysis of economic and political ideas in the period precisely because he tried to combine many of these varied sources in his work. This included, among other sources, his Catholic-based thinking, his connection with personalist debates, his reflections about the individual nuanced by first-hand contact hand with Austrian marginalism (during his sojourn in Vienna in 1934), and a reflection on the functioning of the economy that highlighted the role of structures and took shape in his comparative studies about corporatism on the European continent.

Corporatism was an important, albeit diffuse, focus for the third-way discourse in France in the 1930s, and undoubtedly, Perroux's ideas represented one of the most consistent and influential sources for this debate, particularly after the publication of his book, *Capitalisme et Communauté de Travail*, in 1938. Even though Perroux himself described the work on corporatism in France as "extremely fragmentary, with too inhomogeneous tendencies to speak of a French corporatist movement" (Perroux 1938, 160), it is necessary to re-emphasize the progressive importance of corporatism[8] in the French interwar period as a topic of anti-liberal criticism and third-way discourses.

[8]Variations on the theme of corporatism were frequently evoked in nonconformist debates, in particular in the early 1930s, as an important element for the third-way proposals. Marc and Dupuis, for example, connected the topic to the regional issue in 1932, insisting that: "it is the region which also exercises the property right over all the riches which serve as means of production. Only the regional organization of production makes it possible to break with capitalism; because, at the same time as the system of private capitalism, it excludes, by a corporative organization, all forms of state capitalism" (Marc and Dupuis 1932, 322).

One of the authors highlighted by Perroux in the academic reflection on these ideas and in the analysis reactions of French public opinion about corporatism was Gaëtan Pirou, who, for example, in one of his books sought to recover from René de La Tour du Pin in the nineteenth century to the 1930s the main lines of corporatist ideas in the French context, insisting that until around the 1920s, the debate was still very incipient and that it did not include an effective perception of the economic question involved in all its implications. Even if it served to qualify economic dimensions, the interest of the corporatist perspective of, for example, the *Action française* or defenders of social Catholicism, returned essentially to the question of the search for a way to restore order in modern society (Pirou 1938, 7–15).

Nonetheless, this trend was progressively reversed, making corporatism an important source for third-way discourse. The same Pirou celebrated the proliferation of interest in corporatist themes in the 1930s, showing that this interest permeated different ideological tendencies, particularly highlighting the contribution of Henri de Man (also discussed by Perroux in some works; see Perroux [1936] and [1938]), and included the interests of young people, with particular reference to the group *Ordre Nouveau*:

> A growing number of minds are turning to the corporatist idea and wondering if it is not alone able to solve the current difficulties and put an end to economic and social chaos. (...) the word and the idea of a corporation now find an audience in circles that formerly had disdainfully dismissed them. Thus, the great Belgian socialist Henri de Man (in two articles published in *Le Peuple de Bruxelles* and appropriately reproduced by the *Homme nouveau*) has engaged in a curious rehabilitation of corporatism, and he maintains that he 'does not excommunicate but exorcise it' and means to integrate it into the socialist doctrine... There is more: whereas formerly the seductions of corporatism seemed to try only men of experience and stale meaning, it is today the young people who most willingly let themselves be won by them. The *Ordre Nouveau* devoted to him, on April 15, 1934, a very sympathetic number. (Pirou 1938, 16–17)

This helps us to understand how it was possible for aspects of the discourse of communitarian personalism in relation to the international order to have participated in this relative convergence of perspectives between neo-liberalism, neo-corporatism and neo-syndicalism. Combined and recombined in this period, communitarian personalism offered important elements that, in the immediate postwar period, would be part of the vocabulary and logic through which the integration process would take shape. In the line proposed by Olivier Dard, we can identify among the projects of transformation of the state and societies that marked this context of the 1930s two distinct groups: that of the "realists," who pointed to the modernization of the economy, the reform of the state and the perspectives of European integration, and the "spiritualists," whose beliefs can be directly associated to the personalist movement represented by the *Ordre Nouveau* or *Esprit*, which, in turn, criticized the empire of technique and pointed in the direction of a quest for a renewed humanism founded on spiritual primacy (Dard 2002, 20, 285; Guieu 2010, 6). There were undoubtedly overlaps and variations between these groups, and it is also possible to treat these two perspectives as expressions of the same sum of pessimism with the will for transformation mentioned above, favoring both realistic and spiritualistic perspectives of action at the same time.

Perroux's first studies on corporatism date from the early 1930s (see, for example, Perroux 1933), and they soon expanded as part of his studies on the historical evolution and national structure of contemporary capitalism in Germany, Austria and Italy under the auspices of a fellowship from the Rockefeller Foundation that allowed him to take study and research visits to these countries in 1934 and 1935 (see Brisset and Fèvre 2019) that provided, among other things, the working material for some of the central parts of *Capitalisme et Communauté de Travail* (1938) years later.

Perroux's first trips to Portugal date from that same period and arose in the same way as those in the Austrian case, that is, from an interest in corporatist experiences in Catholic countries. In Portugal, where he gave lectures in Coimbra and Lisbon in 1935 and 1937, Perroux had direct contact with the Portuguese corporatist experience, which, to a large extent, influenced his ideas about the development that corporatism should follow in France.

Perroux published some analyses of the international situation from his personal experience in these different European countries in *Affaires Étrangères*, a monthly Parisian review published between 1931 and 1939. In the November 1935 issue, Perroux published an article on Portugal and referred in the following terms to the head of government, António de Oliveira Salazar (who, until 1928 was the holder of the chair of political economy at the Faculty of Law of the University of Coimbra, the one that Perroux temporarily held between January and May 1935[9]):

> Salazar, a scientist, head of government and great spiritualist, recognized and vigorously affirmed that to accept the national 'vocation' consists of adjusting contradictory interests within a group, of subordinating the diverse opinions to a minimum of values on which everyone can agree, and thus places the human persons who form the nation in an environment favorable to their highest material yield and their most intense spiritual development. This doctrine, which transfers to the account of the person the sacrifices that it imposes on the individual, respects the differences in functions, the diversity of opinions and aspiration, but within moral frameworks considered intangible, and in which an increasing unification of the nation can take place. (Perroux 1935, 524)

The praise for Salazar highlights in particular the importance attributed by Perroux to the connection of the personalist perspective with the concrete experience of corporatism in Portugal. The excerpt, to a large extent, says more about Perroux's own perspectives, however, than about the Portuguese experience itself and helps us to begin to differentiate important aspects in his understanding of the human person as an element that both translates communitarian affiliations and results in a growing unification of the nation. Later in the article, he also insists on the connection between the prerogatives of this legal person who expresses him or herself through different intermediary groups and the revitalization of the State:

> The political reconstruction is attempted according to a formula that is developed on a completely different plan than that of pure individualism or statism and emphasizes the destinies and prerogatives of the person, of intermediate groups (family, '*commune*', professional activity groups). Such a formula invigorates the state, but without deifying it. (Perroux 1935, 528)

The Portuguese experience, marked by a "personalist and communitarian philosophy equally distant from democratic liberalism and collectivist socialism, and even from state socialism" (Perroux 1935, 532), concentrated fundamental aspects of the third-way response to corporatism that Perroux was interested in disseminating in France. In concrete terms,

[9] See Ribeiro (1993, 251).

the Portuguese experience in fact served as a model for different aspects of Vichy's corporatist economic system, enjoying the direct attention of Marshal Pétain himself (Le Crom 1995, 121–22).

Overcoming the problems of the capitalist economy in terms of a third-way perspective was a central theoretical question for Perroux, and his propositions in the field of corporatism, more specifically from the idea of a community of labor (*communauté de travail*), constituted his answer to this problem until the early 1940s. Only when it became clear that France's liberation from Nazi occupation only was a matter of time did Perroux undertake an effort to reorient his prospects, with a view to neutralizing, as much as possible, his involvement with Vichy. He sought a redefinition of his third-way discourse, moving away from corporatism and shaping an idea of "liberal interventionism" (Cohen 2006; see also Cohen 2012). It is important to note, however, that several points of connection remained, particularly in terms of the idea of the "organized market economy," an expression that, at times, recalled his reflection in terms of corporatism (Cunha 2020).

In his works, Perroux highlighted that corporatism was, first and foremost, a product of the Depression and that this context was, above all, what created the opportunity for forms of conservative interventionism. Nevertheless, his original idea of the community of labor differed from both other theoretical perspectives of corporatism and the concrete experiences then lived in Europe, even if it bore similarities to these perspectives and experiences. From his perspective, and taking into account that the crisis that was then occurring should be understood as a crisis of the capitalist system itself, the idea of a community of labor worked as a representation of a possible "regime" in the transformation/metamorphosis of capitalism, along with the partial socialization of state capitalism. In Perroux's exercise of anticipation, the half-century following his period of focus (the 1930s), i.e., the lifetime of the generation that was then 20 or 30 years old, would be marked in the great nations of Western Europe by an "organized market-economy regime" (Perroux 1938, 194–95).

One of the distinctive features of Perroux's vision under corporatism was indeed his attention to the development of the human being as a person and the non-obliteration of the issue of freedom. This would manifest itself, for example, in the very question of the organization of the community of labor, which should be distinguished from simple corporations because of the element of freedom of participation in the organisms of effective worker representation and therefore does not serve as a mere mechanism to enforce the authority and tutelage of the state (Cardoso 2012, 110).[10]

Freedom was a repeated theme in these discussions, albeit fundamentally as an idea of collective freedoms (freedom of persons) and not as an individual freedom. Reflecting on this issue in an article published in *Esprit* in 1936, Perroux asserted that "freedom, as the right to do what pleases, does not lead to anything positive," thus reinforcing the importance of the idea of collective freedoms and connecting the topic to labor law, which, for him, was not simply linked to historical liberalism but could represent an "instrument of a greater sum of effective freedoms, freedoms of persons" (Perroux 1936, 869–70).

In the evolution of Perroux's ideas about corporatism, which would assume their main form in the 1938 *Capitalisme et Communauté de Travail*, there were undoubtedly a series of articulations on the personalist discourse. However, it is also important to note Perroux's deliberate effort to demarcate some differences and distances from Mounier's conceptions, which, to a large extent differed in relation to the "coordinates of the nation in a personalist system" (Perroux 1938, 286). Nonetheless, Perroux also highlighted converging concerns: "Mounier, who heads the group '*Esprit*', denounces the 'duplicates of corporatism' and does not hesitate to proclaim that any liberal or authoritarian corporatism which does not break decisively with the spirit and techniques of capitalism is a deception" (Perroux 1938, 161).

At that time, Perroux embraced the idea of the "person" but not without questioning the usefulness of creating a new terminology. He seemed to resist giving up the idea of the individual (not the one of individualism, but the one in which the multiple spiritual determinations could also be recognized). This movement led him to progressively use the term "man" (instead of person), which would eventually become the basis of one of his most influential formulations, the idea of the

[10] This "humanistic" perspective of corporatism would be present, for example, in a new wave in Portuguese corporatism in the 1950s with strong inspiration from the tradition of social Catholicism and, in particular, the work of Perroux. These authors would have no problem referencing Perroux's works from the 1930s with new works related to economic development that would appear in the 1950s and 1960s (Cardoso 2012, 109–10).

economy of the whole man and of all men ("*de tout l'homme et de tous les hommes*").[11] For him:

> An outdated conception of man (*l'homme*) ruins the state of yesterday and deviates the state of today. A renewed conception of man will bring up the state of tomorrow. Those who cannot be satisfied as citizens of the liberal state, of the proletarian state, or of the totalitarian state will seek to find out how the state must be completely overhauled to meet the material and spiritual demands of the time. (Perroux 1938, 254)

Perroux insisted that the liberal state, authoritarian state, totalitarian state, and proletarian state would all be unable to accurately contemplate the idea of the collective human person that underlies the idea of the community of labor and would ignore it in its "full and irreducible meaning" (Perroux 1938, 255). He finally insisted on the necessity of the affirmation of the rights of the group, of the "human person and not only of the citizen, of the producer [or] of the proletarian" (Perroux 1938, 267).

Nevertheless, the last part of his 1938 book (titled "French Revolution") ends with ideas for a process of profound transformation, of revolution, that Perroux foresaw for France that had the nation (as a collective of intermediate groups of persons) in the center. This emphasis on the nation marked important differences in relation to Mounier's personalist revolution. For Perroux, this "French revolution" would take place on the basis of a communitarian economy, in which the community of labor "is the tool and the means of a communitarian spirit, of a community of persons" (Perroux 1938, 330). In 1938, Perroux already resorted to what, years later, would become Vichy's official slogan: the idea of the "national revolution," but not as a "revolution that closes and locks a nation in on itself. (…) The very particular historical conditions of the fascist and Hitlerian revolution do not allow us to dispute this obvious truth that a nation, to open up to international collaboration, (…) must first benefit from a minimum of security and order" (Perroux 1938, 287).

[11]This formula of the economy of "*tout l'homme et de tous les hommes*" was widely used by Perroux in his studies of economic development from the 1950s onwards and exerted considerable influence on the social Catholicism discourse. Perroux was one of the founders, in Vichy times, of the movement "*Economie et Humanisme*" and close associate of the Dominican priest Louis-Joseph Lebret, which is why these ideas took part in the text of the 1967 encyclical "*Populorum Progressio*" of Pope Paul VI. On the movement "*Economie et Humanisme,*" see Pelletier (1996).

In what would be Perroux's editorial project with probably the most impact and diffusion during the occupation, the *Cahiers d'études communautaires*, which was directed by Perroux and Jacques Madaule between 1941 and 1942, the central message was the national revolution as a communitarian work. Its first issue ("*Communauté et Société*") presented texts by Perroux and Rémy Prieur, a pseudonym of Perroux's beloved pupil, Pierre Uri (behind which Uri disguised his Jewish origins). The final part of Prieur/Uri's article is devoted to a section on "Communauté et personne," in which he discusses in particular the limits of the question of collective personality and problems relating to the unity of the group (Prieur 1941, 46). At that time, Uri actively participated in Perroux's reflections on communitarian topics. This is evidenced, for example, by another text ("Communauté et Communisme"), this one prepared by Uri for an intervention in a study and discussion session with Perroux and others in July 1941.[12] Uri would become Perroux's most important collaborator in the immediate postwar period, just before moved on (causing great resentment on the part of Perroux) to Jean Monnet's entourage at the *Commissariat Général au Plan* (CGP), where he would be one of Monnet's main collaborators in the definitions of the Schuman Plan and in the design of the Economic Community of Coal and Steel (ECCS), which rehabilitated the idea of community in the projects for postwar European integration.

It is important to emphasize, however, the question of how this path of a "National Revolution" was already inscribed in Perroux's work in 1938. This helps us to better understand the circumstances of Perroux's engagement in the Vichy government. We fully agree here with Julian Jackson's line of reasoning that "the fact that someone of Perroux's intellectual distinction could commit himself so totally to Vichy suggests that we take Vichy's National Revolution seriously as an intellectual project, and not see it as merely the rearguard action of a handful of irreducible reactionaries" (Jackson 2005, 157). Although deep, complex, opportunistic to a great extent and certainly not valuable for his future curriculum, there is undoubtedly a component of true conviction in Perroux's connections with the Vichy regime and a belief in a path of renewal for France that was already inscribed in the perspectives he defended throughout the 1930s.

[12] Historical Archives of the European Union at Florence, Italy: Fund "Pierre Uri"—PU-3 ("Réunion du samedi 1 5 juillet 1941" in "Études d'économie avec le professeur F. Perroux").

Perroux had different institutional insertions during the Vichy period, having been part of the constitutional commission of the *Conseil National* created in 1941 and contributed directly to the writing of the Labour Charter ("*Charte du travail*"), a central document for the French corporatist experience in the period that ended up having no effective application (see Dard 2017, 230–32; Cointet 1989, 154–56). His main position, however, starting in 1942, was that of secretary-general of the influential Carrel Foundation (*Fondation française pour l'étude des problèmes humains*), where he also directed the Department of Biosociology (Drouard 1992, 207–69).

His activism as a disseminator of communitarian ideas advanced in parallel with intense academic management activity at the Carrel Foundation in those years. Perroux took advantage of his privileged institutional position to further his research interests, in particular through the team he gathered at the Department of Biosociology and the wide range of contacts he established with prominent social scientists and intellectuals. In an article published in late 1943, Perroux produced a reflection on the possibilities of integrating the "sciences of man" with economic sciences. The extensive discussions and praiseworthy references to the works of Alexis Carrel led Perroux to not even wait for the printing of the book to retract himself, including an erratum in the publication in which he attributed his lack of training in the biological disciplines to his mistake in relation to ideas de Carrel, also saying that "I must therefore, to my great regret, warn the public against an error of which I was, for a time, the victim, and no longer intend to be the propagandist" (Perroux 1943, *erratum*). In addition to the endorsement of Carrel's ideas, other elements of the text were also potentially problematic to Perroux in that moment of personal search for redefinition. In themselves, the analyses follow a coincident line with his other publications in the period, but some statements are much more intense than those in his other works. He wrote about the trends and shape lines of an economy of tomorrow that he defined as "communitarian and authoritarian." For him, "the economy of tomorrow will be communitarian" and "this economy will develop under the sign of authority" (Perroux 1943, 32–34).

The integration of the sciences of man with the economic sciences allowed Perroux to speak of an economy of the complete man, "in contrast to the ideologies of parliamentary democracies and social democracies." He insisted that:

> Biology is breaking into the politics of several large states. (…) The public authorities take care of the child, the mother, the blood, the race, and to achieve this protection for the masses, by mass means. (…) All this is in contrast to the ideologies of parliamentary democracies and social democracies. This conversion takes place at the same time or roughly [the same time] in enemy states. Such a statement by Lenin or Stalin on the construction of solid men with steel nerves echoes those of Hitler or Mussolini. Rome, like Berlin, like Moscow, is finding the meaning of a full life, vigorously animal to be effective and with a tendency for the improvement of man. (Perroux 1943, 29)

In the same way, Perroux sought to bring this idea of a "complete man" (l'*homme complet*), informed by this articulation with the biology that the article extols (and which he worked on at the Department of Biosociology), together with his motto of the economy of the whole man and of all men. His work talks of "an economy of the whole man, of all man, who performs all of his essential functions as a robust and balanced animal, and who also participates in the ascent of the spirit" (Perroux 1943, 30).

This 1943 academic article mobilized a large amount of theoretical content but was still articulated with Perroux's texts and intended for dissemination in the period. These intense activities for disseminating the communitarian perspectives in the period, which included the creation of different groups and publications, culminated in the creation, together with Yves Urvoy, of the so-called *Renaître* group in 1942, which, to some extent, radicalized the discourse of the National Revolution and insisted on the idea of doctrinal work and mobilization of the elite that would lead France to this revolution. The objective of the *Renaître* group was the same as that advocated by Perroux and repeated multiple times in those years: a national communitarian revolution. The tone, however, was more intense and urgent: "Our action has a very limited meaning: Revolution, we specify: National Community Revolution. We find ourselves in the stream of confused aspirations and groping thoughts which for years has prepared the present revolutionary task, and which is the soul of all the important events of our time" (Perroux and Urvoy 1943, i).

The path to the deepening of the national revolution also included, for Perroux, a specific vision on the future of Europe, clearly announced by *Renaître* by attributing a prominent role in this process to the French nation. This idea is in line with other perspectives vehemently supported by Perroux during those years, including ideas such as the idea of a complete man, a new man, a healthy society and, in particular, an unmeasured importance attributed to the nation. For him, the nation is the locus for a synthesis of the different communities that are part of the country, though this does not necessarily unfold within a nationalist discourse. The perspective that the *Renaître* group seemed to sustain, on the contrary, was still associated with the perspective of the 1930s federalist and personalist nonconformist groups that preserved the idea of the nation as a space of belonging and moving away from sectarian perspectives of nationalism. That is, the idea was one of an "integral federalism," built on the basis of the recognition of diverse collective persons, diverse communities, forming multiples and organic bonds among individuals at the local and national levels as well as, by the same reasoning, the international level.[13]

> And if Europe is divided, it is because of these global and confused aspirations, where some focus on one side, others on the other. You have to note that you have to take and keep both, but in a higher order, which will be the European civilization of tomorrow. (…) The first problem, the capital problem, is to remake the unit in the man, to remake the man. (…) The second problem, which is just another side of the first, is to rebuild a healthy society. By remaking a new man, he makes a new society, both a result and a cause, a manifestation and a setting, of a new man. The new man will understand that it is through other men, in common life, that he finds the normal framework for his development and not in sterile isolation. 'Community' is the guiding word for the constructive task. It is complemented by another: 'hierarchical pluralism.' It is by reintegrating man into numerous human communities organically linked within the Nation that

[13] The idea of "integral federalism" (as opposed to the "integral nationalism") was in line with several sources of discourse that understood the nation as a kind of community of communities. It is noteworthy how this type of discourse in the mid-1930s could be appropriated by very different figures in the political spectrum. Here again, the reference to Henri Lefebvre and his 1937 book, *Le nationalisme contre les nations* is of particular interest (see Lefebvre 1988 [1937]). Lefebvre speaks positively of "integralism" and "total man" in his search to find, qualify or requalify terms capable of separating nationalism in its forces that pointed to totalitarianism, of aspects of the term that he understood as positive and that could be associated with the idea of homeland and community. There were undoubtedly many terms in dispute at that time, not only for Perroux or Lefebvre. What seemed to matter was most of all a redefinition of the discourse. Even if polarized on one side or the other of the political spectrum, there is a very broad interest, shared by a whole generation in 1930s France, in redefining the terms of the political discourse at a time when the responses presented seemed insufficient to deal with the various dimensions of a persistent crisis.

> we will give him the possibility of solving the great political, technical and human problems of the hour, of solving them himself, supported fraternally by his companions of destiny. (Perroux and Urvoy 1943, 84–85)

This understanding of Europe as diverse echoed the ideas that Perroux had already insisted on in the mid-1930s that were broadly in consonance, for example, with the federalist perspectives inspired by personalism asserted by Marc, who insisted at that time on topics such as multi-belonging to different communities at different levels. Analyzing the imperial ambitions of Nazi Germany in 1934, Perroux commented that "the pan-German solution is unacceptable because it destroys Europe. Europe is diversity, originality of autonomous elements on a common civilization background. A continuous German band, stretched between Hamburg and Constantinople, irreparably breaks European unity" (Perroux 1934, 530).

A coincident perspective was also present in his arguments in the postwar period. We can thus insist once again on the elements of continuity in Perroux's reflection in the interwar period, in the Vichy years and in the immediate postwar period (even if accompanied by a discourse on which the terms of analysis ended up being redefined or remade). In Perroux's analysis of the postwar period, the perspective of an effective understanding of "cultural pluralism" is a key element for the success of the integration process or, in its own terms, of overtaking the nation (*dépassement de la nation*). Perroux was precisely interested in the criticism of "partial federalism" (as opposed, therefore, to "integral federalism"), which merely proposed the retreat of national borders in the direction of larger territorial units and would simply produce an "expanded nationalism." For Perroux, the answer, on the contrary, was a process of the progressive "devaluation of borders" for the construction of what he called "Europe unbounded by the sea" (*Europe sans rivages*) (Perroux 1954, 295–96).

4 Final Remarks

It is interesting to note how Perroux, in the pages of the *Renaître*, repeatedly used variations of the term "confusion." Perroux, Mounier, Marc and other authors analyzed here tried to understand those confusing aspirations and confusing times and came closer to the coincident perception that not only was action necessary, but also an exercise in interpreting reality, in order to understand which course of action should be taken. It is from this greater unrest that the search for an answer by nonconformist groups in the 1930s in France was born, and third-way perspectives in personalist and federalist discourses were fundamental dimensions of this. Perroux, Mounier, Marc, Dandieu, Aron, Maulnier and others understood that their efforts, always with a view to revolutionary action, included, above all, a "doctrinal stage."[14] Not only did this preliminary step serve to educate and convince a wider audience to engage in the intended revolutionary action but also, and perhaps primarily, that stage was the space to affirm (tentative) responses to a confused and unstable reality. It is not surprising that the answers themselves were also sometimes confusing and unstable. The combination of philosophical, spiritualist, political, economic, and social discourses also contributed to this confusion, which tended to very easily create internal dissonances and sometimes conflicts within these groups.

The present attempt to articulate some of these elements with a particular focus on the personalist sources of the third-way discourse, in different of their appropriations (an in particular in Perroux's political economy of corporatism), leads us finally to a particular conclusion: the enormous plasticity of the personalist argument (which, to some extent, helped to generate confusion in the historiography of this period). The idea of personalism as developed in the French context of the 1930s lends itself easily to both the call for freedom and the call for order. Both the praise of the difference, which is a reaction against the uniformity of the nation, and, on the contrary, the concern with perceiving bonds and elements of belonging shape the collective person and the community. In the end, it was exactly this plasticity that allowed the concepts created in the 1930s context to be used by different groups, with reinforcement from one or the other of its facets, during that decade, throughout the Vichy period, and in the postwar period.

References

Aron, Robert. 1935. "Chronique permanente pour une troisième force: II. Le point de vue de l'Ordre Nouveau." *Esprit* 38 (Nov. 1935): 381–89.

Bastow, Steve. 2001. "Third Way Discourse in Inter-War France." *Journal of Political Ideologies* 6 (2): 169–89.

[14] See for example: Marc (1932, 333) or Aron (1935, 282).

Bernard, Philippe, and Henri Dubief. 1985. *The Decline of the Third Republic, 1914–1938*. Cambridge: Cambridge University Press.

Bernis, Gèrarde Destanne de. 2000. "François Perroux (1903–1987)" In *A Biographical Dictionary of Dissenting Economists*, 2nd ed., edited by Philip Arestis and Malcolm Sawyer, 494–501. Northampton, Mass: Edward Elgar.

Brisset, N., and R. Fèvre. 2019. "Peregrinations of an Economist: Perroux's Grand Tour of Fascist Europe," *GREDEG Working Papers 2019–11*, Groupe de Recherche en Droit, Economie, Gestion (GREDEG CNRS), University of Nice Sophia Antipolis.

Cardoso, José Luís. 2012. "Corporativismo, Instituições Políticas e Desempenho Económico." In *Corporativismo, fascismos, Estado Novo*, edited by Fernando Rosas and Álvaro Garrido. Coimbra: Almedina.

Chavagneux, Christian. 2003. "Perroux l'ambigu." *L'Economie Politique* 20: 44–78.

Cohen, Antonin. 2006. "Du corporatisme au keynésianisme: Continuités pratiques et ruptures symboliques dans le sillage de François Perroux." *Revue française de science politique* 56 (4): 555–92.

———. 2012. *De Vichy à la Communauté européenne*. Paris: Presses universitaires de France.

Cointet, Michèle. 1989. *Le Conseil national de Vichy: vie politique et réforme de l'état en régime autoritaire: (1940–1944)*. Paris: Aux amateurs de livres.

Craiutu, Aurelian. 2017. *Faces of Moderation: The Art of Balance in an Age of Extremes*. Philadelphia, PA: University of Pennsylvania Press.

Cunha, Alexandre Mendes. 2020. "Postwar Third-Way Perspectives: François Perroux on National Income and Planning."*History of Political Economy* 52 (4): 653–82.

Dard, Olivier. 2002. *Le rendez-vous manqué des relèves des années trente*. Paris: Presses Univ. de France.

———. 2017. "Vichy France and Corporatism." In *Corporatism and Fascism: The Corporatist Wave in Europe*, edited by António Costa Pinto. London: Routledge.

Deweer, Dries. 2013. "The Political Theory of Personalism: Maritain and Mounier on Personhood and Citizenship."*International Journal of Philosophy and Theology* 74 (2): 108–126.

Drouard, Alain. 1992. *Une inconnue des sciences sociales: la Fondation Alexis Carrel, 1941–1945*. Paris: Editions de la Maison des sciences de l'homme.

Dupuis, René, and Alexandre Marc. 1933. *Jeune Europe*. Paris: Plon.

Francis, Robert, Thierry Maulnier, Jean Pierre Maxence. 1934. *Demain la France*. Paris: Grasset.

Gosewinkel, Dieter. 2015. *Anti-Liberal Europe A Neglected Story of Europeanization*. New York, NY: Berghahn Books.

Guieu, Jean-Michel. 2010. "Le militantisme européen, une approche générationnelle (des années 1920 au début des années 1950)." *Histoire@Politique* 10 (1): 3.

Hellman, J. 2002. *The Communitarian Third Way: Alexandre Marc's Ordre Nouveau, 1930–2000*. Montreal, QC: McGill-Queen's University Press.

Higgins, Benjamin, and Donald J. Savoie, eds. 1988. *Regional Economic Development: Essays in Honor of François Perroux*. Boston: Unwin Hyman.

Jackson, Julian. 2005. 'Mal embarqué bien arrivé': The Strange Story of François Perroux. In *Vichy, resistance, liberation new perspectives on wartime France*, edited by Hanna Diamond and Simon Kitson. New York, NY: Berg.

Labrousse, Roger. 1938. "Henri Lefebvre: Le nationalism contre les nations." *Esprit* 65 (Feb. 1938): 789–91.

Le Crom, Jean-Pierre. 1995. *Syndicats, nous voilà!: Vichy et le corporatisme*. Paris: Editions de l'Atelier/Editions ouvrières.

Lefebvre, Henri. 1988 [1937]. *Le Nationalisme contre les nations*. Paris: Méridiens Klincksieck.

Loubet del Bayle, Jean Louis. 1969. *Les Non-comformistes des annees 30, une tentative de renouvellement de la pensée politique français*. Paris, Editions du Seuil.

———. 1998. "Le mouvement personnaliste français des années 1930 et sa postérité." *Politique et Sociétés* 17(1–2): 219–237.

Loughlin, John. 1989. "French Personalist and Federalist Movements in the Interwar Period." In *European Unity in Context: The Interwar Period*, edited by Peter M.R. Stirk. London: Pinter.

Marc, Alexandre. "Vers un Ordre Nouveau." *Esprit* 2 (Nov. 1932): 330–34.

Marc, Alexandre and René Dupuis. 1932. "Le Fédéralisme Révolutionnaire." *Esprit* 2 (Nov. 1932): 316–24.

Meardon, Stephen J. 2000. "Eclecticism, Inconsistency, and Innovation in the History of Geographical Economics." In *Toward a History of Applied Economics*, edited by Roger E. Backhouse and Jeff Biddle. *History of Political Economy* 32 (supplement): 325–60.

Mounier, Emmanuel. 1935. "Révolution Communautaire." *Esprit* 28 (Jan. 1935): 548–80.

———. 1936. *Manifeste au service du personnalisme*. Paris: Aubier, Editions Montaigne.

Ordre Nouveau (Coll.). 1933. "Lettre à Hitler." *Ordre Nouveau* 5(15).

Ory, Pascal, and Jean-François Sirinelli. 2004. *Les intellectuels en France: De l'affaire Dreyfus à nos jours*. Paris: Perrin.

Pasture, Patrick. 2018. "Catholic and Christian Democratic Views on Europe Before and After World War II: Continuities and Discontinuities." In *Christian Democracy across the Iron Curtain: Europe Redefined*, edited by Piotr H. Kosicki and Sławomir Łukasiewicz. Cham, Switzerland: Palgrave Macmillan.

Pelletier, Denis. 1996. *Économie et Humanisme. De l'utopie communautaire au combat pour le tiers-monde (1941–1966)*. Paris: Cerf.
Perroux, François. 1933. "Économie Corporative et Système Capitaliste: Idéologie et Réalité." *Revue d'Économie Politique* 47 (5): 1409–478.
———. 1934. "L'Europe Danubienne."*Affaires Étrangères* 4 (Nov–Dec.).
———. 1935. "Une nouvelle doctrine du Droit public. Le Portugal et Salazar: essai d'interprétation." *Affaires Étrangères* 5 (Nov.).
———. 1936. "La Personne Ouvrière et le Droit du Travail." *Esprit* 42 (Mar. 1936): 866–97.
———. 1938. *Capitalisme et communauté de travail*. Paris: Librairie du Recueil Sirey.
———. 1943. "Science de l'homme e science économique." In *Fondation Française pour l'étude des problèmes humains—Conférences*. Paris: Librairie de Médicis.
———. 1954. *L'Europe Sans Rivages*. Paris: Presses Universitaires de France.
Perroux, François, and Yves Urvoy. 1943. *Renaitre: Essais (1er série): La Révolution en Marche*. Monaco: Éditions de la Renaissance Européenne.
Pirou, Gaëtan. 1938. *Essais sur le corporatisme: corporatisme et libéralisme: corporatisme et étatisme: corporatisme et syndicalisme*. Paris: Sirey.
Prieur, Rémy [Pierre Uri], 1941. "Mesure de la Communauté." In *Cahiers d'Études Communauraires: Communauté et société*, edited by François Perroux, Rémy Prieur. Paris: Presses universitaires de France.
Ribeiro, Teixeira J.J. 1993. "A Faculdade de Direito de Coimbra na renovação do ensino e do estudo da Economia." *Boletim de Ciências Económicas* 36.
Siernhell, Zeev. 1984. "Emmanuel Mounier et la contestation de la démocratie libérale dans la France des années trente." *Revue Française De Science Politique* 34 (6): 1141–1180.
Touchard, Jean. 1960. *L'esprit des années 1930 une tentative de renouvellement de la pensée politique française*. Paris: Hachette.

CHAPTER 4

Corporatism and Planning in Monnet's Idea of Europe

Katia Caldari

1 Introduction

Wall Street crash and the Great Depression of the '30s raised serious doubts on the goodness of market capitalism and the effectiveness of the liberal recipes. In Great Britain J.M. Keynes developed his *General Theory*, which underlined the shortcomings of the neoclassical analysis and the limits of laissez-faire and proposed state intervention as the only possible way to overcome the crisis. In the meantime, the economic central planning implemented by Stalin from 1927—after the brief experience of the New Economic Policy and a form of market socialism—was proposed as an alternative to capitalism which was showing its limits and troubles.

The First World War had highlighted a decline of Europe, which became the subject of debates and reflections in the interwar period. The publication of the volumes by Oswald Spengler, *The Decline of the West* (1918, 1922, 1923) was the first of a long series of contributions which

K. Caldari (✉)
University of Padua, Padua, Italy
e-mail: katia.caldari@unipd.it

© The Author(s) 2021

A. M. Cunha and C. E. Suprinyak (eds.), *Political Economy and International Order in Interwar Europe*, Palgrave Studies in the History of Economic Thought,
https://doi.org/10.1007/978-3-030-47102-6_4

raised the issue of the existence of Europe as a community, a culture, a civilization[1] and signed the first important steps towards the idea of a European Union,[2] which would have been developed after WWII.

In the interwar period, therefore, politicians, intellectuals, scholars and economists wondered about the practicable new economic order in the light of the serious crisis of the liberal system and started to conjecture about the possible political order to be given to the European countries that had come out of a terrible fratricidal war.

Concerning the possible new economic order, in most Western countries a vivid debate developed over the conceivable alternative between the rising socialist experience in the Soviet Union and liberal capitalism: if the awareness of the need to find a "third way" solution between the two was largely shared, the suggestions on what shape should take this alternative were highly different and often conflicting. Main issues of discrepancy were the role to be given to the state and the scope to be left to the market.

Although it may seem just a question of different weights to be given to the state and the market, that choice entailed (implicitly or explicitly) a different proposal in terms of political and economic structures. And, if at the theoretical level it was easy to affirm the urgency for something in between capitalism and socialism and to develop some reasonable alternative, most attempts to implement the suggested alternative remained only partially successful (as for planning) and more often resulted into evident failures (as for corporatism).

In France, far more than in other countries, the debate about the third way was particularly intense and, especially from 1932 when in the country the effects of the economic crisis started to be felt, the efforts to practically develop an alternative to liberal capitalism and socialism involved two main different solutions: planning and corporatism. Some form of planning was especially suggested by neoliberals and

[1] As for instance, Paul Valery's essay "La crise de l'esprit" (1919), André Gide's article "L'avenir de l'Europe. Le point de vue d'un français" (1923); Gaston Riu's volume *S'unir ou mourir* (1929); Ortega Y Gasset's book *La rebellion de las masses* (1930) and Julien Benda's "Discours à la Nation européenne" (1933).

[2] Most notably, the idea of "Paneuropa" (1923) suggested by the count Coudenhove-Kalergi who founded the Paneuropean Union and Aristide Briand's proposal of a European Federal Union (1929).

socialist unionists; whereas corporatism was supported by catholic conservatives, anti-communist unionists, academics, royalists and employers (Kuisel 1981, 98–104). Although corporatism had much less influence and support than planning in the interwar period, it became one of the pillars of the Vichy regime during the war.

Corporatism and planning perspectives often overlapped[3] (see Pirou 1933) and since the beginning both of them were imbued with some elements of neoliberalism[4]: such a combination of "corporatism"-"planning"-"neoliberalism" is the backbone of the French design developed for the European construction soon after WWII (see Cohen 2006b). Such a design as originally conceived never succeeded and it was instead replaced by an ordoliberal architecture.

This paper focuses on the European project that was proposed by Jean Monnet soon after the war and aims to underline the strict connection of this idea of Europe with the legacy of both the debates developed in the interwar period on the role of the state and the workable version of capitalism and of the experiences occurred during the war period.

2 Between Neo-Corporatism and Planning

Although during WWI some form of corporatist management was experienced and supported, as for instance in the Clémentel's scheme,[5] soon after the war France returned to liberalism with a national policy characterized by "decontrol and detachment rather than management and

[3] There is not indeed a clear-cut difference between these two perspectives that share the same reproach of the "absence of order and organization" to the capitalist system (Pirou 1933, 15) and oppose the individualistic capitalism with more or less structured forms of state intervention (Pirou 1933, 15).

[4] "Neoliberalism" developed out of the Colloque Lippman organized by Louis Rougier in Paris in 1938 and which gathered together the main representatives of the liberal credo. Since the beginning in France neoliberalism was something pretty compound and manifold that counted people with very different perspectives, from those closest to socialism to those who were supporters of a rather radical laissez-faire. This miscellaneous soul continued to characterize French neoliberalism also after WWII (as it clearly appears at the first meeting of the Mont Pèlerin Society in 1947: see on this Denord 2009) and it explains its intertwining with the corporative and *planiste* ideas (Denord 2009, 2016; Margairaz 2001; Pirou 1939). By using the term neoliberalism therefore it should be kept in mind that it is a term "plus commode que précis" (Margairaz 1991, 722).

[5] Étienne Clémentel was Minister of Commerce and Industry of Government Briand during WWI. In 1917 he presented a reconstruction plan with a strong corporatist frame and with the suggestion of an "inter-allied pooling of scarce materials" (see Kuisel 1981, 37–55). His plan has several resemblances with the planning efforts developed after World War II. See below.

modernization" (Kuisel 1981, 62). During the thirties the corporatist ideas acquired a certain weight and started to be promoted[6]: French conception of corporatism, it was underlined, was to be distinguished from both the system of corporations which had characterized the Ancient Regime[7] and the dictatorial experiments that were going on in Italy or Germany.[8] It was a "neo-corporatism" (Pirou 1939, 73; see also Pirou 1937) which aimed at overcoming the most mischievous effects of the free market, giving voice to both entrepreneurs and workers under the state safeguard. It would assure order, discipline and justice whereas liberal capitalism had produced anarchy, disequilibrium and instability (Pirou 1939, 87). At this time, however, neo-corporatism was just a doctrine of a "few academics and fewer employers" and its possible concrete implementation produced several doubts and perplexities (Kuisel 1981, 104; see also Dreyfus 1988; Loubet del Bayle 1969).

Along with the renovated consideration of corporatism, during the thirties planning was the other important alternative suggested to overcome the economic crisis. Planning was much more supported than corporatism and was sustained by both neoliberals and socialists-syndicalists.[9] The neoliberal conception of planning derived from the rationalization movement of the 20s[10] and fostered the development of a forecasting apparatus, producer's discipline, corporatist networks, and indirect controls (Kuisel 1981, 105). Neoliberal planners—critical of the

[6] Among the others by: Firmin Baconnier, Pierre Lucius, Pierre Gaxotte and Eugène Mathon, who became a crucial reference for the corporatist approach in France (Pirou 1937, 15–16; Brocard 1933).

[7] Neo-corporatists underlined the plasticity of corporations that aimed at "preserving competition which compels everyone to make efforts and at assuring the game of personal interest which is the most important stimulus for economic activity" (E. Mathon, in Pirou 1937, 44).

[8] For instance, the economist François Perroux tried to promote a "French" version of corporatism—to be neatly distinguished from the totalitarian corporatism experiences in Italy and Germany—that was based on the concept of "Communauté de Travail" (1938a, b, c; see Brisset and Fèvre 2019).

[9] As for instance Jean Coutrot, a progressive industrialist; Alfred Sauvy, demographer-statician; Jean Ullmo, economist; and Auguste Detoeuf, industrialist who played an important role during Vichy.

[10] Rationalization and scientific management as the symbol of modern industry were particularly endorsed by French syndicalism (Kuisel 1981; Denord 2001).

traditional liberalism—envisaged an economic duality with the distinction between a free market sector and a corporate sector. Whereas the former—typical of the consumer goods—was to be left to the free play of the market, the latter—for the most vital necessaries—required some form of planning. On the other hand, the socialists-syndicalists—deeply influenced by Henri de Man[11]—advocated a throughout structural reform of capitalism. Among the most significative plans that were proposed, we find: (1) The 1935 Plan of the CGT (*Confédération Générale du Travail*) which promoted a structural reform based on the nationalization of credit and other key industries, the creation of an economic council to control the nationalized sectors and the development of an annual plan to prompt an "organized growth" (Kuisel 1981, 111; Mioche 1984); and (2) The 1934 Plan of *Revolution Constructive*[12]—not so different from the CGT Plan—which gave however less weight to nationalizations and more attention to the sector to be planned.

In the thirties, both planning and corporatism remained however overall on paper without any serious political endorsement.[13] It is only during the "national revolution" prompted by General Pétain (1940–1944) that these two possible alternatives were (partly)[14] implemented.

[11] Belgian socialist who promoted an idea of corporatism based on the importance of self-government for workers and entrepreneurs (Pirou 1937, 17; Perroux 1938a, 175).

[12] A study group founded with the publication of a volume manifesto in 1932 by a number of people that broke with the Socialist Party. Among its founders we find: Georges Lefranc, Pierre Boivin, Claude Levy-Strauss and Robert Marjolin, who was to become Secretary-General of the OEEC (Organisation for European Economic Co-operation) from 1948 to 1955 and Vice-President of the EEC (European Economic Community) from 1958 to 1967. See below.

[13] Most notably the coalition government of the socialist Blum (1936–1938)—due to its different contrasting component parts (i.e. radicals, communists, and socialists)—was uncapable to realize a comprehensive program of structural reforms as it was in its original intention (see on this Kuisel 1981, 121–23; Margairaz 1991, vol. I; Pirou 1939, 169–70; Marjolin 1989). Planning—partly supported by some representatives of the CGT—was rather left aside as well as the program of nationalizations the socialists wished (Asselain 1984, 58). There are however some exceptions: along with the creation of the Wheat Office and the nationalization of some war industries, the most important reform concerns the reorganization of the Bank of France (Margairaz 1991, 232–40), which is herald of the post-war nationalization (Monnet 2018, 44–63).

[14] The only partial realization of the planned structural reforms under Vichy was mainly due to the interference and then the increasing intrusion of Germany into the economic choices of the Petain's regime. Soon after the armistice, the main idea of the Vichy's authorities was to develop a new *politique* based on a sort of "economic collaboration"

The new Vichy regime operated an industrial reorganization (see on this, V.V.A.A. 1943; Dreyfus 1990) based on a (pseudo-)corporatist[15] structure with the creation of: (a) the *Comités d'Organisation* (CO) and (b) the *Office Central de Répartition des Produits Industriels* (OCRPI). The COs were provisional bodies to be incorporated into a more pervasive corporatist reform to develop in the future. There was a CO for each economic sector with the tasks of making industrial census and regulating business operations. COs cooperated with private employers and trade associations and were intermediaries between private enterprises and government. The OCPRI had the power to control the allocation of industrial products and all levels of rationing. Both COs and OCPRI remained more statist than corporatist structures, they largely excluded small firms and workers and assumed a highly bureaucratic character which limited their effectiveness.[16] Moreover, in so far as both COs and OCPRI were under the government control[17] they were expression of a strong *dirigisme* which involved some form of planning.

The "economie dirigée" designed under Vichy finds better expression in two plans to be implemented after the war: (1) The 1942 *Plan d'Equipement National* and (2) the 1944 *Tranche de Démarrage*. Both of them were elaborated by the *Délégation Générale à l'Equipement National* (DGEN) in cooperation with the OCPRI, COs, industrial representatives, scientists and farm leaders. These two plans were directed

with Germany: the creation of the COs and OCRPI was indeed functional to Petain's "politics of presence" in the occupied territory. However this strategy pretty ambiguous since the beginning (Margairaz 1991, 523–90) became a clear failure during the second period of the Vichy regime (1942–1944) when it became completely subjugated to the Germany's choices and directions (Margairaz 1991, 671–715).

[15] This aspect was particularly underlined by Perroux who, commenting on the Vichy's first results, notes for instance that the Reform incorporated in the 1941 Labour Charter was just a pre-corporatist law (1943, 158; 1942, 12) although it marked the way "towards a true corporatist economy" (1943, 186). See on this Margairaz (1991, 564–70); on the outcomes obtained in terms of corporatist reform under the Vichy regime see also Cohen (2006a).

[16] Besides, many COs simply reproduced existing cartels and trade associations (Kuisel 1981, 142).

[17] The Ministry of Industrial Production controlled the OCPRI, selected CO's personnel, appointed a government commissioner and exercised an overreaching surveillance (Kuisel 1981, 135–36).

by François Lehideux[18] who had conceived the DGEN as a small committee of experts which had to order the programs of the different bureaus of central administration into a coherent plan (Kuisel 1977). Although both the plans were never implemented[19] they are of crucial importance for the early post-war period and, as we will see below, it is a necessary reference for the arising French European project.

3 Thinking of the National Reconstruction...

During WWII two main positions developed about how to reconstruct France after the war. Following the distinction made by Villey (1945), there were on the one hand the so-called "architects" (mainly socialists, syndicalists and *planistes*[20]) who proposed structural reforms, and on the other hand the so-called "doctors" (mainly neoliberals[21]) who supported market and private property along with some state intervention and the relevance given to the cooperation with the United States. As a matter of fact, indeed, these two perspectives often overlapped and each of them had elements of the other.

Three chief reports developed in this period are worthy of being recalled:

[18] Former director of the Renault automobile company, he was appointed head of the Commissariat for the Unemployment in 1940; in 1941, Petain assigned him the role of *Délegué general à l'Équipement* for the government.

[19] The DGEN and its plans were openly thwarted by Laval, who became head of government in 1942 and progressively they were marginalized. In 1942, Bichelonne, head of the Ministry of Industrial Production, created the *Conseil Supérieur de l'Économie Industrielle et Commerciale* to deal also with economic planning. However the Conseil dealt with planning only on a very general ground and stressed, instead the importance of strong corporatist bodies to "mediate planning and thus avoid centralized bureaucratic management" (Kuisel 1981, 152).

[20] As André Philip, Georges Boris, Jules Moch, Mèndes-France and Robert Marjolin.

[21] Among the others, H. Alphand, E. Hirsch, R. Courtin and R. Pléven.

1. the Alphand Report[22] (1942) which followed Britain's wartime economic and social policy and, along with the importance recognized to market and free enterprises, it underlined the unavoidability of nationalizations and some form of planning. A subcommittee that included E. Hirsch,[23] who had a corporatist inclination, strongly suggested the creation of a number of new institutions of public management (as the ministry of economy, economic parliament, agencies for the control of monopolies) and urged more pervasive techno-corporatist measures with the conservation of the corporatist bodies developed under Vichy (COs and OCRPI).
2. the Courtin Report[24] (1943) which had noticeable neo-liberal content, although it relied also on corporatist bodies as COs-OCRPI; it proposed the creation of a planning office and of the Ministry of Economy.
3. the Philip Report[25] (1944) which underlined the role of the state, the importance of planning and nationalisations: it suggested Keynesian policies and the conservation of the Vichy's corporatist bodies (COs) to be renamed "industrial groups".

None of these reports was endorsed by General De Gaulle under the provisional government (1944–1946). De Gaulle wanted to gather the largest possible consensus and support and he was particularly prudent especially on questions that produced doubts and objections, as for

[22] Named chief of the Commissariat for Economics and Colonies by De Gaulle in 1941, Alphand was at the head of a Commission that should study post-war economic and social problems. The commission was expression of different orientations, from the more liberal—represented by Alphand and Pléven—to the socialist (with André Philip, Georges Boris and Robert Marjolin) sides.

[23] Étienne Hirsch, former manager of a chemical firm, cooperated with Fighting France during the war and with Jean Monnet in the post-war period. He was General Commissioner for the Second French Plan and President of Euratom from 1959 to 1962. See below.

[24] Developed by a Committee of experts (the Comité Général d'Études) named by the Organisation Civil et Militaire (OCM) which operated in the occupied France. Among its members we find: de Menthon, Paul Bastid, Robert Lacoste, Alexandre Parodi and René Courtin.

[25] André Philip, named by De Gaulle the CFLN's commissaire in charge, organized a study group for the post-war problems with Mendès-France, Albert Gazier and Luis Vallon.

instance that related to the liquidation/conservation of the Vichy corporatist bodies (see on this Mioche 1987; Margairaz 1991, 770–80). Although among his ministers there was a general agreement on the necessity of some measure of dirigisme, planning, and nationalization many differences existed on the weight to give to and the ways to develop them[26] (Kuisel 1981, 189–90).

A project for a new Ministry of National Economy was entrusted by De Gaulle in 1944 to Pierre Mendès-France, who proposed a reform based on two main pillars: (1) austerity monetary measures in the attempt to control the high inflation and (2) economic planning.[27] According to his reform,[28] the Ministry of National Economy had to absorb Vichy's DGEN and OCRPI. Mendès-Frances referred to a three sectors economy: (1) a nationalized sector for the industries that were crucial for the reconstruction as energy, banking, iron and steel; (2) a controlled sector for the rest of the industries and the wholesale trade that should be under the control of the reformed COs; and (3) a free sector for small scale enterprises and farmers, which was under state control for the allocation of raw materials and dissolution of commercial monopolies. These three sectors would be linked through a general economic plan. The proposed plan heavily relied on the Vichy's Tranche de Démarrage, whose text was published by Mendès-France in 1944 under his responsibility (Mioche 1987, 46); moreover several DGEN's proposals were incorporated (Kuisel 1981, 195–96). Mendès-France's project was therefore highly criticized

[26] Under the Provisional Government, in De Gaulle's cabinet a particularly thorny question was indeed related to the problem of what to do with the Vichy's institutions and there was a strong contrast between those who wanted to radically liquidate them because expression of a dictatorial experience (as Paul Giacobbi, commissioner for supply and production) and those who thought it was better to maintain them (as Raymond Offroy, De Gaulle's counselor on economic affairs).

[27] This part of the reform was elaborated in strict collaboration with Georges Boris, who was a very close friend of Mendés-France and played an important role for the emergence of planning in France (see on this Fourquet 1980).

[28] The elaboration of this reform was rather troubled, and it gave rise to a rather struggled debate within the economic committee, which was formed by the main economic ministers (transport, industrial production, agriculture and so forth). See on this Mioche (1987, 37–52).

for its *dirigiste* measures—but also for its austerity recipes[29]—and then rejected by the government[30] (see on this Margairaz 1991, 784–90).

After Mendès-France's attempt, the elaboration of a plan of reconstruction was formally entrusted in June 1945 by Pléven, Minister of National Economy and Finances, to the Council of National Economy which consisted of 15 people appointed by the Minister himself. Indeed, what this Council did was just a sort of inventory of the country's economic situation; Pléven in fact did not aim to particularly foster economic planning.[31] Nonetheless, it is interesting to note that in this period within the Ministry of the Reconstruction and Urbanism (with Raoul Dautry), the Ministry of National Economy (with Gaston Cusin), and the Ministry of the Industrial Production (with Robert Lacoste) there were some attempts to develop some form of planning. As for the Ministry of the Reconstruction and Urbanism, R. Dautry—firmly convinced of the need for a plan[32]—published in November 1945 a report on the Reconstruction which strongly relied upon the Vichy's Tranche de Démarrage; G. Cusin, Minister of National Economy, published at the end of 1945 the Plan d'Équipement 1946 which openly recalled the Vichy's Tranche de Démarrage; R. Lacoste for his part, promoted instead the elaboration of 8 plans, one for each different sector (hydro-electric, commercial marine, automobile, dams, collieries, SNFC, machine-tools and reconstruction); there was not the idea of a comprehensive national coordinated plan but these plans are important in so far they anticipate, as we will see, an aspect of the structure of the Monnet Plan. It is also interesting to note that Lacoste preserved in his Ministry the bulk of the Vichy's administrative structures as OCRPI and the COs, changing them only formally into "Professional Offices" but keeping most of the people who had worked under Vichy.

29 De Gaulle followed instead the suggestions of the liberal Pléven, Minister of Finance, who promoted a softer policy based on the negotiation of prices and wages and the recourse to public debt (Fourquet 1980, 50–51).

30 Consequently, Mendès-France resigned in April 1945.

31 This aspect was critically stressed by Georges Boris and other supporters of planning. In 1945 a debate on planning involved some politicians, university professors, economists like C. Rist, Aftalion, R. Mossé, R. Courtin and others (Mioche 1987, 60–61).

32 In a letter written to Pléven he stresses that "the plan is indispensable" (quoted in Mioche 1987, 62).

However, despite these proposals, the question of planning seemed to be overshadowed by the attention the government gave to the problem of nationalizations that took place in 1945–1946 in the most crucial sectors as banks, electric power, gas, insurance and coal. Nevertheless from January 1946 economic planning was to become the most characteristic element of post-war French economic policy with the creation of the General Planning Commissariat (CGP). Fundamental for this turn towards economic planning was the role played by Jean Monnet.

4 The Directed French "Concert"

An experienced and clever contact between France and the United States,[33] Monnet skilfully linked the American foreign aids to the development of the national economic planning (Lynch 1984, 1997; see also Margairaz 1991, 764–814). The elaboration of a coherent and convincing plan of development was the condition for France to obtain the necessary financial means from the United States[34] with the Marshall Plan (Monnet 1976, 360; 387). This element, along with the urgency to reconstruct the country, was also the decisive reason to get De Gaulle's endorsement of economic planning which became a standard tool of French economic policy for a couple of decades. The first "Modernization and Equipment" Plan (the so-called Monnet Plan, 1947–1952) became a fundamental complementary element of the European Recovery Program

[33] Monnet was very familiar with the American culture and politics. In the interwar period he was a League of Nations official and part of the executive committee in an American bank (Kuisel 1981, 220; Margairaz 1991, 756–57). Between 1943 and 1945 he was in Washington as head of the staff of the French Supply Council and there gathered the people of his post-war team, with among the others Robert Marjolin and Étienne Hirsch (Monnet 1976).

[34] Along with other two crucial conditions that Monnet explicitly mentions in a memorandum dated 24 July 1947 and presented to the Minister of Foreign Affairs Georges Bidault (see on this Margairaz 1991, 892–96): namely the involvement of Germany into the European reconstruction and the financial and monetary stabilization of the country. Monnet as General Planning Commissioner dealt with the first aspect pushing towards the creation of the ECSC; as for the second issue, even more crucial for the problem of the dollar gap (Margairaz 1991, 876–903), Monnet worked towards the stabilization of money, prices and exchange rates without falling into a deflationist policy (Margairaz 1991, 928–31); in order to deal with the latter manifold and difficult problem, Monnet promoted and achieved the creation of the Commission of National Accounting of which he was the president (Fourquet 1980, 74–95) and that became a crucial tool for the CGP.

and was promoted by Monnet as the example to be followed by the other OEEC member countries.[35]

The Plan was promulgated by decree without being submitted to the Parliament. The Plan Commissariat was responsible to the Prime Minister's office and it was considered a permanent delegate of the head of the Government; the General Commissioner had a small staff, a modest budget and did not have a ministerial rank, although he had a large influence on most economic matters. Since the beginning, the General Planning Commissariat, for technical aspects of planning and projections, heavily relied both on qualified specialized groups and on members of the Modernization Commissions and their sub-commissions. The Commissions gathered together representatives of employers, workers and civil servants; they were specialized for sectors of activity. Their structure was made of the Chairman (usually a representative of the Grand Corps d'État); General Rapporteurs with only a few representatives of the private sector; and the members with representatives of employers and trade unions. All of them were appointed by decision of the Minister of Finance on suggestion of the General Commissioner (see on this Hackett and Hackett 1963; Lutz 1969).

It is an "economie concertée"[36] and an indicative form of planning that Monnet proposed in his Plan[37] to be neatly distinguished from the experiences of "economie dirigée" or "economie corporative" that had

[35] According to Monnet's idea, each European recipient country should have an equivalent of the French Plan to ease the distribution of the American aids. These different plans then should be inserted into a "European pyramid of economic control" (Gillingham 2003, 21) through the Organization of European Economic Cooperation (OEEC). However, his idea remained unsuccessful and the European Recovery Program followed its own criteria to distribute money to the European countries, whereas the OEEC became the main promoter of free trade with and within the European countries and in 1961 it was transformed in the Organization for Economic Cooperation and Development which became sponsor of global liberalization (Esposito 1994; Gillingham 2003).

[36] This definition is indeed due to Hirsch, as Monnet recalls (Monnet 1976, 373) and Hirsch himself emphasizes: "C'est moi qui a inventé la formule d'économie concertée, car je considère que dans le monde modern il est indispensable que les différents acteurs de l'économie, étant donnée leur interdépendance, se connaissent et discutent entre eux" (quoted in Fourquet 1980, 56).

[37] The Plan and its revisions were indeed the result of the joint work done by Monnet's small operative team: here we find E. Hirsch, R. Marjolin, A. Sauvy, J. Fourastier, J.-R. Rabier, J. Ripert, P. Denis, R. Auboin, L. Kaplan and J. Vergeot and from 1947 P. Uri (Monnet 1976, 346–378). Monnet was the General Commissioner of the first Plan.

characterized French economy before the end of the war.[38] Accordingly, the plan would be executed with the collaboration of all the national vital elements, that is the cooperation of experts on the one hand and the representatives of trade unions and business associations on the other hand (Monnet 1976, 344). The main goals of the Monnet Plan were the modernization of some basic sectors (coal, electricity, steel, transport, cement and agriculture) and the advancement of a general economic recovery which was deeply necessary after the war: the Plan determined that the outlined targets for the six basic sectors were to be considered *imperative*, whereas for all the other sectors they were simply *indicative* (Premier Plan 1946–1947, 35).

Although Monnet underlines (1976, 372) that the plan did not imply any form of dirigisme, some measures of dirigisme were not excluded in so far as along with some nationalizations—reputed not as aims in themselves but as means for collective progress (Monnet 1976, 345)—the Plan recognized to the state a dominant influence over the direction of investments in all the sectors[39] and several direct and indirect instruments to affect and control national economic activities.[40] Monnet emphasizes that these measures were tools that already existed, they belonged to the administrative power and were only reluctantly accepted by the planning team for which the most important means was "persuasion" (1976, 373). It is undoubtedly true that the General Commissioners who followed Monnet—most notably E. Hirsch for the second and third plan and P. Massé for the fourth plan—have increasingly emphasized the plan as "an effort to convince, clarify and talk" (Hirsch quoted in Fourquet 1980,

[38] In underlining the importance of the synergy between the General Planning Commissariat, the Commissions de Modernisation and the state, it is pointed out: "C'est ainsi seulement que les problèmes pourront être réglés par un échange permanent d'idées entre l'administration et le pays, dans une économie concertée et non pas dans une économie dirigée à caractère bureaucratique ou corporatif (Premier Plan, 101).

[39] It was for instance maintained: "Pour la·mise en œuvre du plan, il faut prévoir des méthodes d'exécution variables suivant les secteurs de l'économie, méthodes qui, cependant, doivent toutes s'inspirer du principe que la modernisation est une obligation pour toutes les activités du pays, et que nos ressources limitées en matières, main d'œuvre et moyens financiers doivent être utilisées en priorité pour l'exécution du plan" (Premier Plan, 102).

[40] Controls of licensing, selective tax treatments, privileged subsidies, financing of (public and private) industry through the Fund for Economic and Social Development (FDES) and so forth.

63–64) and as something "indicative" that "can only effect through persuasion and incitement" (Massé 1965, 83). Nonetheless, in our view, this departure from the idea of dirigisme[41] does not automatically imply the complete remove from the legacy of Vichy, as it is suggested by some authors (most notably Fourquet 1980, 63).

In fact the Monnet Plan has many features that are drawn from the previous experiences, as for instance the "Equipment Plan 1946" which was based on the DGEN's "Tranche de Démarrage" (Kuisel 1977, 1981; Gruson 1968; Paxton 1972) or Pléven's Council of National Economy and Lacoste's Professional Offices (Mioche 1987). Let us see some of them more in detail:

- The DGEN planners defined themselves as "chef d'orchestre"[42]; as we have seen Monnet and his team proposed a "concert" among the parts involved;
- The DGEN planners referred to a sort of indicative planning[43] emphasising the importance of "direction", analogously the Monnet Plan stressed the indicative nature of the planning proposed;
- The DGEN planners were reformers (Paxton 1972) with an expansionary productive perspective (Gruson 1968, 35) as well as the post-war planners;
- the Monnet's Modernization Commissions recall the Vichy COs[44] (Gruson 1968) notwithstanding their several differences (Kuisel 1981): Lacoste's Professional Offices can be indeed considered as a midway transformation (Mioche 1987, 66) of the Vichy's COs into the Monnet's Modernization Commissions; moreover several officers remained the same in this passage (see on this Mioche 1987).

[41] Indeed, even if the most authoritative instruments that had characterized the first Plan disappeared from the Second Plan, several inducement measures continued to be used in order *to direct* economic activities (Bauchet 1966, 118–38). Moreover, some tasks continued to be considered as "imperative".

[42] In the 1942 Plan d'Équipement National (quoted in Kuisel 1977, 79).

[43] In the Tranche de Démarrage where they write: "L'orientation et le contrôle ne doivent pas enserrer étroitement l'action mais lui imprimer l'impulsion necessaire" (quoted in Kuisel 1977, 92).

[44] In fact, the idea of creating those commissions is due to Hirsch who already in the thirties had largely expressed himself in favour of techno-corporatist structures.

- In the Monnet's Modernization Commissions as well as in the Conseil of Plan there are several names that took part also into the Vichy organization both in the COs and in the body of DGEN officers (Boureville, de Garrigue, Bizot, Surleau and many others, see on this Mioche 1987).
- Structure and functioning of the Pléven's Council of National Economy closely resembles Monnet's Council of Plan, most notably the inventory made by the Conseil was an important basis for the initial works of the CGP (Mioche 1987, 59).
- The conception of the national economy organized by different sectors some of them to be directed or even nationalized and some others to be left to the free market was widely shared among the neoliberals during the 20s and 30s, it strongly characterized Mendès-France's 1944 plan, it affected Lacoste's Ministry, and no doubt it represented the core of the Monnet Plan.

These aspects are important in so far as they show a certain continuity in the process that took towards the French post-war planning and help to better understand its originality. There are of course many important differences too; the most significant for the topic in hand is the following one: unlike the previous plans, the Monnet Plan was conceived within a larger architecture which involved the creation of a new international order but especially the foundation of a new Europe.

5 A French "Concert" for Europe?

The need to create a European framework within which to rebuild the destroyed country is the awareness that was widely shared in France, already before the end of the war, by neoliberals, people of the Resistance and Combatting France. Among those people we find Jean Monnet for whom the reconstruction of France had to go hand by hand with the construction of a new European order and who considered the two actions (France reconstruction and Europe construction) as a unique strategy.

Along with his commitment as Planning General Commissioner, Monnet's main efforts were in fact directed towards the creation of the "United States of Europe" (1976, 588). Architect of the Schuman Plan which resulted into the European Coal and Steel Community (ECSC) and of the Pléven Plan for the establishment of the European Defence

Community (EDC), Monnet pursued his idea of European integration according to his functionalist approach, to the relevance he gave to economic planning,[45] and also to the neo-corporatist heritage which never completely disappeared in the French approach to planning and idea of European project of those years.

According to Monnet's functionalist approach, the European economic integration should proceed by economic sectors and gradually reach the political unity into a federation[46] (Monnet 1976, 392–93). The ECSC was proposed in 1950 by the French Minister Schuman and officially embraced in April 1951 by the signatory countries of the Paris Treaty: France, West Germany, Italy, Belgium, Luxembourg and the Netherlands. It aimed at creating a *functional* organization between the different productive centres of coal and steel of the member countries and was conceived as the first one of a long series of pools that would have involved other domains as transports, energy, agriculture, tourism and so forth (see Monnet 1976, 589–91; Marchal 1964, 313–14). The executive body of the ECSC[47] was the *High Authority* (HA) which was conceived as a super-national organism with supra-national powers.[48] Among them we find the important task of organizing and regulating the sector between the members, that is to develop a form of planning to coordinate (*to concert*) production and consumption.[49]

According to the functionalist perspective, the same ECSC schema should have been applied to all the other sectors, one after the other,

[45] This aspect is often ignored by literature, as stressed in Warlouzet (2010, 345).

[46] This idea is stated also in the 9 May 1950 Schuman Declaration with the following words: "La mise en commun des productions de charbon et d'acier assurera immédiatement l'établissement de bases communes de développement économique, première étape de la Fédération européenne" (Schuman 1963, 203).

[47] The other ECSC institutions were: the *Common Assembly*, which was composed of national parliamentarians and had a supervisory power; the *Special Council* of national ministers with the representatives of the national governments and the assignment to issue opinions, and the *Court of Justice*, composed by judges appointed by the national governments and with the task to ensure the observation of the treaty; the *Consultative Committee*, composed by representatives of producers, workers, dealers of the sector that were nominated by the national governments.

[48] These remained however mostly on paper, as thoroughly described by Marchal (1964, 289–311).

[49] The Schuman Declaration explicitly refers to the need for "l'application d'un plan de production et d'investissements".

until the complete economic union that would have finally resulted into a political federation. However, after the ECSC and in the wake of its success, a pool was attempted in a non-economic sector: army. On the basis of the Pléven Plan that proposed the establishment of the European Defence Community (EDC), the ECSC member countries signed in May 1952 the treaty for the constitution of a common super-national army. The EDC treaty substantially followed the ECSC structure but, of course, had a greater political significance, such a great significance that in fact it turned out into a failure[50] (see Gillingham 2003, 29–32; Bossuat 2012, 97–107). After this debacle, Monnet resigned from the HA of the ECSC in 1954 but continued to pursue his ideas through the creation in 1955 of the Action Committee for the United States of Europe (Monnet 1976). Moreover, he prompted the Rome Treaties, especially the one concerning the creation of Euratom.

Euratom clearly followed the functionalist approach in representing a European pool for the atomic energy. Its organization resembled that of ECSC[51] but only formally in so far as the apparently super-national institution (the Commission) had no real supra-national power.[52] It was indeed the result of a compromise between Monnet's original idea and the increasing scepticism towards a possible European political union. As often underlined, Euratom was finally accepted as a major concession conditional to the construction of the common market (Monnet 1976; Marjolin 1989; Uri 1991; Denord and Schwartz 2010; Bossuat 2012). The opposition to a European "political turn" was growing—the failure of the EDC was a clear proof—and it was particularly evident during the negotiations of the Rome Treaties, where many issues appeared critical and dividing[53] but moreover where it was clear that the majority of the countries involved would have accepted only an agreement of a strictly economic nature (see on this Marjolin 1989, 276–306). This explains the

[50] It caused a long debate which culminated with the failure to obtain ratification in the French Parliament on the 30 August 1954.

[51] There were a Commission, made of 5 people independent from the national governments; the Council of ministers; the Assembly which had to control the works of the Commission; the Court of Justice.

[52] As noted by Marchal the Commission could be considered as an industrial administrative council with technical expertise (1964, 318).

[53] As for instance agriculture or overseas' relations.

reasons why the Spaak Report[54]—which was the reference outline for the Rome treatises—was largely amended for the final text that was signed in Rome on the 25 March 1957. The text agreed upon was not made as an extension of the Treaty of Paris (as Monnet wished) and the term HA was carefully dropped out.[55]

Euratom was therefore another failure for Monnet, certainly less searing than that of EDC but probably more significant because it signed the evident marginalization of his idea of Europe. Let us consider more in detail what this idea implied. Europe would have reached the economic union through the functional integration of its different sectors; each of them would have been under the control of a super-national entity called HA. Each pool would have had its own HA whose power was limited to that particular sector. The presence of a super-national power was necessary to channel the private economic interests (the firms involved) towards the general interest of the whole (see Marchal 1964, 294; see also Marjolin 1953). All the different High Authorities would then have concerted the whole economy and cooperated together forming a "European Confederation" (Monnet 1976, 648).

We do not want here to enter the already very much-debated question of the feasibility of this project (see for instance Perroux 1954; Marchal 1964; Gillingham 2003) but just to underline its strict relations with the interwar and war period experiences. As we have seen the consideration of the economy divided by different sectors is a very well-established idea that characterized France since the 30s; Monnet, who followed this idea in the national plan, adopted it also in his European project but with an important difference: if at the national level he distinguished between free and directed sectors, at the European level each sector should be organized according to a mixture of both liberalism and planning within a structure of neo-corporatist nature. Each sector in fact would have been a competitive part into the (international) competitive market but it also would have been under the control of a HA which had the main aim to direct and plan its choices; at the same time the organization of the

[54] It was drafted by the Spaak Committee where a particularly important role was played by Pierre Uri who was one of the closest Monnet's collaborators, economic and financial adviser of the General Planning Commissariat (1947–1952), and director at the ECSC (1952–1959).

[55] The text of the Rome Treaty neglects also other issues included instead in the Spaak Report, as for instance the pooling of the air transport and the creation of a postal union.

economy by sectors reflects a corporative structure to the point that an important role of the HA was that of equilibrating the particular private interests within the sector.[56]

After the EDC failure and the Euratom downsizing, Monnet's conception of European architecture gave way to that of an economic union based on the common market that did not involve too difficult political choices and implications. A last attempt in Monnet's direction was indeed made in the early 60s by Robert Marjolin[57] who tried to spread and to make accepted his idea of Europe as "Europe organisée"[58] by coordinating meetings and seminars and by creating a network of people that shared and sustained the idea of economic planning. Marjolin's "action program" strongly conflicted with the ordo-liberal view that was increasingly prevailing at the European level (Pühringer 2017), and lastly the idea of planning at the European level disappeared[59] whereas Monnet's United States of Europe never materialized. The European integration followed another totally different path.

[56] For the ECSC, the Schuman Declaration stresses in fact that it was "A l'opposé d'un cartel international tendant à la répartition et à l'exploitation des marchés nationaux par des pratiques restrictives et le maintien de profits élevés…".

[57] Socialist, with a Keynesian formation (Arena 2000), since the beginning he played a crucial role in promoting the idea of Common market; he was a strict collaborator of Monnet far before the end of the war: in 1943, in Algiers, Monnet—as member of the First French National Liberation Committee—formed a small group to reflect on the future of France. In this group there were E. Hirsch, R. Marjolin and P. Mendès France (see Dangel-Hagnauer and Raybaut 2007). Marjolin was not a doctrinaire planner (he also participated to the Colloque Lippman in 1938) but he thought that planning was a necessary means to prompt economic progress. He also considered useful some degree of corporatist organization, as in the American experience of the National Recovery Administration (NRA) developed by Roosevelt in 1933 (Marjolin 1935).

[58] Based on the idea of the necessary coordination among the European members of both economic policies of medium and long term and of cyclical and monetary policies.

[59] European integration developed about the coordination of some macroeconomic aspects leaving completely aside most of the elements that the idea of French planning involved and that never again became part of the European agenda. The main ones are the following three that are among them strictly interconnected: (a) long run perspective; (b) consideration of collective and social goods; and (c) discretionary interventions due to the danger and limits of any automatism (see Caldari 2019).

6 Some Concluding Remarks

French post-war economy was imbued since the beginning with a combination of neo-corporatism and planning inherited from the 30s. These two components characterized France but informed also the idea of Europe that, for a period, France tried to promote.

Economic planning was considered as a necessary means to prompt the modernization of the French economy but also and especially as the unavoidable tool to use at European level in order to shape its new economic and political order. The neo-corporatist background developed in the interwar period influenced both the French approach to planning and the French idea of European project promoted by Jean Monnet and his small team.

However, the flavours of "*economie dirigée*" (even when called "*economie organisée*"[60]), the vestiges of neo-corporatist schemes, the role given to state control (emphasized also at supra-national level) contrasted with the arising conception of Europe increasingly based on ordo-liberal perspectives and signed the failure of Monnet's idea of European project.

References

Arena, Richard. 2000. "Les économistes français en 1950." *Revue économique* 51 (5): 969–1007.

Asselain, Jean-Charles. 1984. *Histoire économique de la France du XVIIIe siècle à nos jours*, vol. 2. Paris: Éditions du Seuil.

Bauchet, Pierre. 1966. *La Planification française. Vingt ans d'expérience.* Paris: éditions du Seuil.

Bossuat, Gérard. 2012. *La France et la Construction de l'Unité Européene.* Paris: Armand Colin.

Brisset, Nicolas, and Raphaël Fèvre. 2019. "Peregrinations of an Economist: Perroux's Grand Tour of Fascist Europe." *GREDEG No. 2019–11*, CNRS, University of Nice Sophia Antipolis.

Brocard, Lucien. 1933. "Le concezioni francesi dell'economia regolata." In V.V.A.A., *l'Economia programmatica*, 3–41. Firenze: Sansoni Editore.

[60] Following Brocard (1933), the concepts of "économie concertée" and "économie organisée" are to be taken as synonymous and clearly distinguished from the idea of "économie dirigée". However, as we have seen, a certain degree of dirigisme (never indeed quantified) is implicit in the French idea of "économie concertée" or "économie organisée". In fact, some French authors—as for instance François Perroux (1938a, 298)—use the term "économie dirigée" as a synonymous of "économie organisée".

Caldari, Katia. 2019. "From 'Planning' to 'Programming': A Lost Opportunity for the European Project?" *Forum for Social Economics*, published online.

Cohen, Antonin. 2006a. "Du Corporatisme au Keynésianisme." *Revue française de Science politique* 56: 555–92.

———. 2006b. "De la Révolution Nationale à l'Europe Fédérale. Les metamorphoses de la troisième voie aux origins du movement fédéraliste francais: la Fédération (1943–1948)." *Le Mouvement social* 217: 53–72.

Dangel-Hagnauer, Cécile, and Alain Raybaut. 2007. "French Economists Within Public Institutions. The Making of Economic Policy in Post-Second-World-War France." In *Economics and Institutions. Contributions from the History of Economic Thought*, edited by Pier F. Asso and Luca Fiorito, 163–85. Milano: Franco Angeli.

Denord, Fraçois. 2001. "Aux origines du néo-libéralisme en France: Louis Rougier et le Colloque Walter Lippmann de 1938." *Le mouvement social* 2 (195): 9–34.

———. 2009. "French Neoliberalism and Its Divisions: From the Colloque Walter Lippman to the Fifth Republic." In *The Road from Mont Pèlerin: The Making of the Neoliberal Thought Collective*, edited by Philip Mirowski and Dieter Plehwe, 45–67. Cambridge, MA: Harvard University Press.

———. 2016. *Le néo-libéralisme à la Française: Historire d'une idéologie politique*. Marseille: Agone.

Denord, François, and Antoine Schwartz. 2010. "L'Économie (très) politique du Traité de Tome." *Politix* 1 (89): 35–56.

Dreyfus, François-Georges. 1988. *Histoire del la démocratie chrétienne en France*. Paris: Albin Michel.

———. 1990. *Histoire de Vichy*. Paris: Perrin.

Esposito, Chiarella. 1994. *Americas Feeble Weapon: Funding the Marshall Plan in France and Italy 1948–1950*. Westport: Greenwoods Press.

Fourquet, François. 1980. *Les Comptes de la Puissance. Histoire de la comptabilité nationale et due plan*. Paris: Recherches.

Gillingham, John. 2003. *European Integration, 1950–2003*. Cambridge: Cambridge University Press.

Gruson, Claude. 1968. *Origine et Espoirs de la Planification française*. Paris: Dunod.

Hackett, John, and Anne-Marie Hackett. 1963. *Economic Planning in France*. London: George Allen & Unwin.

Journal officiel de la République française 1964, Rapport sdur les principales options qui commandent la preparation du Ve Plan", 23 Décembre.

Kuisel, Richard F. 1977. "Vichy et les origines de la planification économique (1940–1946)." *Le Mouvement Social* 98: 77–101.

———. 1981. *Capitalism and the State in Modern France*. Cambridge: Cambridge University Press.

Lynch, Frances M. B. 1984. "Resolving the Paradox of the Monnet Plan: National and International Planning in French Reconstruction." *The Economic History Review* 37 (2): 229–43.
———. 1997. *France and the International Economy*. London: Routledge.
Loubet del Bayle, Jean-Louis. 1969. *Les non-conformistes des années 30*. Paris: Seuil.
Lutz, Vera. 1969. *Central Planning for the Market Economy: An Analysis of the French Theory and Experience*. London: Longmans and Green.
Marchal, André. 1964. *L'Europe Solidaire*. Toulouse: Éditions cujas.
Margairaz, Michel. 1991. *L'État, les finances et l'économie. Histoire d'une conversion. 1932–1952*. 2 vols. Paris: Comité pour l'Histoire Économique et Financière de la France.
———. 2001. "Entre Néo-Liberalisme et Corporatisme: Apports et Limites des Deux Trajectoires Singulièrs." *Le Mouvement Social* 195: 3–7.
Marjolin, Robert. 1935. "La N.R.A. aux États-Unis." In *L'Homme Réel*, n. 15–16, 88–95. Syndicalisme et Corporations.
———. 1953. *Europe and the United States in the World Economy*. Durham, NC: Duke University Press.
———. 1989. *Architect of European Unit: Memoirs 1911–1986*. London: Weidenfeld and Nicolson.
Massé, Pierre. 1965. *Le Plan ou l'anti-hasard*. Paris: Gallimard.
Mioche, Philippe. 1984. "Le démarrage du Plan Monnet: comment une entreprise conjoncturelle est devenue une institution prestigieuse." *Revue d'Historie Moderne et Contemporaine* 31 (3): 398–416.
———. 1987. *Le Plan Monnet. Genèse et Élaboration 1941–1947*. Paris: Publications de la Sorbonne.
Monnet, Eric. 2018. *Controlling Credit: Central Banking and the Planned Economy in Postwar France, 1948–1973*. Cambridge: Cambridge University Press.
Monnet, Jean. 1976. *Mémoires*. Paris: Fayard.
Parlement Européen. 1962. *Débats Compte rendu in extenso des séances*, n. 60.
Parlement Européen. 1965. *Cahiers Mensuels de Documentation Européenne*, Julliet n. 7.
Paxton, Robert. 1972. *Vichy France: Old Guard and New Order, 1940–1944*. New York: Alfred A. Knopf.
Perroux, François. 1938a. *Capitalisme et Communauté de Travail*. Paris: Librairie du Recueil Sirey.
———. 1938b. *Syndicalisme et Capitalisme*. Paris: Librairie Génèrl de Droit et de Jurisprudence.
———. 1938c. "Pour et Contre la communauté de Travail." *Archives de Philosophie du droit et de sociologie juridique, Cahier spécial: Le corporatisme* 3–4: 68–99.

———. 1942. "Exposé de M. le Professeur Perroux." *Comité Sociaux d'entreprise. Idéologie et réalité* 2 Julliet, brochure Archive IMEC.
———. 1943. "La Charte du Travail: son contenu et son esprit." In V.V.A.A., *L'économie sans abondance*. Paris: Les Éditions du Cerf.
———. 1954. *Europe sans Rivages*. Paris: Presses Universitaires de France.
Pirou, Gaetan. 1933. "La crisi del capitalismo secondo gli economisti francesi." In V.V.A.A., *La crisi del capitalismo*. Firenze: Sansoni.
———. 1937. *Essais sur le corporatisme*. Paris: Librairie du Recueil Sirey.
———. 1939. *Néo-Libéralisme, Néo-Corporatisme, Néo-Socialisme*. Paris: Gallimard.
Pühringer, Stephan. 2017. "The Success Story of Ordoliberalism as the Guiding Principle." In *Ordoliberalism, Law and the Rule of Economics*, edited by Josef Hien and Christian Jorgers, 143–60. Oxford: Hart Publishing.
Schuman, Robert. 1963. *Pour l'Europe*. Paris: Nagel.
Uri, Pierre. 1991. *Penser pour l'Action*. Paris: Éditions Odile Jacobs.
V.V.A.A. 1943. *L'économie sans Abudance*. Paris: Éditions du Cerf.
Villey, Daniel. 1945. "Pamphlet contre l'idéologie des réformes de structures." *Cahiers Politiques* 11: 29–53.
Warlouzet, Laurent. 2010. *Le choix de la CEE par la France. L'Europe économique en débat de Mendès France à de Gaulle (1955–1969)*. Paris: Comité pour l'histoire économique et financière de la France.

CHAPTER 5

The Construction of an International Order in the Work of Jan Tinbergen

Erwin Dekker

The European Union is now an essential element of the international order. Other contributions to this volume trace the roots of the European Union to ideas of economic integration from the interwar period. But this chapter demonstrates that there was also a vision of international order that was at odds with the formation of a European political and economic unit. Through the study of the work of Jan Tinbergen this alternative vision will be explored. This vision does not eschew supranational economic integration, in fact it regards that as the crucial way forward after the nationalistic 1930s. But Tinbergen's vision of international order suggested that European integration might be an obstacle rather than a stepping stone toward international, or rather global, economic integration.

In this chapter I investigate the sources for his suspicion of European regional integration. Three of which stand out: he came from a

E. Dekker (✉)
Erasmus University Rotterdam, Rotterdam, The Netherlands
e-mail: e.dekker@eshcc.eur.nl

© The Author(s) 2021

A. M. Cunha and C. E. Suprinyak (eds.), *Political Economy and International Order in Interwar Europe*, Palgrave Studies in the History of Economic Thought,
https://doi.org/10.1007/978-3-030-47102-6_5

small open (Protestant) economy, he was influenced by both pacifism and anti-colonialism, and thirdly he was deeply influenced by the League of Nations perspective of a global order. But most importantly Tinbergen drew parallels between the ways in which the national economy was integrated and made more just, and how this could be achieved for the international economy.

Exploring Tinbergen's resistance to the idea of European economic integration helps us, through a method of contrast, better understand what was distinct about those in favor of European integration. And it also helps us understand why other small open economies, including the Scandinavian countries shared a reluctance to the European project. This chapter intends to show at least two competing models of international integration which both came out of different understandings of the interwar experience. The first model sees the interwar period as a period of conflict between the major powers on the European continent, and therefore primarily as a problem of in the power balance between the major forces. The other model sees the interwar period as a period in which the dangers of (economic) nationalism of any kind are exposed, and therefore seeks a global order which keeps national policies in check. This latter model has recently been associated to the neoliberals in the work of Quinn Slobodian (2018), but in this chapter I show that it was a vision shared across the political spectrum. The internationalists, or globalist as Slobodian calls them, who tended to come from smaller countries sought to undo the nineteenth-century model of power balance more deeply.

The chapter will proceed as follows. In the first section I will provide a brief sketch of Jan Tinbergen and his work in economics, particularly as it relates to the creation of an economic order. In the second section we will study his work at the League of Nations to highlight the way in which his vision was shaped there. Section three will demonstrate the elements of the international order for him, and the extent to which he reconsidered the value of the European Union in this order in later years. We will highlight how he sought to convince his fellow economist the Norwegian Ragnar Frisch that the Scandinavian countries should join the European Union.

1 The Hague and an International Order

Jan Tinbergen was born in 1903 in The Hague into an upper middle-class family. The Hague was around that time in the process becoming a hub of international diplomacy. The crowning achievement, after several peace conferences in the city, was the construction of the Peace Palace. The building which housed an international court and a library of international law was made possible through a generous gift by Andrew Carnegie. The Peace Palace, a project of the modern peace movement which sought to organize peace through law, made an explicit connection between this new project and the older project of Hugo Grotius: international law. The Peace Palace was constructed only a stone's throw away from Tinbergen's parental home (Eyffinger and Hengst 1988).

The young Tinbergen was deeply influenced by the peace movement that had supported these initiatives. Such a movement was at home in a neutral country like the Netherlands, which as a naval trading nation had much to gain from peaceful economic relationships. On a personal level the young Tinbergen was faced with the dilemma of whether he should refuse the military draft, something that just a few years earlier would have resulted in a prison sentence. But in the early 1920s things were changing. The social-democratic movement of which he was part, at least temporarily was successful in blocking a new military naval act through a popular petition, and around the same time conscientious objectors could apply for social rather than military service.

Tinbergen was one of the first to apply for this alternative to the military draft, and his request was granted. This strategy of civil resistance was promoted in Christian socialist circles in which Tinbergen moved. These movements occupied a curious position in the intellectual landscape. They were more international in outlook than mainstream political parties, including the social-democratic parties. As such they were often perceived to be close to the communists. But in contrast to the Communists they rejected any violent or revolutionary measures, and instead sought peaceful change from within. From this angle they were much closer to the bourgeois political middle than the social-democratic party which had not shed all its revolutionary aspirations yet.

Unlike most of the socialist movement, these Christian and cultural socialists strongly believed that the emancipation of the working class could and should be achieved within the current society. They were much more optimistic that an enlightened rationalism could overcome class differences than many other socialists. With this aim in mind many new organizations and magazines were founded which sought to promote this emancipation of the working classes and in particular the youth.

The leading light of these movements in the Netherlands, and more widely on the Continent, was Hendrik de Man. He developed important cultural critiques of Marx and the social-democratic movement of his time. Most importantly he argued that a culturally impoverished proletariat could never possibly form the basis for a new society. So, the most urgent task was to combat the cultural degeneration of the working class. De Man, who worked briefly in Frankfurt, was a pioneer in the combination of psychology and Marxism. It was his cultural socialism that inspired the Workers Youth Movement (AJC) of which Tinbergen was a very active member. De Man believed that through incremental change in the order of society social peace could be maintained while socialism could be achieved (De Man 1927). He attempted to transform socialism into a mainly idealistic movement.

A similar idealism, which believed in the power of moral ideals, was found in the pacifist movement. In that movement the ongoing class struggle was frequently compared to war on the international stage. By analogy the pacifism pursued on the international level was translated into a peaceful idealism in the national class struggle. The same way that improved laws and better institutional representation of the suppressed classes could lead to social peace so, so international law, the end of colonialism, and a new international order could lead to international peace. It was therefore that the international Court founded in The Hague was of such great symbolic value, it represented the first step in the direction of this new international legal order (Sluga 2013). Although the pacifists were at the same time deeply disappointed that not more was achieved, and that the Court remained relatively powerless in the first decades of the twentieth century. Nonetheless it was in this perspective that the newly established League of Nations could be the next step forward in what would be a long process of internationalization.

But although he was active in these internationalist circles Tinbergen's early career was dominated by domestic concerns. In the late 1920s he modernized the collection and analysis of statistics at the Bureau of Statistics, and the early years of the 1930s were completely dominated by research into the business cycle. When Tinbergen started working on that subject it was still predominantly theoretical and involved the investigation of potential theoretical explanations of the cycle. But a new generation of ambitious young econometricians sought to overturn this theoretical focus and combine the new tools of mathematics and statistics to revolutionize the way economics was done. They included Tinbergen,

Ragnar Frisch, and Francois Divisia on the continent, and they received support from Charles Roos, Irving Fischer, and Alfred Cowles, who funded much of this new movement.

Many important steps in econometrics followed each other in quick succession around 1930. Inspired by Frisch it was Tinbergen who in a 1935 article Tinbergen for the first time developed a model that incorporated the dynamics of the business cycle within a model of the whole economy (Tinbergen 1935). A year later he would apply a similar model to the Dutch economy (Tinbergen 1936b). In this groundbreaking model the various parameters were estimated statistically and as such it was the first macro-econometric model of an economy. Developed in the midst of the economic crisis, Tinbergen immediately put it to use to investigate the effects of various proposed policies, in the short- and somewhat longer-run.

One of the proposed policies was a set of public works and social legislation known as the Plan of Labor. The plan was modelled after the example set in Belgium by the Plan of Henri de Man (Pels 1985; Dodge 1979). It was part of a wider movement in the mid-1930s in which various reformers in the social-democratic movement across Europe sought to provide a way out of the crisis. The traditional answer to the recent crisis from the socialists had been that little could be done about it, after all crises were endemic to the capitalist system. But those associated with the Plan movement believed not only that the crisis was so urgent that something had to be done right away, but also that reform from within was possible.

The Plan de Man from Belgium was the result of a relatively quick politicization of Hendrik de Man, who had left some of the emphasis on cultural idealism behind and now presented a political action plan. The Dutch Plan of Labor was not merely action plan, but also a document of vision and reorientation of the social-democratic party (Commissie uit N.V.V. en S.D.A.P. 1936). One of the central suggestions of the Plan was that the economic system could be re-ordered, and it contained an entire chapter about Ordening (Ordnung). Ordnung was mainly related to the industrial structure which, they argued, had led to harmful types of competition and waste. But this reordering of the economy was also proposed at the level of national politics, and in particular in relation to economic policy. The Dutch Plan (for consistency) suggested that the response to the crisis had in part been so poor because the contemporary political system was not at all equipped to deal with a complex crisis like this one. Members of parliament were anything but economically literate and the government lacked many of the relevant instruments to counter the crisis. The Plan of Labor, although it is very much a crisis document, in the long term became an important manifesto for embedding economic expertise into the national political structure.

At home this Plan of Labor which was written in close cooperation between Hein Vos and Jan Tinbergen, received a fair deal of criticism. Some of his more cautious academic friends such as Ed van Cleeff was concerned that the Plan was too political, and not sufficiently grounded in an overarching vision of the desirable socio-economic order.[1] But it was also criticized from the side of the internationalists who critiqued the narrow national nature of the Plan. Was it not foolish to believe that a small economy like the Netherlands could do much to combat a crisis that was in origin and essence international? (Verwey-Jonker 1936). Tinbergen was sensitive to both types of criticism.

Although he agreed in spirit with both the academic caution and the internationalist critique, he argued that the present situation was so urgent that something had to be done, and the plan offered such a way forward. Important in the urgency was that he feared fascism would quickly rise in the Netherlands like it had done abroad. As early as 1929 he signed a petition of the anti-fascist society on Hungary, and in the mid-1930s he became involved in various anti-fascist organizations including the committee of vigilance (Tinbergen 1936a). The effects of the Plan on the social-democratic movement, however, were much along the lines the critics suggested. It established a national-oriented course, and the Plan itself quickly became partisan, despite the hope of Tinbergen and other that it could appeal to constructive forces in all democratic parties (Jansen van Galen 1985).

Perhaps nothing more should have been expected in the turbulent second half of the 1930s. But the legacy of the Plan was much longer. After the war partisan concerns had faded into the background. The postwar order in the Netherlands was shaped much along the lines that Tinbergen and Vos had envisioned in their Plan of Labor. New economic institutions were founded which supplemented or even supplanted traditional ways of making economic policy (den Butter 2011). Hein Vos who became minister in the first postwar cabinet asked Jan Tinbergen to head

[1] Van Cleeff to Tinbergen 24 August 1935, Tinbergen Letters, see https://tinbergenletters.eur.nl/theletters/.

the Central Planning Bureau which would become the main organization for economic expertise in the economic order of the Netherlands. Initially it was primarily concerned with the postwar reconstruction but over time it developed, under Tinbergen's lead, policy-models which were based on his famous methodology of targets and instruments. To this day the organization plays a crucial role in the formation of economic policy in the Netherlands.

Here we will not go into the details of this approach policymaking, but rather focus on some of the other organizations which became crucial after the war. The most important of these is the more corporatist socio-economic council. This socio-economic council, sometimes referred to as the "second parliament," consisted of 30 representatives, 10 representatives each from labor, capital, and economic expertise. It became the primary organ for socio-economic policy making and the creation of legitimacy of this policy toward both the business community and the unions (Don 2019). There were further steps in a corporatist direction, supported by Tinbergen or those affiliated with him, most notably the public–private industry organizations (PBO). The PBO's looked from most outside perspectives very much like government approved cartels, but officially were meant to foster cooperation and orderly competition. As industry organizations they were meant to create stability and coordination between different producers.

Such organizations, or rather the reordering of the Dutch economy, was crucial to Tinbergen because he believed that the system of the 1930s was inherently unstable. He even was skeptical of the very modelling techniques that made him famous in economics, as he repeatedly argued: "it is of little use to predict the course of an essentially unstable system." This instability for him was not merely economic, although it was that also. It was also political, because parliament lacked the necessary knowledge and instruments to conduct good economic policy. The expert and policy institutions of the postwar period were expressly founded with the goal in mind of providing the relevant knowledge and instruments to conduct rational economic policy. But most of all the stability of an economic system was an institutional question.

If encased with the right set of (expert) institutions and legal framework the economy could be stable, but it was not naturally so. He explicitly presented that view as a break with the older nineteenth-century perspective on the economy, as a system of natural harmony. And although these ideas were all present in the Plan of Labor it took the formative League of Nations experience for Tinbergen to develop them further into concrete plans and methods.

2 At the League of Nations

Tinbergen was a somewhat unlikely candidate as leading expert for the second report on business cycles at the Economic and Financial Section of the League of Nations. His predecessor Gottfried von Haberler came out of the theoretically minded Austrian School and had inventoried the various "verbal" theories of the business cycle, and attempted to arise at a kind of synthesis (Haberler 1937). Tinbergen knew about these theories, but his work in the early 1930s on business cycle theories had taken a rather different approach. Whereas the verbal theorists, as he called them, had sought to arrive at a theoretically feasible theory of the cycle, Tinbergen instead had been analyzing a few possible *mechanisms* which could explain cyclical behavior.

There was an important similarity between the two endeavors. Both sought to analyze the dynamics of modern economies endogenously: as a dynamic internal to the system. But whereas much of the theorists were concerned with conceptual analysis of natural and market interest rates, length of production, and degree of roundaboutedness, as well as new concepts such as effective demand, Tinbergen was primarily looking for the types of mechanisms that could generate a cycle. Here he was inspired by his training in physics, and the initial mechanisms he proposed were often analogies with physical mechanisms.

And unlike Haberler, and even more so the more famous business cycle theorists of the age such as Keynes, Hayek, Gunnar Myrdal, and Bertil Ohlin, Tinbergen had no "horse in the race." He held no strong opinion whether the cycle was caused by malinvestment, by a lack of effective demand, or other particular factors. Perhaps that was why the choice fell on him to engage in the project of testing the business cycle theories that Haberler had collected (Haberler 1937). But the way Tinbergen conducted the "test" received criticism from virtually every angle. Keynes critical reviews of the volumes are notorious, he compared Tinbergen's methods to black magic and alchemy (Keynes 1939; Boumans 2019). Internally there were fierce debates about Tinbergen's approach, and it was only through the mediation of Dennis Robertson that Arthur Loveday, who headed the Economic and Financial Section, was calmed down enough to let Tinbergen continue.

This had much to do with the approach that Tinbergen took. Rather than testing individual business cycle theories against a dataset, he constructed a model of the U.S. economy and sought to describe its dynamics. Although he had pioneered a similar model for the Netherlands, the approach was new to most of the economists who formed the expert oversight committee (Boianovsky and Trautwein 2006). This method did not at all directly confront the business cycle theories of the age with the data. Rather it sought to describe the dynamics of the U.S. economy since 1920. Although This led to the refutation of some theoretical suggestions because they did not provide a mechanism that could explain both an upswing and/or a downswing, but Tinbergen's study confirmed most theories of the cycle. Tinbergen explicitly hoped to change the terms of the debate. Not *whether* malinvestment or a lack of effective demand caused the crisis was the right framing, instead *how much* each of these factors contributed was the correct way of understanding the problem. The econometricians like him sought to overcome dogmatic disputes and turn them into quantitative disagreements.

But even on his own methodological ground, there was dissatisfaction with his approach. Frisch, who pioneered the modelling approach right alongside him argued that Tinbergen had not made clear why the particular quantitative relationships he found would be stable over time, or whether the same relations would hold in other countries. It was not at all clear how general the relations were, or whether they were purely contingent relationship specific to time and place.

But despite the contested reception of his report, the League of Nations experience was formative for Tinbergen. The report was a collaborative effort, most directly with his assistants Polak (later research director at the IMF) and Tjalling Koopmans (later Nobel Prize winner in economics). But also with the team of experts which reported at various stages on the draft report, which included Ragnar Frisch, Dennis Robertson, Otto Anderson, John Maurice Clark, Leon Dupriez, Alvin Hansen, Oskar Morgenstern, Bertil Ohlin, Charles Rist, Lionel Robbins, and Wilhelm Röpke (Boianovsky and Trautwein 2006). As such the internationalist outlook of the League was reflected in the make-up of its economic expert team. And what made the period unique is that the League managed to attract some of the foremost economic thinkers of the age to work on problems that were directly relevant to the age.

This was, however, not without difficulties. The most important of which was that the League of Nations was officially only permitted to provide "technical" advice, and not political advice (Clavin and Wessels 2005; Clavin 2015). As such it could inventory the various theories of the business cycle, and at least according to Loveday it also allowed for the "testing" of these theories. But what it certainly could not do is advice on the best way to get out of the crisis. This was made very directly clear when Tinbergen investigated the effects of the New Deal policies. He wanted to include this more practical study in his report to show how the dynamics of the U.S. economy were altered by the more structural policies of the New Deal. But this third part never appeared, and Tinbergen was even forbidden to report on the results of the study at talks he gave around the time.[2]

At that point Tinbergen thus had a dual experience. In the Netherlands he had been active in a plan which directly combatted the crisis, but which was deeply caught up in partisan politics. At the League of Nations, he had worked on a report that was supposed to represent the scientific consensus view of the economists of the age who worked on the business cycle, but it was politically completely without consequence. In fact, in retrospect the reports by both Haberler and Tinbergen are remembered for their academic significance and not their policy relevance. In some ways that was the opposite of the ambition of Loveday, who wanted to create an expertise relevant for creating economic stability.[3]

It is strikingly this vision that has the longest effect on the work of Tinbergen. And not just for him. His assistant Polak stayed at the League of Nations and contributed to the two war-time volumes on the link between the creation of economic stability, peaceful relations, and economic expertise is explicitly developed (League of Nations 1943, 1945). The business cycle problem is presented as an international problem, in need not just of international expertise, but also of international politically coordinated policy efforts. The war-time emergency, or perhaps lack of direct supervision, emboldened Loveday to push for these more policy relevant studies. And as such these volumes sketch a clear vision of a new international economic order (De Marchi 1991).

[2] Correspondence with Loveday, and draft Report of the 'third volume', League of Nations Archives, Geneva.

[3] It might also explain some of the dissatisfaction of the more politically minded economists of the time. Keynes wrote highly critical reviews not just of the Tinbergen volume, but also of the preceding Haberler study.

It is striking that quite apart from the League of Nations studies Tinbergen wrote a book along the same lines *International Economic Co-Operation* (Tinbergen 1945). During the War he resumed his work for the Bureau of Statistics in the Netherlands and was largely disconnected from the international developments. But just like the reports of the League he argued that the international economy had to be made stable through new organizations and rules. Tinbergen listed a few organizations which could do so. They included a continuation of the expertise as it was practiced at the League of Nations, and an international monetary policy. Written quite independent of the Bretton-Woods negotiations Tinbergen proposed an international commodity standard, for which his friend Jan Goudriaan, had developed proposals in the 1930s.

In the proposals we find the same combination of expertise and development of instruments through which rational policy could be organized, as he had proposed on the national level. Like the national economy needed additional features of economic organization, so this was true for the international economy. Tinbergen proposed, before they come into existence, an International Equalization Fund for the settlement of international payments, a Bank for Reconstruction and Development, and a continuation of both the Secretariat of the League of Nations and the International Labor Office (ILO), the two Geneva institutions. These are to be the expert institutions, like he had proposed them in the institutional part of the Plan of Labor: "It must be observed that expert knowledge for this work is essential and must not be subordinated to the representation of special interests" (Tinbergen 1945, 170). But pure expertise was not enough. The ILO had a structure like the socio-economic council in Netherlands. This structure was famously symbolized by the gate of the ILO building which required three keys to be opened: one of the workers, one of the employers, and one for the governments. So even in terms of the creation of legitimacy there was similarity.

3 A Globalist of the Left?

Perhaps the overarching metaphor in Tinbergen's thought is peace. That he had been able to "pacify" the social conflict in the socio-economic council was of crucial importance to him. But even before he had been inspired by the pacificist movement at home in The Hague. That same pacifist spirit was vividly present in Geneva, another governmental town in a small country with a history of neutrality. Pacification had also been the solution to the long-standing school struggle in the Netherlands which dated back to the Napoleonic period. It should there not come as a surprise that this is also what he sought to bring about in international relations after 1945.

Then again who was not in 1945? But to understand how the international was shaped, and what was believed to help bring about peace it is of great importance to know how thinkers like Jan Tinbergen, thought peace could be brought about. For him it meant strengthening the weaker parties after which they could be peacefully integrated into the institutional fabric of society. He believed that this had been the great success of the labor movement (and associated movements). It had strengthened the relative position of an underprivileged group (the workers) and only afterwards was it possible to set-up institutions which would generate a more just order. Creating a stable economy was thus a combination of balancing the relative power of entities and setting up institutions for joint decision-making.

Internationally this means for Tinbergen several things. First, it means complete decolonization. This would achieve two things at once, it would strengthen the relative position of the previously colonized countries, and of course it would weaken the relative position of the (former) colonial powers. Over time it would also mean that the 'new nations' could integrate and form more regional powers: he supported the efforts of regional integration in South America, Africa, and Asia. But more importantly he considered European integration as a backward step in the process toward a more just international order. He argues that such a collaboration would be purely defensive: "only a substitute for what they really want: an ordered world economy" (Tinbergen 1945, 181).

He (rightly) feared that European integration would lead to a strong continent which would raise important barriers in trade, and tight border controls. Although Tinbergen was not very explicit in his arguments, it is amply clear that European integration in his vision would undo much if not all the beneficial effects of decolonization. It is important to emphasize that it is also a difficult argument to make at the time. The European powers had not yet accepted decolonization, including the Netherlands. It failed to let go of Indonesia and would be engaged in a backwards and lengthy war from 1945 to 1949, and it did not give up Surinam until 1975. But the idea of restricting European integration and further limiting the influence of Great Britain and France was even more unlikely. Whereas the U.S. pushed for decolonization, it also pushed for more

European integration. And of course, Western integration through the NATO. It was the latter alliance which both for exclusive and militaristic character would never be supported by Tinbergen. He instead favored the United Nations, as a continuation of the internationalist project of the League of Nations.

Tinbergen's own stance on decolonization was not always principled. In 1945 he calculated the total contribution of Indonesia to the Dutch economy, and he kept emphasizing in the Reconstruction years, that the Netherlands faced a particularly difficult challenge because it lost its colony in the East (Derksen and Tinbergen 1945; Tinbergen 1950). And he preferred to not explicitly engage with the question of colonialism. But in between the lines it is clear that his concern with smaller countries and underdeveloped areas lacking capital represents an argument in favor of the (former) colonies (Tinbergen 1945). This concern was not a break, but rather a continuation of the interwar years, much like Hansen and Jonsson have suggested for the European ideal (Hansen and Jonsson 2015).

Building on the cultural socialism of his youth, Tinbergen hoped to spread a kind of rationalization around the world. And he did so as part of an ethic of responsibility, which believed that a cultural elite could help spread this rationalization. When he was involved with the founding of the development aid organization NOVIB (later part of Oxfam-NOVIB), he did so explicitly from a perspective of Christian and Western responsibility (Tinbergen 1966). The former colonies were now independent, but they still required "our" assistance. In line with an emancipatory ideal of education he held, it was hoped that over time this assistance was no longer required and the countries could be fully independent (Tinbergen 1963a). This continuation was nicely reflected in the chair he occupied from 1956 onwards. That chair was formerly for Colonial Economics now it was a chair for Development Economics, or more precisely Development Planning.

Although he was involved in some of the early exploratory studies of European integration in his role as one of the premier economic policy experts in the Netherlands, he kept opposing the idea. In the 1950s he worked on a model of international trade in which he investigated the effect of economic integration on so-called "third countries" (Tinbergen 1960). The results are telling, the third country is most likely hurt by this type of economic integration. It is a thinly veiled criticism of the European Economic Community. More importantly because Tinbergen demonstrated that such harmful effects are even more severe in the case of labor-intensive industries, the type of industry most typically found outside of the European area around that time. It is important to realize that this is in no way an argument against integrated trade more generally, in fact the investigation is premised on the idea that global free trade is the first-best option (Tinbergen 1968).

His opposition to European integration, therefore, did not mean that he was not a great proponent of international economic integration. In the GATT report which features crucially in the Slobodian's (2018) narrative about the construction of a postwar international order Tinbergen is one of the authors. And so is James Meade, another Geneva luminary and man of the left, who has a similarly internationalist outlook (Haberler et al. 1958). For these economic thinkers a global economic integration is a superior form of creating a more just international economic order. The GATT is precisely a step in the direction of a globally order international market and is now typically viewed as a steppingstone toward the international trade organization (ITO) and the later WTO. The goal of international free trade was shared by many of the Geneva experts, not just among the neoliberals.

But there was also a sense in Tinbergen that things were moving slowly, or even in the wrong direction. The Cold War was heating up in middle of the 1950s, and he expressed his discontent that the social-democratic movement in Europe was more focused on national than international issues (Tinbergen 1957). It is for this reason that Tinbergen increasingly placed his hopes elsewhere. If the West was unwilling to create a more balanced international order, this had to been done by strengthening the less developed countries. And after 1955 his career is mostly devoted to the fate of the underdeveloped countries, and attempts to strengthen international institutions, most prominently the United Nations.

Tinbergen decided that the only way to strengthen the relative position of the underdeveloped nations is by strengthening their internal constitution. Much like the social-democratic movements had succeeded in strengthening the national position of the workers, after which a peaceful integrative solution was possible, so the developing countries now had to be strengthened. During his work on development economics he kept appealing to the developed world for development assistance, and his models inevitably pointed out that part of the development plan had to be financed externally. But development economics was crucially a national project in its execution (if clearly not in its near universal reach).

It thus put him in the same difficult position as the Plan of Labor had done before. The danger of economic nationalism was lurking and would indeed plague many approaches in development economics. Elsewhere I have studied in detail his work in Turkey (Dekker 2021, Chapter 14). Tinbergen also worked in Egypt, Venezuela, Surinam, Indonesia and about a dozen other countries. His students served as economic experts in many of them. And the United Nations development decades were clear evidence that this was an international policy concern, but solutions were sought at the national level. In other words, much like the Great Depression of the 1930s, the problem was international, but the solution was primarily sought at a national level.

The goal, however, remained similar in Tinbergen's vision. The individual units of the international order had to be strengthened so that a more just overall order could be created. A clear outcome of this development is the Group of 77 (G77), an organization which sought to further the interests of the developing countries within international politics. It was symbolically housed in Geneva but drew members mostly from the "Global South." It was this type of integration that Tinbergen fostered first in his *Shaping the World Economy* (Tinbergen 1962) and later in his book written in alignment with the goal of an alternative economic order of the G77 in his *Reshaping the International Order* (Tinbergen 1976). It was also evident in his support for the movement of non-aligned countries, headed by India. These countries sought a development path that was not capitalist or communist but represented a kind of third way. It was here that Tinbergen identified a new role for Europe.

4 Second Thoughts About Europe

At that point Tinbergen's view of Europe was also changing significantly. Whereas in the first decade after WWI it was clear to him that an economically integrated Europe would be an obstacle to global economic integration, rather than a steppingstone he was not so sure anymore. He started to suggest that some level of integration between the global and the national might be useful and perhaps even necessary. This was directly linked to this theory of the optimal level of decision-making, or as he sometimes puts it the optimal level of centralization (Tinbergen 1954). But more importantly he rethought the role of Europe in the global economy.

Amid the Cold War, which facilitated dichotomous thinking about East and West, communist and capitalist, he suggested that Europe might offer a third way between the two. Theoretically Tinbergen links this to his theory of the optimal economic order, a conception of the optimal institutional decision-making structure in the economy. This optimum is neither socialist, nor capitalist, but rather a pragmatic combination of both, based on their relative strengths (Tinbergen 1959). Tinbergen argued that the postwar economies in Europe were closer to this optimum than the regimes of the United States or the USSR. This would become a hallmark of his thought in his theory of convergence (Tinbergen et al. 1966; Linneman et al. 1965).

This idea came to prominence in the context of a debate over the so-called undecided or 'uncommitted' countries. These countries were not formally in the capitalist (U.S.) or the communist (U.S.S.R.) camp yet, and hence were believed to be able to choose an optimal path toward development, independent of dogma and ideology. It is particularly for this group that Tinbergen believed that Europe could function as an alternative model. He often framed the argument in an idealistic manner, as if Europe presented a clear unified alternative economic model, but it should also certainly be read in the context of spheres of influence and power politics.

This becomes all the more clear in a lecture Tinbergen gives in Sweden, in the Wicksell lecture series, in 1963 (Tinbergen 1963b). He was invited to deliver this lecture series by his good friend, and later co-recipient of the first Nobel Prize in economics, Ragnar Frisch. Frisch was a committed opponent of the European Union, who valued the relatively young independence of Norway (in 1905), but also argued that Scandinavian countries more generally might credibly live out this alternative third way independent of the great powers. Tinbergen's lecture is thus best read as an explicit argument to convince Frisch, and other Scandinavians like him, to join the European Community. That context is all interesting because much like the Netherlands the Scandinavian countries have always been somewhat peripheral to the major European conflicts and are all small open economies. In other words, arguments that should compel the Netherlands to join should also be convincing to Scandinavians.

Initially the lectures focused on economic factors. Tinbergen defined the essence of the European Economic Community to be the elimination of national trade borders, which could over time come to include the harmonization of tax regimes and the integration of currencies. But on that front is not where the underlying difference of opinion lies between Tinbergen and Frisch. The contested issue is the extent to which the EEC is a democratic entity, and even more so whether the progressive and protestant forces will win out from the more conservative catholic forces, what Tinbergen in the lecture called the "black forces." Tinbergen tried to identify as many progressive trends in the social policies, a rather heroic given the fact that De Gaulle at that moment represented the clear antithesis of such modern social policy to both Tinbergen and Frisch: "all of us hope that France will soon again show it real face- which, by democratic measures, is federalist" (Tinbergen 1963b, 38). De Gaulle was a kind of antithesis of the progressive democratic future that Tinbergen and Frisch envisioned. De Gaulle, a general, represented militarism and conservative social policy from the top, rather than the democratic, and progressive social policy and awareness that Tinbergen and Frisch favored. But most importantly De Gaulle represented French nationalism, rather than a unifying European or internationalist spirit.

At the heart of the disagreement between Frisch and Tinbergen is the fact whether the EEC can provide a credible alternative, and exemplar for the non-committed countries. Frisch remained unconvinced and believed that Norway and Sweden as such represented more of an exemplar than the EEC could ever be. He actively contributed to the political debate surrounding this issue and rejoiced when the Norwegians rejected membership in the 1972 referendum. For Tinbergen small countries, however, could hardly represent a viable alternative. Given his recent work in India, and involvement with the United Nations he was looking for bigger exemplars than some small Northern European countries. The EEC was therefore of key importance, to demonstrate the viability of an international Third Way.

The idealist socialism and pacificism of his youth had always made Tinbergen sympathetic to the idea that one should lead by example. It was something he practiced in everyday life, and it was something that Frisch was equally sympathetic to. But what that entailed had become unclear. For Frisch a small but pure example set by Norway or another small country could be enough. Tinbergen had become convinced that to truly compete with the models of the United States and the USSR, Europe needed to set a credible, imperfect, large-scale example. For this it was essential for the Scandinavian countries to join, for only that way Europe might be steered in a credibly progressive direction.

In some sense Tinbergen's initial fears about economic integration materialized. The initial set-up of the EEC which included three small countries (and economies), the Netherlands, Belgium, and Luxemburg, and three larger one's France, Germany, and Italy proved to be unbalanced. The drive to expand the European Union on the side of Tinbergen and the smaller countries more generally should be read as similar in spirit to Tinbergen's initial plea for decolonization. An integrated global order was only possible if the underlying units were of somewhat comparable strength and size. Since further breaking up France or Germany was not feasible, the solution was to attempt to enlarge the number of smaller partners to create a better underlying structure.

His vision in development economics was undergirded by the same idea. It was only through the strengthening of the constitutive parts that a more balanced and just international order could be created. This vision of the global economy thus sought to break radically with the ideas about global order from before. It was no longer a balance between great colonial powers, keeping each other in check, but rather an order of small relatively powerless units who had much to gain from international economic integration, and which would ultimately be willing to accept a form of world government. But before that was feasible one could already start with the design of global policy institutes which should prevent economic crises from happening: the spread of business cycles (instability) from one country to another, as well as the return of economic nationalism through raising tariffs. These were existential fears for Tinbergen, aspects of the 1930s which had to be avoided at all costs.

5 Conclusion

The 1930s were a formative decade for thinking about international order, because many of the aspect of the international order which had been taken for granted, or which had been regarded as natural, broke down. This has been well recognized on the level of economic ideologies, liberalism lost terrain to both socialism and fascism, but it has been much less studied what this meant for thinking about international economic order. The great merit of Slobodian's work as well as that of others on the League of Nations during the interwar period is that has put concerns about international economic order back on the research agenda. Slobodian's story about the neoliberals who had seen the Habsburg Empire wither and therefore sought to secure international order on a higher level is correct, it is also incomplete. Similar impulses came from the internationalist left, which was equally present in Geneva, especially from the smaller countries in Europe. They equally believed that an integrated, stable, and just economic order could only be achieved at the international, and perhaps the global level.

Tinbergen is one thinker who fits this profile well, and this chapter has sought to analyze the view of international order which was underlying his work on economic integration. It has been demonstrated that he regarded large powerful nations as the most important obstacle toward such international economic integration, and he worried that an integrated Europe would pose a formidable obstacle of precisely this kind.

That also explains why at the same time he favored regional economic integration in other parts of the world. These parts were comparatively weaker and therefore strengthening their relative economic position would be a steppingstone toward an international economic order. The underlying model in his thought was that of an international order made up of economic units of relatively comparable size and strength, this would create the most solid support for an integrated world economy and an optimal international division of labor (Tinbergen 1968).

References

Boianovsky, Mauro, and Hans-Michael Trautwein. 2006. "Haberler, the League of Nations, and the Quest for Consensus in Business Cycle Theory in the 1930s." *History of Political Economy* 38 (1): 45–89.

Boumans, Marcel. 2019. "Econometrics: The Keynes-Tinbergen Controversy." In *The Elgar Companion to John Maynard Keynes*, edited by Robert W. Dimand and Harald Hagemann, 283–89. Cheltenham, UK: Edward Elgar.

Clavin, Patricia. 2015. *Securing the World Economy: The Reinvention of the League of Nations, 1920–1946*. Oxford: Oxford University Press.

Clavin, Patricia, and Jens Wilhelm Wessels. 2005. "Transnationalism and the League of Nations: Understanding the Work of Its Economic and Financial Organisation." *Contemporary European History* 14 (4): 465–92.

Commissie uit N.V.V. en S.D.A.P. 1936. "Het Plan van de Arbeid." Amsterdam.

Dekker, Erwin. 2021. *Jan Tinbergen (1903-1994) and the Rise of Economic Expertise*. Cambridge, MA: Cambridge University Press.

Den Butter, Frank A. G. 2011. "The Industrial Organisation of Economic Policy Preparation in the Netherlands." In *The Politics of Scientific Advice: Institutional Design for Quality Assurance*, edited by J. Lentsch and P. Weingart, 177–214. Cambridge, UK: Cambridge University Press.

Derksen, J. B. D., and Jan Tinbergen. 1945. "Berekeningen over de Economische Betekenis van Nederlands-Indië Voor Nederland." *Maandschrift van Het C.B.S.* 40 (10/12): 210–16.

Dodge, Peter. 1979. *Hendrik de Man, Socialist Critic of Marxism*. Princeton, NJ: Princeton University Press.

Don, F. J. H. 2019. "The Influence of Jan Tinbergen on Dutch Economic Policy." *De Economist* 167 (3): 259–82. https://doi.org/10.1007/s10645-019-09333-1.

Eyffinger, Arthur, and Jan den Hengst. 1988. *Het Vredespaleis*. Amsterdam: Sijthoff.

Haberler, Gottfried, James E. Meade, Roberto Oliveira de Campos, and Jan Tinbergen. 1958. *Trends in International Trade*. Geneva: GATT.

Haberler, Gottfried von. 1937. *Prosperity and Depression: A Theoretical Analysis of Cyclical Movements*. Geneva: League of Nations: Economic Intelligence Service.

Hansen, Peo, and Stefan Jonsson. 2015. *Eurafrica, the Untold History of European Integration and Colonialism*. London: Bloomsbury.

Jansen van Galen, John. 1985. "Doorbraak: Het Plan in de Herinnering van Tijdgenoten." In *Het Moet, Het Kan! Op Voor Het Plan!*, 156–93. Amsterdam: Bert Bakker.

Keynes, John Maynard. 1939. "Professor Tinbergen's Method." *The Economic Journal* 49 (195): 558–77.

League of Nations. 1943. *The Transition from War to Peace Economy*. Geneva: League of Nations.

———. 1945. *Economic Stability in the Post-War World*. Geneva: League of Nations.

Linneman, H. J., P. Pronk, and Jan Tinbergen. 1965. *Convergence of Economic Systems in East and West*. Rotterdam: Netherlands Economic Institute.

De Man, Hendrik. 1927. *Zur Pscyhologie Des Sozialismus*. Jena: Eugen Diederichs.

De Marchi, Neil. 1991. "League of Nations Economists and the Ideal of Peaceful Change in the Decade of the Thirties." In *Economics and National Security*, edited by Crauford D. Goodwin, 143–78. Durham: Duke University Press.

Pels, Dick. 1985. "Hendrik de Man En de Ideologie van Het Planisme." In *Het Moet, Het Kan! Op Voor Het Plan!*, edited by J. Th. J. Van den Berg, 124–55. Amsterdam: Bert Bakker.

Slobodian, Quinn. 2018. *Globalists: The End of Empire and the Birth of Neoliberalism*. Harvard: Harvard University Press.

Sluga, Glenda. 2013. *Internationalism in the Age of Nationalism*. Philadelphia: Penn University Press.

Tinbergen, Jan. 1935. "Quantitative Fragen Der Konjunkturpolitik." *Weltwirtschaftliches Archiv* 42: 366–99.

———. 1936a. "Fascistische Economie." *Anti-Fascistische Stemmen* 1 (2): 2–3.
———. 1936b. "Kan Hier Te Lande, Al Dan Niet Na Overheidsingrijpen, Een Verbetering van de Binnenlandse Conjunctuur Intreden, Ook Zonder Verbetering van Onze Exportpositie?" In *Prae-Adviezen Voor de Vereeniging Voor de Staatshuishoudkunde En de Statistiek*, 62–108. Den Haag: Nijhoff.
———. 1945. *International Economic Co-Operation*. Amsterdam: Elsevier.
———. 1950. "Het Evenwicht in de Dollarbalans." *Internationale Spectator* 4 (17): 1–4.
———. 1954. *Centralization and Decentralization in Economic Policy*. Amsterdam: North Holland.
———. 1957. "Internationale Socialistische Politiek." *Socialisme En Democratie* 14 (11): 666–71.
———. 1959. "The Theory of the Optimum Regime." In *Selected Papers*, edited by L. H. Klaassen, L. M. Koyck, and H. J. Witteveen, 264–304. Amsterdam: North Holland.
———. 1960. "The Impact of the European Economic Community on Third Countries." In *Sciences Humaines et Intégration Européene*, edited by H. Brugmans, L. Cerych, and M. J. Lory, 386–98. Leyde: A.W. Sythoff.
———. 1962. *Shaping the World Economy*. New York: Twentieth Century Fund.
———. 1963a. "Introductory Remarks on the 'Ization Problem.'" *Zeitschrift Für Die Gesamte Staatswissenschaft* 119 (2): 328–33.
———. 1963b. *The European Community: Conservative or Progressive?* Stockholm: Almqvist & Wiksell.
———. 1966. "Ontwikkelingshulp in Wereldperspectief." In *10 Jaar Novib 10 Jaar Ontwikkelingshulp*, 52–55. 's-Gravenhage: NOVIB.
———. 1968. "The Optimal International Division of Labour." *Acta Oeconomica* 3: 257–82.
———. 1976. *Reshaping the International Order: A Report to the Club of Rome*. New York: New American Library.
Tinbergen, Jan, H. Linneman, and J. P. Pronk. 1966. "The Meeting of the Twain." *The Columbia Journal of World Business* 2 (1): 139–49.
Verwey-Jonker, Hilda. 1936. "Plan En Internationalisme." In *Handboek Voor Het Plan van de Arbeid*, edited by Floor Wibaut, 135–42. Amsterdam: Arbeiderspers.

CHAPTER 6

At the Origins of European Monetary Cooperation: Triffin, Bretton Woods, and the European Payments Union

Pierre-Hernan Rojas

1 Introduction

Robert Triffin (1911–1993) is best remembered for having diagnosed the inconsistency of the gold-dollar exchange standard in his major and most influential work, *Gold and the Dollar Crisis* (1960). His diagnosis, known as the Triffin dilemma,[1] can be explained as follows: if the United States stops running balance of payments deficits, other countries will see the main source of international liquidity diminish, thereby limiting the expansion of world trade and potentially leading to worldwide deflation. Contrariwise, excessive US balance of payments deficits fuel world economic growth with international liquidity but undermining

[1] It was not Triffin but Oscar L. Altman (1961, 164) who first used the term "dilemma."

P.-H. Rojas (✉)
Catholic Institute of Paris, Paris, France
e-mail: ph.rojas@icp.fr

© The Author(s) 2021

A. M. Cunha and C. E. Suprinyak (eds.), *Political Economy and International Order in Interwar Europe*, Palgrave Studies in the History of Economic Thought,
https://doi.org/10.1007/978-3-030-47102-6_6

other countries' confidence in the convertibility of dollar balances into gold.

A purely historical analysis, as carried out by Allan H. Meltzer (2009, 221) and leading us to think back to the circumstances of the time, presents the Triffin dilemma as the consequence of the growing role the dollar played in the international monetary system after the 1950s. Another way to understand Triffin's critique of the Bretton Woods system is to analyze his concrete proposals for European monetary integration in the late 1940s and the 1950s. As far as regional unification was concerned, Triffin was a successful instigator, contributing to both the setting up of a number of regional bodies for economic cooperation and to the consolidation phase in Europe. One decisive experiment in this connection was the European Payments Union (EPU), which came into effect in 1950. The EPU (1950–1958) was a major step toward West European integration, an essential factor in expanding trade among those countries receiving Marshall Plan aid, and a key factor in making their currencies convertible. As the architect of the EPU (Eichengreen 1993) and one of the instigators of the postwar European monetary order, Triffin was a distinctive figure since in his close talks with governments and politicians, he continually reinterpreted economic developments within their historical context in order to demonstrate how they related to the "essential" problems of the present. His method and insights regarding regionalism can best be understood by analyzing his career as an economist and policy adviser between the 1930s and 1950s.[2]

Triffin's works aimed at defeating what were once widely shared opinions, beliefs, and perceptions, which, he argued, underpinned policies that would cause the opposite effect to that intended. For instance, the traditional approach to a balance of payments adjustment required deflation in the event of any misalignment between domestic prices and world prices. Such a policy was supposed to restore equilibrium. In the cases of Belgium in the 1930s and Latin America in the 1940s, Triffin managed to show these analyses were invalid by taking into account the specificities of these economies. Maes (2013) rightly points out the continuity of Triffin's thinking in terms of "the vision that the international adjustment process was not functioning according to the classical mechanisms" (Maes 2013, 1145). This consistency throughout Triffin's career in the 1930s

[2] For a Triffin's biography, see Maes (2013), Maes and Pasotti (2018) and Wilson (2015).

and the 1940s, pointing out the discrepancy between economic theory and facts, provides a better understanding of his analysis of the instability surrounding the gold exchange standard. For that reason, Jacques de Larosière wrote of Triffin's "pragmatism as a practitioner" and referred to him as "a man of action" (1991, 136). Triffin adopted the same attitude when dealing with economic problems in Europe after the Second World War when he became Director of Exchange Control at the International Monetary Fund (IMF) in 1946.

The young Bretton Woods institution was a real breakthrough embodying the recognition that an orderly functioning of the international monetary system required international agreements, universal rules of behavior, and an appropriate framework for their implementation. The agreed rules were mainly directed against what had been deemed the major sources of international monetary disruption in the interwar period, i.e., competitive exchange rate devaluations and the imposition of exchange restrictions on current transactions. The issues of exchange rate, international liquidity and short-term balance of payment balance were under the responsibility of the IMF. However, it failed to provide a multilateral system of payments based on full currency convertibility. Triffin claimed that because countries were not prepared to trade on dollar-convertibility, bilateralism and trade and exchange restrictions were unavoidable in the immediate postwar years. As a remedy, Triffin made reform proposals for European countries to cope with the IMF's structural inability to eliminate exchange restrictions on current transactions and to outlaw bilateral payment arrangements. In a series of IMF memoranda released between 1947 and 1949, Triffin advocated a European clearing union, similar to Keynes' International Clearing Union, aimed at fostering and liberalizing European trade while economizing international reserves. First at the IMF and then at the Economic Cooperation Administration—which administered the Marshall Plan—Triffin succeeded in promoting his ideas, giving rise to the European Payments Union (EPU) in 1950.

The EPU paved the way to a European monetary order with the same objective—promoting a multilateral payments system—of the IMF but with a different modus operandi. His aim was to promote multilateral offsets and payments between the member countries and supervised by institutional machinery: a Managing Board and the Bank for International

Settlements. The institution's success during the 1950s strengthened Triffin's belief that the architecture and functioning of the Bretton Woods system should be decentralized, pointing out that an international monetary system centralized around US currency and policy would not promote its flexibility and stability.[3] In the second half of the 1940s, Triffin was pragmatic and tackled the policy problem in Europe. His experience in Europe and his further reflections on the operation of the monetary system were to provide Triffin with arguments enabling him to propose in the early 1950s the analysis and remedies that were subsequently to be set out in his 1960 book. In point of fact, the formulation of the Triffin dilemma in 1960 was the consequence and not the cause of Triffin's involvement in broader regional monetary integration.[4]

Throughout our analysis, we shall highlight the fact that the international liquidity[5] issue—its use, its provision and its composition—was at the core of Triffin's analysis when he questioned the ability of the gold exchange standard to square the conduct of discretionary national economic policies with the observance of the balance of payments equilibrium. European countries were his laboratory. The emergence of a monetary order at the European level acted more effectively toward multilateralization that the IMF. The second section deals with Triffin's background at Louvain University in the 1930s where he was tutored in Dupriez's methodology and business cycle analysis, and where he developed his scientific approach to practical problems. The third section investigates Triffin's critique in the 1940s of the supposed working of the international gold standard. Indeed, Triffin attempted to highlight the discrepancy between the theory and the facts, questioning the automatic and symmetric features of such a system. He pointed out the

[3] This idea was suggested by Guido Carli, former President of the EPU and Governor of the Bank of Italy: "(…) it is probable that Triffin's close involvement with and understanding of the EPU led to his early diagnosis of the ills that would eventually undermine the system of stable but adjustable exchange rates based on the dollar as the primary reserve asset" (1982, 167).

[4] Maes and Pasotti (2018) show how the EPU led to a shift in Triffin's view of the geography of the international monetary system, considering a regional approach of international monetary integration.

[5] International liquidity has to be understood as resources readily available for monetary authorities in order to finance balance of payments deficits and defend exchange rate stability. These resources could be liquid assets, such as gold and foreign exchange, or facilities for borrowing abroad.

necessity of a flexible international monetary system providing sufficient international liquidity to enable countries to conduct counter-cyclical monetary policies. The fourth section examines Triffin's first proposal for a European clearing union in order to promote trade liberalization and provide international liquidity. The fifth section presents Triffin's continuous involvement in deeper regional monetary integration in order to cope with the inconsistency of the Bretton Woods system. The sixth section concludes.

2 The Crisis in the 1930s: Triffin and the Case of Belgium, a Small Open Economy

Triffin studied the theory of economic cycles under Léon H. Dupriez, who introduced a statistical method to test business cycle theory in Europe.[6] Triffin's first experience at the ISE (*Institut des Sciences Économiques*), headed by Dupriez, is crucial to understanding his insight into international economics during the interwar years.

Economic research in the interwar period was strongly focused on understanding the business cycle, especially in the United States. At Charles Jesse Bullock's initiative, the *Harvard Committee on Economic Research* was created in 1917 with the aim of studying economic statistical series dating back to the nineteenth century to describe business cycles. The *Review of Economic Statistics* was founded in 1919 to disseminate the results of its work. This innovation at Harvard was imitated by other US universities (Princeton, Columbia) and led to the establishment of an official department with the same objective in 1920, the *National Bureau of Economic Research*. These initiatives were followed in France, Great Britain, Germany, and Austria. In 1928, Dupriez established the ISE at Louvain which became the first "modern" research center in economics in the small countries. Léon H. Dupriez soon came to be the dominant voice in the institute. Under his leadership, Louvain economists gained international status in the 1930s.[7]

[6] Léon H. Dupriez (1901–1986) was a Belgian economist, Doctor of Law, Doctor of Political and Social Sciences. He studied at Harvard in 1918–1919 before returning to Belgium. He was one of the pioneers of the introduction of statistical methods in economics, importing US methods from Harvard.

[7] In order to finance its theoretical research, the ISE produced business cycle analyses and forecasts, which were sold to private and (semi-) public corporations and institutions

In 1930 Dupriez published "*Les méthodes d'analyse de la conjoncture économique et leur application à la Belgique depuis 1897.*" Adhering to the methods developed by the *Harvard Committee Society*, Dupriez drew in this book a complete panorama of the general characteristics of the Belgian economy, enabling the real-time analysis of contemporary phenomena. The book set out a method of systematic organization of the collection of information on the conduct of business cycles in Belgium. With this methodological basis, the ISE enhanced the statistics available for establishing a "diagnosis of economic problems."

The economic context in Belgium during the interwar years was peculiar to that country. Dupriez highlighted a structural failure of the Belgian economy that had tended, since the early 1920s, to become more competitive than its British counterpart. Far from attributing this movement to improved productivity, Dupriez and his team quickly showed that Belgium was developing a tendency to reproduce the pattern of less-developed countries. Production was centered on basic products for which competition was more intense. Indeed, Belgium could be defined as a small economy. Production was concentrated in industries like steel, coal, and textiles and during the interwar period these sectors became even more important. Modern industrial products and raw materials were imported, semi-finished products were exported. This structure made Belgium's economy increasingly vulnerable to external shocks. The consequences of the devaluation of the pound in September 1931 confirmed this diagnosis. Belgium was confronted with an enormous price fall for the output of its most important competitor, British industry. The effect of the fall of the pound rippled throughout the British Empire and other countries with close ties with the UK economy. Prices on the international markets dropped in terms of gold with the exchange rate of sterling. The Belgian franc became overvalued. Profit margins having already melted, the necessary new cost reductions had to come from wages. The recession slowly took the form of a severe recession. This shift was not self-evident,

(Maes et al. 2000). But the influence of the ISE on economic policy went far beyond that. Dupriez and several other members of the institute combined their academic careers with senior positions in Belgium's central bank. Moreover, several members, such as Albert-Edouard Janssen and Paul van Zeeland, occupied key positions in different governments (Maes 2009).

however, because the balance of trade remained in equilibrium. Companies preferred to absorb the shock by reducing costs rather than reducing their activity.

To study the Belgian case, Dupriez turned to theories of purchasing power parities. This tool made it possible to illustrate the divergent paths of the price structures of two countries and to deduce from them an exchange rate policy likely to favor a coherent stabilization for both countries. The theory of purchasing power parities was devised by Cassel in 1920 and states that exchange rates must allow the parity of purchasing power of monies in different countries. This theory can be used to determine either the degree of deflation to restore the pre-war gold parity, or the degree of devaluation necessary to avoid deflation. The ISE opposed the deflationary solution which generated unemployment, opting for devaluation instead. Nevertheless, Dupriez and the ISE highlighted two major shortcomings with Cassel's theory. First, it was based on wholesale prices, which were largely defined on the international market and could not alone account accurately for particular national circumstances. Second, Cassel thought of the analysis of purchasing powers as a comparison of two monolithic price blocks and disregarded the possible internal tensions between the various price indices (wholesale prices, cost of living, etc.). This factor, though, seemed decisive for explaining the disparity of purchasing power and the tension that this disparity could cause. Even so, Dupriez was convinced of the relevance of the path taken by Cassel and focused on reworking this approach. It was in this context that Triffin, assisting Dupriez from 1933, played a major role in analyzing the Belgian situation in the 1930s.

In his first analysis, "*Les mouvements différentiels des prix de gros en Belgique de 1927 à 1934. Calcul et interprétation d'indices de groups comparables*" (1935), Triffin presented the movements of 25 agricultural product indices and 28 industrial product indices for the period 1927–1934. He drew a distinction between raw materials, semi-finished products, and finished products to highlight the Belgian price structure. He also compiled separate indices for imported and exported industrial products and imported agricultural products. Following the devaluation of sterling, Triffin pointed out that prices of manufactured products had declined more steeply than domestic costs, leading to serious losses in

Belgian manufacturing and firm closures (Triffin 1935, 290). By concentrating on the price structure, and distinguishing (rigid) wages from (flexible) wholesale prices, Triffin demonstrated the superiority of price adjustment (devaluation) over demand adjustment (deflation). Deflation could not solve the problem of the Belgian price structure. Triffin's results were used for the scientific study of the level of devaluation to be applied to the Belgian franc.

In 1937, Triffin published another article—*La théorie de la surévaluation monétaire et la dévaluation belge*—going further into the theoretical and empirical background of the Belgian devaluation. Triffin's fundamental criticism, in line with his earlier article, was that Cassel did not look at the structure of prices in a country. Like Dupriez, he made a distinction between "sheltered" and "non-sheltered" sectors of the economy. In the non-sheltered sector of the economy, prices had to be aligned with world prices. However, costs in the non-sheltered sectors were largely determined by domestic factors, especially wages, leading to a profit squeeze. Consequently, the Belgian economy's loss of competitiveness, due to the devaluation of the pound sterling, was reflected not so much in the producer prices of the non-sheltered sectors or the trade balance as in a decline in profits in the non-sheltered sectors, a decline in production, and an increase in unemployment. Moreover, the decline of industry had significant consequences for the financial system, as the banks made large losses on the loans they had extended to industry.

The analysis of the economic situation and the theorization of the business cycles enabled the ISE, including Triffin, to establish reliable forecasts on which to base coherent decision making. The Louvain school was becoming a reference not just in Belgium but in Europe and even worldwide. According to Sauvy (1984, 169), "in the history of the interwar economy there are few examples of scientific reasoning dictating, in this fashion, a political decision (…) Thereafter Belgian policy would long be inspired by the Louvain institute." The pioneering nature of the Belgian devaluation, based on a scientific approach to economic realities, deeply influenced Triffin in later works, especially his concern for peripheral countries. However, even if the devaluation of the Belgian franc helped Belgium out of the deflationary spiral, the 1931 monetary crisis revealed the incapacity of the decision makers to devise unanimously a new international monetary order. This failure became obvious during the 1933 London international conference on economic and monetary problems. It made a lasting impression on Triffin who remained obsessed with the monetary problem of the interwar period and it drove his voluntarism after the war.

3 Toward a More Flexible International Monetary System: The Case of Latin America

Triffin's academic career at Harvard was interrupted during the summer of 1942 when the United States entered the Second World War.[8] To work on postwar reforms, US government administrations, including the Treasury and the OSS, launched a large surge of recruitment in American universities. Triffin accepted to join the Federal Reserve Board (FRB) where he was to head the new Latin America section. Between 1942 and 1946, Triffin led money doctor missions in Paraguay, the Dominican Republic, Ecuador, and Guatemala among other countries.

3.1 Criticism of the Orthodox View of the Workings of the Gold Standard

From his thorough empirical analysis of the Latin American countries' circumstances, Triffin described the balance of payments adjustment mechanism within the orthodox theory, based on the hypotheses of automatism and symmetry. The orthodox theory ascribed balance of payments disequilibria to domestic price and cost levels and to interest-rate disparities between countries. A deficit in the balance of payments, resulting in gold exports, could only be absorbed by a contraction of the domestic money supply. According to Triffin:

> The automatic adaptation of the money supply to the fluctuations of the balance of payments was, of course, considered as perfectly normal and desirable in the orthodox gold-standard theory. A favorable or unfavorable

[8] After obtaining his Ph.D. at Harvard, Triffin returned to Belgium in the fall of 1938 but failed to find any position because of the recruitment policy of Belgian institutions at that time. Triffin (1981, 241) recollected that "a decent number of Flemings would have to be appointed first in order to approximate parity with the Walloons, who had up to then filled most of the existing openings." Later, Triffin pointed out that Dupriez was disappointed that he did not continue the industry localization studies at Harvard. Moreover, Dupriez wanted him to complete another Ph.D. at Louvain. See Ferrant et al. (2010, 27). Therefore, in 1939, Triffin accepted an appointment as instructor in economics at Harvard.

> balance-of-payments was taken as a sign of a fundamental disequilibrium in international price and cost levels, and it was assumed that the disequilibrium would be corrected by the domestic expansion or contraction brought about by the inflow or outflow of exchange. (Triffin 1944, 108)

The automatic adjustments of the balance of payments relied on market forces and central banks were supposed to follow the rules of the game, which deprived them of "any real control over the supply of money and credit" (Triffin 1944, 96).Triffin rightly recalled that this pattern of thought "inspired so much of the academic thinking and legislative controversies regarding national and international monetary mechanisms during the nineteenth and even the twentieth century" (Triffin 1947a, 49) while it offered an unrealistic description of the way the gold standard operated. In the 1920s and the early 1930s, this view was the cornerstone of the money doctoring missions led by US officials, such as Edwin W. Kemmerer in Latin American countries which set up rigid monetary systems, such as currency boards or gold exchange standards (for more details, see Gomez Betancourt 2008).

Triffin objected to the orthodox theory, pointing out that it developed only one special category of disequilibrium, "originating in cost maladjustments between a single country and the rest of the world" (Triffin 1947b, 322). The assumption that economic imbalances were only national did not stand up to scrutiny. According to Triffin:

> The most cursory examination of statistical data clearly shows that many of the most spectacular disequilibria in balance of payments are *worldwide* in scope, and must be traced to cyclical fluctuations of an international character rather than to national price and cost maladjustments. (italics in the text, Triffin 1947a, 55–56)

Triffin pointed out another category of disequilibrium which resulted from the international business cycle. International monetary relations were structured asymmetrically between the center—industrial and capital exporting countries—and the periphery—primary goods producing and capital importing countries. Given the leading position of London as an international financial center, the orthodox theory failed to describe the British adjustment mechanism, nor the way global cycles originated from changes in the British discount rate. The international gold standard was in fact a gold-sterling exchange standard with the Bank of England as the leader. In order to meet domestic goals (stabilizing domestic prices and making the money market more liquid), the Bank of England conducted its monetary policy in such a way as to control domestic credit. But changes in this policy also impacted the financial circumstances of foreign countries in that a part of their bills were contracted in London in order to finance international trade (Triffin 1947a, 59, 62–63).

The contraction of international credit, understood as British credit, reduced not only British but also international demand for goods, tending to force down foreign prices. As a financial center, Britain was able to improve its terms of trade—domestic prices relative to foreign prices—and attract short-term capital to restore the balance of payments equilibrium without resorting to the deflationary policies advocated by the orthodox theory.

Moreover, the balance of payments fluctuations in peripheral countries, especially in Latin America, were not governed by international cost comparisons but "dominated by the international movements of capital and by the fluctuations of imports and exports" (Triffin 1944, 104–5), as a consequence of the international business cycle. The peripheral countries were often poorly diversified economies, specialized in the production of one or two goods whose supply "may be determined by the vagaries of the weather" and demand for which "is predominantly influenced by the state of the business cycle in the buying countries" (Triffin 1944, 108). The fluctuations in their balance of payments were reinforced by violent shifts in capital flows resulting from speculation. Contrary to the core countries, in peripheral countries, "capital tended to flow toward them in times of prosperity and away from them in times of depression, irrespective of their discount policy" (Triffin 1947a, 60).

3.2 *Advocating Counter-Cyclical Monetary Policies*

Triffin's analysis and bold reform proposals were facilitated by the development of a new neighborhood policy by the US administrations.[9] According to Helleiner (2003, 255), the US policy-makers' stance evolved during the 1930s. Following the demise of the international gold standard in 1931 and the effects of the Great Depression in the

[9] This change in thinking of US financial diplomacy vis-à-vis Latin American countries probably explains why the FRB gave Triffin full autonomy and independence during his money doctoring missions, not given any prior instructions. See Triffin (1981, 242).

1930s, US officials from the Treasury and the Fed became aware of the vulnerability of the southern countries' economies, most of them being agricultural and suffering largely from volatile capital flows. They considered that orthodox policies "magnified—rather than minimized—the impact of international instability on the domestic economy in this context" (Helleiner 2003, 251) and failed to promote domestic economic activity and high employment.[10]

It was against this backdrop of a break in US financial diplomacy that Triffin began his work at the FRB. Triffin insisted that peripheral countries' specificities differed from those of the core countries. Their financial and banking systems were not so developed as those of Great Britain or the United States, making the control of the money supply via the discount rate and open market policies inoperative. Moreover, foreign banks financed development in peripheral countries, making the latter heavily dependent on capital flows from financial centers. In the event of external disequilibrium in a peripheral country, the orthodox rules of the game strengthened domestic instability.

> The classical prescription for remedial policy becomes as misleading as the diagnosis on which it is based. Deflationary efforts at readjustment by individual countries are largely self-defeating because they aggravate the depression rather than cure the disequilibrium. Any initial success that they may have in curbing imports or expanding exports aggravates the difficulties in their supply and exports markets as well as in competing countries, and leads to similar and mutually offsetting measure of defense or retaliation. (Triffin 1947a, 57)

To avoid the propagation of the cycle from the center to the peripheral countries that accentuated world economic fluctuations, Triffin advocated establishing central banks capable of managing the monetary and banking system through a variety of instruments: changes in reserve requirements, quantitative and qualitative banking loans, empowerment by the central bank to undertake open market operations to control money and credit. Triffin's reforms were grounded on the loosening of the

[10] The US cooperation policy toward Latin America was not only driven by the desire for economic development. Reminding us of the geopolitical issues in the context of the Second World War, Helleiner (2009, 6) writes that "this shift [in neighborhood policy] emerged partly in the context of US worries about growing German influence in the region."

rigid link between legal tender money/deposits and international reserves (gold and foreign exchange).[11] Triffin developed other tools, such as multiple exchange rates and exchange control,[12] to relieve the burden of international instability for Latin American countries.

According to Triffin, not only did peripheral countries have to promote a form of monetary management that insulated the national economy from international disturbances, but also the core countries had responsibility for smoothing worldwide fluctuations. Since the cyclical disturbances originated from their leading position, the core countries had to follow a new set of economic policies stabilizing the purchasing power of money and income. On that topic, Triffin was clear:

> The only satisfactory corrective of cyclical disequilibria in the balance of payments which are not due to fundamental maladjustments in international price levels thus lies for most nations, not in internal deflation according to the "rules of the game" recipe, but in *the restoration of economic activity and purchasing power in the centers of the cyclical disturbance.* (emphasis added, 1947a, 64)

The peripheral countries would have to resort to international reserves, such as gold and foreign exchange, to cope with worldwide fluctuations in economic activity if they wanted to preserve domestic stability. Indeed, if a country ran into balance of payments difficulties, its monetary authorities would have to meet the substantial demand for foreign currency. Since the country did not tighten domestic credit, the depletion in international reserves could lead to liquidity difficulties and a foreign exchange crisis. Triffin was aware of that problem, noting that the general adoption of counter-cyclical monetary policies "would tend to amplify the instability of national reserves of gold and foreign exchange" (1947a, 64). That was

[11] As developed earlier, this set of ideas was not so new when we analyze US monetary thinking in the 1930s, especially at the US Treasury. Like Triffin, Harry D. White, one of the architects of the Bretton Woods system and a member of the US Treasury, recommended in the 1930s control of capital flows or changes in reserve requirements in order to manage the US monetary and banking system (Rojas 2016). Helleiner (2014, 86) showed that White was also committed to this new approach of money doctoring in Latin American countries, leading missions to Cuba in the second half of the 1930s.

[12] Triffin considered that these measures were more effective alternatives than traditional policies, such as deflation or devaluation, which did not sufficiently target the categories of transactions. For instance, the foreign exchange control could reduce the balance of trade deficit by restricting less essential imports, such as luxury goods.

why this kind of policy “requires a high level of international reserves (…) and the willingness to spend these reserves liberally in times of crisis (…)” (Triffin 1947a, 80).

During his money doctoring missions, Triffin raised awareness of how much Latin American countries were suffering from the spillovers of the Great Depression, which included declining world trade flows, falling commodity prices, and increasing capital outflows. This is why Triffin forcefully advocated a general revision of the workings of the international monetary system and the design of monetary policies in order to reconcile national objectives with international balances. In the mid-1940s, the Bretton Woods system seemed to offer the framework in which the global monetary order would avoid economic isolationism, depression and instability.

4 Triffin’s Advocacy of European Monetary Integration

The previous section examined the reasons why Triffin supported the use of international reserves. In the event of temporary deficits of the balance of payments, linked to the global economic cycle, countries should not reduce the deficit by conducting a deflationary policy but rather finance it by resorting to international reserves. The present section tackles a complementary issue: the provision of international liquidity. Did the Bretton Woods agreements set up a financial mechanism making additional international reserves available to the member countries in times of need? It did in theory since the innovation of the agreements was the establishment of the IMF whose purpose was to supply additional international reserves to deficit countries. According to Triffin (1947a, 80), “when reserves are insufficient, foreign or international assistance—such as is contemplated under the International Monetary Fund—will be necessary.” This assistance would both provide reserves for deficit countries without resorting to internal deflation or foreign exchange control and protect other countries from being impacted by the effects of these measures. However, the international monetary system that prevailed after the Second World War was very different from the system that the Anglo-American delegations foresaw. Actually, the IMF was unable to carry out its missions of overseeing the international monetary system—reducing exchange restrictions and providing the return to currency convertibility—and smoothing countries’ external adjustment. In times of bilateralism and dollar shortages, characteristic of the second half of the 1940s, Triffin, then Director of Exchange Control at the IMF, supported a clearing mechanism to facilitate the implementation of the Marshall Plan in European countries.

4.1 Bilateralism and Liquidity Shortage: The IMF's Failure

The Bretton Woods system was an unprecedented experiment in the implementation of rules and international institutions to reconcile international equilibria and autonomous national economic policies. Briefly, the purposes of the IMF (Article I, IMF Articles of Agreement), were to promote (i) international monetary cooperation, (ii) to facilitate the maintenance of full employment and rapid growth, (iii) to maintain stable exchange rates and avoid competitive devaluations, (iv) to provide a multilateral system of payments and eliminate exchange restrictions, (v) to provide resources to meet balance of payments disequilibria without resort to drastic measures, and (vi) to shorten the duration and lessen the degree of payments disequilibria. The IMF articles developed the necessary means to achieve these goals. Firstly, Article IV of the Agreement seeks to ensure exchange rate stability by requiring members to agree on a par value for their currency either in gold or in dollars. This was achieved at the end of 1946 by major European countries. Secondly, the IMF aims at establishing a multilateral system of payments based on currency convertibility for current account transactions (Article VIII) while allowing capital control (Article VI, Section 3). However, the IMF allows its member countries to postpone the return to convertibility for current account transactions for an indefinite transition period (Article XIV). Actually, the currencies inconvertibility period lasted until 1958. Finally, the IMF offers facilities to finance short-term balance of payments disequilibria (Article V). Indeed, countries could borrow a foreign currency from the IMF in exchange for its own in order to settle a deficit with a particular country.[13] To avoid the shortage of a particular currency in IMF resources, the IMF could activate the scarce currency clause (Article VII). When it appeared to the IMF that its holdings of a particular currency were likely to be exhausted—a creditor country's

[13] According to Article III, each country could borrow from the IMF up to an amount limited by its quota. The IMF's resources are made up of countries' initial contributions—equal to the borrowing rights—divided up as 25% in gold and 75% in national currencies.

currency—the Board of Directors should propose to declare this currency scarce and above all, authorize other countries to limit and ration exports from the country whose currency has been declared scarce. This clause was designed to avoid perpetuating an overall surplus of a country toward the world.

Despite the innovative nature of such an institution empowered to foster international monetary cooperation, the IMF failed to achieve its objectives. Actually, the economic environment in which the IMF was supposed to intervene was very different from that to be found in the immediate postwar period. According to Tew (1952, 94), "many of the Fund's failures have undoubtedly been due to the fact that it has had to bat on a bad wicket: the stresses and strains of the post-war years have been of such unparalleled severity that the new organization has never had the chance of proving its value in relatively normal circumstances." Far from promoting multilateralism and providing sufficient international reserves, the IMF failed to avoid a bilateral approach to economic relations and a world liquidity shortage.

After the war, only the dollar was both convertible into gold at a fixed parity ($35 per ounce of gold) and into other currencies.[14] When the IMF officially got under way in March 1947, most countries decided to extend their exchange and trade controls, postponing the return to full currency convertibility. The reason is to be found in the economic consequences of the war. Indeed, following the destruction of European industry and the growing needs for consumption and capital goods, European countries ran a structural current account deficit with the United States until mid-1951. According to Eichengreen (1993, 11), this deficit amounted to $5.6 billion in 1947, $3.4 billion in 1948, and $3.2 billion in 1949.[15] In that context, exchange and trade restrictions enabled

[14] We follow Triffin's distinction (1950, 5–6) between gold convertibility of currency—the ability for private individuals to freely convert national currency into gold at the official fixed price—and convertibility on the foreign exchange market, which referred to the ability for private individuals to buy and sell freely the national currency for the currency of another country. Under the Bretton Woods system, except for the United States, countries were only concerned with the second form of convertibility.

[15] European countries needed immediate key imports such as foodstuffs to meet their basic needs. Moreover, European industry did not produce exports that could have financed this increase in imports. To boost industrial activity, new and improved capital was required. The need for both primary and capital goods explains the extent of the European current account deficit.

countries to allocate the sole means of settlement acceptable by all, the dollar. However, these measures were supplemented by bilateral arrangements that were negotiated between each pair of countries and consisted of licenses and quotas for imports and exports. But these agreements resulted in a trade-diverting policy and strengthened the reallocation of international reserves:

> To maximize the availability of hard currency [gold and dollars] that might be used to purchase from the dollar area the imports to which they attached priority, European countries restricted their imports from the rest of Europe to the value of their receipts in each European trading partner's currency. (Eichengreen 1993, 13)

Bilateralism enabled a resumption of trade between partner countries thanks to the opening of mutual credit lines allowing them to dispense with the strict bilateral balancing of their imports and exports. These reciprocal overdraft rights were promoted on the idea that surpluses and deficits would alternate between countries, enabling a deficit country to repay its credit when later it had a surplus. But these bilateral agreements were restrictive because there were no surpluses and deficits alternating between countries, leading to credit lines' being exhausted:

> Experience demonstrated (...) that some countries tended toward persistent deficits, others toward persistent surplus. Once credit ceilings were reached, additional credits were not forthcoming. And once credits were exhausted, bilateral clearing became increasingly constraining. (Eichengreen 1993, 16)

The dollar shortage, fueled by the structural current account deficit from European countries toward the United States, was reinforced by the overvalued official parities established late in 1946. Bordo (1993, 39) points out that the IMF put pressure on member countries to declare the parity of their currencies as soon as possible. In this context of general disequilibria, the IMF considered the scarce currency problem in 1947 but decided not to take action under Article VII, nor did it take action later. The Executive Directors of the IMF were aware of the origins of the gap between the demand for and the supply of dollars, that resulted "from a shortage of productive facilities, particularly in European countries, with which dollars could be earned. The real scarcity therefore was one of production, and not of dollars" (Horsefield 1969, 193). Since the

IMF was "not intended to provide facilities for relief or reconstruction or to deal with international indebtedness arising out of the war" (Article XIV, Section 1), European countries hardly drew any resources from this institution during the second half of the 1940s.

Facing the gap between the resources of the IMF and the challenges of the postwar years to restore an international economic and monetary system, the Truman administration decided to implement the European Recovery Program, better known as the Marshall Plan. It has to be highlighted that the US desire to finance European reconstruction and foster a resurgence of European trade was grounded on a proactive policy of containing Communism.[16] As a condition for US help, European countries had to agree on a program to allocate US loans and donations.[17] A Conference on European Economic Cooperation (CEEC) was held in Paris in July 1947, giving rise to an official committee of western European governments that had to agree on a four-year program. Simultaneously, the US Congress authorized the creation of the Economic Cooperation Administration (ECA) to administer the Marshall Plan. From early summer 1947, the IMF entered the discussions between the United States and European countries, under the leadership of the new Managing Director, Camille Gutt, the former Belgian Minister of Finance.

[16] After an official visit to Moscow early in 1947, Marshall, Secretary of State, realized that Joseph Stalin did not intend to reduce his influence on European territories occupied by the Soviet army, quite the contrary. According to. Kaplan and Schleiminger (1989, p. 15), "Regardless of Soviet behaviour to their east, economic hardship seemed to strengthen the appeal of western European Communist parties, particularly in France and Italy. Thus a westward expansion of Soviet hegemony appeared within the realm of the possible."

[17] Marshall's speech on 5 June 1947 at Harvard was explicit: "It is already evident that, before the United States Government can proceed much further in its efforts to alleviate the situation and help start the European world on its way to recovery, there must be some agreement among the countries of Europe (…) This is the business of the Europeans. The initiative, I think, must come from Europe."

4.2 *A Multilateral Approach: Triffin and the European Payments Union (EPU)*

After four years at the FRB, Triffin was recruited by the IMF in July 1946 and appointed Director of Exchange Control. Until mid-1947, Triffin continued the projects started during his years at the FRB, especially the Latin American missions. Immediately after the IMF joined the negotiations between the CEEC and the ECA, Gutt and Edward M. Bernstein—then Research Director at the IMF—asked Triffin to work on the first European proposals. According to Kaplan and Schleiminger (1989, 362), the first plans for the multilateralization of payments, based on the clearing mechanism, were supported by Felix LeNorcy, an official at the French Ministry of Finance, and by the Benelux officials during the CEEC meeting in July 1947. Despite the failure of these first proposals, Triffin studied them, especially the Benelux plan, and began to shape his first proposal for a European clearing union (Wilson 2015, 461). Between 1947 and 1949, Triffin issued a series of eight IMF memoranda to promote multilateralization in Europe.[18]

In his first memorandum, *The Unresolved Problem of Financing European Trade*,[19] written in September 1947 but released by the IMF in December 1947,[20] Triffin indicated that "the difficulty to be met here is one of providing adequate machinery [to boost European trade], and not merely financial assistance in terms of gold and dollars" (RTPY, Triffin 1947, 1). Indeed, financial assistance was required to supply European countries with hard currency to meet the deficit with the dollar area, but Triffin considered that a mechanism should be implemented between European countries to avoid resorting to reserves. According to Triffin (RTPY 1947, 2), "as long as gold and dollar reserves remain at their present low level, only further credits can relieve the pressure for bilateral balancing of inter-European trade." So he proposed to multilateralize all

[18] RTPY, box 19, "Summary of Triffin's IMF memoranda and proposals for the multilateralization of Intra-European credits and settlements (September 1947–December 1949)."

[19] RTPY, box 19, "Triffin's EPU proposals... 1947–1948," *The Unresolved Problem of Financing European Trade*, December 16, 1947, IMF Staff Memorandum No. 160.

[20] According to Wilson (2015, 460–61), the IMF staff were not enthusiastic about Triffin's proposal because they considered that a clearing mechanism favored the exchange of non-essential goods, delaying European economic reconstruction. Moreover, since the debate on implementing the Marshall Plan was a political issue, outside the scope of the IMF, the IMF staff felt uncomfortable.

European claims and debts, and to extend credit lines within a multilateral framework. In other words, this multilateral agreement would transfer the credit commitments which existed under the bilateral agreements from individual countries to all countries participating in a clearing house, entitled the "European Clearing Union" (RTPY, Triffin 1947, 4).

> The total credit commitments made by each country to other Clearing members would be paid into the Clearing in its own currency, and the country would receive an equivalent balance in the Clearing which it could then use to settle current account deficits with any Clearing member. (RTPY, Triffin 1947, 4)

The primary feature of Triffin's plan was the compensation mechanism which could offset a large part of bilateral imbalances between countries and the European Clearing Union. The benefit of the clearing house was the saving made on means of settlement (gold and dollar) coupled with the participating countries' renouncement to discriminate against European partners. Moreover, balances in the Clearing should be expressed in a new unit of account:

> This essential aspect of the Clearing's mechanism could be dramatized by the introduction of an inter-European currency unit, equal in value to one American dollar, and called, let us say, "European dollar" or "interfranc". (RTPY, Triffin 1947, 4)

According to Triffin (RTPY 1947, fn1, 4), the bookkeeping nature of this new unit might change in the future if European countries took their monetary integration further. For the time being, Triffin did not propose a European currency. Clearing's assets would remain in participating countries' currencies and national currencies would retain their existing independence and autonomy.

The second feature of Triffin's plan was the payment mechanism of net balances. Indeed, even if a large part of European trade were to be settled, some European countries would have a net overall deficit or surplus toward other European countries; this was the case for respectively France and Belgium. One of the objectives of the US aid was to provide European countries with dollars in order to finance these net balances within the European Clearing Union framework. But Triffin raised a second issue: since European countries were running an overall deficit with the United States, it would deteriorate both the European Clearing Union's and countries' reserves without any certainty of replenishing them later. To avoid jamming the whole clearing machinery, the US aid needed to be large enough. In connection with the problem of the amount of the US aid, Triffin pointed out the need to "define, for each European country, the maximum deficit which could be reasonably and safely incurred" (1947b, 7) but without defining any clear rule. In a second memorandum, released in May 1948 and entitled *Multilateralization of European Payments Agreements among Fund Members*,[21] Triffin did not support an automatic rule in additional credits granted by European surplus to deficit countries:

> Further credits may be required in the meanwhile, but their amount will necessarily depend on the prospective lenders' appraisal of the efforts made by each country to redress its situation. (RTPY, Triffin 1948, 423)

In later memoranda, Triffin discussed rules of the financial machinery, especially the proportion of the deficit that could be financed with credit and the proportion that should be paid in gold and dollars.

Although Triffin never mentioned Keynes's pioneering work on that topic, his proposal for a clearing house fitted in with his International Clearing Union as a remedy for bilateralism and exchange and trade restrictions.[22] However, Triffin did not yet propose to replace the dollar by a supranational currency; his innovative idea lay in the regional monetary approach to solve concrete European problems. Triffin was pragmatic considering that "[the IMF's] administrative machinery had been planned for a world order in which the Fund could deal with one country at a time in isolation from the others" (Triffin 1952, 270). Triffin asserted that this institution was ill-adapted to regional issues, here the structural European deficit toward the United States. The US Treasury and the Fed were strongly opposed to Triffin's proposal for a European Clearing Union. They argued that this "regional liberalization of intra-European trade and payments (...) would stifle worldwide competition and create a high-cost

[21] RTPY, box 19, "Triffin's EPU proposals...1947–1948," *Multilateralization of European Payments Agreements among Fund Members*, May 7, 1948, IMF Staff Memorandum No. 226.

[22] According to Wilson (2015, 369), Triffin learned of the Keynes Plan in September 1942 when his hierarchical superior at the FRB, Walter Gardner, forwarded him a copy.

uncompetitive European area, condemned to increasing discrimination and protectionism to fight its deficits with the rest of the world, particularly the United States" (RTPL N782, Triffin 1977, 1). Moreover, Triffin's proposal was seen as nose-thumbing to the IMF while the latter was unable to promote trade liberalization and a payments mechanism in Europe. To be fair to Triffin, it should be said that he always tried to integrate the IMF in his proposals for a clearing union in Europe, especially in making the IMF the supplier of scarce currencies along with US aid. However, the IMF remained wary of Triffin's proposals (see Wilson 2015, 472–501). But the ECA and the State Department shared the same view as Triffin about solving European payments disequilibria. After being first sent to Paris by the IMF in 1948 to follow European negotiations,[23] Triffin left the IMF in December 1949 because he was asked to come up with concrete proposals in the name of the United States—within the ECA—to negotiate with the Organization for European Economic Cooperation (OEEC).[24] After nine months of negotiations, eighteen OEEC countries signed the European Payment Union Agreement on 19 September 1950 with retroactive effect from July 1, 1950. Triffin's involvement in the multilateralization of European payments was significant enough for him to be considered one of the EPU's architects. One cannot deny the importance Triffin had in the debates within the ECA in establishing the EPU in the face of the reluctance of many officials in US administrations and at the IMF.

The EPU incorporated the broad lines of proposals outlined by Triffin a few years previously. Under the compensation mechanism, at the end of each month, each EPU member country's net balances with each other country were reported to the Bank of International Settlements,[25] the EPU's financial agent, which offset claims not to individual countries but to the Union as a whole. All that mattered was the net position of each

[23] It was Triffin's request to be the first technical representative of the IMF in Western Europe. Triffin (1981, fn2, 243) recalled that he was appointed "Roving Technical Head of the IMF in Europe," reflecting the absence of a clear definition of his role there. Actually, he took the opportunity to follow closely the discussions between European countries and to develop his own ideas on possible remedies, prompting calls to order by Bernstein, his IMF superior (Wilson 2015, 484–96).

[24] This CEEC was converted into the Organization for European Economic Cooperation in April 1948.

[25] Even in the EPU operation, the IMF decided not to play a role.

country vis-à-vis the rest of the group. Under the payment mechanism, net debts could be financed initially with credits, but eventually these liabilities had to be settled in dollars and gold. As in Keynes' plan, the weight of the external adjustment was borne by both the deficit countries and surplus countries. The payment in gold or dollars was determined by a quota allocated to members and by a scheme of borrowing rights and lending obligations (see Appendix). Contrary to Keynes' proposal, the EPU architects, including Triffin, rejected the idea of an automatic mechanism in the credits granted by surplus to deficit countries beyond the quota credits. They advocated a case by case evaluation of the opportuneness of granting credits, through the control of the EPU's Managing Board. Moreover, the Board was empowered to monitor the economic policies of member countries and to formulate recommendations in the event of a permanent balance of payments disequilibrium.

Triffin's criticisms of the inadequacy of the IMF architecture for promoting multilateralization echoed the debates between Keynes and White in the early 1940s. The international monetary system did not provide a mechanism to meet European demand for dollars. In the absence of such a system and to reduce this demand, the EPU coupled with the Marshall Plan were set up and temporarily solved the scarce currency problem. The ECA allocated dollars to the estimated needs, i.e., to buy US goods, and allowed additional funds to cover the probable net outgoing of dollars from the system.[26] To a certain extent, the EPU completed its task successfully and while it was expected to come to an end in 1952, the EPU was continued until 1958 when the participating countries restored current account convertibility. Between 1950 and 1958, three quarters of participating countries' balances were offset, the remaining quarter necessitated payment in gold and dollars. The savings in means of settlements was obvious. Moreover, over the same period, European trade had more than doubled in value. The EPU Agreement helped to stimulate trade between European countries, to deter them from discriminating among their trading partners and tended to reduce trade and exchange transactions between participating countries. Nevertheless, Triffin acknowledged that even if the "EPU system

[26]The Marshall Plan helped to establish the EPU's working capital ($350 million) and in addition gave assistance to structural debtor members. In his 1948 memorandum, Triffin (RTPY 1948, 5) had proposed an external aid of $338 million to constitute the Clearing's working capital.

has restored multilateralism over a wide area, [it] has left intact—and might even increase—discrimination against the dollar area" (1952, 299). Indeed, in the EPU framework, European countries were able to maintain their exchange and trade restrictions toward the United States. Triffin pointed out that the absence of trade liberalization toward the United States by European countries was no more than the scarce currency clause (Article VII of the IMF) put into practice:

> I argued that mutual preferences decided by the EPU were only the equivalent of the clause 7 of scarce currencies, but expressed in a positive form rather than negative, and therefore more readily acceptable to public opinion and the US Congress. (our translation, Triffin, in Ferrant et al. 2010, 39)

Without resorting to full currency convertibility and relying on the clearing mechanism in a framework of regional cooperation, European countries succeeded in coping with the dollar shortage and bilateralism. Although Triffin was not the first to propose a clearing mechanism,[27] he became a leading figure in both negotiating the EPU at the end of the 1940s and promoting the idea of multilateralization of payments.

It is worth recalling that Triffin met Jean Monnet for the first time in 1948 in Paris during the OEEC discussions. From the outset, they disagreed over the tactics to be adopted to promote Monnet's ultimate aim: the completion of the European Monetary Union as an essential element of his political union; the United States of Europe. Triffin shared his enthusiasm but considered that the monetary integration of European countries should be accomplished by stages, starting with the EPU. Monnet was skeptical about the Triffin project, which was considered too modest and insufficient. The success of the EPU swept away Monnet's skepticism.

[27] See Kaplan and Schleiminger (1989, 360–63) for an account of the source of ideas at the origin of the EPU.

5 Triffin's Support for Closer European Integration

In this section, we examine Triffin's further reflections and proposals for closer monetary integration in Europe in the 1950s. According to Triffin (1960), the gold exchange standard was unable to provide a sustainable amount of international liquidity without impeding the stability of the whole international monetary structure. The composition of international reserves appeared problematic in the late 1950s since the dollar shortage was replaced by a dollar glut, weakening the net reserve position for the United States. Further provision of international reserves appears to have arisen from the United States' decision to run a large deficit in its current account or to export capital to foreign countries. In other words, under the gold exchange standard regime, the international liquidity issue was tied entirely to the circumstances and policy of the United States.

Before presenting the problem—the Triffin dilemma—in those terms in his 1960 book, Triffin developed in the early 1950s a bottom-up approach to reforming the international monetary system: his involvement in the EPU provided him with the theoretical and empirical basis for advocating first the systematic extension of the compensation mechanism to third countries and second the development of another form of liquidity. In a November 1951 memorandum sent to the ECA, entitled *The Path from EPU to European Monetary Integration*, Triffin argued that worldwide cooperation was to be decentralized, "promoting a closer integration between neighboring countries than would be either objectively desirable or politically feasible in a broader framework" (1951, 451). The EPU was an example of a first step toward regional monetary integration and was not considered by Triffin to be an alternative to the IMF's objectives. On the contrary, far from being the IMF's rival, the EPU was an integral part of the international cooperation framework. So, the formulation of the Triffin dilemma results from his willingness to further regional monetary integration under the leadership of a reformed IMF. As stated earlier, the formulation of the Triffin dilemma was the consequence and not the cause of Triffin's involvement in regional monetary integration.

As one of the EPU architects and the US representatives at the OEEC since 1949, Triffin became the US alternate representative on the EPU's Managing Board. In disagreement with the instructions he received from the new US administration, Triffin resigned in August 1951[28] and was made professor at Yale University until 1977. After several years of negotiations about international monetary issues, both in Washington and in Europe, Triffin strengthened his conviction that monetary reforms had to be implemented at the regional level. In a memorandum, dated July 31, 1953 and entitled *Convertibility and the EPU*, Triffin saw Keynes' Clearing Union as an "ideal one" (RTPL N593, Triffin 1953, 9) but regarded it "as still premature and utopian" (ibid.). Moreover, Triffin remained pragmatic and pointed out the practicability of closer regional integration rather than the centralized approach promoted in Keynes' plan:

> (…) It is extremely difficult to create an effective form for quick negotiation among fifty countries or more, on the multiple issues for discretionary decisions by the Union: monetary policy, commercial policy, exchange rates, etc. Such discussions and negotiations can be conducted effectively only between a limited number of participants, all interested in the question at issue, highly interdependent on one another's decisions, keenly aware of this interdependence, and willing to trust one another to fulfill the obligations assumed. (RTPL N593, Triffin 1953, 9)

The degree of coordination to be pursued should depend upon a weighing of the advantages and urgency of centralized decisions against the real costs and friction inseparable from such centralization. Triffin understood well that many issues of trade or exchange policy arise primarily among a limited group of countries and could be most fruitfully explored first through regional negotiation. An agreement to resurge trade between European countries was not forced to wait upon the agreement of a landlocked country, such as Australia. About two-thirds of EPU trade took place within the EPU area. Considerable progress was achieved with greater ease and speed by direct discussion among countries vitally concerned and should not be delayed or impeded unnecessarily by insistence on a worldwide negotiation of all the issues involved.

Along the same lines, Triffin considered that the generalization of EPU principles to a decentralized international monetary system was a better

[28] Triffin recalled this event in his career without shedding light on the content of US instructions. However, it could be assumed that the US administration wanted to undermine the EPU. See Ferrant et al. (2010, 41).

way to prepare the return to full currency convertibility. From the early 1950s, Triffin never stopped believing that "the EPU Agreement [was] only the first of many steps on a long road toward the eventual integration of European monetary policies and institutions" (Triffin 1966, 449).

On a regional scale, Triffin proposed to deal with monetary integration in depth. His final objective was to transform the EPU into a European Central Bank (ECB), able to lend and rediscount to national central banks, with a unit of account that could also be a means of payment between countries and centralizing participating countries' international reserves. These three features of such an institution could lead to the creation of a single currency area in which a European currency would be used for international transactions without removing national currencies for national transactions. Triffin acknowledged that this would be the natural way forward for the EPU:

> The evident value of EPU to its members will ensure their loyalty and their desire to strengthen and develop it themselves, as required by the logic of events. I, for one, feel confident that this will transform fairly rapidly EPU into a Central Reserve Bank for Europe, and may even end up in something approximating a single currency area. (Triffin 1951, 458)

This long-run view shaped Triffin's proposals to deepen European monetary integration. The first step toward fuller monetary integration in Europe was to build a joint reserve fund for European countries:

> Such centralization of reserves is certainly one of the first prerequisites and functions of a European Central Bank. (Triffin 1951, 459)

The concentration in the hands of the ECB of international reserves originally held by European countries in their own central banks would be a means to save on gold and dollars. The excess credit, for countries running a net surplus position beyond the quota against other European countries would be settled in convertible accounts rather than in dollars or gold. The cash saved could guarantee those accounts. According to Triffin:

> Unspectacular in itself, the convertible account technique would set in motion the very mechanism out of which modern banking actually developed over the course of history. (Triffin 1951, 459)

The second step toward fuller monetary integration was the strengthening of the EPU managing board's influence over its member countries' monetary policies to avoid excessive current account deficits or surpluses. Indeed, according to Triffin, one of the major shortcomings of the IMF agreed rules was the reaffirmation of untrammeled national sovereignty on international monetary policy and exchange rates. The incompatible use of national sovereignty by member countries could be truly effective for most of them. A stable European order supposed that incompatible policies were bound to be made compatible through effective harmonization and mergers of ex ante policies which were mutually supporting. With the centralization of reserves and the convertible account technique, the ECB "could place [gold and dollars] at the disposal of its members in case of need" (Triffin 1951, 459). In that way, it could reinforce the influence of the EPU managing board by placing at their disposal larger financial resources to "back up its advice to members" (ibid.).

The perpetuation of the EPU through the centralization of reserves was a recurrent idea in Triffin's works during the 1950s. Triffin recalled the importance of creating convertible accounts to facilitate monetary transfers inside the EPU and with the dollar area. In order to strengthen the ability of the EPU to lend more to member countries, the latter would have to contribute to the increase in the EPU's working capital "to finance automatic or special assistance overdraft facilities to the countries whose convertible account is exhausted, and who lack other resources or current earnings to replenish it" (RTPL N593, Triffin 1953, 13). By centralizing EPU members' reserves, "the convertible account system should develop EPU into a major monetary center attracting a portion at least of the monetary reserves of non-member countries as well as of member countries" (ibid.). This would require the development of the EPU unit of account into a regional means of exchange and store of value (Triffin 1951, 452). Drawing on his experience, Triffin tried to set up an institution in charge of monetary flows between Europe and the Dollar area through the collective management of national reserves (Bussière and Feiertag 2012, 76). This European monetary framework would aim at avoiding the dollar shortage experienced by European countries in the second half of the 1940s while reinforcing monetary integration at the regional level. It should be noted that Triffin advocated the creation of European liquidity without yet considering the suppression of the dollar and gold, that is to say, the pillars of the gold exchange standard.

Triffin's advocacy of a European reserve fund was reiterated in 1955 when the European Monetary Agreement was signed with a view to replacing the EPU in time.[29] This agreement provided for a fund to lend short term to weaker European countries. These loans enabled them to achieve the return to currency convertibility. According to Triffin, this fund was not ambitious enough and he "advocated the transformation of the EPU into a European Clearing House that would also pool about 20% of the total gold and foreign exchange reserves held by European central banks" (Maes and Buyst 2004, 433). Despite Triffin's warnings, in December 1958, the EPU was cleared and all European countries returned to full currency convertibility. At that point, Triffin tried to warn that the risk of returning to full currency convertibility without more cooperation between countries to ensure the operation of the international monetary system would be a blind alley. This analysis was expounded in his 1960 *Gold and the Dollar Crisis*.

As reminded by Bordo (1993, 61), the IMF questioned the level of international liquidity to meet countries' need at a time when world trade was increasing. In a 1958 report, the IMF recommended the increase in members' quotas to face the return to currencies convertibility in an expanding world. In his 1960 book, Triffin tackled the same issue asserting that the whole international monetary system was not adequate to the growing needs of international liquidity. Indeed, making his diagnosis on the evolution of the international monetary system, Triffin forecasted that if the United States corrected its persistent balance of payments deficit,[30] the gold production at 35$ an ounce would not be sufficient to meet the growth of the needs of international reserves and lead to a deflationary bias. On the other hand, if the United States kept running deficits, its foreign liabilities—dollars balances held by foreign countries—would excess by far the American ability to convert these assets

[29] Monnet supported Triffin's proposal to transform the UEP into a European reserve fund with conviction and enthusiasm.

[30] We need be more precise when we use the term "persistent balance of payments deficit." Indeed, until the early 1970s, the US ran a current account surplus with the world. When Charles de Gaulle's Finance Minister, Valéry Giscard d'Estaing, spoke of the US "exorbitant privilege" in the 1960s, he referred to the ability for the United States to borrow on short term easily and at low cost to lend on long term to the rest of the world. In other words, "the source of the dollar balances accumulated abroad was net capital outflows, nor current account deficits" (Portes 2012, 196).

in gold on demand and resulting in the suspension of the gold exchange standard by the United States.

> The most fundamental deficiency of the present system, and the main danger to its future stability, lies on the fact that it leaves the satisfactory development of world monetary liquidity primarily dependent upon an admittedly insufficient supply of new gold and an admittedly dangerous and haphazard expansion in the short-term indebtedness of the key currencies countries. (Triffin 1960, 100)

This diagnosis was at the core of Triffin's analysis when he pointed out the dangerous state and prospects of international liquidity: higher will be the growth of world trade, the more international reserves countries will need (Triffin 1960, 49). According to Triffin (1960, 61), since the end of the 1940s, the American gold reserves decreased from $24.6 billion in 1949 to $20.6 billion in 1958. At the same time, dollar balances held by foreign countries for official and private transactions shoot up from $6.4 billion in 1949 to $15.6 billion in 1958. The haphazardly development of this structure of international reserves threatened all of the international monetary and financial architecture, which would lead to the collapse of the gold exchange standard in a case of a confidence crisis. Triffin explicitly drew the parallel between 1931 and a probable demise of the Bretton Woods system:

> This [the run on key currencies and flight to gold] happened to the United Kingdom in 1931. The collapse was then brought about by large shifts of sterling balances into gold and dollars, leading to the devaluation of sterling. (Triffin 1960, 67)

Triffin put to the light the inconsistency of the gold exchange standard. To some extent, the threat of a crisis confidence in dollars denominated assets holdings increased the instability of all the international reserve system.[31]

[31] In his 1957 *Europe and the Money Muddle*, Triffin already forecast the formulation of the dilemma: "The enormous improvement of foreign countries' reserves which has taken place in recent years has been primarily the result of vast redistribution of net reserves from the United States to the rest of the world (…) it is evident that such a movement could not continue indefinitely without eventually undermining confidence in the dollar itself" (Triffin 1957, 296–97).

This diagnosis was not only an alarming observation of the actual working of the Bretton Woods system and its prospects, but also an acknowledgment of failure of the regional monetary integration. Indeed, *Gold and the Dollar Crisis* has to be read in a historical perspective, that is to say the abandonment of the EPU when European countries returned to currency convertibility. As clearly summarized by Maes and Buyst (2004, 433):

> It is very remarkable that, in 1955-1957, the six "Schuman" countries made two very different choices: a regional one for the integration of goods markets, with the Rome Treaty, and a worldwide one for monetary integration, with complete convertibility in the framework of the Bretton Woods system.

To get out of the dilemma, Triffin strengthens his former proposals to reform the international monetary system.

The first level would be the development of regional monetary integration, on the European example. In that scale, a regional central bank would offset balances between countries, centralize reserves and grant credits to deficit countries. Actually, Triffin iterated the same propositions as before:

> The participating countries would establish jointly a Clearing House centralizing all payments among their separate central banks. These payments would be effected through corresponding debits and credits to the account maintained by each central bank with the Clearing House. (Triffin 1960, 124)

The resources of the clearing would be made up of gold and convertible foreign currencies, in order to maintain the convertibility of participating countries' accounts. As highlighted by Triffin, this reform proposal for European countries "would be regional, rather than world-wide in scope, (...), and could probably negotiated and implemented more easily, more rapidly and more fully within such a framework" (1960, 125). So Triffin supported regional monetary integration, on the European example, but for others regional zones like Latin American and African Countries.[32]

[32] Triffin's efforts to promote regional trade and payments agreements in Latin American countries, Asia or Africa were important since the 1950s. See Triffin (1966, Chaps. XII and XIII).

However, Triffin's plan suffers from defects, rightly highlighted by Maes (2016), concerning the ins and outs of closer regional monetary integration. Indeed, Triffin did not make a significant distinction between a monetary union and a fixed exchange rates system explaining that in both case, countries have to "subordinate their internal monetary and credit expansion to the maintenance of equilibrium in their balance of payments" (Triffin 1957, 289). In the light of the recent euro zone crisis, Maes (2016, 65) reminded that, under a monetary union with capital flows, disequilibria are not necessarily corrected between countries. Moreover, monetary union in Triffin's view did not imply fiscal federalism. Again, Maes (ibid.) points out "a major weakness of Triffin's analysis."

The second level of reform is an international one and consisted in a reform of the IMF's structure. To cope with the instability of using national currencies as international money, Triffin advocated to replace gold and foreign currencies balances, such as dollar and sterling ones, by gold-guaranteed deposit accounts at the IMF (Triffin 1960, 102). These IMF balances would be gradually the major source of increase of international reserves. In other words, the IMF would control the expansion of world liquidity to countries' needs. As the EPU for European countries, the IMF would be able to clear balances between countries and propose credits from the net surplus to the net deficits countries (Triffin 1960, 115).

Triffin saw the new IMF as a central bank of the national central banks, whose objective would be to regulate disequilibrium between regional monetary zones. Gold would remain an international reserve but the IMF would create a new international money, consisting in bank deposits. In the end, the IMF would act a clearing house, centralizing countries' reserves. It has never been mentioned that this proposal was already developed by Triffin in the early 1950s, especially in a OEEC memorandum, released on 8 August 1952 and entitled *Major Proposals for E.P.U. and I.M.F. revision*.[33] In parallel to a reform of the EPU, Triffin advocated yet a reform of the IMF to establish a mechanism that enable countries to draw on the IMF to settle any balance with another member country:

> Emphasis in Fund transactions should shift from individual salvage operations to triangular or multilateral operations designed to maintain a

[33] RTPY, box 19, "EPU revision 1952," *Draft Outline of Major Proposals for E.P.U. and I.M.F. Revision*, August 8, 1952, N° 00005.

> multilateral framework for monetary settlements. (…) the Fund should give maximum attention and automaticity to the mobilization of bilateral earnings necessary to cover bilateral deficits in other directions. (RTPY, Triffin 1952, 13)

Far before the dollar glut, Triffin attempted to "reintroduce in the I.M.F. operations some essential features of the Keynes Clearing Union Plan" (RTPY, Triffin 1952, 15). Nevertheless, as reminded in his 1990 interview (Ferrant et al. 2010, 48–49), Triffin considered the creation of a supranational central bank as a pious hope but regional central banks, on the EPU model, could be feasible. In the end, the management of the new international monetary system would be decentralized, regional monetary zones acting under the leadership of the IMF.

6 Conclusion

Being quite convinced that his 1947 plan for a European clearing mechanism was the solution to boost European trade and permanently reduce the demand for dollars from European countries, Triffin began to consider regional monetary integration as a solution to the flaws in the Bretton Woods system. His proposals to create alternative forms of liquidity to the dollar and gold demonstrate his commitment to improving the use and provision of international liquidity. Fearing the unilateral return to full currency convertibility within the Bretton Woods framework, Triffin tirelessly promoted closer European monetary integration and cooperation as complementary to a reform of the international monetary system. Guided by the EPU achievements, Triffin became aware of the inability of the gold exchange standard to provide both sufficient international liquidity and stability in the making of external payments.

Triffin's method was to question the facts so as to determine whether the common institutions and knowledge could solve the problems facing countries. He did so in the Belgian case concerning devaluation, in Latin American countries with respect to monetary reforms, and in European countries. In each case, commonly accepted solutions did not solve the problem. This approach to and understanding of the international economic system, especially the position of peripheral countries, enabled Triffin to be innovative on issues of international economic integration. European integration was a way of overcoming the shortcomings of the Bretton Woods system.

The monetary order that should have emerged from the Bretton Woods agreements was unrealistic. The IMF was not equipped to deal with postwar economic and monetary difficulties. It could take no initiative itself in requesting a readjustment in any currency's par value, no matter how disruptive it might become for other countries and for the world community. Moreover, the transitional period granted by the Article XIV left, in effect, all countries free to disregard for a long time to come the Fund's provisions concerning exchange controls. Progress toward the restoration of currency convertibility by the major countries of Western Europe was made possible by actions taken outside the IMF itself.

As explained, the EPU devised and implemented the concrete steps toward the gradual, mutual dismantlement of controls which Article XIV of the IMF had failed to spell out. The EPU negotiations tackled first with the immediate and complete elimination of all bilateral trade and exchange restrictions, and secondly, the gradual relaxation of other forms of restrictions and trade protection (direct, administrative trade and exchange controls in particular). The issue of fluctuations of exchange rates was secondary in the trouble times of the 1950s. The worldwide attempts at postwar cooperation followed the exactly reversing order, negotiating exchange rate commitments before tariff commitments; the elimination of discrimination before the elimination of bilateralism. According to Triffin, this way of addressing issues stimulated the regional forms of cooperation which were responsible for most of the postwar progress toward economic integration, trade liberalization and currency convertibility.

Moreover, Triffin's method of promoting the construction of regional unions resembles Monnet's strategy in the political arena.[34] Indeed, in the situation of extreme uncertainty and growing Franco-German tension that characterized postwar Europe, Monnet proposed tackling the international global situation by building the European Coal and Steel Community (ECSC). The creation of ECSC saw the beginning of cooperation between France and Germany, and the process of European unification. Triffin took the same approach, explaining "The agreement on the European Payments Union consisted of an exceptionally clear and

[34] Thanks to the success of the EPU, Triffin became the monetary expert of the action committee for the United States of Europe of Monnet. From 1957, he also became Robert Marjolin's adviser at the European Commission.

simple document, incorporating flexible and precise undertakings of a quite revolutionary nature, which drastically altered the entire structure of bilateral and multilateral regulations within Europe from one day to the next" (1957, 161). The EPU was the first step toward closer monetary integration, as explained earlier. The next step would be the creation of a European Central Bank whose features would be a multilateral system of payments among member states of the union; the definitive consolidation of rates of exchange by means of a single currency, to circulate initially alongside the national currency, issued by this new institution.

Again, the OEEC and the EPU demonstrated that regional and worldwide agreement scan be fully complementary and mutually supporting, rather than alternative policies. The agreements and commitments that could be negotiated on a worldwide basis at any point of time do not exhaust the possibilities for further and beneficial cooperation and integration on a regional scale between countries more keenly interdependent on one another, and aware of this interdependence. Despite the fact that the OEEC and the EPU did not promote removal of the trade discrimination to the United States, rather it temporary admitted discrimination to the United States, the United States regarded the existence of these institutions as essential to the multilateral liberalization of Western World. Triffin had recognized the fact that regional framework was the right setting to multilateralism.

The EPU was a successful pioneering effort in economic and monetary cooperation. To a greater extent, the EPU, and the European Coal and Steel Community, were the "pillars of the reconstruction" of Western Europe. As Triffin said (1960, 14), "in the 1950's the European Payments Union played a more effective role than the IMF in the changeover of Western Europe from bilateralism to world convertibility, and [...] the regional trade-liberalization agreements of the Organization for European Economic Cooperation (OEEC), and later the European Economic Community, have certainly proved 'trade creating' rather than 'trade diverting' as initially feared by Jacob Viner, Gottfried Haberler, and *tutti quanti*." The EPU was designed not just to enable but also to encourage national policies of expansion. Moreover, its positive spillovers meant that the EPU was critical for both domestic and international political economy. These spillovers in turn contributed substantially to the process of postwar growth and to European construction.

To conclude, the EPU constituted the embryo of a "clearing union" for the central banks of the participating countries, and for Triffin, the best point of departure for the European monetary union. Essential in this respect was the partial settlement of surpluses in the forms of reserve claims on the EPU, rather than exclusively in gold, dollars, and other national currencies. According to Triffin, this crucial feature of the EPU agreement should have been implemented by the IMF itself. This is the reason why Triffin considered that the EPU, as one of the main institutions of the postwar monetary order, as a key element of the global monetary order.

Appendix

See Table 1.

Each country received a quota of 15% of its total trade in goods (visible and invisible transactions) with EPU member countries in 1949. Each country's quota limited its rights to borrow or obligations to lend. The settlement of balances—in gold or dollars—worked as follows.

See Table 2.

To illustrate the mechanism, let us take the example of West Germany, with a quota of $500 million, which runs a deficit vis-à-vis the EPU of $100 million during the first period. Since its deficit comes to 20% of its quota, it is entirely financed by credit. Let us now assume that, during the next period, West Germany accumulates a deficit amounting to $200

Table 1 European Payments Union quota (in million US$)

Sterling area	*1060*
France	520
West Germany	500
Belgium Luxembourg	360
Netherlands	355
Sweden	260
Switzerland	250
Italy	205
Norway	200
Denmark	195
Austria	70
Portugal	70
Turkey	50
Greece	45
Iceland	15

Source Author's own creation

Table 2 Borrowing rights and lending obligations

% of Quota	*Debtors*		*Creditors*	
	Credit	*Gold payment*	*Credit*	*Gold payment*
20	20	–	20	–
20	16	4	10	10
20	12	8	10	10
20	8	12	10	10
20	4	16	10	10
100	60	40	60	40

Source Author's own creation

million, that is, 40% of its quota. In that case, it can borrow a further $80 million ($\frac{16}{20}$ × $100 million) and pay $20 million ($\frac{4}{20}$ × $100 million) in gold or dollars to the EPU. The larger the country's deficit with the EPU, the greater the proportion of its debt it has to pay in gold/dollars. For creditor countries, the mechanism is the same: the larger the surplus a European country runs with the EPU, the smaller the proportion it is paid in gold/dollars.

Archival Sources

RTPL: Robert Triffin Papers, Robert Triffin International Foundation, University of Louvain, Louvain-La-Neuve, Belgium.

RTPY: Robert Triffin Papers (MS 874). Manuscripts and Archives, Yale University Library, United States.

References

Altman, Oscar L. 1961. "Professor Triffin on International Liquidity and the Role of the Fund." *IMF Staff Papers*, 8.

Articles of Agreements. 1944. *International Monetary Fund and International Bank for Reconstruction and Development*. United Nations Monetary and Financial Conference, Bretton Woods: New Hampshire. Federal Reserve Bank of St. Louis.

Bordo, Michael D. 1993. "The Bretton Woods International Monetary System: A Historical Overview." In *A Retrospective on the Bretton Woods Systems: Lessons for International Monetary Reform*, edited by Michael D. Bordo and Barry Eichengreen, 3–104. Chicago: University of Chicago Press.

Bussière, Eric, and Olivier Feiertag. 2012. "Triffin et la construction monétaire européenne." In *In Search of a New World Monetary Order*, edited by Jean-Claude Koeune and Alexander Lamfalussy, 73–96. Bern: P.I.E. Peter Lang.

Carli, Guido. 1982. "From the European Payments Union to the European Monetary System." In *The International Monetary System under Flexible Exchange Rates: Global, Regional and National*, edited by R. N. Cooper et al., 161–69. Cambridge: Ballinger Publishing Company.

De Larosière, Jacques. 1991. "Robert Triffin and the Reform of the International Monetary System." In *Evolution of the International and Regional Monetary Systems, Essays in Honour of Robert Triffin*, edited by Alfred Steinherr and Daniel Weiserbs, 134–43. London: Macmillan.

Dupriez, Léon. H. 1930. *Les méthodes d'analyse de la conjoncture économique et leur application à la Belgique depuis 1897*. Louvain: Librairie universitaire.

———. 1993. *Reconstructing Europe's trade and payments: The European Payments Union*. Manchester: Manchester University Press.

Ferrant, Catherine, Sloover Jean, Michel Dumoulin, and Olivier Lefebvre. 2010. *Robert Triffin, conseiller des princes*. Bern: P.I.E. Peter lang.

Gomez Betancourt, Rebeca. 2008. *Edwin Walter Kemmerer, Théoricien et Médecin de la Monnaie*. Thesis (PhD). Paris I Panthéon-Sorbonne University.

Helleiner, Eric. 2003. "The Southern Side of Embedded Liberalism: America's Unorthodox Money Doctoring During the Early Post-1945 years." In *Money Doctoring: The Experience of International Financial Advising 1850–2000*, edited by Marc Flandreau, 249–74. Abingdon: Routledge.

———. 2009. "Central Bankers as Good Neighbours: US Money Doctors in Latin America during the 1940s." *Financial History Review* 16 (1): 5–25.

———. 2014. *Forgotten Foundations of Bretton Woods: International Development and the Making of the Postwar Order*. Ithaca: Cornell University Press.

Horsefield, John K. 1969. *The International Monetary Fund, 1945–1965. Vol. 1: Chronicle*. Washington, DC: The International Monetary Fund.

Kaplan, Jacob J., and Gunter Schleiminger. 1989. *The European Payments Union: Financial Diplomacy in the 1950s*. Oxford: Clarendon Press.

Maes, Ivo. 2009. "On the Origins of the BIS Macro-Prudential Approach to Financial Stability: Alexandre Lamfalussy and Financial Fragility." Working Paper Research, N°176, National Bank of Belgium.

———. 2013. "On the Origins of the Triffin Dilemma." *The European Journal of the History of Economic Thought* 20 (6): 1122–50.

———. 2016. "Robert Triffin: The Arch Monetarist in the European Monetary Integration Debates?" In *Architects of the Euro: Intellectuals in the Making of European Monetary Union*, edited by Kenneth Dyson and Ivo Maes, 53–84. Oxford: Oxford University Press.

Maes, Ivo and Eric Buyst. 2004. “Triffin, the European Commission and the project of a European Reserve Fund.” In *Economic Networks and European Integration*, edited by Michel Dumoulin, 431–44. Bern: P.I.E. Peter Lang.

Maes, Ivo, Eric Buyst, and Michel Bouchet. 2000. “The Post-1945 Development of Economics in Belgium.” In *The Development of Economics in Western Europe since 1945*, edited by Alfred W. Coats, 94–112. London: Routledge.

Maes, Ivo, and Ilaria Pasotti. 2018. “The European Payments Union and the Origins of Triffin’s Regional Approach toward International Monetary Integration.” *History of Political Economy* 50 (1): 155–90.

Meltzer, Allan H. 2009. *A History of the Federal Reserve. Vol. 2, Book 1, 1951–1969*. Chicago: The University of Chicago Press.

Portes, Richard. 2012. “A Reassessment of the Triffin Dilemma.” In *In Search of a New World Monetary Order*, edited by Jean-Claude Koeune and Alexander Lamfalussy, 195–99. Bern: Peter Lang.

RTPL, N593. *Convertibility and E.P.U.* July 31, 1953.

RTPL, N782. *The European Payments Union*. Informal introductory remarks presented at the Marshall Plan session for the Eastern Economic Association, Hartford, April 1977.

RTPY, box 19, “Summary of Triffin’s IMF Memoranda and Proposals for the Multilateralization of Intra-European Credits and Settlements (September 1947—December 1949”.

RTPY, box 19, “Triffin’s EPU Proposals…1947–1948.” *The Unresolved Problem of Financing European Trade*, December 16, 1947, IMF Staff Memorandum N° 160.

RTPY, box 19, “Triffin’s EPU proposals…1947–1948.” *Multilateralization of European Payments Agreements among Fund Members*, May 7, 1948, IMF Staff Memorandum N° 226.

RTPY, box 19, “EPU Revision 1952.” *Draft Outline of Major Proposals for E.P.U. and I.M.F. Revision*, August 8, 1952, N° 00005.

Tew, Brian. 1952. *International Monetary Co-Operation, 1945–52*. London: Routledge.

Triffin, Robert. 1935. «Les mouvements différentiels des prix de gros en Belgique de 1927 à 1935. Calcul et interpretation d’indices de groups comparables.» *Bulletin de l’Institut des Sciences Economiques* 6 (3): 267–95.

———. 1937. «La théorie de la surévaluation monétaire et la dévaluation belge.» *Bulletin de l’Institut de Recherches Economiques* 9 (1): 19–52.

———. 1944. “Central Banking and Monetary Management in Latin America.” In *Economic Problems of Latin America*, edited by S. E. Harris, 93–116. New York: McGraw-Hill.

———. 1947a. “National Central Banking and the International Economy.” In *International Monetary Policies*, edited by L. A. Meltzer, Robert Triffin, and

Gottfried Haberler, 46–81. Postwar Economic Studies 7. Washington, DC: Board of Governors of the Federal Reserve System.

———. 1947b. "International versus Domestic Money." *The American Economic Review* 37 (2): 322–24. Papers and Proceedings of the Fifty-ninth Annual Meeting of the American Economic Association.

———. 1950. «La Multilatéralisation Progressive des Devises en Europe.» *Economia Internazionale* 3 (2): 1–28.

———. 1951 [1966]. "The Path from EPU to European Monetary Integration. Memorandum for the ECA." In *The World Money Maze: National Currencies in International Payments*, edited by Robert Triffin, 450–62. New Heaven and London: Yale University Press.

———. 1957. *Europe and the Money Muddle: From Bilateralism to Near-Convertibility, 1947–1956*. New Heaven and London: Yale University Press.

———. 1960. *Gold and the Dollar Crisis*. New Heaven, CT: Yale University Press.

———. 1966. *The World Money Maze: National Currencies in International Payments*. New Heaven and London: Yale University Press.

———. 1981. "An Economist's Career: What? Why? How?" *BNL Quarterly Review* 138: 239–59.

Triffin, Robert, and Anne Winslow. 1952. *Monetary Reconstruction in Europe*. International Conciliation 482. New York.

Sauvy, Alfred. 1984. *Histoire économique de la France entre les deux guerres*. Tome I. Paris: Economica.

Wilson, Jérôme. 2015. *Robert Triffin: Milieux académiques et cénacles économiques internationaux (1935–1951)*. Questions monétaires internationales n°1. Versant Sud.

PART II

Democracy and Technocracy

CHAPTER 7

Technocracy, Corporatism, and the Development of 'Economic Parliaments' in Interwar Europe

António Costa Pinto

Corporatism put an indelible mark on the first decades of the twentieth century, both as a set of institutions created by the forced integration of organized interests (mainly independent unions) in the state and as an "organic-statist" type of political representation alternative to liberal democracy.[1] As the German political scientist Karl Loewenstein wrote in 1937, 'Economic instead of political representation, partly mystical, partly technological and rational in character, proved to be so tempting

[1] Like Alfred Stepan (1978) and Juan Linz (2000, 215–17), we use this expression to refer to the 'vision of political community in which the component parts of society harmoniously combine… and also because of the assumption that such harmony requires power and the unity of civil society by 'the architectonic action of public authorities-hence 'organic-statism'".

A. C. Pinto (✉)
University of Lisbon, Lisbon, Portugal
e-mail: acpinto@ics.ulisboa.pt

© The Author(s) 2021

A. M. Cunha and C. E. Suprinyak (eds.), *Political Economy and International Order in Interwar Europe*, Palgrave Studies in the History of Economic Thought,
https://doi.org/10.1007/978-3-030-47102-6_7

that many countries suffering from the defects of political parliamentarism began to experiment a occupational representation'. Variants of corporatism inspired conservative, radical right, and fascist parties, not to mention the Roman Catholic Church and the 'third way' options of segments of the technocratic elites. It also inspired dictatorships—stretching from António de Oliveira Salazar's Portuguese New State through Benito Mussolini's Italy and Engelbert Dolfuss' Austria right across to the new Baltic states to create institutions to legitimate their regimes. The European variants spread throughout Latin America and Asia.[2]

When we look at twentieth century dictatorships we note some degree of institutional variation. Parties, cabinets, parliaments, corporatist assemblies, juntas, and a whole set of 'parallel and auxiliary structures of domination, mobilization and control' were symbols of the (often tense) diversity characterizing authoritarian regimes (Perlmutter 1981, 10). These authoritarian institutions, created in the political laboratory of interwar Europe, expanded across the globe after the end of the Second World War: particularly the personalization of leadership, the single-party, and the 'organic-statist' legislatures. Some contemporaries of fascism had already realized some of the institutions created by the interwar dictatorships could be durable. As the committed early twentieth century observer, Romanian academic and politically authoritarian Mihail Manoilescu, noted, 'of all the political and social creations of our century – which for the historian began in 1918 – there are two that have in a definitive way enriched humanity's patrimony… corporatism and the single party' (Manoilescu 1936, viii). Manoilescu dedicated a study to each of these political institutions without knowing in 1936 that some aspects of the former would be long-lasting and that the latter would become one of the most durable political instruments of dictatorships (Manoilescu 1934, 1936).

Interwar dictatorships were personalized authoritarian regimes (Pinto et al. 2007). Even those regimes that were institutionalized following military coups or military dictatorships gave rise to personalist regimes and attempts to create single or dominant regime parties. The personalization of leadership within dictatorial regimes became a dominant characteristic of the fascist era. However, autocrats need institutions and

[2] For a development of the themes of this chapter, see Pinto (2017a), Pasetti (2016), Pinto and Finchelstein (2019) and Pinto (2020).

elites to exercise their rule and their role has often been underestimated as it has been taken as a given that decision-making power was centralized in the dictators (Pinto 2009). To prevent the undermining of their legitimacy and the usurpation of their authority, dictators need to co-opt elites and to either create or adapt institutions to be the locus of the co-optation, negotiation, and (sometimes) decision-making: 'without institutions they cannot make policy concessions' (Geddes 2006, 185). On the other hand, and as Amos Perlmutter has noted, no authoritarian regime can survive politically without the critical support of such modern elites as bureaucrats, managers, technocrats, and the military (Perlmutter 1981, 11).

If the typical fascist regimes of' Italy and Germany were based on a takeover of power by a party, many civilian and military rulers of interwar Europe did not have a 'ready-made organization upon which to rely' (Gandhi 2008, 29). In order to counteract their precarious position, dictators tended to create regime parties. Some fascist movements emerged during the interwar period either as rivals to or unstable partners within the single- or dominant-government party, and often as inhibitors to their formation, making the institutionalization of the regimes more difficult for the dictatorial candidates. Interwar dictators also established controlled parliaments, corporatist assemblies, or other bureaucratic-authoritarian consultative bodies. The political institutions of the dictatorships, even those legislatures some authors have described as 'nominally democratic', were not just window dressing: they did affect policy making. Autocrats also need compliance and co-operation and, in some cases, in order 'to organise policy compromises, dictators need nominally democratic institutions' that can serve as forums in which factions, and even the regime and its opposition, can forge agreements (Gandhi 2008, viii). 'Nominally democratic institutions can help authoritarian rulers maintain coalitions and survive in power' (Geddes 2006, 164), and 'corporatist parliaments' are legitimating institutions for dictatorships and are also sometimes the locus of that process.

In this Chapter we will examine the role of corporatism as a political device against liberal democracy that permeated the political right during the first wave of democratization, and especially as a set of authoritarian institutions that spread across interwar. Powerful processes of institutional transfers were a hallmark of interwar dictatorships, and we argue corporatism and 'Economic Parliaments', in the words of Karl Loewenstein, was at the forefront of this process of cross-national diffusion, both as a new form of organized interest representation and as an authoritarian alternative to parliamentary democracy.[3]

1 Social and Political Corporatism During the First Wave of Democratization

Corporatism as an ideology and as a type of organized interest representation was initially promoted by the Roman Catholic Church from the late-nineteenth through to the mid-twentieth century as a 'third way', in opposition to socialism and liberal capitalism (Conway 2004). Much of the model predates the Papal encyclical, *Rerum Novarum* (1891), and was due to the romanticizing of medieval Europe's feudal guilds by nineteenth century conservatives who had become disenchanted with liberalism and fearful of socialism and democracy. However, 'the church's explicit endorsement surely moved corporatism from seminar rooms to presidential palaces', especially after the publication of the encyclical, *Quadragesimo Anno* (1931) (Morck and Yeung 2010, 4).

Corporatism became a powerful ideological and institutional device against liberal democracy during the first half of the twentieth century, but the neo-corporatist practices of some democracies during its second half—not to speak of the more recent use of the word within the social sciences (Cardoso and Mendonça 2012)—demands a definition of the phenomenon being studied, and for the sake of conceptual clarity, to disentangle social from political corporatism:

> *Social corporatism* 'can be defined as a system of interest representation in which the constituent units are organized into a limited number of singular, compulsory, non–competitive, hierarchically ordered and functionally differentiated categories, recognized or licensed (if not created) by the state and granted a deliberate representational monopoly within their respective categories in exchange for observing certain controls on their selection of leaders and articulation of demands and support'. (Schmitter 1974, 94)

> *Political corporatism* can be defined as a system of political representation based in an 'organic-statist' view of society in which its 'organic'

[3] For a typology of outcomes of diffusion in this period, see Weyland (2010).

> units (families, local powers, professional associations and interest organizations and institutions) replace the individual-centered electoral model of representation and parliamentary legitimacy, becoming the primary and/or complementary legislative or advisory body of the ruler's executive.[4]

A central ideal of corporatist thinkers was the organic nature of society in the political and economic sphere. This was based on a critique of what Ugo Spirito called the egotistical and individualist *homo economicus* of liberal capitalism, which was to be replaced by an *homo corporativus*, which would be motivated by the national interest and common values and objectives (Bastien and Cardoso 2007).

During the interwar period corporatism permeated the main political families of the conservative and authoritarian political right: from the Catholic parties and social Catholicism, to radical right royalists and fascists, not to speak of Durkheimian solidarist and supporters of technocratic governments. Royalists, republicans, technocrats, fascists, and social Catholics shared 'a notable degree of common ground on views about democracy and representation' and on the project of a functional representation as an alternative to liberal democracy, namely, as constituencies of legislative chambers or councils, that were established in many authoritarian regimes during the twentieth century (Williamson 1989, 32). However, there were differences between the Catholic corporatist formulations of the late-nineteenth century and the integral corporatist proposals of some fascist and radical right-wing parties. When we look at fascist party programs and segments of the radical right, like the Action Française-inspired movements, the portrait is even clearer, with many reinforcing 'integral corporatism' vis-à-vis a social Catholicism. Although part of the same ideological magma, social, and political corporatism did not necessarily follow the same path in twentieth century politics.

The historical experience with corporatism has not been confined to dictatorships, and in liberal democracies 'implicit tendencies toward corporatist structures developed both before and concurrently with the emergence of fascism' (Panitch 1977, 62). In fact, occupational representation was not limited to the world of dictatorships, with several democracies discovering complements to the typical parliamentary representation. Corporatist ideology was particularly strong in Ireland's 1937

[4] My definition in Pinto (2017b, 89).

constitution, for example, which called for the election of groups representing 'interests and services', while several other interwar bicameral democracies introduced corporatist representation to their upper chambers (Lowerstein 1937, 426).

Many ideologists of social corporatism—particularly within Catholic circles—advocated a societal corporatism without an omnipresent state, but the praxis of corporatist patterns of representation was mainly the result of an imposition by authoritarian political elites 'to civil society' (Stepan 1978, 47). Under interwar dictatorships corporatism became synonymous with the process of forced unification of organized interests into single units of employers and employees that were closely controlled by the state, and which eliminated their independence: especially that of trade unions. Social corporatism offered autocrats a formalized system of interest representation to manage labor relations, legitimizing the repression of free labor unionism by the co-optation of some of its segments through state-controlled unions, often with compulsory membership. Last but not least, corporatist arrangements also sought to 'allow the state, labor and business to express their interests and arrive at outcomes that are, first and foremost, satisfactory to the regime' (Kim and Gandhi 2010, 648).

However, during this period corporatism was also (and in some cases mainly) used to refer to the comprehensive organization of political society beyond state-social groups relations seeking to replace liberal democracy with an anti-individualist system of representation. In fact, in many cases the corporatist, or 'economic parliaments', either co-existed with and assisted parliaments or replaced them with a new legislature with consultative functions, and which provided the government with technical assistance. The most influential theorist of *Quadragesimo Anno*, the Jesuit Heirich Pesch, did mention the 'economic parliament' as a 'central clearing house' of his organic view, but he left its structure to the future (Misner 2003, 77). In 1937 Karl Loewenstein saw 'this romantic concept of organic representation', in new legislatures trying to be a 'true mirror of the social forces of the nation and a genuine replica of its economic structure' (Lowerstein 1937, 423). However, the role of corporatist bodies within the dictatorships was certainly much less romantic.

George Valois, the syndicalist ideologist of Action Française and founder of one of the first French fascist movements, encapsulated the functions of corporatist legislatures when he proposed the replacement of parliament with general estates (*etats géneraux*). 'This body was not to be an assembly in which decisions were made based on majority votes or where the majority would be able to overwhelm the minority; rather, it was to be an assembly in which the corporations adjusted their interests in favor of the national interest' (Chatriot 2011, 65). In 1926, the Spanish general, Miguel Primo de Rivera, was not engaging in intellectual romanticism when he introduced corporatist principals in his dictatorship, proclaiming: 'The parliamentary system has failed and no-one is crazy enough to re-establish it in Spain. The government and the Patriotic Union call for the construction of a state based on a new structure. The first cell of the nation will be the municipality around which is the family with its old virtues and its modern concept of citizenship'.[5] In Austria in 1934, Chancellor Englebert Dolfuss reaffirmed the words of the Spanish general, words that many dictators were either thinking privately or repeating publicly: 'this parliament... will never, and must never, return again' (Wohnout 2004, 184). In this perspective, corporatism was a powerful agent for the institutional hybridization of interwar dictatorships, largely surpassing the ground from which it sprang. As the Portuguese Dictator Oliveira Salazar wrote "despite politics, as a human art [being] forever necessary as long as mankind exists; government... will increasingly be a scientific and technical function". The constitutions, constitutional revisions, and their authoritarian equivalents are a clear indication of this dynamic. In the immediate aftermath of the First World War and the early 1920s, with the exception of the short-lived regimes of Sidónio Pais in Portugal and Gabriel D'Annunzio in the Italian regency of Carnaro, no corporatist parliament was provided for in any of the new constitutions, but by 1938 the number had risen exponentially.[6]

Since representation was an essential element of modern political systems, authoritarian regimes tended to create political institutions in which the function of corporatism was to give legitimation to 'organic' representation and to ensure the co-optation and control of sections of the elite and organized interests. 'Working out policy concessions requires an institutional setting: some forum to which access can be controlled, where demands can be revealed without appearing as acts of resistance,

[5] Cited in Gómez Navarro (1991, 234).

[6] See Mirkine-Guetzevitch (1928) and the revised and expanded edition of 1938, and Velez (2018).

where compromises can be hammered out without undue public scrutiny and where the resulting agreements can be dressed in a legalistic form and publicized as such' (Gandhi and Przeworski 2007, 1282). The tendency of interwar dictatorships toward the creation of 'organic' legislatures should not be separated from the creation of regime parties—whether single or dominant—that provided legitimation for the abolition of political pluralism, forcing the authoritarian coalition to merge in a single or dominant party under personalized rule.

Another implicit goal of the adoption of corporatist representation, Max Weber noted, was to disenfranchise large sectors of society (Weber 1968, 1, 298). As Juan Linz notes: 'corporatism encourages the basic a-politicism of the population and transform issues into technical decisions and problems of administration'.[7] Institutionalized in the wake of polarized democratizations, interwar dictatorships tended to choose corporatism both as a process for the repression and co-optation of the labor movement, interest groups and of elites through 'organic' legislatures. It is from this perspective we revisit the processes of the institutional crafting of some interwar European dictatorships, observing in particular the adoption of social and political corporatist institutions and regime parties.

2 Interwar Dictatorships and Corporatist Institutions

2.1 The Primacy of Italian Fascism

In the celebrated Futurist manifesto of 1918, Filippo Marinetti announced the 'transformation of parliament through the equitable participation of industrialists, farmers, engineers and businessmen in the government of the country' (Gagliardi 2010, 4; Adinolfi 2019). However, even before their fusion with the Fascist Party, the nationalists of Enrico Corradini and Alfredo Rocco were the most systematic ideologists of integral corporatism and national syndicalism. For Rocco, this integral syndicalism represented both the integration into the state of organized interests and the elimination of parliament and senate in favor of bodies

[7] And 'those chambers are only components in their regimes…no legislature in an authoritarian regime has either the formal or de facto power to question the ultimate authority of a ruler or ruling group'. See Linz (1979, 91, 95).

representing professions and other functional groups (De Grand 1978, 100). Rocco's statism was perhaps the most different from Catholic corporatism, since it was a strategy for the passive and subordinated integration of the masses into the state.

Many authors stress the primacy of institutional reform over the 'economic' question in Italian Fascism. In the inaugural speech of the *Fasci di Combattimento,* Mussolini immediately referred to the need for the 'direct representation of interests', which was also noted in the Fascist Party's 1921 program (Perfetti 2011; Gagliardi 2010). Mussolini and the National Fascist Party (PNF—Partito Nazionale Fascista) had institutional reform and the elimination of liberal representation in mind ever since the March on Rome of 1922; however, the 'legal' nature of the Fascist seizure of power and the presence of a monarch who was heir of the liberal period ensured the process was slow and full of tension.

The Fascists' first concern was to secure political control of the parliament, which they quickly achieved, while eliminating its capacity for legislative initiative and declaring the independence of the executive and the head of government (Musiedlak 2003). Following this, corporatist representation was an ever-present in the proposals for the abolition of a parliament that managed to continue existing—at least formally—for a few more years. In 1929 elections were replaced with plebiscites in which Italians could respond 'yes' or 'no' to a list of candidates chosen by the Fascist Grand Council from a list of names put forward by the PNF, the Fascist syndicates and business organizations. In this way representation became 'organic', accompanied with the corporatization of interest organizations, as outlined in the 1927 Carta del Lavoro (labor charter), and the chamber dominated by the PNF. As a declaration of the principles of Fascist corporatism, the labor charter fell short of the aspirations of Fascist syndicalism; however, it was the most influential document within those dictatorships that adopted social corporatism (Roberts 1979).

In 1931 Mussolini called on the Fascist Grand Council to begin reforming parliament. The secretary of the PNF, Giovanni Giuriati, who was also president of parliament, was charged with the project. At the beginning of the 1930s the debate around corporatism and the reform of representation was a hot topic. There were several options evident within the limited pluralism of the regime, with the former nationalist, Rocco, calling for a model of corporatism that was restricted more to labor relations, while Giuseppe Bottai called for a more decentralized model without forgetting the manifest desire of the PNF to dominate the future chamber. Farinacci opposed the proposal to turn the National Council of Corporations into a corporatist chamber because he thought this would undermine the PNF. Giuriati finally proposed the establishment of a 'Fascist legislative assembly' and the dissolution of the senate; however, Mussolini, possibly in order not to enter into conflict with the king, opposed the abolition of the upper house of the liberal era, which the PNF subsequently 'fascistised' (Colombo 2010, 105).

Another commission was then created by hierarchies of Fascism and jurists, supported by functionaries who studied the systems in Germany, Poland, Portugal, and Austria (Di Napoli 1998, 257). It was not until 1936—14 years after taking power—that Mussolini was finally able to announce the establishment of the Fascist and Corporatist Chamber (Camera dei Fasci e delle Corporazioni), and with it the corporatization of political representation. This chamber became the functional representation of the PNF's national council and National Council of Corporations, while members of the Fascist Grand Council became ex-officio members. A survey of its members in 1939 allows us to note a difficult balance between counsellors of the PNF and the corporations, with the latter being—at least formally—dominant. In practice the situation was different, since the PNF was also represented within the corporatist structures (Musiedlak 2011; Dormagen 2008; Gagliardi 2010). Because he had to recognize all national counsellors by decree, Mussolini had the last word.

While initially underestimated by many historians, the importance of the work carried out by the National Council of Corporations and later by the chamber, and its co-opting and negotiating functions, has been stressed both by contemporary observers and in some more recent historiography (Field 1938; Di Napoli 1998). Organized in 12 'standing committees' the meetings of which were not public, the chamber had very few legislative powers: in practice it was the cabinet that initiated legislation. Due to the variation in the leadership of PNF and corporations, the turnover of counsellors was high. According to a report on the first three years of activity submitted to Mussolini by Grandi, ten days were enough to pass 80% of the bills, with just 23% amended (Di Napoli 1998, 261). Legislation was often discussed and amendments completed. However, as one student of the theme—citing Bottai—notes, this was clearly without 'exceeding the limits of a technical and conceptual critique', and always within the regime's boundaries (Musiedlak 2011, 151).

2.2 *Fascism and Social Catholicism in the Iberian Peninsula*

If we exclude the one year presidentialist dictatorship of Sidónio Pais in Portugal (1918), the dictatorship of Miguel Primo de Rivera in Spain (1923–30) was probably the first to replace parliamentarianism with a unicameral system based on corporatism and by the creation of the Patriotic Union (UP—Unión Patriotica) a regime party endowed with a well-defined political doctrine. While Sidónio Pais had earlier outlined a program for corporatist representation, the truth is that the Catalan general introduced a political formula for modern dictatorships in which corporatism was a central element of its legitimation. In September 1923, Miguel Primo de Rivera led a coup against the liberal regime, issuing a manifesto to the country in which he denounced social agitation, separatism, and clientelism. His imposition of 'order' was justification for a transitional dictatorship; however, he held a plebiscite on a plan to change the constitutional order and institutionalize a new regime. This was quickly implemented through the creation of a party, the UP, which was controlled by the government, of a corporatist parliament with limited powers and an attempt to integrate all organized interests into the state with the abolition of class-based unions (Perfecto 1991, 2011).

A national consultative assembly was established in 1927 which, as its name suggests, collaborated rather than legislated. The National Consultative Assembly, the first corporatist chamber in interwar Europe, consisted of 400 representatives of the state, local authorities, the party, municipalities, and professional groups, in a process controlled by the interior ministry. Even while participating in this corporatist assembly, some conservatives remained suspicious of its 'rubber-stamp' functions. On the eve of the dictatorship's collapse in 1929, the project for the new constitution that would result in a dramatic increase in the executive's powers and the establishment of a single chamber, the members of which were to be nominated by the UP and elected by direct and corporatist suffrage in equal measure, was presented to the public.

Some of the institutional traces of this early dictatorial experiment in the Iberian Peninsula were also present in Portugal, which experienced one of the longest dictatorships of the twentieth century, and which until the end claimed a corporatist legitimacy (Lucena 1976). On 28 May 1926 a military coup put an end to Portugal's parliamentary republic. Between the end of the republic and the institutionalization of Salazar's New State there were seven unstable years of military dictatorship; however, it is worth citing the project for a new constitution that the leader of the military uprising, General Manuel de Oliveira Gomes da Costa, presented to the first government of the dictatorship just one month after the coup: 'A new constitution based on the following principles: national representation by direct delegation from the municipalities, the economic unions and the educational and spiritual bodies, with the absolute exclusion of individualist suffrage and the consequent party representation' (Madureira 1978, 243).

Other projects were discussed during the years that followed, but this example demonstrates the importance of corporatist alternatives in Portuguese anti-democratic elite political culture. In fact in 1918, during the brief dictatorship of Sidónio Pais, a parliament controlled by a dominant party formed by the government co-existed with a senate with corporatist representation; however, it lasted only briefly.

The first political institution to be created by the dictatorship was the single-party, the National Union (UN—União Nacional). Created by Oliveira Salazar in 1930, this accompanied the dissolution of political parties—including the Catholic Party, of which Salazar had been a member. The impetus for its formation came from Salazar and the government, with decisive aid from the state apparatus, especially the interior ministry and its local delegations. Both in the UN's manifesto and in Salazar's inaugural speech to the UN in 1930, the future dictator's intention was already clear as he announced the 'creation of the social and corporatist state that would closely follow the natural constitution of society' (Salazar 1934, 87).

The foundation stone of social corporatism in Portugal was contained in the 1933 National Labour Statute (ETN—Estatuto Nacional do Trabalho). As a declaration of corporatist principals the ETN owed a great deal to Italian Fascism's labor charter, although tempered by the ideals of social Catholicism (Patriarca 1995). With the ETN approved unions were the first sector to be affected, and subsequent legislation foresaw a long series of intermediate bodies that would lead to the constitution of the corporations (Schmitter 1999; Wiarda 1977). Social corporatism was strongly institutionalized in the Portuguese case, with agencies to encompass virtually all social groups and professions, but, until the 1950s, when the corporations were finally created, a sizeable part of the representation of the 'organic elements of the nation' was chosen by the corporatist council, made up by Salazar and ministers connected with the sector.

The development of Salazar's constitutional project at the beginning of the 1930s and the institutions defined by him were symptomatic of the role of the various conservative currents supporting the dictatorship and the role of the military. The first project called for a corporatist system for the election of both the president and parliament; however, between this and the project presented to the public in 1932 many changes were introduced by Salazar and his 'council of notables' (Araújo 2007; Estevão 2009). In the 1932 project there was a legislature of 90 deputies, half elected by direct suffrage and half by 'corporatist suffrage'. This project was strongly criticized by some republican military officials as well as by the Integralists and by Francisco Rolão Preto's fascists, while the Church was more concerned with the absence of God in the constitution (Pinto 2000).

The final version approved by Salazar and submitted to a plebiscite was a compromise. Portugal became 'a unitary and corporatist republic', but the president and the National Assembly were elected through direct—not corporatist—suffrage. In fact, the constitution opted for a single chamber, with a national assembly occupied exclusively by deputies selected by the single-party and elected by direct suffrage; however, it also created a consultative corporatist chamber composed of functional representatives. The National Assembly had few powers before an executive free of parliamentary ties; however, the corporatist chamber was to be an auxiliary and consultative body. The Portuguese corporatist chamber, which consisted of 109 procurators and whose meetings were held in private, remained a consultative body for both the government and the National Assembly.

The longevity of the Portuguese regime and some research into Salazar's corporatist chamber allows us to reach some conclusions (which, unfortunately, cannot be generalized given the absence of comparative data) about functional representation. Despite the great majority of procurators in the chamber representing functional interests, a small group of 'administrative interests' were nominated by the corporatist council that was led by the dictator and which constituted the chamber's elite (Castilho 2010). In practice, these 'political procurators', making up an average of 15% of all procurators, controlled the chamber.

An analysis of a large number of the corporatist chamber's advisory opinions during the first decade of its operation allows us to conclude that its function within the framework of the dictator's consultation system, 'permitted it a first hearing of the impact of public policies and to make suggestions about the implications of the measures to be adopted' (Estevão 2009). Finally, it also underlined its subordinate character compared to the National Assembly, given that its advisory opinions were not necessarily taken into account during debates in the National Assembly (Castilho 2010). However, it is worth highlighting that the National Assembly was also given a subordinate role as an adviser on legislation and was closely integrated with the executive and subservient to it in a regime, not of separation of powers but of 'organic unity' (Wiarda 1977, 101).

While during their long existence Salazar's regime and Francoism converged as forms of authoritarianism, their markedly different origins were evident, as they were from the Primo de Rivera dictatorship. However, this apparent continuity between some of the figures and institutions of twentieth century Spanish authoritarianism cannot hide the fact the origins and original configuration of Francoism had little in common with the Primo de Rivera dictatorship, with that of Salazar in Portugal, or indeed with any of the central and eastern European dictatorships.

The product of a bloody civil war, the main characteristic of the first years of the Franco regime was its radical break with democracy and the fact it was inspired by the dynamics of fascism to a much greater degree. As Stanley Payne notes, during the early years of Francoism 'the nominal structure of the Franco regime was the most purely arbitrary of the world' (Payne 1987, 323).

Social corporatism was an essential component of Francoism and its institutions, which began to be sketched out in Nationalist-controlled areas during the civil war, where tensions existed between the FET's 'national syndicalist' model and those of groups closer to conservative Catholics. Not all of these conflicts were doctrinal in nature; some were expressions of the fears within FET that its role in the creation of the new corporatist structure would be reduced. However, these fears were not confirmed, as both the 1938 Fuero del Trabajo and the definition of the institutional structure of the Francoist labor organization gave the Falange a central role (Payne 2000; Molinero 2005). In 1940, when the Law of Syndical Union required most workers, technicians and employers to join one of the 27 multi-function, vertical and sectoral syndicates, the process was controlled both at the state and party level by the Falangists (Garcia 2010). Despite the fascist rhetoric accompanying the creation of the corporatist system being powerful, with the removal in 1941 of Salvador Merino, the FET's director of syndicates, the party's influence was to diminish and, more significantly, the original concept of 'vertical' syndicates was to be replaced, with employers and workers being represented in separate sections.

Under Ramón Serrano Suñer's leadership, in 1940 FET's political committee outlined the first project of constitutional laws, which also anticipated the establishment of a corporatist parliament. A total of 20 of the draft's 37 articles were devoted to it. As Stanley Payne notes, Serrano Suñer backed a 'more fully fascist' political system than Franco was willing to permit' (Payne 1987, 285). The most controversial proposal contained in this project was the institutionalization of FET's political committee as a collegiate co-ordination body between the state and the movement: a kind of Francoist version of Mussolini's Fascist Grand Council. Conservatives viewed this body as the 'interjection of the party' in the state, and Franco dismissed it (260).

Franco's decision to create a corporatist parliament in 1942 was an important step in the consolidation of his regime—particularly given the tide of the Second World War was turning against fascism—and the chief institutional innovation of this phase of redefinition of legitimacy. Religion and 'organic-statist' views of state-society relations did play a central role (Linz 1979). The Spanish Christian roots, the exceptional historical position of the Caudillo and representation of 'the people' through a system of 'organic democracy', were to be the main elements of legitimacy of consolidated Francoism after the era of Fascism.

The Spanish corporatist parliament, the Cortes, was established as an instrument of collaboration with Franco. According the law governing the Cortes this new legislature was to serve 'for the expression of contrasting opinions within the unity of the regime'. Franco, the head of state, would continue as 'the supreme power and to dictate legal norms', but Cortes would represent 'a valuable instrument of collaboration in that task' (Gómez Navarro 1991, 2). The first Cortes consisted of around 423 procurators, made up of 126 members of the single-party's national council, 141 from the syndical organization, 50 designated by the Caudillo and the remainder representatives of the municipalities, 'families' and associations of liberal professions, etc. (Diaz-Nosty 1972). Cabinet ministers and the head of the judiciary were also members (Morales 1977). The large majority of procurators were public servants; consequently, the weight of the bureaucracy within it was very significant (Martinez 1978). The only change in the composition of the Cortes, was the introduction in 1967 of 108 'family representatives', formally elected through a restricted electoral system. Needless to say the cabinet was responsible to the head of state and Cortes was designed to advise and to deliberate upon proposed laws coming from the government. To avoid the creation of 'informal' factions within Cortes, its president was nominated by Franco and the heads of commissions were nominated by the president of Cortes. Few institutional changes took place during the dictatorship's *long durée* (Lasus 2019).

2.3 Dolfuss' Austria

The brief institutionalization of Englebert Dolfuss' dictatorship in Austria was the most complete expression of an attempt at the authoritarian fusion of social and political corporatism under the hegemony of conservative Catholicism (Botz 2017). From the beginning of the 1920s the Social Christian Party advanced proposals for the partial corporatization of political representation and, by the beginning of the following decade, under the leadership of Ignaz Seipel, the Social Christians moved away from democracy. This social Christian leader was one of the most important supporters of the corporatist option as the 'true democracy' in Austria (Von Klemperer 1971, 247).

In 1929 the Social Christians repeated some of their 1919 proposals for a corporatist upper chamber, a proposal that was rejected by the Socialists. However, when Dolfuss suspended the constitution, dissolved parliament, banned the political parties and began governing with emergency powers, the transition to authoritarianism was enabled through the institutionalization of corporatist representation formalized in the 1934 constitution. In this context, the influence the Heimwehr fascists had on the corporatist option cannot be underestimated, since it coincided with the time they had their greatest political influence within the new regime. As they were closer to the Italian fascist model and to Othmar Span, they had been proposing projects for the corporatization of the political system since 1930.

The 1934 constitution established a period of transition, and when Hitler invaded Austria in 1938 a large part of the corporatization process was still only on paper. According to the new constitution, the duumvirate of the president and the chancellor gave powers to the latter. In electoral terms, the 'organic' vote was established and the legislature replaced by four advisory bodies representing the state, culture, the economy, and the regions. These advisory bodies sent delegates to the federal diet of

59 members. The corporatist bodies had only one more delegate than the others within the federal diet; however, we should not forget that, as elsewhere, with the absence of organized corporations these bodies were composed of members appointed by the president and the chancellor, since only two of the seven professional corporations had been created by 1938. The Social Christians were dominant in many of these advisory bodies, although during the first two years of the regime the Heimwehr had more places within them than their electoral strength in the old parliament of the democratic period (Pasteur 2007, 160).

The government had a great deal of autonomy in relation to these advisory bodies, which had only limited and partial veto powers that could be circumvented by the executive. The subjection of the legislative branch to the government left little room for the expression of opinion on public policy not sanctioned by the executive (Diamant 1960, 269). In fact, between 1938 and the end of the regime following the Nazi invasion, 69.31% of the legislation was adopted directly by the council of ministers (Wohnout 2003, 151).

2.4 *The Challenges of Corporatism in the Competitive Authoritarianisms of Central and Eastern Europe*

Some interwar regimes were 'able to work within a formal parliamentary framework with a dominant-government party that obtained a majority through corrupt electoral practices, co-optation of some political elites and outlawing or harassing those that oppose them, and by tolerating a weak and tamed opposition' (Linz 1979, 91). While the form of government divided conservatives and the radical right, as Andrew Janos correctly notes, these regimes incorporated significant compromises that even led to the establishment of poorly institutionalized regimes (Janos 2000). Interwar Hungary and Poland are the closest examples of this.

The stabilization of Hungary following the successful counter-revolution gave rise to a hybrid regime under the paternal but firm leadership of Admiral Miklós Horthy; however, it was under the premiership of Count Stephen Bethlen in 1921 that the new regime was consolidated. Bethlen, as with so many European conservative leaders, believed democracy was 'suitable only for rich, well-structured and highly-cultured countries', which was not true of Hungary in the 1920s. Hungary needed to be somewhere 'between unbridled freedom and unrestrained dictatorship' (Janos 1982, 210). He carried out a program of electoral reform that reconciled a reduction in the electorate with a clientelist 'open vote' in the rural districts while retaining the secret ballot in the major cities.

The second step was the creation of a government party that would ensure, through political pressure and clientelistic procedures, its domination of the system. This was achieved with the creation of the Unity Party (EP—Egységes Párt), which from 1922 won successive semi-competitive elections during the Bethlen era (Batkay 1982). To the EP dominated house of representatives was joined an upper house that was restored in 1925 along corporatist lines, with representatives of the three religious denominations, 36 professional and economic chambers, 76 representatives of the counties and municipalities, 48 life members appointed by Horthy and 38 aristocrats.

When in 1932 Horthy reluctantly appointed Gyula Gömbös prime minister despite the fragmentation of the Hungarian extreme right, the regime began to move to the right. Gömbös had been the leader of a right-wing paramilitary association and was a close associate of Horthy, who nevertheless mitigated the most radical parts of the former's strategy. He reorganized the EP, renamed it the Party of National Unity (NEP—Nemzeti Egység Pártja), gave it more responsibilities in respect of extra-electoral political mobilization, provided it with a small paramilitary section and turned its attention to mass mobilization. Gömbös also planned a system of compulsory organized interest representation based on 'vertical corporatism' inspired by the Italian labor charter, with several professional chambers in which representatives of both employers and employees would handle labor issues. He attempted to suppress the bicameral parliament (through the creation of a council of state to replace the senate) and presented plans for the creation of a new parliament consisting of elected representatives and delegates from the municipalities, state departments, and professional corporations (Berend 1998; Vonyó 2006, 59; Ormos 2008, 254–58). In 1935 plans for the institutionalization of a single-party dictatorship were announced to Goering; however, Gömbös died the following year, and with him his plans, which had in any event been blocked for some time when 'the corporatist system was taken off the agenda' and the reorganization of the party suspended (Romsics 1995, 335). Some of the party's organizations were dismantled, and it was restored to its 'original condition of an electoral machine based on the local bureaucracy' (Janos 1982, 290).

Somehow anticipating the academic discussion on hybrid or semi-democratic regimes that was to take place at the beginning of the twenty-first century, in 1972 one historian of Poland defined the interwar Polish regime as a 'semi-constitutional guided democracy' (Polonsky 1972, vii; Levitsky and Way 2010). In fact, when Józef Pilsudski led the coup d'état that overthrew Poland's parliamentary democracy in 1926, it did not lead to a rapid transition to dictatorship. With his origins in democratic nationalism, which was very different from the counter-revolutionary origins of the Hungarian leading elite at the same time, some of the dilemmas in classifying Pilsudski's regime do not differ greatly from those of Bethlem's Hungary. The concentration of power, the creation of a coalition party, the Non-partisan Bloc for Co-operation with the Government (BBWR—Bezpartyjny Blok Wspólpracy z Rzadem), to support the general in parliament and, finally, the presentation of a new constitution and of a more coherent dominant party were the marks of his governance.[8]

While Pilsudski had many powers, parliament—despite having been diminished and controlled—continued to be a problem for the president, given that it still represented a very significant degree of pluralism. In 1935 a new constitution attempted to limit much that was already the functional praxis of the regime. The executive was made responsible to the president rather than parliament, with article two stating the president was responsible only 'to God and history' for the fortune of the state (Wynot 1974, 24). The constitution provided for a bicameral system; however, the amount of legislation that could be decided by decree was increased. The decisive break with liberal parliamentarism was nevertheless adopted by the electoral laws defining the legislature's composition. The innovation was in the definition of the electorate, which remained individual and direct, although candidates were to be nominated 'organically'.

The parliament (Sejm) had 209 deputies, with the country divided into 104 two-member constituencies in which the candidates were selected by local commissions led by a president nominated by the government and comprising of delegates from local government, corporations, the chambers of commerce, industry and agriculture, the liberal professions and

[8] The predominance of Roman Catholicism in Poland did not give rise to strong Catholic parties, and although the 'detailed model of a corporatist system that made provision for setting a new vertical power system at whose head would be a corporatist national chamber' was part of the small Christian Democratic Party's program, this did not influence Pilsudski's institutional reform. See Kuk (2004, 157).

trade unions. The scope of manipulation by the government was impressive and a homogeneous and obedient Sejm was assured. The upper house was later reduced to 96 members with one-third appointed by the president and two-thirds by electoral councils elected by similar 'organic' institutions.[9] Opposition parties reacted by boycotting the elections.

In the case of Romania, the short dictatorial experiment did not lead to a consolidated regime, but the clear goal was to institutionalize a single-party regime. When, on 10 February 1938, King Carol II suspended the constitution and inaugurated a period of 'royal dictatorship', his first steps were to abolish the political parties, create a single-party—the Front of National Rebirth (FRN—Frontul Renasterii Nationale)—and hold a plebiscite on a new corporatist constitution. All of this took place in the same year. The fascists of Corneliu Zelea Codreanu's Iron Guard, the Legion of the Archangel Michael, did not respond to the royal coup d'état, and initially accepted the Legion's dissolution. The royal dictatorship sought to steal some of the Iron Guard's ideological appeal, adopting the propaganda of 'organic nationalism, family, church and the gospel of work' (Rothschild 1974, 311).

According the constitution, the new parliament was selected according to the sectoral categories of agriculture, industry, commerce, the professions, and the intelligentsia. Ministers were chosen by the king and were responsible only to him, while legislative initiative was transferred from parliament to the king. Manoilescu, the theoretician of corporatism, was an eminent strategist of the royal dictatorship's economic policy. Following the execution of Codreanu and other fascist leaders, and coming under Nazi pressure to integrate them into the regime, King Carol II reorganized his single-party, renaming it the Party of the Nation (PN—Partidul Natiunii), which incorporated the remaining fascists and to which membership was compulsory for all public and corporatist office holders. Corporatism was a minor ideological component for Codreanu's Iron Guard. As the legionary leader Ion Mota stated, corporatism 'is entirely colorless from a folk point of view' (Roberts 1951, 231).

While the Romanian Dictatorship proved to be poorly institutionalized, the same cannot be said of Catholic Slovakia. When the Slovak state was created as a German protectorate in 1939, the expanded heir

[9] The general electorate could send a delegate to these electoral commissions only with 500 notarised signatures, which was a worthless procedure. See Polonsky (1972, 397) and Wynot (1974, 26).

of Andrej Hlinka's Slovak People's Party (HSLS—Hlinkova slovenská l'udová strana) became the single-party led by his successor and vice-chairman, the Catholic priest Jozef Tiso, under the motto 'One God, one people, one party' (Hoensch 1987, 174). However, despite being the 'guide' of the dictatorship and of the single-party, Tiso always had to share power with Vojtech Tuka, who was more radical and had been appointed prime minister, and whom the Germans wished to retain.

The 1939 constitution proclaimed Slovakia a Catholic state in which 'the nation participates in power through the HSLS', and in fact the single-party took control of parliament (Soubigou 2010, 79). The newly created state council developed into a corporatist upper house to advise Tiso, who had in the meanwhile become president. Members of this privy council included the prime minister, the president of parliament, and members nominated by Tiso, the single-party and each corporation: also, similarly to Mussolini's Fascist Grand Council, this council chose the candidates for parliament (Hoensch 1987, 180; Poli and Salmi 2006). As Tiso noted in 1930, the nation was a single set of origins, customs, and language, constituting an 'organic whole' and the implantation of a corporatist system called 'Christian solidarism' were programmed (Nedelsky 2001, 221). All Slovaks were obliged to join one of four corporations that replaced the unions, and the political cadres within these corporations had to be members of the single-party (Soubigou 2010, 76). The new constitution, inspired by Salazar's Portugal and Dolfuss' Austria, sought to conciliate liberal parliamentarism with corporatism and within the single-party, the Party of National Unity (SSNJ—Strana Slovenskej Národnej Jednoty), the pro-corporatist 'clerical faction' was the most important (Jelinek 1976, 47–51; Poli and Salmi 2006, 173). The regime's brief existence, Tuka's more radical faction and the influence of Nazi Germany and of the German minority prevented the rapid evolution toward a corporatist and 'organic' system.

In south-eastern Europe corporatism also made a brief appearance in Bulgaria and in Metaxas' Greece. In Bulgaria, following Colonel Damian Velchev's 1934 coup d'état, both parliament and the political parties were dissolved with the proposal to institute corporatist representation through the creation of seven corporations (estates) that were to provide the basis for the election of three-quarters of the members of the new parliament (Crampton 2005, 159). Plans for a single-party were blocked by the king. Feeling his position threatened, King Boris assumed full power, inaugurating a period of royal dictatorship the following year, with a controlled parliaments and electoral laws that were 'carefully constructed' to ensure government control of the Chamber (162).

The 'Fourth of August' Regime in Greece, was established in the wake of a coup d'état led by the prime minister, Ioannis Metaxas, who was head of a small conservative, anti–parliamentary and royalist party (Kallis 2017). Metaxas did not create a single-party following the dissolution of parliament and the political parties, as this would have been difficult for the king to accept; however, he did place great hope in the creation of an official youth organization, the National Youth Organization (EON—Ethnikí Orgánosis Neoléas), which was inspired by the fascist model. A few weeks after the 1936 coup, Metaxas' program was clear, with its 14th point indicating the 'the remodeling of society by easy stages on a corporatist national basis so that a truly national representation may emerge' (Kofas 1983, 65). In fact, the regime embarked on a 'programme of "horizontal" restructuring of economic and labour relations in a pattern that revealed the influence of the Italian Fascist' and Portuguese Salazarist experiments with corporatism, with this latter being particularly evident in his plans for constitutional reform (Kallis 2010). The plans became more concrete in the political arena when Metaxas designed a 'new system of national delegation' supported by two bodies: the Great Council of National Labour and the Assembly of the Professions (Sarandis 1993, 156; Papacosma 2006, 187). According to several sources, the king's strong opposition to corporatist representation led to the postponement of the project.

2.5 Corporatism and the Presidential Dictatorships of the Baltic Countries

The construction of personalized authoritarian regimes in the young Baltic countries was rapid (Kasekamp 2017). In 1926 a military coup d'état in Lithuania brought Antanas Smetona to power, while in 1934 an almost syncretic series of coups led to the institutionalization of presidentialist dictatorships in Estonia and Latvia, which were only brought to an end with the Soviet invasion of 1940. The most elaborate attempt to institutionalize corporatist regimes in the region took place under Päts in Estonia and Karlis Ulmanis in Latvia.

Despite the influence of the Catholic Church and a generous concordat in Lithuania, the swift concentration of power to President Smetona caused a number of conflicts between the now dominant party, the

Tautininkai, and the Christian Democrats, which had initially been involved in the pro-authoritarian coalition. By the end of the 1930s this party had a youth wing and a militia. Parliament eventually became a consultative body only, and the president elected by 'extraordinary representatives of the nation' selected by the dominant party; however, despite this, pressures for the official party to have a more active role were not supported by the president (Eidintas 1997).

Corporatist economic bodies were established during the 1930s, but it was the opposition Christian Democrats who explicitly advanced the idea for the 'creation of an organic state' against Smetona (Eidintas 1997, 121). The strategy for controlling parliament involved an electoral process in which the candidates were selected by the municipalities and not the political parties that had in the meanwhile been dissolved. The dominant party obtained an overwhelming majority in the parliament that had mere consultative powers. With Smetona being glorified as the 'leader of the people', Lithuania became the first authoritarian single-party state of the Baltic countries (Von Rauch 1995, 164).

After the silencing of parliament following the 1934 coup d'état in Estonia, in 1935 Konstantin Päts dissolved the political parties and sought to create a single-party, the Fatherland League, to support the president. This party was not so very different in its origins and initial functions from those of its peers, such as the UN in Salazar's Portugal. Organization by occupational groups was promoted as an alternative to parties and parliamentarism, since corporatist organizations 'had been a pet concept of Päts' for quite some time' (Kasekamp 2007, 121). Between 1934 and 1938 the regime created 15 professional chambers, representatives of which would later be assigned seats in the upper house of the national assembly. In 1935 a transitional institution to advise the government was also created, with 15 members elected by the occupational chambers and ten appointed by the president. The political system was not made wholly corporatist with the 1938 constitution that created a bicameral system, with a chamber of representatives of 80 directly elected deputies and a corporatist upper house of 40 members representing administrative departments, professional bodies, and ecclesiastical and secular organizations.

In Latvia, Karlis Ulmanis, leader of the main right-wing Agrarian Union, declared a state of siege after several attempts to revise the constitution to limit parliamentary power. Parliament was eventually dissolved, along with the political parties—including his own; however, unlike his

Baltic neighbors, Ulmanis did not create an official political party. Nevertheless, mobilization of the members of the previous party elite was significant. Ulmanis initially ruled via the government, and once the presidential mandate was over he combined the office of the prime minister with that of the president.

The institutionalization of corporatism in Latvia was the most complete of all of the Baltic States and historians have debated the external influences on it, including the Italian and the Austrian (Plakans 1995). A total of six corporations were created between 1934 and 1938, and the old associative and syndical structures were abolished, with the corporatist chambers being placed under the control of the respective ministries that nominated a large number of their members. The regime also created a National Economic Council and a National Cultural Council to supervise the activities of the different chambers. While some observers have noted the fact Ulmanis wished to create a corporatist parliament, replacing for good the 'plenary meeting of political parties', this never saw the light of day (Von Rauch 1995, 166).

3 Concluding Remarks

Corporatism has frequently, and legitimately, been associated with the Catholic political culture of the beginning of the twentieth century, even although fascism had also codified it as an authoritarian alternative to liberal democracy. Although it had a presence in the institutions of some democratic regimes, it is mainly in dictatorships that a serious effort was made to organize political regimes according to corporatist representation (Linz 2000, 214). These experiences also illustrate their use by dictators with no link to the cultural background of the Catholic or fascist corporatism of southern Europe, which suggests it was, in fact, the outcome of a process of diffusion during the interwar period. While there was some variation, the ideology of a single national interest, typical of the a-politicism of military thinking and of anti-democratic conservative elites was very compatible with the 'organic-statist' core of corporatist representation, and the 'successful practical experience' of some regimes lead to its rapid diffusion in Europe and in Latin America as well (Stepan 1978; Weyland 2010, 1167).

Institutional transfer was a hallmark of interwar dictatorships, but the diffusion was differentiated. In the case of social corporatism it is clear that the influence of Italian Fascism plays a central role. In its apparent totalitarianism, the first principle of Italian Fascism's Labour Charter was replicated across interwar European dictatorships: 'The Italian nation… is a moral, political and economic union that is globally realised in the fascist state'. The projects of authoritarian constitutions and labor charters, albeit in less statist versions, generally began with the 'organic' principle. Social corporatism as a form of state-led forced integration of interest groups in para–state structures and of the decapitation of autonomous union movements largely transcends the interwar period; however, the process of political engineering through which these dictatorships provided a channel for complex interest groups structure co-optation and its legitimizing discourse became a blueprint of the 1930s. The comparative analysis of the labor charters or equivalent legislation of these regimes demonstrates the role-model function of the Italian Fascist Carta del Lavoro in 11 dictatorships, the national adaptations of which were an expression of the original coalition that formatted them. Thus in the Portuguese New State, in Dolfuss' Austria, in Tizo's Slovakia and even in Spain under Franco, political Catholicism has a greater presence than, for example, it had in Vichy France or in eastern Europe. However, this mark is already a determinant in the design of a common heritage for the creation of structures of interest intermediation, for the dissolution of independent unions and the establishment of state-led bargaining structures created to defend the regime. Even when such institutions remain on paper, as in the case of Greece under Metaxas or in Velchev's Bulgaria, the outlines are very similar.

Despite the primacy of social corporatism, the constitution of an 'organic' political representation as an alternative to parliamentary democracy also plays a central role in the processes of the institutional development of interwar dictatorships, transcending, and in many cases incorporating, historical fascism. However, Mussolini's Italy has a much more limited role in the spread of 'corporatist legislatures': as we saw above, a comparative analysis of the constitutions and processes of institutional reform show that Portugal under Salazar and Austria under Dolfuss had a more important role. Moreover, Italian Fascism was undergoing institutional reform right up until the end of the 1930s with the creation of the Fascist and Corporatist Chamber. We should not underestimate these authoritarian constitutions since they serve to consolidate autocratic coalitions in power. Uncertainty is very great at the beginning of a new authoritarian regime and constitutions represent 'one key mechanism through which political actors other than the dictator can codify their right and interests' (Albertus and Menaldo 2011, 5). At the same time, the power of parties and legislatures is often designed by the constitutions, making the boundaries of the ruling group less fluid.

The diversity of legislatures designed by authoritarian constitutions suggests the domination of mixed systems of single or dominant party legislatures with corporatist chambers. Very few dictators in interwar Europe had, at the outset, the concentration of power that General Franco had in 1939, and the majority of them had great difficulty with the institutional design of their regimes and had to accommodate the more prominent members of the coalitions that brought them to power into their new institutions. Nevertheless, however appealing the principle of corporatist representation may have been for authoritarian rulers, the creation of corporatist legislatures was much more difficult to implement in several dictatorships, even when it had been part of the dictators' program. In some countries, such as in Greece and Bulgaria, it was blocked by monarchs who feared losing their power, while in others, such as in Horthy's Hungary, it was paternalistic rulers, or, as in Portugal, it was the initial compromise with segments of conservative liberal parties that led to the institutionalization of bicameral systems with a corporatist chamber and a parliament controlled by the dominant or single-party.

To conclude, as far as can be observed from the case-studies analyzed above, the political institutions of the dictatorships—even authoritarian legislatures—were not as many students of fascism have suggested, merely window dressing. Dictators also need 'compliance and co-operation' and in some cases, in order to organize policy compromises, dictators need these institutions that can serve as forums in which factions, and even the regime and its opposition, 'can forge agreements', that can help authoritarian rulers maintain coalitions and survive in power (Gandhi 2008, viii). As we have seen, corporatist parliaments are not just institutions for legitimizing dictatorships, they can also be the locus of that process. If this is so, corporatism, with a single or dominant party, was the interwar dictatorships' most powerful institutional device and certainly their lowest common denominator (Pinto 2011).

References

Adinolfi, Goffredo. 2019. "Corporatism and Italian Fascism." In *Authoritarianism and Corporatism in Europe and Latin America: Crossing Borders*, edited by Antonio C. Pinto, and Federico Finchelstein, 10–26. London: Routledge.

Albertus, Michael, and Victor Menaldo. 2011. "Dictators as Founding Fathers? The Role of Constitutions Under Autocracy." Available at SSRN: http://ssrn.com/abstract=1794281.

Araújo, Antonio. 2007. *A lei de Salazar*. Lisbon: Tanácitas.

Bastien, Carlos, and José L. Cardoso. 2007. "From Homo Economicus to Homo Corporativus: A Neglected Critique of Neo-Classical Economics." *The Journal of Social Economics* 36 (1): 118–27.

Batkay, William M. 1982. *Authoritarian Politics in a Transitional State: Istvan Bethlen and the Unified Party in Hungary, 1919–26*. New York: EEM-Columbia University Press.

Berend, Ivan T. 1998. *Decades of Crises: Central and Eastern Europe Before World War Two*. Berkeley, CA: California University Press.

Botz, Gerhard. 2017. "'Corporatist State' and Enhanced Authoritarian Dictatorship: The Austria of Dollfuss and Schuschnigg (1933–38)," In *Corporatism and Fascism: The Corporatist Wave in Europe*, edited by Antonio C. Pinto. London: Routledge.

Cardoso, José. L., and Pedro Mendonça. 2012. "Corporatism and Beyond: An Assessment of Recent Literature." ICS Working Papers, no. 1.

Castilho, José M. T. 2010. *Os procuradores à câmara corporativa, 1935–74*. Lisbon: Texto.

Chatriot, Alain. 2011. "Georges Valois, la representation professionelle et le syndicalisme." In *Georges Valois, intinéraire et receptions*, edited by Olivier Dard. Berne: Peter Lang.

Colombo, Paolo. 2010. *La Monarchia fascista, 1922–1940*. Bologna: Il Mulino.

Conway, Martin. 2004. "Catholic Politics or Christian Democracy? The Evolution of Interwar Political Catholicism." In *Political Catholicism in Europe, 1918–45*, vol. 1, edited by Wolfram Kaiser, and Helmut Wohnout, 235–51. London: Routledge.

Crampton, Richard J. 2005. *A Concise History of Bulgaria*. Cambridge: Cambridge University Press.

De Grand, Alexander J. 1978. *The Italian National Association and the Rise of Fascism in Italy*. Lincoln, NE and London: The University of Nebraska Press.

Di Napoli, Mario. 1998. "The Italian Chamber of Fasci and Corporazioni: A Substitute for Parliament in a Totalitarian Regime." In *Repräsentation in Föderalismus und Korporativismus*, edited by Wilhelm Brauneder, and Elisabeth Berger. Frankfurt am Main: Peter Lang.

Diamant, Alfred. 1960. *Austrian Catholics and the First Republic: Democracy and the Social Order, 1918–34*. Princeton, NJ: Princeton University Press.

Diaz-Nosty, Bernardo. 1972. *Las Cortes de Franco*. Barcelona: DOPESA

Dormagen, Jean-Yves. 2008. *Logiques du fascisme: L'état totalitaire en Italie*. Paris: Fayard.

Eidintas, Alfonsas. 1997. "The Presidential Republic." In *Lithuania in European Politics: The Years of the First Republic, 1918–40*, edited by Alfonsas Eidintas, Vytautas Zalys, and Alfred E. Senn, 111–37. Vilnius: Valga.

Estevão, Nuno. 2009. "A câmara corporativa no Estado Novo: Composição, funcionamento e influência." PhD Dissertation, Instituto de Ciências Sociais, Universidade de Lisboa.

Field, G. Lowell. 1938. *The Syndical and Corporative Institutions of Italian Fascism*. New York, NY: Columbia University Press.

Gagliardi, Alessio. 2010. *Il corporativismo fascista*. Rome: Laterza.

Gandhi, Jennifer. 2008. *Political Institutions Under Dictatorship*. Cambridge: Cambridge University Press.

Gandhi, Jennifer, and Adam Przeworski. 2007. "Authoritarian Institutions and the Survival of Authocrats." *Comparative Political Studies* 40 (11): 1279–1301.

Garcia, Francisco B. 2010. *El sindicalismo vertical: Burocracia, control laboral y representación de interesses en la España franquista (1936–51)*. Madrid: Centro de Estúdios Políticos e Constitucionales.

Geddes, Barbara. 2006. "Stages of Development in Authoritarian Regimes." In *World Order After Leninism*, edited by Vladimir Tismaneanu, Marc M. Howard, and Rudra Sil. Seattle, Washington, and London: The University of Washington Press.

Gómez Navarro, José L. 1991. *El Regimen de Primo de Rivera*. Madrid: Catedra.

Hoensch, Jorg K. 1987. *Catholics, the State and the European Radical Right, 1919–45*. New York: SSM-Columbia University Press.

Janos, Andrew. 1982. *The Politics of Backwardness in Hungary, 1825–1945*. Princeton, NJ: Princeton University Press.

———. 2000. *East Central Europe in the Modern World*. Stanford, CA: Stanford University Press.

Jelinek, Yeshayahu. 1976. *The Parish Republic. Hlinka's Slovak People's Party*. New York, EEM-Columbia University Press.

Kallis, Aristotle. 2010. "Neither Fascist nor Authoritarian: The 4th of August Regime in Greece (1936–41) and the Dynamics of Fascistisation in 1930s Europe." *East Central Europe* 37: 303–30.

———. 2017. "'Ideas in Flux…': The '4th of August' Dictatorship in Greece as a Political 'Departure' in Search of 'Destination'." In *Corporatism and Fascism: The Corporatist Wave in Europe*, edited by Antonio C. Pinto, 272–91. London: Routledge.

Kasekamp, Andres. 2007. *The Radical Right in Interwar Estonia*. London: Macmillan.

———. 2017. "Corporatism and Authoritarianism in the Baltics Päts' Estonia in Comparison." In *Corporatism and Fascism: The Corporatist Wave in Europe*, edited by Antonio C. Pinto, 257–71. London: Routledge.

Kim, Wonik, and Jennifer Gandhi. 2010. "Co-opting Workers Under Dictatorship." *The Journal of Politics* 72 (3): 646–58.

Kofas, Jon. 1983. *Authoritarianism in Greece: The Metaxas Regime*. New York: EEM-Columbia University Press.

Kuk, Leszek. 2004. "A Powerful Catholic Church, Unstable State and Authoritarian Political Regime: The Christian Democratic Party in Poland." In *Political Catholicism in Europe, 1918–45*, vol. 1, edited by Wolfram Kaiser, and Helmut Wohnout. London: Routledge.

Lasus, Carlos D. 2019. *Dictatorship and the Electoral Vote: Francoism and the Portuguese New State Regime in Comparative Perspective, 1945–1975*. Brighton: Sussex Academic Press.

Levitsky, Steven, and Lucan A. Way. 2010. *Competitive Authoritarianism: Hybrid Regimes After the Cold War*. New York: Cambridge University Press.

Linz, Juan J. 1979. "Legislatures in Organic-Statist-Authoritarian Regimes: The Case of Spain." In *Legislatures in Development: Dynamics of Change in New and Old States*, edited by Joel Smith, and Lloyd D. Musolf. Durham, NC: Duke University Press.

———. 2000. *Totalitarian and Authoritarian Regimes*. Boulder, CO: Lynne Rienner.

Lowerstein, Karl. 1937. "Occupational Representation and the Idea of an Economic Parliament." *Social Science* 12 (1): 420–32.

Lucena, Manuel. 1976. *A Evolução do Sistema Corporativo Português. 1-O Salazarismo*. Lisbon: Perspectivas e Realidades.

Madureira, Arnaldo. 1978. *O 28 de Maio. Elementos para a sua compreensão*. Lisbon: Presença.

Manoilescu, Mihail. 1934. *Le siècle du corporatisme*. Paris: Librairie Felix Alcan.

———. 1936. *Le parti unique: Institution politique des regimes nouveaux*. Paris: Les Oeuvres Françaises.

Martinez, Rafael B. 1978. *Poder de la burocracia y cortes franquistas, 1943–71*. Madrid: Instituto Nacional de Administración Publica.

Mirkine-Guetzevitch, Boris. 1928. *Les Constitutions de l'Europe Nouvelle*. Paris: Delagrave.

Misner, Paul. 2003. "Christian Democratic Social Policy: Precedents for Third-Way Thinking." In *European Christian Democracy: Historical Legacies and Comparative Perspectives*, edited by Thomas Kselman, and Joseph A. Buttigieg. Notre Dame, IN: Notre Dame University Press.

Molinero, Carme. 2005. "'Sindicalisme Nacional': Una anàlise comparativa entre Itàlia e Espanya." In *Nou Estat, nova política, nou ordre social Feixisme en una perspectiva comparada*, edited by Giuliana Di Febo and Carme Molinero, 45–77. Barcelona: CEFID-UAB.

Morales, Angel G. 1977. *Autoritarismo y control parlamentário en las Cortes de Franco.* Murcia: Departamento de Derecho Político.

Morck, Randall, and Bernard Yeung. 2010. "Corporatism and the Ghost of the Third Way.' *Capitalism and Society* 5 (3): 1–61.

Musiedlak, Didier. 2003. *Lo stato fascista e la sua classe politica, 1922–43.* Bologna: Il Mulino.

———. 2011. "Le corporatisme dans la structure." In *Les experiences corporatives dans l'aire latine*, edited by Didier Musiedlak, 102–15. Berne: Peter Lang.

Nedelsky, Nadya. 2001. "The Wartime Slovak State: A Case Study on the Relationship Between Ethnic Nationalism and Authoritarian Patterns of Governance." *Nations and Nationalisms* 7 (2): 215–34.

Ormos, Maria. 2008. *Hungary Between the Wars.* New York: EEM-Columbia University Press.

Panitch, Leo. 1977. "The Development of Corporatism in Liberal Democracies." *Comparative Political Studies* 10 (1): 61–90.

Papacosma, S. Victor. 2006. "Ioannis Metaxas and the 'Fourth of August' Dictatorship." In *Balkan Strongmen: Dictators and Authoritarian Rulers of South-East Europe*, edited by Bernd Fischer. London: Hurst.

Pasetti, Matteo. 2016. *L'Europa corporativa: Una storia transnazionale tra le due guerre mondiali.* Bologna: Bononia University Press.

Pasteur, Paul. 2007. *Les états autoritaires en Europe, 1919–45.* Paris: Armand Colin.

Patriarca, Fátima. 1995. *A questão social no salazarismo, 1933–47.* Lisbon: Imprensa de Ciências Sociais.

Payne, Stanley G. 1987. *The Franco Regime, 1936–75.* Madison, WI: The University of Wisconsin Press.

———. 2000. *Fascism in Spain.* Madison, WI: The University of Wisconsin Press.

Perfecto, Miguel A. 1991. "Influências Ideológicas no Projecto de Corporativismo Político-Social da Ditadura de Primo de Rivera (1923–1930)." *Penélope* 5: 99–108.

———. 2011. "La droite radicale espagnole et la pensée antiliberale française durant le premier tiers du XX siècle." In *Georges Valois, intinéraire et receptions*, edited by Olivier Dard. Berne: Peter Lang.

Perfetti, Francesco. 2011. "La discussion sul corporativismo in Italia." In *Les experiences corporatives dans l'aire latine*, edited by Didier Musiedlak, 102–15. Berne: Peter Lang.

Perlmutter, Amos. 1981. *Modern Authoritarianism: A Comparative Institutional Analysis*. New Haven: Yale University Press.

Pinto, Antonio C. 2000. *The Blue Shirts: Portuguese Fascism in Interwar Europe*. New York: SSM-Columbia University Press.

——— ed. 2009. *Ruling Elites and Decision-Making in Fascist-Era Dictatorships*. New York: SSM-Columbia University Press.

——— ed. 2011. *Rethinking the Nature of Fascism*. London: Palgrave.

——— ed. 2017a. *Corporatism and Fascism: The Corporatist Wave in Europe*. London: Routledge

———. 2017b. "Fascism, Corporatism and the Crafting of Authoritarian Institutions in Inter-War European Dictatorships." In *Corporatism and Fascism: The Corporatist Wave in Europe*, edited by Antonio C. Pinto. London: Routledge.

———. 2020. *Latin America Dictatorship in the Era of Fascism: The Corporatist Wave*. London: Routledge.

Pinto, António C., and Federico Finchelstein, eds. 2019. *Authoritarianism and Corporatism in Europe and Latin America: Crossing Borders*. London: Routledge.

Pinto, Antonio C., Roger Eatwell, and Stein U. Larsen, eds. 2007. *Charisma and Fascism in Interwar Europe*. London: Routledge.

Plakans, Andrejs. 1995. *The Latvians: A Short History*. Stanford, CA: The Hoover Institution Press.

Poli, Davide and Stefano Salmi. 2006. "Lo Stato corporativo. Una comparazione fra i casi italiano, portoghese e slovacco." In *Progetti Corporativi tra le due guerre mondiali*, edited by Matteo Pasetti, 165–86. Rome: Carocci editore.

Polonsky, Antony. 1972. *Politics in Independent Poland, 1921–39: The Crisis of Constitutional Government*. Oxford: Clarendon Press.

Pope Leon XIII. 1891. *Rerum Novarum*, Vatican City.

Pope Pius XI. 1931. *Quadragesimo Anno*, Vatican City.

Roberts, Henry L. 1951. *Rumania: Political Problems of an Agrarian State*. New Haven, CT: Yale University Press.

Roberts, David D. 1979. *The Syndicalist Tradition and Italian Fascism*. Chapell Hill: The University of North Carolina Press.

Romsics, Ignác. 1995. *István Bethlen: A Great Conservative Statesman of Hungary*. New York: EEM-Columbia University Press.

Rothschild, Joseph. 1974. *East Central Europe Between the Two World Wars*. Seattle, WA, and London: University of Washington Press.

Salazar, Antonio de O. 1934. *Discursos e notas politicos*, vol. 1. Coimbra: Coimbra Editora.

Sarandis, Constantine. 1993. "The Ideology and Character of the Metaxas Regime." In *Aspects of Greece: The Metaxas Dictatorship*, edited by Robin Highan, and Thanos Veremis. Athens: ELIAMEP.

Schmitter, Philippe. C. 1974. "Still the Century of Corporatism?" In *The New Corporatism: Social-Political Structures in the Iberian World*, edited by Frederick B. Pike, and Thomas Stritch. Notre Dame, IN: Notre Dame University Press.

———. 1999. *Portugal: Do autoritarismo à democracia*. Lisbon: Imprensa de Ciências Sociais.

Soubigou, Alain. 2010. "Le 'clerico-fascisme' slovaque fut-il une religion politique?" In *Vers un profil convergent des fascismes? 'Nouveaux consensus' et religion politique en Europe central*, edited by Traian Sandu. Paris: L'Harmattan.

Stepan, Alfred. 1978. *The State and Society: Peru in Comparative Perspective*. Princeton, NJ: Princeton University Press.

Velez, Pedro. 2018. *Das Constituições dos Regimes Nacionalistas de entre-guerras*. Lisbon: Imprensa de Ciências Sociais.

Von Klemperer, Klemens. 1971. *Ignaz Seipel: Christian Statesman in a Time of Crises*. Princeton, NJ: Princeton University Press.

Von Rauch, Georg. 1995. *The Baltic States: The Years of Independence, 1917–40*. New York: St Martin's.

Vonyó, Jószef. 2006. "Tentative de l'organization totale de la société hongroise sous le gouvernement de Gyula Gömbös." In *La périphére du fascisme*, edited by Catherine Horel, Traian Sandu, and Fritz Taubert. Paris: L'Harmatan.

Weber, Max. 1968. *Economy and Society: An Outline of Interpretive Sociology*. Berkeley: The University of California Press.

Weyland, Kurt. 2010. "The Diffusion of Regime Contention in European Democratization, 1830–1940." *Comparative Political Studies* 43 (8–9): 1148–176.

Wiarda, Howard J. 1977. *Corporatism and Development: The Portuguese Experience*. Amherst, MA: The University of Massachusetts Press.

Williamson, Peter J. 1989. *Corporatism in Perspective*. London: Sage.

Wohnout, Helmut. 2003. "A Chancellorial Dictatorship with a 'Corporative' Pretext: The Austrian Constitution Between 1934 and 1938." In *The Dollfuss/Schuschnigg Era in Austria: A Reassessment*, edited by Gûnther Bishof, Anton Pelinka, and Alexander Lassner. New Brunswick, NJ: Transaction.

———. 2004. "Middle-Class Governmental Party and Secular Arm of the Catholic Church: The Christian Socials in Austria." In *Political Catholicism in Europe, 1918–45*, vol. 1, edited by Wolfram Kaiser, and Helmut Wohnout. London: Routledge.

Wynot, Edward D., Jr. 1974. *Polish Politics in Transition: The Camp of National Unity and the Struggle for Power, 1935–39*. New York: SSM-Columbia University Press.

CHAPTER 8

Pluralism, Tripartism and the Foundation of the International Labour Organization

Valerio Torreggiani

1 Introduction

On the 8th of June 2018, the 107th International Labour Conference concluded its annual works adopting seven different resolutions. Among them, with the *Resolution concerning the second recurrent discussion on social dialogue and tripartism* the delegates gathered in Geneva reaffirmed and reinforced one of the founding principles of the International Labour Organization (ILO) and its ideology. The text of the resolution reported that "social dialogue and tripartism are essential for democracy and good governance" within a society where "free, independent, strong and representative employers' and workers' organizations, together with trust, commitment and respect by the governments for autonomy of the social partners and social dialogue outcomes are key conditions for effective social dialogue" (ILO 2018, 1). Therefore—the resolution concluded—"the tripartite constituents renew and reaffirm their commitment to promote and apply the principles of social dialogue and

V. Torreggiani (✉)
Institute of Social Sciences, University of Lisbon, Lisbon, Portugal

© The Author(s) 2021

A. M. Cunha and C. E. Suprinyak (eds.), *Political Economy and International Order in Interwar Europe*, Palgrave Studies in the History of Economic Thought,
https://doi.org/10.1007/978-3-030-47102-6_8

tripartism" (ILO 2018, 1). One year later, marking the centenary anniversary of the ILO, the 108th International Labour Conference approved the *ILO Centenary Declaration for the Future of Work*, once again re-stating the fact that "social dialogue, including collective bargaining and tripartite cooperation, provides an essential foundation of all ILO action" (ILO 2019, 5).

Initially set up in 1919 within the framework of the peace treaties ending World War I, the ILO was conceived as an agency of the League of Nations with the objective of dealing with labour problems and socio–economic policies. Since then, tripartism has remained one of its most singular and jealously safeguarded features: article 3 of the ILO Constitution states that "the General Conference [...] shall be composed of four representatives of each of the Members, of whom two shall be Government delegates and the two others shall be delegates representing respectively the employers and the workpeople of each of the Members" (ILO 1919, Art. 3).

In 1919, this tripartite-corporatist interest representation solution represented a clear novelty among the political economic answers to the problems arisen by the industrial development of western societies. Overall, since the late nineteenth century, on the dramatic background constituted by the continual escalation of tension between labour and capital, coming to terms with rapidly changing societies became the core preoccupation of the founding fathers of the modern social sciences. Thinkers such as Durkheim, Weber, Pareto, Mosca, Veblen, Michels or the Webbs tried, from their specific disciplinary and political angle, to solve the problem of how societies cohere when traditional customs no longer led to a pacific acceptance of social hierarchy; and specifically, of how societies cope with the unforeseen challenges posed by industrial development, mass democracy and socio–economic grouping.

At the beginning of the twentieth century, and even more in the interwar period, one of the outcomes of these new challenges was precisely the flowering of corporatist, tripartite and economic democracy models across Europe, in both democratic and fascist regimes (Costa Pinto 2017; Pasetti 2016). A great theoretical and political variety characterized the movement (Williamson 1985), ranging from the German *ZAG* in the 1920s, to the Portuguese constitutional reform signed by Sidónio Pais in 1918; from the anti-capitalist syndicalism of Georges Sorel, Hubert Lagardelle, Sergio Pannunzio and Edmondo Rossoni, to the technocratic project of Walter Rathenau; from De Ambris' constitutional experiment in Fiume in 1920, to the Weimer Republic constitution; from the Belgian Henri de Man, to the German socialist trade union proposals in the 1920s, and to many others (Schmitter 1974; Schmitter and Lehmbruch 1979; Moses 1978). Overall, therefore, if "implicit tendencies towards corporatist structures developed both before and concurrently with the emergence of fascism" (Panitch 1977, 629), during the interwar period a corporatist form to imagine and reshape such a troubling scenario assumed a great importance putting, as recently stated by Costa Pinto, "an indelible mark on the first decades of the twentieth century" (Costa Pinto 2019, 7).

Furthermore, at the end of World War I the emergence of ideas and procedures of interest representation in the European political culture coincided with, and was reinvigorated by, the conservative, business-led decontrol movement, which rapidly gained the uppercut in the post-war reconstruction projects, both in continental Europe (Maier 1975; Tooze 2014) and in Britain (Cronin 1991). Here, for instance the "Treasury view" of austerity promptly succeeded to roll back labour gains achieved during the war (Mattei 2017b), leading to an undisputed conservative hegemony in the interwar period.

State retrenchment and cost-cutting processes are particularly relevant for the comprehension of how post-war institutions and stabilizing strategies were imagined and shaped. As R.H. Tawney affirmed in 1943, although the spectacle of dismantling state intervention was certainly less impressive of its creation, it was equally important (Tawney 1943). This chapter places the creation of the ILO and its tripartite structure in the wider context of the post-war anti-revolutionary and conservative momentum. In this context, the self-reflexive stabilization efforts pursued by the conservative political and economic elites of the western societies took the form of a "variety of different strategies of stabilization, repression, demobilization, depoliticization and reorganization" (Tooze and Fertik 2014, 232) of which the ILO was an important element. This perspective is consistent with an expanding historiography that stresses the increasing importance of interwar international organizations directed by a technocracy of experts (Laqua 2011; McCarthy 2011; Gorman 2012; Sluga 2013; Cabanes 2014; Jackson and O'Malley 2018). In the post-war context, these civil servants came to believe that their key international function was not just to organize global intelligence, but also to mitigate economic turmoil, restore social order and make international capitalism feasible once again (Clavin 2013). Together with the spreading of American rationalization and scientific management discourses, these characteristic figures of the twentieth century were crucial in uniting the European establishment against social revolution under the flag of a technocratic truth. Through the inaccessible language of expertise, the new technocrats were in the frontline in conceptualizing and building a post-war global order, which required new modes of governance and regulation, both at national and international level (Maier 1987; Cayet 2010; Nyland et al. 2014; Mattei 2017a).

It is against this flourishing historiographical backdrop that this chapter investigates the theoretical sources of the tripartite idea, whose historical roots in relation to the foundation of the ILO deserves to be better understood (Croucher and Wood 2015).

In this chapter, the notion of tripartism to which the ILO was committed since the beginning of its operations refers to the idea that employers, employees and governments should work as social partners, creating socio–economic policy through formal and informal consultation, cooperation, compromise and negotiation (Nyland et al. 2014; Crouch and Wood 2015). In line with this argument, I consider ILO tripartism as a regime of codetermination that is to be viewed against the background of the transformations of the capitalist ecosystem between the two world wars. In this sense, I assume that the terminological historical variety adopted in the period 1919–1945 to indicate this type of political economy procedures—which ranges from tripartism to corporatism, industrial democracy, guild system, participatory management, economic planning, coordinated economy and others—hides a certain degree of homogeneity of practices and ideas. Eventually, crediting ILO tripartism as a part of a wider multi-political interwar corporatist movement consents to look at the long-term connections between interwar institutions, ideas and projects, and the emergence of the post-1945 coordinated capitalist system (Maier 1987; Eichengreen 2007).

More specifically, as the post-war British civil service acted as "a sounding board for transnational social ideas" (Hidalgo-Weber 2012, 17), I intend to explore one of the many genealogical paths of the ILO tripartite formula, investigating a series of theoretical developments and transfers occurred in Britain during the first two decades of the twentieth century which exerted their influence over the functioning and structure of the ILO. In this regard, the analysis will be centred on a network of British intellectuals, technocrats and civil servants—those who "whisper in the ear of the Wilsons and the Lloyd Georges of this world," as recalled by Lord Esher in 1919 (Jackson and O'Malley 2018, 1)—exploring their asymmetric and different roles in debating, promoting and eventually establishing the tripartite structure of the ILO and its ideology.

As a result, I will demonstrate how British pluralism offered a model of democratic governance predicated upon a specific conception of political economic organization, i.e. a system of codetermination between interest groups and governments. I will prove how, at the end of the war, British civil servants and technocrats exploited the pluralist model as a tool for creating an international organism aimed at depotentiating socialist-revolutionary impulses, which after 1917 were threatening the capitalist order. In so doing, I will supplement and reinforce the thesis of the ILO as an agency created in order to offer a compromise with moderate trade unions and to contrast violent social revolution (Shotwell 1933). In this sense, the entire post-war conservative reconstruction movement, of which the ILO was part and parcel, is not here interpreted as a simple return to a pre-1914 normalcy, but rather as a way of reinventing and renewing conservative stability, capitalism and social order. As Maier wrote, "stabilization [...] does not preclude significant social and political change but often requires it" (Maier 1987, 154). According to this, international tripartism is intended as a new technology of corporatist governance aimed at mitigating intra-group contrasts, eradicating class struggle and promoting international social order. In addition, I will explore the enduring fortune of tripartite practices, examining possible historical connections between ILO tripartism, interwar corporatist projects and post World War II coordinated capitalism.

In order to reach its objectives, the chapter tries to reconstruct the process through which the tripartite idea emerged and developed in Britain since the beginning of the twentieth century, determining the elements of continuity between the following phases: (a) the early twentieth century British pluralist theory, with its attached political, economic and institutional model of group cooperation; (b) the wartime industrial relation system and the reconstruction projects elaborated by the Reconstruction Committee between 1916 and 1917 with the aim of projecting wartime industrial cooperation in times of peace; (c) the efforts of the Intelligence Division of the Ministry of Labour and of the British labour delegation in Paris to establish a tripartite international labour organization between 1918 and 1919. The idea here is neither to argue that tripartism was a specific British intellectual product, nor that the ILO tripartite structure and ideology was exclusively the resultant of British efforts and ideology. Nonetheless, due to the great importance that historiography has already ascribed to the British civil service in launching and designing the ILO, I contend that the cultural pluralist background of the British stakeholders, as well as the tripartite-corporatist planning experience developed during the war, critically influenced the British labour delegation in Paris and, consequentially, the ILO's institutions and ideology.

2 A Society of Societies

In general terms, empowering representatives of interest groups with political powers is a way to put in question the idea of state monopoly of political representation and authority. A theoretical challenge of this kind circulated in British academic and intellectual circles since the beginning of the twentieth century. These theories were based on the notion of a society built not exclusively around the atomistic and individualist political representation, uniquely channelled into a traditionally elected parliament, but on the idea of a society established around the institutional collaboration between organized socio–economic interests and the state. The reference goes naturally to the pluralist movement. As recognized by a recent historiographical literature (Bevir 2012; Enroth 2010; Stears 2006; Runciman 2005; Laborde 2000; Nicholls 1994), "pluralism refers to a belief in or sensitivity to diversity in society and government" (Bevir 2012, 2) and, as many other concepts in the history of political and economic thought, it is best illustrated in terms of family resemblance. In this sense, although the label pluralism ends up hiding a plurality of theoretical outcomes, overall it seems to be characterized by a common suspicion, when not an explicit antipathy, towards the idea of a homogeneous nation ruled by a centralized, uniform, monopolistic state. The reasons behind this suspicion/antipathy were certainly multiple, but all of them appear to have arisen both as a reaction to the omnipotent nineteenth century nation-state, and to its parallel individualist and utilitarian philosophical dogma.

Arising out of an intense crisis of the liberal political and economic model, the pluralist agenda started to spread the idea that a post-liberal democracy had to include the representation of non-political interests—in particular organized economic interests—as a way of complementing the traditional mechanisms of elections, parties and political parliaments. That appeared to be even more necessary in the light of the unprecedented expansion of organizations such as trade unions and employers' federations in the first decades of the twentieth century. In fact, as the massive waves of workers' turmoil of 1910–1914 clearly demonstrated, the gap between the socio–economic power and influence of non-political actors and their actual political power was widely and dangerously growing.

This development posited a serious challenge on the liberal tradition of political economic studies. If the liberal benthamite creed, and thereafter the marginalist economists, neglected the existence and importance of groups in society, considering worthy of analysis only the isolated individual in an international context of competing nation states, the first pluralist school openly rejected these positions and started to defend the standing, autonomy and legitimacy of groups within society. If capitalism was changing society, society required a different political framework. Riding the wave of overcoming economic laissez-faire, and in synergy with similar proposals emerging in continental Europe—e.g. Durkheim, Duguit and La Tour du Pin in France, Giuseppe Toniolo and Santi Romano in Italy, Von Ketteler and Von Gierke in Germany—thinkers such as Frederic W. Maitland and John N. Figgis argued for the existence of a moral and legal legitimacy of groups broadly understood. Thereafter, authors such as G.D.H. Cole began to endorse the idea according to which the process of government should depend on the activity of coordinated and cooperative economic groups, autonomously or alongside parliament. In both cases, the idea of the insufficiency of the existing constitutional structure to reflect the complexity of modern industrial societies permeated the pluralist intellectual climate of the first two decades of the twentieth century. It was a reaction against those theoretical explanations posing the hedonistic felicific calculus at the core of any human actions and crowning the state—intended as government and parliament—as the sole political decision-maker.

Overall, the pluralist project was a challenge to rethink the conceptual categories of the individual, the group and the national community, in order to establish a different, decentralized and functional institutional architecture. In this regard, one of the first pluralist attacks was unleashed against the so-called concession theory, championed by jurists such as Savigny and Blackstone. According to this theory, one of the attributes of state sovereignty was its right to bestow on or withdraw legal personality from other interest groups or associations, exercising the power to recognize an entity's rights and interests. Contrary to this opinion, pluralist writers led by Maitland affirmed the natural existence of groups in society, granting them a real juridical personality independent from the acts of other political authorities. Largely referring to the work of the German thinker Von Gierke, in his Sidgwick Lecture held at the Newnham College of Cambridge in 1903, Maitland affirmed that "if *n* men unite themselves in an organised group, jurisprudence, unless it wishes to pulverise the group, must see *n*+1 persons" (Maitland 1911, 316). Hence the group had a reality that simultaneously was composed of individuals and transcended them.

One of the consequences of this perspective was that, in a world crowded with non-governmental economic organizations, pluralist theory recognized that socio–economic associations had their own autonomous life and activities, existing per se and not by the concession of a prince, a state, or any other type of superior political authority. For pluralist authors the process according to which men associate themselves in a stable association in order to reach a common scope—i.e. the process of forming a corporation, to use Maitland's lexicon—was a natural fact of the human society. Thus law had the duty of recognize the resultant group as a "right-and-duty-bearing unit" (Maitland 1911, 307).

However serious the political repercussions of this approach might have been, Maitland never took his legal and sociological reasoning to an explicit political or institutional level, leaving his teaching apolitical, open-ended, and essentially ambiguous. A step towards a clearer political direction was taken by one of his associates, John N. Figgis, who in 1896 took up a job as lecturer in history at St. Catherine's College at the University of Cambridge. Figgis did not share Maitland's hesitancy in embracing the political implications of the pluralist legal thinking. In 1913 he espoused his own political theory in a volume titled *Churches in the Modern State*. Among Figgis' references, a part from Maitland and Von Gierke, an important place was occupied by the seventeenth century German jurist and philosopher Johannes Althusius who, in Figgis' opinion, had the merit of envisaging a state composed of associations operating in a true cooperative society (Figgis 1913a, 202).

Therefore, armed with a medieval corporatist understanding of the society—what Maitland defined as "a 'communitas communitatum', a system of groups [standing] between the state and the individual" (Maitland 1911, 310)—Figgis commenced his battle "against an abstract and unreal theory of state omnipotence on the one hand and the artificial view of individual independence on the other" (Figgis 1914, 206). Combining

Maitland, Gierke and Althusius, Figgis advocated an idea of society as formed by self-governing associations, co-existing in a broader national framework with the central state. It was, as Figgis put it, a "society of societies" (Figgis 1913b, 49), where men's corporate life had to constitute the foundation of a new kind of state. Moving from a critique to the liberal foundations of the nineteenth century Victorian Britain, Maitland and Figgis started to look back to medieval England and early modern Europe in order to explore the metaphysical and legal status of various associations, thereby opening a research path for a different understanding on the relationship between individuals, intermediate bodies and the state (Runciman 2005).

Among this path, although similar in the general outlook, a different perspective on pluralism was provided by G.D.H. Cole, a second-generation pluralist thinker based at the University of Oxford, whose literary exordium is dated in 1913 with the publication of *The World of Labour*. Two distinctive features mark Cole's theoretical journey towards what has been called socialist pluralism, officially known as guild socialism (Stears 1998, 2006). First of all, Cole always defined himself a socialist: not, therefore, an apolitical animal as Maitland, nor a catholic medieval nostalgic as Figgis. Secondly, Cole was a very particular kind of socialist, for he always refused to believe that the solution to working class impoverishment and grievances had to be inevitably a centralized omnipotent collectivist state.

Cole's challenge to the Fabian Society and the Webbs' dominance of British socialist thinking coincided with the outbreak of World War I. The deep alterations brought about by the wartime economic and political system exerted a great influence on his thought, marking a decisive step forward in differentiating his proposals from the ones of the older pluralist theorists. Cole's most relevant works on guild socialism were published between 1917 and 1920. Nonetheless, what it is worth to underline is that, even before the war, Cole had already recognized the mounting importance of the economic groups. In his 1913 volume he explicitly wrote that "everywhere we are faced by the uprising of the group" (Cole 1913, 19), substantially following Maitland and most of all Figgis in contrasting the conviction that group activities were by definition a conspiracy against the public interest. On the contrary, what Cole sustained was that a flourishing associational activity within the political national community was not incompatible with an ordered communal life;

rather, it was considered both natural and beneficial in terms of guaranteeing a more democratic and inclusive decision-making process. If Cole shared Maitland and Figgis' attention to group formation, behaviours and accomplishments, what distinguished his guild socialist theory was an understanding of the group as economically—or functionally, as he put it—defined. In this sense, the guild model frequently recalled by Cole was bound up with a broader interest in the medieval period that intensified in the early twentieth century. If this medieval nostalgia can be traced back to a moral and spiritual critique of the capitalist system—which had a good fortune during the rest of the century (Rogan 2017)—Cole's most famous sources in this sense were Thomas Carlyle, John Ruskin and William Morris (Cole 1951, 3). In Cole's case, however, the guild idea referred not to the relationship between the church and the secular power, as in Figgis, but specifically to the political economic medieval system of the guilds, highlighting its prowess to efficiently orient the overall decision-making process.

It was with this philosophical baggage that Cole witnessed the outbreak of World War I in 1914. Everywhere the conflict shattered the traditional system of policy-making, multiplying the centres of powers and diverting decision-making from the normal channels of party and parliamentary competition into direct bargaining by organized interests and the state. In Britain, since the famous Treasury Agreement of March 1915, which secured the cooperation of organized labour to the war effort, the wartime corporatist edifice grew rapidly. Especially after 1916 and the appointment of Lloyd George as Prime Minister, several new ministries and technical committees were created, incorporating representatives of business and labour, as well as scholars and experts (Burk 1982; Cronin 1991, 58–81). As the war progressed, therefore, Cole observed the emergence of a system of compulsory cooperation imposed by Lloyd George's war cabinet on certain key areas of the economy. In the context of this wartime patriotic alliance, although Cole feared an institutional development where trade union representatives were co-opted by the government, he also praised the increasing public recognition of the role of economic groups and associate life.

As a consequence, since the war period Cole started to deepen his guild socialist proposals, imagining a complex institutional system where economic groups, whose behaviours and actions were democratically controlled by its members, had to fulfil the political role of expressing the needs and concerns of specific socio–economic sections of the national community. Specifically in the works published between 1917 and 1920, Cole endorsed a political economic model ensuring, on the one hand, the individual freedom of choice and expressions—evident in the continuously restated democratic control of the guilds by their members—and facilitating, on the other hand, the integration of the parts in the whole.

Forging a distinctive socialist tradition of pluralism, Cole and his guild socialist colleagues, somehow paradoxically, provided a hyper-individualistic account of the society stressing, as R.H. Tawney put it, the infinite diversities of individuals (Tawney 1931, 208) and their freedom to continuously re-order their associational priorities. However, what stands out for its importance is that individuals were not left isolated in their liberty; they were not imagined as atoms living in a void. Quite the opposite, individuals were understood as strongly interconnected throughout a highly organized society composed by scope-oriented socio–economic groups operating under the general principles of interdependence, complementary, cooperation and coordination.

As different as they might be, the British pluralist traditions of early twentieth century embodied by Maitland, Figgis and Cole betray a common attitude to crucial problems of economic governance, authority and sovereignty. All the pluralist writers, in fact, directed their protests towards the idea of state and central government as the sole authoritative centres, denouncing the inefficiency of liberal democracy to accurately represent a modern industrial society structurally composed of socio–economic associations. On the political economic side, this rationale was hinged on a lively British and European tradition of debating economic democracy, co-partnership, cooperative movement and profit sharing as alternatives both to unregulated capitalism and to nationalization and central planning. Although there was a certain degree of ambiguity in defining what economic democracy means (Poole et al. 2001; Rousselière 2009), in Britain this kind of proposals stretches back to the nineteenth century and relates to the works of John Stuart Mill—on this matter deeply influenced by Fourier, Saint Simon and Owen—and then Henry Fawcett, John E. Cairnes and Alfred Marshall, but also of Sidney and Beatrice Webb, although the Webbs supported a different, consumer-citizen and state-centred perspective (Claeys 1987; Goodway 2016; Persky 2016). As a matter of fact, if the Webbs suggested that the only purpose of trade unions was to fight the employers within a wider socialist-collectivist state context, for Cole labour organizations had to be considered the harbinger of a completely different economic and political order based on productive industrial organisms (Wright 1979, 29). More focused on the productive side of the economic problem, Cole identified the cure to the liberal state maladies in giving an active political role to the same organizations that were threatening its existence.

Notwithstanding, although the undeniable theoretical richness of the pluralist thinking and Cole's writing prolificacy between 1914 and 1921, a void concerning concrete political proposals persisted. As Cole admitted in 1915, "it remains [...] the philosopher's task to say where sovereignty should lie, and the business of the practical man to find the requisite machinery" (Cole 1914–1915, 157). In the next paragraph, we will see how during the war these "practical men" took the baton and started to investigate into concrete institutional solutions to the issues arose by pluralism, applying its teachings to the problems of state, economic groups, industrial relations and post-war reconstruction.

3 Pluralism and Post-War Reconstruction

Already in the first years of the war, contemporary observers recognized the conflict as a historical turning point that would lead to a post-war scenario completely different from all that was known. Nonetheless, the actual nature of this changing, the peculiarity of the new scenario and the solutions proposed to deal with the post-war challenges, did not meet unanimous agreement. One thing was clear: as recalled by a group of young conservatives in retrospect, the conflict "shattered preconceived economic notions, removed irremovable barriers, and created new and undreamt of solutions" (Boothby et al. 1927, 35). Debates and disputes were indeed frequent. Intellectuals and politicians dedicated a great amount of thinking to discuss what kind of answers had to be provided in order to solve the political, economic and social rebus that would emerge from the rubble of the conflict. In this sense, the war in the trenches was mirrored at home by a parallel, bloodless, battle of ideas—"a professors' war," to use the words of Delisle Burns (Delisle Burns 1915, 91)—in which the opponents were arguing on how post-war British and international society had to be imagined and reshaped (Cline 1982).

If this "professors' war" took place primarily within the traditional academic boundaries, taking the shape of conferences, debates and symposiums, the discussions were not caged within the walls of prestigious colleges at Oxford or Cambridge, but soon invaded other areas of the civil society. Trade unions, industrial federations and other economic associations, in fact, financed and promoted meetings for debating post-war problems, also at the international level (Tosstorff 2005). Moreover, the theoretical skirmish penetrated several government departments, signalling the emergence of the figure of the intellectual-civil servant, who was becoming the main channel of communications between the academic world and the governmental arena. These highly educated civil servants formed a new class of knowledge-based experts that occupied a middle area suspended between state and society, fulfilling crucial positions in key ministries and committees. Connecting universities, enterprises, trade unions, industrial federations, lobbying groups and public administration, these new technocrats started to play a fundamental role, which would reveal all its relevance as the twentieth century progressed (Maier 1987; Clavin 2013; Kohlrausch and Trischler 2014; Kaiser and Schot 2014; Martin 2016).

This said, it is important to underline that almost all the belligerent countries developed new and similar institutional solutions to meet the demands of war between 1914 and 1918. These innovations seriously challenged the functioning of the old-fashioned structure of the liberal state. Overall, the technological and economic demands of the conflict led to establish a new typology of relations between the industrial and military apparatus. When it became clear that the final outcome of the war would have been the resultant of the comprehensive efficiency of the industrial-military national chain, governments started to erect an institutional mechanism of decision-making in key productive sectors involving the representatives of the socio–economic organized forces of the society. In order to efficiently and rapidly allocating resources and raw materials in a coordinated national effort, an unprecedented wartime alliance was forged between governments, employers and workpeople. In Britain, the Treasury Agreement of 1915—a voluntary deal through which trade unions and employers' federations decided to suspend restrictive practices and to settle disputes by arbitration, not by strikes—represented perhaps the most symbolic moment. Among its numerous effects, this cooperative effort was crucial in generating a spirit of national inter-class cooperation that produced non-secondary theoretical consequences. In the last three years of war, in fact, a great amount of time was precisely dedicated to discuss the option of continuing the wartime tripartite employers–workers–government cooperation in times of peace. In this sense, the war became a powerful example in class collaboration and economic codetermination.

Overall, war economy gave the world a screenplay for a new approach to the resolution of social conflict based on the dialogue between highly empowered economic groups on both sides of industry (workers and employers), and between them and the State. In this respect, unfolding the movement of ideas and projects circulating between the pluralist tradition and those units of the British civil service more committed to drafting post-war schemes means disentangling a complex series of networks, individuals and institutional organisms that, between 1916 and 1919, were working on the ideas of industrial harmony, class cooperation and social dialogue, laying the ideological foundations for the creation of a new variety of capitalism and, more specifically, of one of its post-war element, i.e. the ILO.

Among the individuals committed to elaborate a tripartite post-war reconstruction plan, a key role was played by Arthur Greenwood, who was fundamental in channelling a pluralist approach into the ministerial spheres, specifically in the Reconstruction Committee and in the Intelligence Division of the Ministry of Labour.

Born in Leeds in 1880, in the 1920s Greenwood became one of the second-generation Labour Party's leaders, even though he always remained more of a back-room intellectual than a politician (Pimlott 1977, 26). Before the party adopted a new constitution in 1918, Labour was far from a coherent national political organization. It amounted more to an agglomeration of linked but distinct sections, societies, local groups and trade unions. Within this fragmented organization, each part brought its own traditions and cultures, its own political priorities and blueprints (Pugh 2002; Worley 2005). Therefore, for a long time, Labour encapsulated a countless variety of socialisms, for the most part non-Marxist (McKibbin 1984), conformed to a rather abstract set of values, assumptions and ethical references, such as the notions of social justice, equality and improvement. Other than that, however, there were numerous and very different concrete political proposals. Within this context, Greenwood was part of the (dominant) non-collectivist, non-Marxist and moderate trade unionist section of the Labour party. Lecturer of Economics at the University of Leeds, he was close to the Workers' Educational Association, where he met Alfred Zimmern—a historian and political scientist of Oxford, who lately contributed to the foundation of the League of Nations and UNESCO. Zimmern eventually introduced Greenwood to the socialist pluralist tradition and to the thought of G.D.H. Cole. Both Zimmern and Greenwood were also connected to the early activities of guild socialism in Oxford and London, directly participating to the foundation of the National Guild League in 1915 (Stitt 2006, 64).

In July 1916, Greenwood was invited to participate in a conference organized at the Ruskin College of Oxford on *The Reorganisation of Industry*. In his paper—titled *How Readjustment could be Facilitated after the War*—Greenwood's intimate affinity with socialist pluralism clearly emerged. His main intent was to apply Cole's ideas to the "sombre and less spectacular problems of reconstruction" (Greenwood 1916, 18). Greenwood believed that the issue had to be discussed with "a greater degree of open-mindedness than has hitherto been shown" (Greenwood 1916, 19). Understanding the global conflict as a sort of forerunner of the future on many different levels, Greenwood emphasized the extraordinary intensity and duration of the war effort that led to an unprecedented mobilization of economic and industrial resources. Consequentially, state authority grew massively and the British government became involved in almost every economic area, taking control of transport, coal, armaments, iron and engineering industries to the extent that by the end of the war the ministry of munitions had become the largest employer in the nation. At the same time, Greenwood highlighted, new forms of workers–employers–government relations were being experimented. In this respect, he described how the Treasury Agreement of 1915, which banned strikes and other forms of restrictive practices and aggressive industrial relations, was a landmark moment in facilitating the subsequent creation of joint trade councils. Here, representatives of both sides of the industrial world were attached to government departments as semi-public agencies of industrial controls with a certain amount of self-government powers in their respective sectors.

In so doing, if the war experience certainly set up a formidable example concerning new techniques of government, its legacy resulted more ambiguous than it could appear, especially in terms of actual socio–economic policies. As a matter of fact, basic concepts such as national efficiency, social peace, industrial cooperation and economic codetermination—all widely applied and applauded during the war—could result in very different intellectual reasoning and concrete political outcomes. In few words, wartime economic system produced a twofold theoretical heirloom. On the one hand, the state emerged highly empowered from the war, with new and unprecedented regulatory economic powers. However, on the other hand, self-governing workers-employers experimentations paved the way to a stream of thought that, retrieving the socialist pluralist tradition, was based on the rejection of the overwhelming role of the state and looked to alternative sources of power to counter-balance and integrated the supremacy of central government.

Various narratives of the war, each showcase unique and novel forces, crucially shaped post-war reconstruction proposals concerning the institutional architecture of the country. Majoring on one element of the wartime organization or another could have led to very different set of post-war institutions. In this sense, in 1916, Greenwood argued that it was absolutely "necessary to observe the changes which have taken place during the war" (Greenwood 1916, 19) looking primarily to the problem of democratization in the economic sphere: "industry—he protested—alone of all departments of national and social activity, shows few signs of becoming democratic" (Greenwood 1916, 24). Here, the model of wartime economy stood out as a real breaking point in the history of humanity. As Greenwood phrased in a 1915 co-edited book, "the society of yesterday can never return [...] because of the growth of new ideas under the stimulus of the war" (Greenwood 1915, 303). Those ideas, as well as their concrete resultant and institutional experimentations, suggested to Greenwood that a true democratic control of industry could be achieved only delegating economic decision power to a permanent mechanism of institutional cooperation between labour and capital. The instrument through which this goal could be achieved was the establishment of sectorial and national representative bodies jointly set up by trade unions, industrial associations and the government. Debating the creation of such a bodies, Greenwood argued that "if there is to be anything approaching satisfactory reconstruction, it can only be by the organised workers of this country being taken into full consultation on equal terms with the employers," thereby stressing "the importance of national joint conferences of each industry" (Greenwood 1916, 26).

It was in this respect that Greenwood's pluralist and guild socialist backgrounds became more explicit. As wartime political and socio–economic experience became a giant example in terms of harmonic national cooperation, social peace and class collaboration, in Greenwood's opinion wartime economic model represented only the first step towards the establishment of a full functioning industrial democracy based on socialist pluralist guild principles. The way of achieving such a goal was extending the war political novelty of tripartite-corporatist institutional cooperation in peacetime. Since "the reorganisation of each industry is a matter which affects the workers as much as the capitalists and the managers," Greenwood affirmed (Greenwood 1916, 25), the wartime industrial relation system had to be interpreted as the base of a new kind of society characterized by a distribution of legislative and authoritative powers among organized economic groups. Trying to envisage the new institutional landscape, Greenwood proposed to establish a Ministry of Labour having the duty of coordinating and controlling the functioning of local, regional and national industrial councils. In this way a continuous and permanent negotiation between officially recognized organized interests and the state would be created, ensuring harmony and progress for the entire national community (Greenwood 1916, 25).

4 The Reconstruction Committee and the Whitley Report

Apart from serving as a powerful political and economic model, the war also offered a group of intellectuals and scholars the opportunity to actually undertake concrete actions to develop post-war reconstruction projects.

In March 1916, the Prime Minister Herbert H. Asquith set up the Reconstruction Committee, an organism aimed at considering problems and solutions concerning industrial and economic policy to be conducted after the end of the war (Johnson 1968; Stitt 2006). Led by Asquith's former private secretary Vaughan Nash, the Reconstruction Committee had a slow start during the spring and summer of 1916, commencing to appoint specific working sub-committees only during the fall of the same year. In this occasion, a specific Sub-Committee for the Study of the Relations between Employers and Employed was created in October 1916, chaired by the liberal politician John H. Whitley, future speaker of the House of Commons during the 1920s. Among the members of the sub-committee, there were important personalities of the academic world, such as S.J. Chapman and J.A. Hobson; two female social reformers, Susan Lawrence and Mona Wilson; and representatives of the most important industrial sectors of the wartime period, namely Sir Thomas Redcliffe-Ellis from the mining industry, Sir George Claughton from the rail industry, Sir George Carter from shipbuilding, and Allan Smith, chairman of the powerful Engineering Employers' Federation. The sub-committee, which soon became known as the Whitley Committee, eventually produced a memorandum in March 1917, known as the Whitley Report, which was made public in October of the same year.

During the second half of 1916, Greenwood was appointed general secretary of the Reconstruction Committee, probably under Zimmern's recommendation, who had already been working for the British civil service since 1912. The choice also coincided with a more vigorous attempt conducted by Cole and his movement to influence governmental initiatives concerning post-war reconstruction plans. In order to increase the influence exerted by guild socialism on the political scenario—"we are a tiny body of intellectuals setting out of what seems an impossible task,"[1] lamented Cole in a letter to Zimmern in April 1915—Greenwood and Zimmern became the most relevant channels through which guild socialism tried to wedge itself into the Reconstruction Committee, bending post-war reconstruction schemes, and especially the Whitley Report, towards socialist pluralist proposals.

As mentioned, the Whitley Report was firstly delivered on the 17th of March 1917 but it was publicly disclosed by the government only in October, right after the conclusion of the strikes in the engineering industries. The report was released on the 19th of October 1917, accompanied by an official letter signed by the recently appointed ministry of labour George H. Roberts. The Whitley Report was a quite simple and thin document. As some commentators pointed out, it seemed that the report was formulated as a discussion basis, more than as a technical operative document. However, it contained several points of interest. Once again the war was indicated as a crucial turning point, a period of important experiment in managing industrial mass society. The ministry himself explained this perspective in the letter coming with the publication of the report, arguing that, with regard to the political situation, "the experience of the war has shown the need for frequent consultation between the government and the chosen representatives of both employers and workmen" (Roberts 1917, 3). In this sense, the report presented a very positive judgment of the wartime industrial relations system. Indeed, the war offered "a great opportunity" (Committee on Relations Between Employers and Employed 1917, 8) and the continuation of its decision-making mechanisms into the future was more than desirable. The statement in this sense was rather explicit and left room for no doubt: "in the interest of the community—the report stated—it is vital that after the war the co-operation of all classes, established

[1] *Letter of G.D.H. Cole to Alfred Zimmern*, April 18, 1915, in Bodleian Library Special Collection, Oxford, Zimmern Papers, Ms. Zimmern 14.

during the war, should continue, and more especially with regard to the relations between employers and employed" (Committee on Relations Between Employers and Employed 1917, 9). In this way, the wartime socio–economic and political model of continuous bargaining and inter-class cooperation became the ultimate panacea of all the problems of the capitalist society.

Overall, if the conflict was interpreted as a ground breaking event in the history of human societies, and in particular in the history of industrial relations, it simultaneously represented a sort of confirmation of the early twentieth century pluralist predictions concerning the insufficiency of the liberal state and the relevance of groups in society. More specifically, the conflict certified that central government alone was unable to improve industrial efficiency and ensure social peace; on the other hand, the war proved how a decentralized system, supported by an active embroilment of labour, capital and government, could yield positive results, both from a social and economic viewpoint. The observation of such a development strengthened a theoretical narrative of transforming and adjusting old paradigms, converting the organized interest group—generated outside the traditional juridical borders of liberal state and economy—into permanent sources of political power aimed at complementing the authority of the traditional elected parliament.

However, in order to avoid sparking alarmism among the entrepreneur community, the ministry's letter specified that the plan intended to limit a further expansion of state economic intervention, somehow anticipating the post-war conservative stabilization impetus. The joint industrial councils proposed in the report "would be autonomous bodies, and they would, in effect, make possible a larger degree of self-government in industry than exists to-day" (Roberts 1917, 2). In this sense, the report located the technical and political skills needed to guarantee a durable and peaceful post-war industrial reconstruction "among those directly connected with the trade" (Committee on Relations Between Employers and Employed 1917, 9), thereby enhancing the social as well as the political role of an economic community organized in trade unions and employers' federations. The representatives of industry, in fact, were the only ones possessing the "intimate knowledge of the facts and circumstances of each trade" (Committee on Relations Between Employers and Employed 1917, 9) needed in order to enact a useful economic legislation. In other words, the committee proposed a balancing mechanism of distributing powers between political and technical bodies, thus establishing a multilevel and coordinated system of decision-making founded on the transformation of private economic organizations into reliable sources of power and instruments of authority.

Although certainly poor and vague, the report presented a first sketch of the post-war institutional scheme desired. The ultimate objective was "the establishment for each industry of an organisation, representative of employers and workpeople, to have as its object the regular consideration of matters affecting the progress and well-being of the trade from the point of view of all those engaged in it" (Roberts 1917, 2). To do so, the authors recommended the creation of a three-level structure for each industrial sector, whose representatives of employers and employed had to cooperate in joint councils on a national, district and workshop level. The scheme suggested the institution of a decentralized decisional machinery, where national industrial councils had to deal with matters of national importance, while the district councils had to manage district matters within the limits laid down at a national level, and finally the workshops committees had to take care of problems peculiar to a single workshop without altering the national and district framework. The proposed joint industrial council chain had to be in charge of a great number of issues affecting their respective industries, from questions of training, education and industrial research, to other key elements in the life of the workshops, such as the conditions of labour, wages, methods of negotiation and arbitrating (Committee on Relations Between Employers and Employed 1917, 10–12).

Although the report received a quite positive evaluation both from the government and the organizations of employers and workpeople, its actual adoption in the post-war years was rather weak, especially due to the mutated socio–economic and political scenario of the 1920s and the 1930s. Nonetheless, the Whitley Report marked an important step in the direction of affirming the institutional cooperation of workers, employers and government—a formula that would soon be known as tripartism or corporatism—as a possible solution to industrial problems and social conflict. Overall, the wartime industrial system came to represent a feasible model for governing the multiplicity of actors already acknowledged by the pre-war pluralist tradition, or at least it showed a viable way towards it. Furthermore, the Whitley Report constituted an important step in combining wartime lessons of class cooperation and pluralist thinking, emphasizing the political role of the socio–economic organized groups within a non-monopolistic, coordinated and decentralized institutional framework. Ironically, the society of societies imagined by Figgis in 1913 and the tripartite formula proposed in the Whitley Report of 1917 would not be implemented at home, but it would be adopted as the basic working principle by a completely new international organization created in Paris in 1919 with clear anti-revolutionary intents: the International Labour Organization.

5 Tripartism and the Foundation of the International Labour Organization

The treaty of peace ending World War I established the ILO as an international organism devoted to promote fair labour conditions, sound industrial relations, effective social dialogue and international peace. The basic principle of its functioning was the cooperation between the representatives of governments, employers and workpeople in all its official organisms, i.e. the general assembly, the governing body and the international labour office. In order to understand how this mechanism of decision-making process was debated and approved, this paragraph focuses on the process through which the tripartite idea came to influence the proposals of the British delegates to the Commission on International Labour Legislation that inaugurated the ILO in 1919. More precisely, the analysis will be centred on the internal dynamics of the British civil service during the two final years of the war, focusing on key individuals serving into two crucial ministries of the time, the Ministry of Labour, created at the end of 1916, and the Ministry of Reconstruction, which evolved in 1917 from the previous Reconstruction Committee.

As we already saw, between 1916 and 1917 Arthur Greenwood played a crucial role in connecting the socialist pluralist tradition of G.D.H. Cole and the Sub-Committee for the Study of the Relations between Employers and Employed working under the Reconstruction Committee umbrella. Between 1917 and 1919, Edward Phelan—a civil servant of the ministry of labour, future director of the ILO between 1941 and 1948—performed an equally important linking function. Born in the south of Ireland in 1888, Phelan graduated in mathematics and physics at the University of Liverpool, where he moved with his family in 1895. Just before the war, he joined the civil service, where he occupied the role of researcher at the Board of Trade conducting an enquiry into the housing conditions in Britain (Van Goethem 2010). The outbreak of the conflict led to a suspension of the enquiry, but when Lloyd George became Prime Minister in December 1916, Thomas Jones—one of Lloyd George's closer advisers—called Phelan to organize the Intelligence Division of the newly created Ministry of Labour (Lowe 1974 and 1986).

Phelan was not a theoretician or an academic. Often described as an intelligent, hardworking, capacious and practical man, during his career he developed no taste for abstract plans with no foreseeable application. At the same time he always showed a keen fascination for "the vanguard of original thought expressed in practical terms" (ILO 2009, 1). Possessing the sensibility and intuition for establishing a fruitful dialogue between state bureaucracy and high theory, between public servants, political scientists and economists, Phelan seems to fit perfectly the portrait of the "practical man" that Cole was looking for since 1915 (Cole 1914–1915, 157). In this sense, Phelan showed a remarkable aptitude for anchoring intellectual reasoning to the ground transforming abstract projects into reality. Besides, Phelan's importance in structuring the ILO is above question. In his autobiography, James T. Shotwell, an American history professor who participated at the Paris Conference and in the foundation of the ILO, affirmed that "the International Labour Organization owes more to him [Phelan] than will probably ever be widely known" (Shotwell 1961, 97). More specifically, Phelan is credited both with developing the tripartite formula in the context of the peace negotiations, and with ensuring the principle as the base functioning of the ILO.

In 1916 Phelan was assigned by the Board of Trade to the study of the British industrial capacity of producing war material with special concern to the wage rate fixing issue. As such, he regularly cooperated with other governmental departments interested in the matter, such as the Home Office, the Ministry of National Service, and the Ministry of Reconstruction. In the same period, between 1916 and 1918, as the war went on and new ministries and governmental organisms were established, a small group of civil servants started to made a practice of lunching together once a week in Westminster in order to informally discuss problems of administration and institutional architecture (ILO 2009, 97–98). Arthur Greenwood, who was then working at the Reconstruction Committee, had already met Phelan years before in Oxford at the local meetings of the Oxford Group of the Workers' Educational Association (ILO 2009, 66) and introduced him to the group. These weekly luncheons at Westminster turned out to be fundamental for Phelan's career. In fact, during these occasions he became acquainted with Thomas Jones, Deputy Secretary to the Lloyd George's cabinet. In this capacity, at the beginning of 1917, Jones confessed to Phelan Lloyd George's plan to establish a Ministry of Labour, asking him to organize a new labour intelligence division. Phelan welcomed the idea, enthusiastically accepting the position. He considered essential that governments equip themselves with official departments aimed at studying labour issues, compiling statistics and analyzing industrial relation legislations and practices, both about Britain and abroad. Thus, in his opinion, the new Ministry of Labour "should be given the function of studying every aspect of them [labour questions] and watching developments both at home and abroad." Therefore, such a ministry should have "a labour intelligence division which would keep under review the whole subject" (ILO 2009, 98). Consequentially, in the following months Phelan, together with Charles MacMullan, was put in charge of organizing the Intelligence Division of the Ministry of Labour, which became one of the most important research sections under the control of the government, with its headquarters located at the Montagu House.

The Intelligence Division was headed by the Liberal politician Sir John Hope Simpson and devoted all its energies to studying matters of general policy linked with labour issues. It was organized in two sections, one led by MacMullan, which had to deal with home matters, and the other headed by Phelan, with the aim of analyzing foreign material and problems. The Intelligence Division started to produce a weekly report on labour conditions in Britain and abroad, jointly prepared by MacMullan and Phelan. The working procedure of the division was uncommon. A member of what Phelan called the "production staff"—i.e. university professors and lecturers with whom the division was in touch—was summoned in order to study a particular topic. After receiving general instructions and all the information the division possessed, the researcher was left free to conduct whatever other research might be necessary and to write a report without interference. The process was then concluded holding a final meeting with the division's officials in order to collectively discuss the conclusions reached by the investigation (ILO 2009, 101). Phelan was rather proud of this procedure. In his opinion, this method had the merit of initiating a socially profitable "system of bringing academic scholarship and administrative experience into collaboration to explore problems of social policy" (ILO 2009, 101).

By the late summer of 1918, as the war seemed to be closer to a conclusion, the entire governmental community became more preoccupied by problems that could arise in the post-war period, and more generally by the social, economic and political equilibrium that had to be re-constructed after the unprecedented and tragic experience of conflict. Phelan and the Intelligence Division of the Ministry of Labour were not an exception and, confident of their well established system of combining academic knowledge and administrative experience, they started to draft schemes to bring to the attention of the incoming peace conference, especially in regards to labour and industrial relation issues. Reflections on these matters started to occupy the pages of the Intelligence Division weekly reports, but more importantly constituted the central concerns of a memorandum redacted by Phelan and issued in October 1918, titled *Memorandum on character and status of an International Labour Commission*[2] and known as the Phelan Memorandum, which eventually received the support both of the Ministry of Labour and the Home Office.

The Phelan Memorandum of October 1918 was prepared with the help of Hector Hetherington, a former student at Oxford University and Professor of Logic and Philosophy at University College Cardiff since 1915. The document strongly stated the necessity and urgency of establishing an international labour commission in order to study, debate and advance labour legislation at a supranational level. Precise political and economic reasons underpinned the particularly special effort of the British government in endorsing such an international labour organism. After four years of war, imposed social peace and restrictions, Lloyd George could not refuse to include labour issues in the peace conference without a risk of antagonizing labour circles that were currently supporting the government, thereby producing undesirable consequences menacing the on-going social order and industrial peace. Furthermore, from a purely economic point of view, Lloyd George was perfectly aware that, once international free competition would be restored after the war, British exporting industries could only benefit from an international agency ensuring supranational standards on wages and conditions of labour,

[2] *Memorandum on character and status of an International Labour Commission*, October 1918, in Shotwell Papers, 1.03.P01, Archives of the International Labour Organization (AILO), Geneva.

thereby reducing the impact of foreign industrial competition (Alcock 1971, 19).

In order to reach these objectives, the Phelan Memorandum recommended the implementation at a supranational level of a new mechanism capable of achieving an appropriate and effective international labour legislation. At this regard, the Intelligence Division of the Ministry of Labour embraced the view already expressed by the Whitley Report, enhancing the political and decision-making role of the socio–economic interest groups. With remarkable similarities also in relation to the phrasing, the Phelan Memorandum argued that only the industrial delegates could represent those "authoritative men of wide knowledge and experience who are in immediate contact with industry."[3] Only they could be instrumental in securing an economically appropriate and politically viable international labour legislation. In this sense, Phelan appeared to be quite aware of the necessity of a new kind of constituency. However, his more urgent problem did not seem to be whether the delegates had to be selected among the three classes of governments, employers and workpeople, rather what balance had to be established between them. Scaling up the issue, the memorandum stated that "the real question [...] is not whether representatives of all three classes should be sent—it is manifestly necessary that the knowledge and experience of all three should be available—but whether or not all should go with equal status."[4] Therefore, in October 1918 the question was not anymore whether tripartism had to be the proper response to the crisis of the liberal parliament, state and economy, but in what form tripartism should be concretely implemented: what balances had to be conceived in order to reach a new socio–political equilibrium.

In his unfinished memoirs published by the ILO in 2009, Phelan described the choice for tripartism as an obvious one, a logical solution based on the fact that in order to deal with labour matters the new organism "would have to bring together technically qualified representatives of the interests involved, namely workers, employers and government departments concerned with industrial matters" (ILO 2009, 141). Nonetheless, the technical motivation was coupled with a more political

[3] Ivi, 2.

[4] Ivi, 7.

reason, which expanded the list of the virtues of tripartism. Pre-war industrial struggles clearly demonstrated the conflicting potentialities of the modern capitalist society. In order to undermine them, therefore, political decisions had to be observed by the majority of citizens, without causing any form of social upheavals or industrial turmoil. Consequentially, the memorandum of October 1918 took particular care in explaining how only a tripartite organization would have both the technical capacity and political authority to reach this fundamental objective: "if the enactments of the Commission are to be effectively observed, a great deal will depend on their loyal acceptance by both the workpeople and the employers of every country. This is less likely to be secured unless those who are to speak for each party are the nominees of each party and of full rank in the Councils of the Commission."[5]

Overall, the similarities between the Phelan Memorandum and the results of the Whitley Report are significant, thereby suggesting a direct line of influence. Moreover, a same theoretical viewpoint—that is political pluralism generally understood—appeared to underpin both the projects, framing their thinking and proposals. In fact, both the joint industrial councils recommended by the Whitley Report and the international labour commission outlined by the Intelligence Division had as its core the notion that governments alone did not possess neither the authority nor the technical skills necessary for implementing and enacting a valuable labour legislation able to support a non-socially disrupting economic progress, guaranteeing at the same time a wide-ranging welfare and private property, social order and individual profit.

Another proof of the connections existing between the Whitley Report and the Phelan Memorandum is given by the personal relationship between Arthur Greenwood—who, as we saw, was the mastermind behind the Whitley Report, as well as the linking figure between Cole's guild socialism and the Reconstruction Committee—and Edward Phelan, the author of the Phelan Memorandum. That closeness emerged quite clearly if we look at the process of getting the memorandum approved by the governmental departments involved as described by Phelan in his memoirs. The process was quite slow at the beginning. As the war ended on the 11th of November 1918, the British government was facing a rather chaotic situation, mainly caused by the rising discontent of the

[5] *Memorandum on character and status of an International Labour Commission*, October 2018, 7.

population due to housing conditions, unemployment, dissatisfaction and resentment of ex-soldiers. In this context, during the last days of October, Phelan was convinced that the Ministry of Labour did not properly prioritize the discussion on his memorandum. Hoping to speed up the issue, Phelan decided to resort to his personal connections, directly approaching Greenwood, who had recently been appointed Deputy Permanent Secretary of the Ministry of Reconstruction, and asking him whether the matter debated in his memorandum was receiving sufficient consideration (ILO 2009, 142–43). After a couple of days, Greenwood arranged a meeting between him, Phelan and Vaughan Nash, now Permanent Secretary of the Ministry of Reconstruction, in order to discuss the issues rose by memorandum. After that, the text started to rapidly circulate within the Home Office, arriving in the hands of Malcom Delavigne, who had a great experience in international labour issues having been the British delegate to international conferences on labour regulations in Bern between 1905 and 1913 (Van Daele 2005).

In this way, thanks to Greenwood's early approval and intervention, Phelan's document and ideas circulated in various departments. At the end of 1918, the text arrived on Lloyd George's desk. The Prime Minister, knowing that a general election had to be held soon after the conclusion of the war, immediately backed the idea of creating an international labour organism, mainly to avoid alienating moderate trade unionists' and labour circles' support. Eventually, the Cabinet decided to create a special labour section of the British delegation sent at the Peace Conference in Paris. The labour section was then formed by George Barnes, a trade unionist who was a Minister without portfolio in the Lloyd George Cabinet; Malcolm Delavigne of the Home Office; and finally, by Harold Butler and Edward Phelan of the Ministry of Labour. The Phelan Memorandum became the official British proposal to the Paris negotiations concerning international labour questions.

6 Conclusions

The British delegation arrived in Paris in January 1919. After several internal meetings, held between the 15th and the 25th of January, a polished version of the Phelan Memorandum was drafted. The new document—officially called the *Draft convention creating a permanent organization for the promotion of the international regulation of labour conditions*—incorporated all the basic ideas and principles of the first memorandum, specifically stressing the importance of the tripartite constituency proposal.[6] On the 2nd of February, the draft was placed before the members of the Labour Commission of the Peace Conference, where it was debated until the 24th of March 1919. After the discussion and the final approval, the International Labour Organization was established and the results of the Labour Commission were included in the sections I and II of the Part XIII of the Treaty of Versailles. Section I, composed by forty articles, was and continues to be nowadays the ILO's constitution.

The text formally realized the first pillar of the ILO, i.e. international tripartism. As we saw, the formula was an experiment in codetermination, balancing the need of representing the economic forces of the society—at the time identified in industrial federations and trade unions—with the necessity of having equally strong governmental representation. The final result was the so-called 2:1:1 formula, namely two votes for governments and one each for employers and workpeople, a scheme also proposed by Phelan (ILO 2009, 19–20). This asymmetric allocation of powers was considered necessary in order to guarantee the overall feasibility of the project, as the ILO architects realistically understood that labour legislation, although approved by an international institution, had to be concretely pursued and enacted by national governments.

Insofar as social and political practices require their participants and creators to possess a certain understanding of the world, we examined the historical roots of the tripartite practice by asking how the underlying specific understanding arose. Investigating the intellectual origins of the ILO tripartite formula, this chapter has identified three crucial and interconnected moments constituting its historical development: first of all, the British pluralist re-evaluation of the political relevance of the socio–economic group; secondly, the various wartime discussions among intellectuals, politicians and civil servants about post-war reconstruction plans; finally, the role played by the labour British delegation in Paris in shaping the philosophy of inter-class collaboration and economic codetermination, concretely mirrored in the ILO tripartite functioning.

In the post-war context, international tripartism appeared to be a powerful conceptual instrument, developed by a group of British civil

[6] *Draft convention creating a permanent organization for the promotion of the international regulation of labour conditions*, January 26, 1919, p. 2, in Shotwell Papers, 1.07.S01, AILO, Geneva.

servants within a cultural environment dominated by the fall of the traditional liberal political explanations and socio–economic convictions, and by the emergence of the multifaceted pluralist tradition. Then, if tripartism made its first explicit appearance during the war as an emergency tool of war economy management, the idea was warmly embraced by a group of moderate socialists, public servants, and technocrats. For them, tripartism represented a perfect instrument to unleash their attack both against the old-fashioned laissez-faire capitalism of the nineteenth century, and against the collectivist socialist state brandished by the Bolsheviks in Russia, thereby triggering a narrative of a national salvific inter-class cooperation between government, employers and workpeople, to be reproduced in the post-war world. At this point, pluralism served as a strong reference benchmark used by key men within the Ministry of Reconstruction in order to draft post-war projects, such as the Whitley Report and the joint industrial councils herein proposed.

At the end of the conflict these two elements—pluralism and wartime industrial relations—provided the key principles underpinning the scheme elaborated by the Intelligence Division of the Ministry of Labour—i.e. the Phelan Memorandum—for creating an international organism specialized in labour legislation based on an original tripartite government-employers–workpeople constituency. Therefore, not only it is possible to recognize a conceptual *fil rouge* running among the three different but connected moments of the elaboration of the tripartite idea—that is between British pluralism, post-war Reconstruction Committee's project, and the Intelligence Division of the Ministry of Labour—but it is also possible to stress a profound unity of problems, solutions, and individuals involved in the entire process.

Nonetheless, if Cole's socialist pluralism was always leaning towards a quasi-libertarian approach (Goodway 2016, 28), the actual concretization of the empowerment of the economic groups in the ILO resulted instead in a technocratic and anti-revolutionary experiment. This outcome was fully consistent with a post-1918 international conservative momentum in search of new governing techniques to secure a bourgeois stability against the backdrop of a dramatically escalating social conflict (Haimson and Sapelli 1992; Wrigley 1993). Therefore, in their transportation from the British scenario to the international level at the ILO, pluralist and guild socialist ideas were blended to a wider reconstruction design, where labour representation was put at the service of a larger capitalist stabilization policy. In this sense, the war had both innovatory and conservative outcomes. In fact, if on the one hand the conflict generated a movement towards labour empowerment, governance experimentation and institutional creativity, on the other hand the results of this imaginative effort were used in order to ensure a new form of social order functional to the post-war survival of the capitalist system.

Therefore, in 1919 the creation of a tripartite international organization for labour legislation represented a tentative answer to the social crisis of the liberal state and economy, stemming the spreading of a Bolshevik-type revolution. Regardless of its concrete results, at its outset the ILO came to represent a social liberal laboratory, mostly European—neither the United States nor Soviet Russia joined it—for experimenting a variant of capitalist international management (Hall and Soskice 2001) in which a certain amount of legislative power was delegated to the representatives of national economic organizations. In this sense, tripartism became a way of exploring a form of regulated market capitalism, grounded on a culture of coordination and codetermination between economic groups and the state, as opposed to a liberal market system subject to a philosophy of individualism and deregulation (Regini 2003).

Another element that emerges from the analysis is that the most prominent ILO interwar voice, its first director Albert Thomas, played no role in securing the ILO tripartite governance. Although profoundly involved in French wartime tripartite organizational practices (Walter-Busch 2006; Blaszkiewicz-Maison 2015) as well as in the European labour network (Aglan et al. 2008), Thomas did not participate to the Labour Commission in Paris or to the Washington first ILO conference (Maul 2019, 36). In the period 1918–1919 the entire process of creating the ILO and its tripartite structure was monopolized by British civil servants, leading us to the necessity of scaling down Thomas' influence over the creation of the ILO.

In conclusion, tripartism at the ILO came to represent, as the Belgian socialist Emile Vandervelde put it, the triumph of the British revolution over the Soviet revolution (Alcock 1971, 37), or, to use the words of James Shotwell, it provided an alternative to violent revolution, a way to "prove the workers of the world that the principles of social justice might be established under the capitalist system" (Shotwell 1933, 18). In so doing, a procedure of social concertation and codetermination was inaugurated; a procedure that would reach its apogee after World War II. As well known, in fact, the spectacular growth of the post-1945 period was hinged on an array of variants of tripartism, neo-corporatist intermediation, codetermination and economic concertation. Despite the lexical heterogeneity of the twentieth century, a conceptual uniformity permeated the new practices of governance of a different typology of capitalism. After 1945 the key element of an ordered and non-conflicting capitalist society was indeed found in a set of institutions and informal practices grounded on the principle of tripartite codetermination, that is trade unions, employers associations and growth-minded governments cooperating in order to mobilize credit for investments and stabilizing wages in a full employment effort. At this regard, historians have long comprehended that the norms and principles underpinning the post-1945 neo-corporatist coordinated capitalist institutional framework did not appear overnight, but they were instead inherited from the past (Maier 1987; Eichengreen 2007). The formation of the ILO and the pluralist understanding of the reality of its architects were part and parcel of this wider story: a piece in the transformation of the international capitalist system along the twentieth century.

References

Aglan, Alya, Freiertag, Olivier, and Kevonian Dzovinar, eds. 2008. "Albert Thomas, société mondiale et internationalisme: réseaux et institutions internationales des années 1890 aux années 1930." *Les Cahiers Irice* 2 (2).

Alcock, Antony. 1971. *History of the International Labour Organization*. London: Palgrave Macmillan.

Bevir, Mark, ed. 2012. *Modern Pluralism: Anglo-American Debates Since 1880*. Cambridge: Cambridge University Press.

Blaszkiewicz-Maison, Adeline. 2015. *Albert Thomas: le socialisme en guerre, 1914–1918*. Rennes: Presses Universitaires de Rennes.

Boothby, Robert et al. 1927. *Industry and the State: A Conservative View*. London: MacMillan.

Burk, Kathleen, ed. 1982. *War and the State: The Transformation of British Government, 1914–1919*. London: Routledge.

Cabanes, Bruno. 2014. *The Great War and the Origins of Humanitarianism, 1918–1924*. Cambridge: Cambridge University Press.

Cayet, Thomas. 2010. *Rationaliser le travail, organiser la production. Le Bureau international du Travail et la modernisation économique durant l'entre-deux-guerres*. Rennes: Presses Universitaires de Rennes.

Claeys, Gregory. 1987. "Justice, Independence, and Industrial Democracy: The Development of John Stuart Mill's Views on Socialism." *The Journal of Politics* 49 (1): 122–47.

Clavin, Patricia. 2013. *Securing World Economy: The Reinvention of the League of Nations, 1920–1946*. Oxford: Oxford University Press.

Cline, Peter. 1982. "Winding Down the War Economy: British Plans for Peacetime Recovery, 1916–1919." In *War and the State: The Transformation of British Government, 1914–1919*, edited by Kathleen Burk, 157–81. London: Routledge

Cole, G. D. H. 1913. *The World of Labour: A Discussion of the Present and Future of Trade Unionism*. London: G. Bells & Sons.

———. 1914–1915. "Conflicting Social Obligations." *Proceedings of the Aristotelian Society* 15: 140–59.

———. 1951. *British Labour Movement—Retrospect and Prospect*. London: Fabian Publications.

Committee on Relations Between Employers and Employed. 1917. *Industrial Councils: The Whitley Report Together with the Letter of the Ministry of Labour Explaining the Government's View of Its Proposals*. London: HMSO.

Costa Pinto, António, ed. 2017. *Corporatism and Fascism: The Corporatist Wave in Europe*. London: Routledge.

———. 2019. *Latin America and Dictatorship in the Era of Fascism: The Corporatist Wave*. New York-London: Routledge.

Cronin, Edward J. 1991. *The Politic of State Expansion: War, State, and Society in Twentieth-Century Britain*. London-New York: Routledge.

Croucher, Richard, and Wood, Geoffrey. 2015. "Tripartism in Comparative and Historical Perspective." *Business History* 57 (3): 347–57.

Delisle Burns, Cecil. 1915. "When Peace Breaks Out." *International Journal of Ethics* 26 (1): 82–91.

Eichengreen, Barry. 2007. *The European Economy Since 1945: Coordinated Capitalism and Beyond*. Princeton: Princeton University Press.

Enroth, Henrik. 2010. "Beyond Unity in Plurality; Rethinking the Pluralist Legacy." *Contemporary Political Theory* 9 (4): 458–476.

Figgis, John Neville. 1913a. *Churches in the Modern State*. London: Longsman Green and Co.

———. 1913b. *A Free Church in a Free State*. In *Churches in the Modern State*, edited by John Neville Figgis, 3–53. London: Longman Green & Co.

———. 1914. *The Divine Right of King*. Cambridge: Cambridge University Press.

Jackson, Simon, and O'Malley, Alanna. 2018. *The Institution of International Order: From the League of Nations to the United Nations*. Abingdon: Routledge.

Johnson, Paul B. 1968. *A Land Fit for Heroes: the Planning of British Reconstruction*. Chicago: University of Chicago Press.

Kaiser, Wolfram, and Schot, Johan. 2014. *Writing the Rules for Europe: Experts, Cartels, and International Organizations*. London: Palgrave Macmillan.

Kohlrausch, Martin, and Trischler, Helmuth. 2014. *Building Europe on Experts; Innovators, Organizers, Networkers*. London: Palgrave Macmillan.
Goodway, David. 2016. "G.D.H. Cole: A Socialist and a Pluralist." In *Alternative to State Socialism in Britain: Other Worlds of Labour in the Twentieth Century*, edited by P. Ackers and A. J. Reid. London: Palgrave Macmillan.
Gorman, Daniel. 2012. *The Emergence of International Society in the 1920s*. Cambridge: Cambridge University Press.
Greenwood, Arthur. 1915. "Social and Economic Aspect of the War." In *The War and Democracy*, edited by R. W. Seton-Watson, J. Dover Wilson, A. E. Zimmern, A. Greenwood. London: MacMillan.
———. 1916. "How Readjustment Could Be Facilitated After the War." In *The Reorganisation of Industry*. Council of Ruskin College: Oxford.
Haimson, Leopold, and Sapelli, Giulio eds. 1992. *Strikes, Social Conflict and the First World War: An International Perspective*. Milan: Feltrinelli.
Hall, Peter A., and Soskice, David eds. 2001. *Varieties of Capitalism: The Institutional Foundation of Comparative Advantage*. Oxford: Oxford University Press.
Hidalgo-Weber, Olga. 2012. "Social and Political Networks and the Creation of the ILO: The Role of British Actors", In *Globalizing Social Rights: The International Labour Organization and Beyond*, edited by Sandrine Kott and Joëlle Droux, 17–31. London: Palgrave Macmillan.
———. 2013. "Social and Political Networks and the Creation of the ILO: The Role of British Actors." In *Globalazing Social Rights: The International Labour Organization and Beyond*, edited by Sandrine Kott and Joëlle Droux, 17–31. New York: Palgrave.
International Labour Organization (ILO). 1919. *Constitution of the International Labour Organization* in *Treaty of Versailles*, part XIII.
———. 2009. *Edward Phelan and the ILO: Life and Views of an International Social Actor*. Geneva: International Labour Organization.
———. 2018. *Resolution Concerning the Second Recurrent Discussion on Social Dialogue and Tripartism*. Geneva: International Labour Organization.
———. 2019. *ILO Centenary Declaration for the Future of Work*. Geneva: International Labour Organization.
Laborde, Cécile. 2000. *Pluralist Thought and the State in Britain and France, 1900–25*. Basingstoke: MacMillan.
Laqua, Daniel, ed. 2011. *Internationalism Reconfigured: Transnational Ideas and Movements Between the World Wars*. London: I.B. Taurus.
Lowe, Rodney. 1974. "The Ministry of Labour, 1916–1924: A Graveyard of Social Reform?" *Public Administration* 52: 415–38.
———. 1986. *Adjusting to Democracy: The Role of the Ministry of Labour in British Politics*. Oxford: Clarendon Press.

Maier, Charles S. 1975. *Recasting Bourgeois Europe: Stabilization in France, Germany, and Italy in the Decade After World War I. Princeton: Princeton University Press*. Princeton: Princeton University Press.

———. 1987. *In Search of Stability: Explorations in Historical Political Economy*. Cambridge: Cambridge University Press.

Maitland, Frederick William. 1911. "Moral Personality and Legal Personality." In *The Collected Papers of Frederic William Maitland*, edited by Herbert Albert Laurens Fisher, 304–20. Cambridge: Cambridge University Press.

Martin, James R. 2016. *Experts of the World Economy: European Stabilization and the Reshaping of International Order, 1916–51*. Doctoral dissertation, Harvard University, Graduate School of Arts & Sciences.

Mattei, Clara E. 2017a. "The Guardians of Capitalism: International Consensus and the Technocratic Implementation of Austerity." *Journal of Law and Society* 44 (1): 10–31.

———. 2017b. "Treasury View and Post-WWI British Austerity: Basil Blackett, Otto Niemeyer and Ralph Hawtrey." *Cambridge Journal of Economics* 42 (4): 1123–44.

Maul, Daniel. 2019. *The International Labour Organization: 100 Years of Global Social Policy*. Berlin: De Gruiter.

McCarthy, Helen. 2011. *The British People and the League of Nations: Democracy, Citizenship and Internationalism, c.1918–45*. Manchester: Manchester Univeristy Press.

McKibbin, Ross. 1984. "Why Was There No Marxism in Great Britain?" *The English Historical Review* 99 (391): 297–31.

Moses, John A. 1978. "The Concept of Economic Democracy Within the German Socialist Trade Unions During the Weimar Republic: The Emergence of an Alternative Route to Socialism." *Labour History* 34: 45–57.

Nicholls, David. 1994. *Pluralist State: The Political Ideas of J.N. Figgis and His Contemporaries*. Basingstoke: MacMillan.

Nyland, Chris, Kyle Bruce, and Prue Burns. 2014. Taylorism, the International Labour Organization, and the Genesis and Diffusion of Codetermination. *Organization Studies* 35 (8): 1149–1169.

Panitch, Leo. 1977. "The Development of Corporatism In Liberal Democracies." *Comparative Political Studies* 10 (1): 61–90.

Pasetti, Matteo. 2016. *L'Europa corporativa. Una storia transnazionale tra le due guerre mondiali*. Bologna: Bononia University Press.

Persky, Joseph. 2016. "Producer Co-Operatives in Nineteenth-Century British Economic Thought." *The European Journal of the History of Economic Thought* 49 (1): 1–22.

Pimlott, Ben. 1977. *Labour and the Left in the 1930s*. Cambridge: Cambridge University Press.

Poole, Michael et al. 2001. "A Comparative Analysis of Developments in Industrial Democracy." *Industrial Relations* 40 (3): 490–25.

Pugh, Martin. 2002. "The Rise of Labour and the Political Culture of Conservatism, 1890–1945." *History* 88: 514–37.

Regini, Marino. 2003. "Tripartite Concentration and Varieties of Capitalism." *European Journal of Industrial Relations* 9 (3): 251–63.

Roberts, George Henry. 1917. "Letter Addressed by the Minister of Labour to the Leading Employers' Associations and Trade Unions." In *Industrial Councils: The Whitley Report Together with the Letter of the Ministry of Labour Explaining the Government's View of Its Proposals*, edited by Committee on Relations Between Employers and Employed, 1–6. London: HMSO.

Rogan, Tim. 2017. *The Moral Economists: R.H. Tawney, Karl Polany E.P. Thompson, and the Critique of Capitalism.* Princeton: Princeton University Press.

Rousselière, Damien. 2009. "What is Economic Democracy? An Inquiry Into French Cooperatives." *Studies in Political Economy* 84: 29–46.

Runciman, David. 2005. *Pluralism and the Personality of the State.* Cambridge: Cambridge University Press.

Schmitter, Philippe C. 1974. "Still the Century of Corporatism?" *The Review of Politics* 36 (1): 85–131.

Schmitter, Philippe C., and Lehmbruch, Gerhard eds. 1979. *Trends Towards Corporatist Intermediation.* Beverly Hills: Sage.

Shotwell, James T. 1933. "The International Labour Organization as an Alternative to Violent Revolution." *The Annals of the American Academy of Political and Social Science* 166: 18–25.

———. 1961. *The Autobiography of James T. Shotwell.* Indianapolis: Bobbs-Merril.

Sluga, Glenda. 2013. *Internationalism in the Age of Nationalism.* Philadelphia: University of Pennsylvania Press.

Stears, Marc. 1998. "Guild Socialism and Ideological Diversity on British Left, 1914–1926." *Journal of Political Ideologies* 3 (3): 289–06.

———. 2006. *Progressives, Pluralists, and the Problems of the State: Ideologies of Reform in the United States and Britain, 1909–1926.* Oxford: Oxford University Press.

Stitt, James W. 2006. *Joint Industrial Councils in British History: Inception, Adoption, and Utilization, 1917–1939.* Westport: Praeger.

Tawney, Richard H. 1931. *Equality.* London: George Allen and Unwin.

———. 1943. "The Abolition of Economic Control, 1918–1921." *The Economic History Review* 13 (1–2): 1–30.

Tooze, Adam. 2014. *The Deluge: The Great War, America and the Remaking of the Global Order, 1916–1931.* New York: Penguin.

Tooze, Adam, and Fertik, Ted. 2014. "The World Economy and the Great War." *Geschichte und Gesellschaft* 40 (2): 214–38.

Tosstorff, Reiner. 2005. "The International Trade-Union Movement and the Founding of the International Labour Organization." *The International Review of Social History* 50 (3): 399–33.

Van Daele, Jasmien. 2005. "Engineering Social Peace: Networks, Ideas, and the Founding of the International Labour Organization." *International Review of Social History* 50 (3): 435–66.

Van Goethem, Geert. 2010. "Phelan's War: The International Labour Organization in Limbo (1941–1948)." In *ILO Histories. Essays on the International Labour Organization and Its Impact on the World During the Twentieth Century*, edited by Van Daele, Jasmien et al. Bern: Peter Lang.

Walter-Busch, Emil. 2006. "Albert Thomas and Scientific Management in War and Peace, 1914–1932." *Journal of Management History* 12 (2): 212–31.

Williamson, Peter J. 1985. *Varieties of Corporatism: A Conceptual Discussion.* Cambridge: Cambridge University Press.

Worley, Matthew. 2005. *Labour Inside the Gate: A History of the British Labour Party Between the Wars*. London: Tauris.

Wright, A. W. 1979. *G.D.H. Cole and Socialist Democracy*. Oxford: Clarendon Press.

Wrigley, Chris, ed. 1993. *Challenges of Labour: Central and Western Europe 1917–1920*. London: Routledge.

Archival Documentation

Alfred Zimmern Papers, Ms. Zimmern 14, Bodleian Library Special Collection, Oxford.

James T. Shotwell Papers, 1.03.P01, Archives of the International Labour Organization, Geneva.

CHAPTER 9

Pluralism and Political Economy in Interwar Britain: G. D. H. Cole on Economic Planning

Carlos Eduardo Suprinyak

1 Introduction

The spectacle of World War I produced a wave of strong reactions against the nefarious consequences of a political system built around the notion of state sovereignty, and the several nineteenth-century political philosophies that seemed to legitimize such a system. In Britain, interwar commentators already had a philosophical tradition on which to base their criticism of the sovereign state: political pluralism. Building on the work of F. W. Maitland and J. N. Figgis, interwar pluralists such as Harold Laski, G. D. H. Cole, and R. H. Tawney called attention to

The author wishes to thank Liane Hewitt, Joseph Persky and participants at the Jean Monnet Workshop 'Interwar Economics and the Intellectual Origins of European Integration' for their comments on an earlier version of this manuscript.

C. E. Suprinyak (✉)
Federal University of Minas Gerais, Belo Horizonte, Brazil

© The Author(s) 2021

A. M. Cunha and C. E. Suprinyak (eds.), *Political Economy and International Order in Interwar Europe*, Palgrave Studies in the History of Economic Thought,
https://doi.org/10.1007/978-3-030-47102-6_9

the multiplicity of loyalties and obligations inherent in any society and posited that the state had no legitimate claim to precedence over other forms of associative life. Nevertheless, the war not only illustrated the dangers of state sovereignty, but also the extent to which the state could, under modern conditions, manage the course of social life to suit its own purposes. War mobilization had shown how effectively the state could take the reins of the economic machinery into its own hands, while the economic difficulties that beset Britain from the mid-1920s onward, capped by the trauma of the 1929 crash, eroded confidence in the capacity of the capitalist system to function properly when left alone. The Soviet experiment offered to socialists and non-socialists alike the prospect of a new world made rational and stable through extensive economic planning. Insofar as this amounted to an increase in the power and functions of the state, advocates for political pluralism and economic planning would seem to be tugging at the opposite ends of the rope.

Such, however, was not necessarily the case. There was much interaction between economists and political theorists in Britain during the interwar years, so that issues of sovereignty, economic organization, technocratic rule, and international order were often part of the same scholarly conversation (Suprinyak and Oliveira 2018; Godden 2013). In this chapter, my purpose is to contribute to the history of the social sciences during the interwar era by weaving together the separate histories of economics, political philosophy, and international studies.[1] The case of G. D. H. Cole offers fertile material for this exercise. One of the foremost exponents of political pluralism and an engaged activist for the Guild Socialist movement, Cole was also a lecturer, political advisor, and popular writer on economic subjects, who wrote extensively during the early 1930s on the nature and practical implications of economic planning. Cole's appeal to the notion of social function as a device for reconciling political decentralization and economic planning foreshadowed future developments in the post-WWII European settlement, when functionalism became a strategy for curbing state sovereignty in the name of a more rational management of economic life across national borders.

[1] For a recent argument in defense of a cross-disciplinary history of the social sciences during the twentieth century, see Backhouse and Fontaine (2018).

2 Pluralism and Political Economy in Interwar Britain

Pluralism drew its inspiration from several different intellectual sources. The idealist vogue that swept British philosophy during the late nineteenth century established, contra utilitarian individualism, that individual personalities could only develop to their full potential when immersed in a social setting. To philosophers like T. H. Green, the towering figure of British idealism, it was meaningless to discuss freedom merely as the absence of external interference. True freedom, on the contrary, had to do with the capacity to bring one's own personality to bear on the pursuit of common purposes and the improvement of common life—a message that struck a chord with intellectuals who sought to address the social dislocations of late Victorian and Edwardian Britain (Den Otter 2009). In the Hegelian tradition, however, idealism implied a conception of the state as the ultimate source of all social meaning and purpose, a feature mostly evident in Britain in the works of Bernard Bosanquet, one of the favorite targets of pluralist-inspired critique. The tradition of legal historical scholarship initiated by F. W. Maitland, and further developed by J. N. Figgis, provided an antidote to the idealist overemphasis on the state as an agent of social cohesion. Maitland excavated medieval public records to show how English law had always recognized a distinct group personality in different forms of associative life, rather than conceiving them, in contractualist language, as an artificial creation of the state. Writing on the eve of World War I, Figgis developed this insight to argue that associations had a moral personality distinct from—and not subordinate to—the state (Runciman 1997, 89–149).

Harold Laski, G. D. H. Cole, and R. H. Tawney, the most prominent advocates for the pluralist cause during the interwar years, differed from Maitland and Figgis by adhering to a distinctly socialist perspective. Often referred to as the "Red Professors," Tawney, Cole, and Laski were also united in their belief in associational life as an effective remedy for the deficiencies of liberal representative democracy. Alarmed by the enormous concentration of power in the hands of state machineries ever more removed from the effective control of their citizens, they postulated that individuals held simultaneous allegiances to multiple social groups, and questioned whether the state could rightfully claim priority over other forms of association on grounds of principle (Stears 2002, 88–123). In their hands, pluralism thus became an alternative to the binary opposition between laissez-faire individualism and the several brands of collectivism that had gained ground by the early twentieth century, both left and right. Their approach, however, diverged from other "third way" platforms that emerged in Europe at the time in important respects. In contrast to corporatism, their emphasis on individual freedom and self-determination bordered on libertarianism, as especially evident in the case of Cole. Conversely, they distanced themselves from anarchism and syndicalism by positing the need for integrating the different forms of associational life into a set of common social purposes (Laborde 2000, 69–100).

Though professing socialist ideas, the three authors had strong reservations to centralized and bureaucratic models of the Soviet variety. For similar reasons, in the immediate aftermath of World War I, they were strongly opposed to the philosophy and tactics embraced by the Fabian Society, which put great emphasis on the role of a strong state in directing the course of economic life in a reformed socialist commonwealth (Stears 2002, 89–90). To the "socialist pluralists," the Fabian model was willing, in good utilitarian fashion, to condone worker's alienation in the name of productive efficiency (Rogan 2017, 20–22; Laborde 2000, 70–72). By focusing on increased consumer satisfaction through income redistribution and broader social policies, they disregarded the conditions under which human labor was performed. Moreover, by subordinating industry to the imperative of maximum productivity, they introduced obstacles to the expression of individual initiative and personality through labor. A true democratic society, so the pluralists argued, began in the workplace. Worker's control of industry should never be sacrificed in the name of some monolithic notion of the "common good" emanating from the state. In contrast with earlier pluralists like Figgis, the new generation stressed how the same individual could hold multiple simultaneous social allegiances and should thus decide for herself which of these were the most important in any concrete situation (Runciman 1997, 170–73). In other words, there was nothing that legitimately compelled people to value their interests as consumers above their interests as producers. A pluralist democracy, recognizing the whole spectrum of associational forms that existed to fulfill different human purposes, should safeguard the right of individuals to judge for themselves and make their own choices (Stears 2002, 96–104).

The pluralists sought to give concrete expression to these principles through their involvement with the British labor movement, offering a first glimpse of their engagement with interwar political economy. This was especially evident in the case of the National Guilds League, founded by Cole in 1915. The guild socialist movement sought to counter attempts by the British central government to encroach on the autonomy of trade unions.[2] Cole was the foremost public voice of guild socialism in Britain, but Tawney was also closely involved with the movement (Rogan 2017, 35–36). Differently from other variants of labor activism at the time, guild socialism did not advocate the transfer of ownership of industrial enterprises to the workers themselves. Its platform focused instead on industrial democracy, the effective seizing of control and management by the workers. Industrial self-government promised to redress the democratic deficit inherent in liberal political institutions without relying on a highly bureaucratized and potentially authoritarian central government (Laborde 2000, 76–77). In the early twentieth century, as the trade union rose to become the modern form of association par excellence, industrial management and democratic ideals suddenly found themselves in the same playing field.

The socialist pluralists' involvement with political economy was not restricted, however, to labor activism. In their careers as scholars and political advisors, they were also routinely drawn to the discussion of topics that fell within the purview of economics. In Britain, politics still lacked at the time a distinct disciplinary identity. Political theorists and philosophers typically worked as academic "generalists" with a background in law, history, and classical humanism (Adcock et al. 2009, 99–100). Moreover, the nature of the challenges posed by the interwar context prompted arguments that encompassed a broad spectrum of social scientists, offering fertile ground for the interplay between economists and political theorists (Suprinyak and Oliveira 2018). The Fabian Society was one privileged space for such cross-disciplinary interaction: even if Cole, Laski, and Tawney largely disapproved of the Fabian approach during the heyday of socialist pluralism, they still held rather close ties with the society at different moments in their lives (Holthaus

[2] The cause had been brought to the center of public discussion by a 1908 legal decision forbidding the Railway Servants Union from charging a contribution to the British Labour Party from its members. Building on other contemporary disputes concerning the freedom of activities for churches and religious groups, this gave rise to a broader political agitation in defense of the autonomy of voluntary associations (Stears 2002, 91–92).

2018, 13–14; Hickson and Beech 2007, 63–65; Rogan 2017, 19–20).[3] The London School of Economics and Political Science—an institution where disciplinary boundaries were notoriously looser than in traditional British universities—was another focal point. One of the LSE founders, social psychologist Graham Wallas, provided a common intellectual reference for pluralist political theory, insisting that "human nature" at once shaped and was shaped by the evolution of society (Rogan 2017, 38–39). Both Laski and Tawney were affiliated to the LSE for most of their careers, as professors, respectively, of political science and economic history.

Cole was never formally attached to the London School of Economics. Still, a young Lionel Robbins expressed his wonder at Cole's "apparently effortless command of his subject and superiority of manner," which seemed to him "beyond the ambition of any ordinary mortal to achieve" (Howson 2011, 54–55). Robbins became a member of the National Guilds League after returning from the war, and when he resumed his studies at the LSE in the early 1920s, he was tutored by Laski in the history of political ideas—an experience that seems to have played a role both in his moving away from socialism and in his growing interest in economics. Robbins' and Cole's paths would cross once again, however, when both were enlisted to work for the Labour government newly created Economic Advisory Council, in 1930. Cole had been one of the driving forces behind the creation of the council, which sought to bring together government officials and persons that possessed "special knowledge and experience of industry and economics" (Howson and Winch 1977, 24). He joined Tawney and John Maynard Keynes as one of the senior economists working for the council.

Despite his credentials as a political theorist, the appointment was not out of character. In his first major work, *The World of Labour* (1913), Cole seemed much more concerned with analyzing the economic underpinnings of industrial democracy than with exploring the finer philosophical aspects of political pluralism that would later occupy his mind (Runciman 1997, 165–66). Even his subsequent guild socialist writings continued to exhibit a wealth of economic content (Persky and Madden 2019). When he distanced himself from political agitation and

[3] Before finally resigning from the Fabian Society in 1915, Cole and some of his associates had in fact attempted to take it over for the guild socialist cause (Carpenter 1973, 28–32).

returned to academia in 1925, he took up a readership in economics at Oxford, a position he retained until being appointed for the university's first-ever chair in political and social theory, in 1945. During this time, he was also a popular writer on economic subjects, publishing dozens of newspaper articles and a handful of volumes explaining the ongoing economic predicaments to a non-specialist audience (Snowden 2009). This coincided with his work at the Economic Advisory Council, where he came in direct contact with the ideas of Keynes about the depression. Cole was also an admirer of John Hobson—another intellectual who effortlessly melded economic and political considerations—using the latter's underconsumption thesis to advocate for expansionary economic policies (Holthaus 2018, 155–62). In short, Cole belonged to a class of interwar scholars who worked in the boundaries between political theory and economics, looking for answers to the dilemmas facing Western civilization. In his specific case, this meant reconciling a profound distrust of the sovereign state with the reality of an increasingly complex and interconnected economic machinery.

3 Cole's Pluralism

Among the socialist pluralists, Cole was certainly the most committed to radical notions of industrial democracy, both at the practical and at the theoretical levels. In *Self-Government in Industry* (1917), he clearly established his opposition to the Fabian route to socialism, arguing that the "fundamental evil in our modern society" was not poverty, but rather slavery (Cole 1917 [1920], 34). The modern industrial system of highly bureaucratized, centralized decision-making militated against workers' emancipation, tending instead to perpetuate slave habits and virtues. "Socialists," said Cole, "have all too often fixed their eyes upon the material misery of the poor without realising that it rests upon the spiritual degradation of the slave" (35). "Machinery and Capitalism," he continued, "between them have made the worker a mere serf" (38). When reformist socialists sought to redress the problems of capitalism by redistributing income in favor of the poor, they struck at the symptom, not the underlying cause. By relying on the state to fulfill this task, they focused exclusively on the needs of individuals as consumers, leaving aside the other essential dimension of their economic life as producers. A collectivist solution, even if it managed to distribute wealth more equally, would essentially maintain the worker as "a wage-slave, subject to the will of a master imposed on him from without" (38).

Cole thus proclaimed that "the crying need of our days is the need for freedom." True freedom, however, required "an all-round [...] development of personality" focused on the "more positive and assertive virtues," instead of the "one-sided development of the virtues of self-repression" stimulated by the present industrial system (Cole 1922, 413–14). Much of Cole's inspiration for his ideas on freedom came from Rousseau, whose works he translated into English. Rousseau provided Cole with a framework for criticizing the shortcomings of liberal representative democracy without diluting individual will into some overriding social organism, as was usual in much of idealist philosophy (Holthaus 2018, 124–28; Laborde 2000, 77–95). Human will and personality could never be represented in their entirety, and a political system based on representation necessarily involved systematic distortion of individual dispositions. The alternative was direct involvement in collective decision-making through participatory democratic arrangements. Cole followed Rousseau's contractualist approach when arguing that individuals come together in associations by force of their rational will, which entitled them to direct participation in common deliberations. Through such democratic engagement, they could then develop the "positive and assertive virtues" that led to the full realization of their freedom.

In contrast to Rousseau, however, Cole believed the state could no longer function as the privileged locus for democracy in modern society. His argument was at the same time political and economic. On one hand, the modern state had become far too bureaucratic and complex in its operations to allow the ordinary individual to develop any meaningful identification with its purposes. On the other, the most consequential decisions for the everyday life of common people were not reached at the level of the state, but at the workplace. It was here that the "slave virtues" of self-repression did most of their harm, for someone who behaved as a slave in economic life would never have a chance to develop the necessary values and skills to act as a free person in the political arena (Holthaus 2018, 128). Cole thus employed the pluralist framework to argue that democracy and freedom in modern society could only hope to develop within the far more restricted scope of associational life. Rather than threats to the coherence and stability of the state, as posited by Rousseau, associations in fact represented a multitude of equally legitimate social allegiances. While the conceptual language was borrowed from Figgis, Cole showed very little interest in the types of moral and spiritual associations that had mostly concerned the latter. In his view, the quintessential association of industrial society was the trade union, through which one could envisage the emergence of the self-governing guild (Runciman 1997, 168–69).

This was not the only point in which Cole diverged from the path open by Figgis. In common with the other socialist pluralists, he firmly rejected the notion that associations possessed a moral personality of their own, which risked simply replacing the state by the group as a source of tyrannical rule over the individual. Associations existed simply for their capacity to help individuals pursue their purposes through cooperation and collective action—in other words, they could not be justified by purposes that transcended those of the individuals who composed them. In contrast to the strongly idealist concept of freedom espoused by Figgis, Cole sided with Rousseau to deny that freedom lay in allegiance to any given social morality. In the words of Cécile Laborde (2000, 82), Cole interpreted freedom as "an individualistic, subjective experience," which meant that associations were only legitimate to the extent they helped individuals fulfill their own goals. This point was elaborated by Cole in his 1915 paper "Conflicting Social Obligations," presented before the Aristotelian Society. Taking his cue from Rousseau's discussion of the relations between the "general will" and the several "particular societies" that make up the body politic, Cole argued that "all social machinery, alike in its agreements and its conflicts, is a partial and more or less successful expression of a General Will which every community possesses" (Cole 1915, 151). Such machinery, however, was "necessarily imperfect, because all machinery tends to standardise what is, in its real nature, infinitely various" (156). The will of any association, including the state, was therefore only partial and imperfect. "A well-organised Society," Cole concluded, "will admit the ultimate possibility of conflict, but will try to reduce the need for conflict to a minimum" (158).

The multiple allegiances inherent in human personality reinforced the case that freedom and democracy could only find their full expression in the individual. Associations existed because certain purposes were too complex for being pursued individually, therefore requiring some form of social collaboration. They should thus be autonomous to decide their own goals, methods, and practices. At the same time, there always remained much about human personality that could not be expressed through any form of association. Similarly, when different allegiances came into conflict, it fell to the individual to decide which of them should prevail in each concrete circumstance. Associational democracy, including the right to free enter and exit, was thus important to safeguard individual freedom against any unwarranted encroachment by the group (Stears 2002, 104–14). Nevertheless, if the state had no claim to priority over other forms of association, and if the actions of an association were only constrained by the purposes of its members, it remained unclear how society could "reduce the need for conflict to a minimum"—in other words, how one could prevent different associations from pursuing their aims at the expense of society. Cole's answer to this conundrum involved the key concept of function.

As mentioned above, individuals formed associations to pursue a common purpose. "Every such purpose or group of purposes," Cole explained in *Social Theory*, "is the basis of the *function* of the association which has been called into being for its fulfillment" (1920a, 49). Function was thus not an ethical principle, but a principle of social organization. "Every individual is in his nature universal," comprising an enormous variety of functions, and "it is just in the choice of and between functions and in assigning their relative places to the many functions, social and personal, of which we are conscious, that our selfhood appears as a coordinating principle beyond any of them" (50). An association, by contrast, was "specific and functional" by its very nature. Nevertheless, the functionality of associations did not involve simply their capacity to help fulfill the purposes of their members, but also their relations to other associations imbued with their own functions. Cole thus uses the concept of function to introduce a "standard of value" through which one can judge whether a specific association is acting in a way that furthers the coherence of society or detracts from it. In line with his commitment to an individualist notion of democracy, however, he stressed that function in this broader sense "can only be based upon a purpose." When assigning a function to any association, we are limited "to the purposes which its members have set before themselves in creating and maintaining it" (54).

Functional representation, therefore, was the only truly democratic form of representation, since it asked each one "not to choose someone to represent him as a man or as a citizen in all the aspects of citizenship," but only "his point of view in relation to some particular purpose or group of purposes, in other words, some particular *function*" (Cole 1920b, 32–33). The state, in Cole's view, should be regarded simply as one specific form of functional association—*primus inter pares*, at the most (1917

[1920], 136). The function of the state was to "represent those elements in the common life which are best represented on a geographical basis," meaning the purposes that are "distributed with some approximation to equality among all the citizens" (1915, 151–52). Being thus partial in its function, the state did not have the authority to coordinate the actions of other associations, but rather should strive to have its own actions aligned with those of other social bodies (Runciman 1997, 170–72). Functional devolution should be the norm, relying on councils for arbitrating eventual disputes that might emerge between different associations (Laborde 2000, 85–88).

Cole was aware that his use of function as a "standard of value" could open the door to idealist-inspired notions of social purpose or the "common good." His response was to reaffirm that such judgments pertained not to any higher authority, but rather to the individuals who could, from their multiple allegiances, devise "some conception of the sort of social life which is ultimately desirable" (Cole 1920a, 54). Cole's faith that functional coherence would ultimately trump factional strife arose from his view of associational democracy as a process through which individuals could gradually develop a greater sense of community. As described by Leonie Holthaus, Cole conceived voluntary associations as "hubs for democratic education and the development of social values transcending egoism" (Holthaus 2018, 130). Industrial democracy permitted individuals to understand and perfect their own personalities, thus coming closer to the realization of their best-selves (Stears 2002, 119–20). Community, to Cole (1920a, 28), was a "center of feeling," and the personal emotional attachments necessary for social cohesion could only blossom with democratic participation.

4 Planning the Route to Industrial Democracy

In light of all that has been discussed so far, it may come as a surprise to hear Cole proclaim, roughly a decade later: "The source of our present troubles is not that States interfere too much, but that their interference remains external and mainly negative" (Cole 1933a [1934], 37). The verdict was pronounced in a piece entitled "Economics in the Modern World," originally published in the *Political Quarterly*, in which Cole argued that standard economic and political theories were faltering because they had been conceived for "an age of successful individualism." Free market utilitarian economics and representative democracy were the twin intellectual pillars of this tradition, and the reorientation of value theory toward consumer decisions, effected by Jevons and his followers, guaranteed that individual interests were essentially harmonious, not conflictive. In the modern world, however, the economy was not a collection of individuals freely exchanging goods and services, but rather of "groups, institutions, associations, and classes which cohere in varying degrees, and by their cohesion shape the conditions of exchange" (36). "What is called monopoly," continued Cole, is an "omnipresent condition varying in strength and degree from case to case." In these conditions, the cause of *laissez-faire* economics was "mere inverted Utopianism." The alternative required using "the State as an instrument of economic regulation," since "the only way in which the conflict of sectional interests can be transcended is by merging the rival groups in a wider collective unit" (40).

Cole's newly found faith in the State as an agent of social and economic coherence did not arise out of the blue. Much had changed in the intervening decade, forcing him to reconsider some elements of his earlier quasi-libertarian approach to industrial organization. The collapse of the National Building Guild in 1922, and the later failure of the 1926 General Strike, led to disillusionment with the Guild Socialist movement and the broader prospect of social transformation by way of trade union activism. By the end of the 1920s, Cole recognized he had been over-optimistic in his earlier belief that workers could gradually "encroach" the control of industry and make capitalist management redundant. Industrial laborers, he now realized, regarded their work as an obligation rather than an active interest, while their political instincts were not strong enough for them to dedicate their leisure time to guild affairs (Riddell 1995, 939–40). As a result, Cole was now convinced that "socialization must come as a political measure, rather than as a product of direct action in the industrial field" (Cole 1935, 336). Accordingly, he came around on his antagonism to the British Labour Party and the Fabian Society, even helping to establish the New Fabian Research Bureau in 1931 (Hickson and Beech 2007, 38–54; Holthaus 2018, 156). The results of the first Soviet Five-Year Plan also seem to have captivated Cole's imagination for the potential inherent in state-led economic planning (Cole 1934, 168). Undoubtedly, however, his interest in the latter subject was sparked, first and foremost, by the dire economic conditions prevailing in Britain during the latter half of the 1920s, further aggravated by the 1929 crash. In his numerous writings from the early 1930s, Cole seemed convinced that untrammeled capitalism was no longer capable of adequately using the productive forces of society to generate material welfare—"economic faith in Providence," in his own words, "is at a discount" (1934, 11).

He thus turned to the study of economic planning—its promises and challenges, instruments and requirements—in a rapid succession of works, culminating with the bulky *Principles of Economic Planning* (1935). If our collective goal was to use available resources as best as we can to satisfy human needs, then recent developments made clear that some form of planning was needed. Capitalist planning, however, was "a highly paradoxical idea" (1934, 11), indicating how grossly inadequate our current concepts were to face the new reality. Cole was here at his most comfortable as an economic analyst, presenting broad overviews of recent developments and competing currents in economic theory, and delving extensively into stock-in-trade topics such as the determination of prices, income distribution, capital accumulation, international trade and finance. Most importantly, however, he seemed convinced that the relevant political unit for economic planning was the state. "National economic planning," he argued in the popular *The Intelligent Man's Guide Through World Chaos* (1933b), "involves public ownership of industry and at the same time public control of the distribution of income," which meant "the State shall itself be in control of the normal means of providing work" (615). In apparent stark contrast to his earlier pluralist writings, Cole now contended that the world needed "a new set of incentives, which will fit in with the advancing technique of collectivisation." "These new incentives," he added, "must be collective rather than individual in their appeal" (Cole 1932 [1934], 89).

Concern with the pervasive influence of monopoly power on modern capitalist economies seemed to add a pessimistic twist to Cole's prior arguments about the role of associations in society. The "sectional monopolies" that controlled production appeared as a doppelgänger to the functional associations of a coherent and harmonic pluralist society. Their inevitable result was conflict and dispute, and "the tendencies to disequilibrium arising from the unequal pulls of conflicting groups and classes," Cole believed, "can be overcome only by the supersession of these sectional forces by an inclusive public monopoly" (Cole 1933a [1934], 39–40). The new conditions required a new economic theory, where the individualist values of capitalism would be replaced by the collective values of socialism. Instead of social function following individual purpose, as in the model developed in *Social Theory*, the "social product" should now become "a matter for collective decision and not for individual consumer's choice" (Cole 1934, 256). While individual preferences should not be completely disregarded, they would be "valid only within the limits set by [the] collective judgment of the needs of the community." This new approach, in other words, involved "substituting the Society as a whole for the individuals who compose it as the authority which is to settle the use to be made of the available productive resources" (261).

Even though we can trace Cole's gradual recognition of a larger role for the state back to some of his writings from the early 1920s, the key to reconcile his ideas on pluralist politics and economic planning lies in another paper read before the Aristotelian Society in 1926, entitled "Loyalties." Reflecting on the topics addressed in "Conflicting Social Obligations" a decade earlier, Cole considered the language of "obligations" to have been an unfortunate choice. In the concept of "loyalties," by contrast, he believed to have found the "clue to the problem of sociality." The shift in terminology meant speaking "in terms not of the Kantian imperative, but of that common sentiment of us all which is the whole basis of our capacity to live and work together" (Cole 1934, 271). It allowed one to conceive the problem in terms of a positive force that could hold together different forms of association. Even if this did not eliminate the possibility of conflict between different loyalties, it helped shift the emphasis to the "positive contributions which all these different loyalties can make to the common good" (276). What, then, was necessary for the various loyalties to coalesce around a socially beneficial pattern? In his reply, Cole weaved together his time-honored beliefs and the concerns that would soon come to the fore in his work:

> The condition clearly is harmony. In order that there may be a common good to which all can know how to contribute, there must be at least the broad conception of a common plan. The association, like the individual, must have some knowledge of his 'place' if it is to set up for itself any satisfactory standard of social behaviour. In other words, the interworking of the associative life must be consciously and purposefully promoted. The doctrine of 'function', Plato's master-concepts in politics, is vital for the association as well as for the individual. (Cole 1934, 278)

"Loyalty," Cole continued, "is essentially a matter of will, and the voluntary principle is therefore vital to it." Social harmony therefore depended "not merely on the avoidance of conflicts and clashes of loyalties in men's minds or between rival groups and associations, but still more on the positive evocation of many different loyalties in the common service" (280). A pluralist society, where individuals conduct their lives according to multiple loyalties, is a society that compels "comparison, choice, judgment," thus contributing to the formation of a rational citizenry. Social coherence depended on the capacity of this society to elicit loyalty to "a set of social institutions which most people regard as, in essence, fair and reasonable" (283). The monolithic forms of social organization then arising in Europe were based on an irrational loyalty that was "concentrated on the general by the suppression of the particular," and they foreshadowed disaster. What we need, argued Cole, is "rational loyalty to the whole," but this could only be achieved "through a harmony of diversified loyalties to the parts." "The freedom of voluntary association," he concluded, "is the life-breath of its being" (285).

Cole thus envisioned economic planning not only as a practical solution to the shortcomings of modern capitalism, but also as an instrument for developing the communal values necessary for a new economic order. Given present conditions, planning would doubtless have to be carried forward by a centralized political authority. "At the time when planning is being first introduced," he argued, "it may be necessary to carry centralization a good deal further than will be desirable when the system has settled down to work" (Cole 1935, 324). A planned economy, however, "when it has had time to get into working order, should be far more effective than any other system in diffusing responsibility over a wide field." Flexible operation would require decentralization and properly trained local leadership. To Cole, "if a planned economy is to work well, adapting itself to constantly changing conditions and opportunities, and acting on the spirit rather than the letter of the plan when things go wrong, there must be within it a widespread devolution of responsibility and power" (326).

This was not, however, simply an instrumental argument for the successful working of a planned economy. "The object of a planned society," asserted Cole, "is gradually to replace the monetary incentives on which Capitalism relies for getting the world's work done by other incentives more consistent with the social interest." The moral transformation that economic planning could bring about involved heightening in each citizen "the will to do good service to society and the sense that each man has his definite part to play in the promotion of the happiness and well-being of all" (327). To bring such loyalties forward, society must give people the power "to play a real part in its control." An autocratic system of planning will not solve the problem of social coherence, for it will continue to make the individual worker feel like "a slave of the mass-machine, even if that machine is used, far more than now, to produce real utilities for the common enjoyment." Economic planning without industrial democracy would produce "a disastrous *malaise* and disillusionment, which no enlargement of wealth and leisure will suffice to prevent," thus opening the way to "an unhealthy and neurotic community" (330–31).

The goal of a planned society, therefore, should be to "make men and women citizens of industry as well as of the State." Technical considerations of productive efficiency were, of course, important in collective decisions, but "the technicians should serve and advise, [...] never rule." The sort of industrial citizenship envisioned by Cole promised to imbue in each worker "a sense that the success of the plan of socialised production depends upon their co-operation." This was the ultimate rational loyalty to the whole, "a collective sentiment of responsibility and interest in the success and efficiency of their work." Once this loyalty was robust enough, the state could then gradually recede into the background and devolve to people the responsibility to manage their own affairs. "In the long run," said Cole, "the aspiration of a planned economy must be to make each industry to the fullest possible extent a democratic self-governing Guild, responsible in matters of public policy to society as a whole," but left free "to manage its internal affairs mainly in its own way" (338). Economic planning under a centralized authority was thus, at bottom, simply a transitional device, responsible for planting the seeds of the new spirit of industrial democracy.

5 Concluding Remarks

In line with the mood of the times, G. D. H. Cole came increasingly to believe, as the interwar years advanced, that the state was still a pivotal actor in modern society. The pluralist rebellion against state sovereignty gradually gave way to a more pragmatic attitude that saw the state as a necessary instrument to face the irrational workings of a capitalist order predicated not on competition, but on widespread monopolistic dispute. Economic planning provided the key to ensure that social resources would be adequately used to serve human needs, and the state was the only institution capable of carrying out planning on the necessary scale. Even then, however, Cole did not lose sight of the greater goal: the development of a new set of motivations that would render individuals more willing to serve the community and fulfill their social responsibilities (Stears 2002, 187). In capitalist society, economic interests tended to impose themselves over political alignments, so that "the transformation of politics can in fact only follow, not precede, the socialisation of the economic life of the community" (Cole 1933a [1934], 40). The subsequent socialization of politics, however, sustained by the cultivation of civic loyalties, could only be accomplished through democratic participation. "On this issue," said Cole, "I remain an unrepentant Guild Socialist, though I am conscious that the way to industrial self-government in any full sense may be longer and more difficult than I used to think" (1935, 339).

The British pluralist approach to political philosophy went into hibernation with World War II, only to be reinvented in the United States a few years later (Gunnell 1995). In British Labour politics, Cole's legacy was absorbed into variants of corporate socialism that departed significantly from his radical democratic ideals, such as Evan Durbin's Keynesian-tinged approach to economic planning, or the autonomous public corporation model advocated by Herbert Morrison and Barbara Wootton, managed by a technocratic elite and properly insulated from workers' control (Foote 1997, 158–82). In the realm of international politics, on the other hand, Cole's concept of function enjoyed a very fruitful afterlife. David Mitrany, whose *A Working Peace System* (1943) is often credited with having introduced the so-called functionalist approach in the study of international relations, was a direct heir to the British pluralist tradition, insisting on the arbitrariness of national boundaries to define the scope of political action (Long 1993). Economic and political integration, in Mitrany's view, could take place effectively through the definition of clear social functions best fulfilled at a level transcending the national state, thus dispensing with the need for an overarching political authority. As they found concrete expression in post-WWII Europe, however, these ideas departed significantly from Cole's view of social function as a gateway to the development of a communal spirit. Here too, technocratic rule and the persistence of "democratic deficits" seem to indicate that post-war functionalism has failed to generate new kinds of supranational loyalties, thus leading even farther away from Cole's promised land.

References

Adcock, Richard, Mark Bevir, and Shanon C. Stimson, eds. 2009. *Modern Political Science: Anglo-American Exchanges Since 1880*. Princeton, NJ: Princeton University Press.

Backhouse, Roger, and Philippe Fontaine. 2018. "Economics and Other Social Sciences: A Historical Perspective." *Annals of the Fondazione Luigi Einaudi* 52 (2): 7–44.

Carpenter, Luther P. 1973. *G. D. H. Cole: An Intellectual Biography*. Cambridge: Cambridge University Press.

Cole, George D. H. 1913 [1920]. *The World of Labour*. 5th ed. London: G. Bell & Sons Ltd.

———. 1915. "Conflicting Social Obligations." *Proceedings of the Aristotelian Society* New Series, 15: 140–59.

———. 1917 [1920]. *Self-Government in Industry*. London: G. Bell & Sons Ltd.

———. 1920a. *Social Theory*. New York: Frederick A. Stokes Company.

———. 1920b. *Guild Socialism Re-Stated*. London: Leonard Parsons.

———. 1922. "'Slave Virtues' and Other Virtues." *The New Statesman* 18: 412–14.

———. 1932 [1934]. "The End of the Bourgeoisie." In *Studies in World Economics*, edited by George D. H. Cole, 80–90. London: Macmillan.

———. 1933a [1934]. "Economics in the Modern World." In *Studies in World Economics*, edited by George D. H. Cole, 28–41. London: Macmillan.

———. 1933b. *The Intelligent Man's Guide Through World Chaos*. London: Victor Gollancz Ltd.

———. 1934. *Studies in World Economics*. London: Macmillan.

———. 1935. *Principles of Economic Planning*. London: Macmillan.

Foote, Geoffrey. 1997. *The Labour Party's Political Thought: A History*. 3rd ed. London: Macmillan.

Godden, Chris. 2013. "Observers, Commentators, and Persuaders: British Interwar Economists as Public Intellectuals." *History of Political Economy* 45 (Annual Supplement): 38–67.

Gunnell, John G. 1995. "The Declination of the 'State' and the Origins of American Pluralism." In *Political Science in History: Research Programs and Political Traditions*, edited by James Farr, John Dryzek, and Stephen Leonard, 19–40. Cambridge: Cambridge University Press.

Hickson, Kevin, and Matt Beech. 2007. *Labour's Thinkers: The Intellectual Roots of Labour from Tawney to Gordon Brown*. London and New York: Tauris Academic Studies.

Holthaus, Leonie. 2018. *Pluralist Democracy in International Relations: LT Hobhouse, GDH Cole, and David Mitrany*. Cham: Palgrave Macmillan.

Howson, Susan. 2011. *Lionel Robbins*. Cambridge: Cambridge University Press.

Howson, Susan, and Donald Winch. 1977. *The Economic Advisory Council, 1930–1939: A Study in Economic Advice During Depression and Recovery*. Cambridge: Cambridge University Press.

Laborde, Christine. 2000. *Pluralist Thought and the State in Britain and France, 1900–25*. London and New York: Macmillan Press and St. Martin's Press.

Long, David. 1993. "International Functionalism and the Politics of Forgetting." *International Journal* 48 (2): 355–79.

Mitrany, David. 1943. *A Working Peace System: An Argument for the Functional Development of International Organization*. London: The Royal Institute of International Affairs.

Den Otter, Sandra M. 2009. "The Origins of a Historical Political Science in Late Victorian and Edwardian Britain." In *Modern Political Science: Anglo-American Exchanges Since 1880*, edited by Richard Adcock, Mark Bevir, and Shanon Stimson, 37–65. Princeton, NJ: Princeton University Press.

Persky, Joseph, and Kirsten Madden. 2019. "The Economic Content of G.D.H. Cole's Guild Socialism: Behavioral Assumptions, Institutional Structure, and Analytical Arguments." *The European Journal of the History of Economic Thought* 26 (3): 427–63.

Riddell, Neil. 1995. "'The Age of Cole'? G. D. H. Cole and the British Labour Movement, 1929–1933." *The Historical Journal* 38 (4): 933–957.

Rogan, Tim. 2017. *The Moral Economists: RH Tawney, Karl Polanyi, EP Thompson, and the Critique of Capitalism*. Princeton, NJ: Princeton University Press.

Runciman, David. 1997. *Pluralism and the Personality of the State*. Cambridge: Cambridge University Press.

Snowden, Nicholas. 2009. "Depression Economics Before the General Theory: The Order in Cole's Chaos." *Oxford Economic Papers* 61 (3): 415–39.

Stears, Mark. 2002. *Progressives, Pluralists, and the Problems of the State: Ideologies of Reform in the United States and Britain, 1909–1926*. Oxford: Oxford University Press.

Suprinyak, Carlos E., and Thiago D. Oliveira. 2018. "Economists, Social Scientists, and the Reconstruction of the World Order in Interwar Britain." *The European Journal of the History of Economic Thought* 25 (6): 1282–1310.

CHAPTER 10

Ordoliberalism and the Rethinking of Liberal Rationality

Timo Miettinen

Ordoliberalism is best known as one of the central traditions of European neoliberalism and the official economic ideology of post-WWII Germany. Following the German experience of the interwar period, ordoliberal theory is known for its emphasis on the role of state and a strong legal framework for free market economy. Traditionally, ordoliberals have been in favour of strong competition laws that regulate markets by dismantling monopolies, preventing the abuse of controlling market positions, and limiting state aid (see e.g. Brunnermeier et al. 2016; Dullien and Guérot 2012; Demetriades 2015). Ordoliberal theorists have favoured a rule-based approach to macroeconomic coordination and emphasized the neutrality of monetary policy. In the research literature on the European economic model, ordoliberalism is often viewed as the key ideology behind the rule-based economic constitution of the European Union

T. Miettinen (✉)
University of Helsinki, Helsinki, Finland
e-mail: timo.pa.miettinen@helsinki.fi

© The Author(s) 2021

A. M. Cunha and C. E. Suprinyak (eds.), *Political Economy and International Order in Interwar Europe*, Palgrave Studies in the History of Economic Thought,
https://doi.org/10.1007/978-3-030-47102-6_10

(Tuori and Tuori 2014, 231ff. See also e.g. Streit and Mussler 1994; Hien and Joerges 2017).[1]

Although economic policies can hardly be explained on the basis of a single intellectual tradition, many claim that ordoliberalism is more relevant than ever. Mechanisms such as the 2012 Fiscal compact have strengthened the implementation of rule-based economic coordination and the future of French-style fiscal union looks bleak (Young 2014). On a more general level, ordoliberal ideas of individual responsibility and moral hazard have surfaced particularly in the German or "Northern" narrative according to which the irresponsible behaviour of problem countries constituted the key cause of the Euro crisis (Fourcade 2013). In this regard, concepts such as authoritarian liberalism or executive federalism are more and more discussed in connection to the contemporary European economic policy (see e.g. Bonefeld 2017; Habermas 2012; Haselbach 1991).

Although the COVID–19 virus has challenged some of the political principles of ordoliberal governance—such as budget rules and limitations on state aid—it has not changed the fundamental division between Northern and Southern Europe and their approaches to economic governance. On the contrary, stark divisions persist between North and South on the viability and scope of EU level fiscal responses. Thus, ordoliberal ideas and policies are thus absolutely crucial for any discussion on national sovereignty, democratic accountability, and the future of liberalism in today's Europe.

Despite this relevance, the concept itself lacks analytic clarity. Ordoliberalism is frequently conflated with Germany's political and economic interests, or, it is simply seen as a more socially oriented version of neoliberalism. The story has been primarily institutional with a strong focus on political and economic ideas (for a classic presentation, see Blum 1969. See also Meiers 2015; Hall 2012; Katzenstein 1997).[2]

[1] In the context of the EMU, the influence of ordoliberalism is present in at least three central components: (i) The Stability and Growth Pact (SGP) that focuses on fiscal discipline; (ii) the rejection of joint liability in the Treaties (e.g., Art. 123 & 125 TFEU); and (iii) the mandate of the European Central Bank that focuses on price stability. See also Biebricher (2013) and Ryner (2015).

[2] In more popular debates, ordoliberalism is often scorned for being "wacky economics" (*Financial Times 16.11.2014*) that is slowly "decoupling [...] Germany from the rest of the world" (*The Economist 9.5.2015*). For a critical analysis on the recent emphasis on ordoliberalism, see Hien (2013), Hien and Joerges (2018), Wegmann (2000).

The recent surge of academic literature on the genealogy of ordoliberalism (e.g. Blyth 2013), however, has broadened our understanding on this idea. It is now acknowledged that ordoliberalism was more than a political-legal doctrine: a broader cultural programme with religious, moral-philosophical, and existential underpinnings (Hien 2017; Bonefeld 2017; Slobodian 2018; Goldschmidt 1998. See also Ptak 2009).

This article offers a complementary narrative. Instead of a political or economic doctrine, the article examines ordoliberalism as a *philosophically motivated theory* that emerged as a response to the crisis of economics and scientific reason in general. Its key context was not only the collapse of the Weimar Republic but also the interwar crisis of science as articulated by philosophers and academics of the time (see e.g. Dekker 2016). This crisis, although having its origins in the late nineteenth century debates on the differences between the natural and the human sciences, was not only about theoretical knowledge but about the role or status of science within culture as a whole. Science had lost not only its unity but also its normative task as the driving force of rational humanity.

Ordoliberalism was not the only variant of neoliberalism, but it was intellectually one of the most radical ones (see Plickert 2008). Unlike many of the representatives of the Austrian School who saw themselves continuing the programme of classical liberalism—or defending it against "foreign ideas" (Tribe 2009, 71)—ordoliberalism presented itself in an explicit opposition to eighteenth and nineteenth century liberalism.[3] Instead of a political-economic doctrine, it formulated a philosophical and moral programme that aimed at a fundamental revision of the ontological and epistemological foundations of liberalism. It did this by reinterpreting some of the key concepts and ideas of the political domain and articulating a new philosophy of history that was critical of the progressive narrative of classical liberalism. It presented an all-encompassing vision of a functioning institutional order supported by a moral philosophy of an autonomous individual. By doing so, it employed theoretical and conceptual resources from a variety of philosophical and intellectual traditions such as Neo-Kantianism, Max Weber's theory of ideal types, phenomenology, and to some extent, Protestantism and philosophy of life.

[3] For an extensive comparison between ordoliberals and the Austrian School, see Kolev (2015).

The key argument is the following: Unlike classical liberalism that defined itself as moral-philosophical project or an ideology, ordoliberalism employed these philosophical ideas to redefine liberalism as a scientific theory with normative implications. Its political and economic programme was based on a radical rethinking of the ontological and epistemological foundation of liberalism and a thorough critique of the optimistic philosophy of history characteristic of classical liberalism. In the end, the normative appeal of the liberal project was not to be based on moral-philosophical ideas such as freedom or responsibility. Instead, liberalism was to be based on the new idea of economics as a *normative science*.

1 Ordoliberalism and the Market as a Political Event

Ordoliberalism is not a single and unified movement. Its roots can nevertheless be traced back to the so-called Freiburg School of National Economics, in particular, to the work of economists Walter Eucken (1891–1950), Adolf Lampe (1897–1948), and Friedrich Lutz (1901–1975) as well as jurists such as Franz Böhm (1895–1977) and Hans Großmann-Doerth (1894–1944). Together with sociologists such as Alexander Rüstow (1885–1963) and Wilhelm Röpke (1899–1966), often referred to as the Cologne School, the ordoliberal collective strived for a radical rearticulation of the basic principles of liberalism. One of the key platforms for the renewal of liberalism was the German Economic Association (*Verein für Sozialpolitik*) that gathered together a wide variety of intellectuals from Lujo Brentano and Max Weber to Austrian economists Ludwig von Mises and Friedrich Hayek. The association also served as a springboard for the Walter Lippmann Colloquium of 1938, often referred to as the key event in the formation of the "neoliberal thought collective" (Mirowski and Plehwe 2009).

Although the influence of ordoliberals in the interwar period was limited, they played a central role in the transition from the planned wartime economy to the post-war "social market economy"—a term coined by Alfred Müller-Armack—and the creation of the so-called *Wirtschaftswunder*, the German economic miracle (see e.g. Sally 1996; Goldschmidt and Wohlgemuth 2008). Ludwig Erhard (1897–1977), who served as a Minister of Economics under Chancellor Adenauer from 1949 onwards—and became the chief economic architect of the Federal

Republic—was a strong proponent of ordoliberal policies, contributing to the post-war currency reforms, the first antitrust laws, and the creation of a politically neutral Bundesbank in 1957. In the context of the European Economic Community, the ordoliberals influenced significantly the implementation of competition laws from late 1950s onwards.

Although ordoliberalism gained political success only after the WWII, its emergence was closely tied to the collapse of the liberal order in the interwar period. Ordoliberals criticized both fascism and socialism for their trust in central planning, and were critical of Keynesian approaches to macroeconomic adjustment (see Eucken 1948; Allen 2005). Eucken, for one, saw a clear link between full employment policies and central planning, although his position seemed to have become more moderate during the 1930s (Hutchison 1979).

This did not mean, however, that liberalism could have done away with the state. The conscious shaping of political institutions and legal culture, rather than mere trust in the invisible hand of the market place, was to be made the basic principle of market economy.

The representatives of the ordoliberal movement aimed at reconfiguring classical liberalism both theoretically as well as from a practical standpoint. From a theoretical perspective, they criticized classical liberalism for its trust in *laissez-faire* ideology and naturalistic concepts. According to them, the market was to be seen as an *artificial* construction that is constantly in danger of losing its essential principle, that of competition. As Leonhard Miksch, one of the leading economists of the Freiburg School put it, economic freedom is a "political event" (Miksch 1947, 9). Rather than growing spontaneously from the natural interaction of humans, it is based on a voluntary choice. From a more practical perspective, liberalism was to be provided with a new, stable foundation that would have secured the success of market economy through changing political trends. Legal or constitutional order, rather than democratic politics, became the central mechanism through which this continuity is secured (Vanberg 2001).

The ordoliberal doctrine became, as Werner Bonefeld puts it, one of *strong state and free economy* (Bonefeld 2017). Market economy needs the state in order to protect itself against the concentration of power both politically as well as from the point of view of producers. The state needs to be protected from interest groups and lobbyists, and the dynamism of market economy needs to be protected against the concentration of power through monopolies and cartels.

Thus, although the ordoliberals were among the first to use the concept of neoliberalism, their views on the role of state and social policies differed substantially from the more free market oriented versions of neoliberalism. Market economy, according to ordoliberals, could only function within a competitive environment that is sustained by a strong and effective legal framework—what both Eucken and Böhm called an "economic constitution" (*Wirtschaftsverfassung*) (Eucken 1989, 52ff.; Böhm 1937, xix). Constructing such a constitution and giving it a robust theoretical-scientific foundation became the central task of the ordoliberal project.

2 Between Norms and Reason

Ordoliberalism was not purely a rationalistic movement. It emerged from a combination of several intellectual strains such as the natural law tradition, humanism, deontic moral philosophy (e.g. Kant), and of course classical liberalism. Protestantism was another important source of influence, particularly through the so-called *Bonhöffer Kreise*, led by Protestant theologian Dietrich Bonhöffer from 1938 and 1944, that brought together several Protestant economists, jurists and historians—among them Eucken, Böhm and Miksch (Hien 2017). Protestant virtues such as hard work, ascetism and self-responsibility—rather than Catholic ideas of social justice and redistribution—were at the core of ordoliberal doctrine.

As recent scholarship has shown, ordoliberals believed in the Protestant idea that the essence of human being is fundamentally "empty" or undefined in character. In the words of Luther, the human being is *simul justus et peccator*, both a saint and a sinner, and therefore he needs to be guided by proper societal structures. In this regard—particularly through the works of Rüstow and Röpke—Protestantism coincided with the ordoliberal interest in the concept of biopolitics (*Vitalpolitik*). Politics is not only about institutional design but about shaping the human being. This was not to say, however, that ordoliberalism would have been in conflict with Catholic teachings. The concept of *ordo* itself had of course deep Catholic roots particularly in the Thomist tradition, although

Eucken seems to have distanced himself from the naturalistic interpretations of this concept.[4] Concepts such as Müller-Armack's "social market economy" were of aid in promoting ordoliberal ideas among the Catholic voters of the CDU. All in all, unlike the kind of market fundamentalism that is sometimes associated with neoliberalism, the ordoliberals emphasized that the legitimation of liberal economy cannot rest solely on the market. It needs a "sociological basis" anchored in cultural and moral values (Goldschmidt 1998; Manow 2001).

Despite this emphasis on culture and morality, the ordoliberal movement was defined, above all, by a firm belief in science. A key part of the ordoliberal narrative was the idea that classical liberalism had failed because it lacked solid foundations in science. It should be recalled that in the context of the nineteenth century, political economy was still conceived a subfield of moral philosophy. The study of production, consumption and exchange within a particular nation was of course conducted with the help of analytic categories, but rarely as distinct from normative issues of justice, equality, honesty, and fairness. The question of values was primary. The modern idea of economics as a value-free science arose not only from this tradition of political economy, but from the more practically oriented fields such as German cameralism (*Kameralismus*), the science of administration (Langewiesche 2000). Many of the ordoliberals actually worked with concrete issues of public administration from nationalization of the Ruhr Area (Rüstow) to economic governance (Böhm) and competition policy (Miksch).

In this regard, the emphasis on science did not mean a complete break from ethics; rather, scientific arguments played a key part in the intellectual differentiation from ideological or interest-based approach. Science was important because it provided the ordoliberals an aura of neutrality with regard to politics. As the ORDO manifesto of 1936 put it:

> If men of science relinquish this role [of serving as experts of national economy] or are deprived of it, then other less competent advisers take over – the interested parties. They are certainly expert in the technical details of their professional field, but equally certainly they are not, nor can they be, competent to assess overall economic interrelationships. Moreover, they are incapable of divorcing themselves from their own economic interests

[4] See especially Eucken's manuscript Morphologische Studien, BL 21–23, Walter-Eucken-Archiv, Jena. See also Johnson (1989).

> which, as a rule, inevitably results in the welfare of their own professional field being confused with that of the national economy as a whole. (Böhm et al. 2017, 27)

In the eyes of the authors of the manifesto, political actors always have a particular interest when it comes to economic matters. In fact, this is what politics is all about: a battle of individual interests, not a formation of a general will. According to the popular analysis of philosophers such as José Ortega y Gasset, the emergence of mass society in the late nineteenth and early twentieth centuries had brought within itself an almost paradoxical atomization of society whereby classical liberal virtues of responsibility for the self and for others seemed to had lost their ground. The liberal state had vanished and was replaced by a mass state with its mass politics, mass parties and mass men. In this situation, the liberals could no longer rely on the idea of a benevolent elite at the heart of state machinery (Bonefeld 2017, 39). Instead, it had become a short-sighted contest of short-term advantages for individual interest groups.

Science, however, is a way to overcome this interestedness. This is because scientists have the possibility of becoming the general representatives of reason who are able to overcome their particular interests and base their views on objective knowledge. What sets the scientists apart from typical interest groups is their ability to view the domain of economy from the perspective of *totality*. Other groups may also be directed to totalities, but usually from the perspective of their particular interest. In this sense, scientists constitute what Röpke called a "nobilitas naturalis" (Röpke 1998, 130), a natural aristocracy of the public spirit. This class derives its legitimacy from both supreme, disinterested knowledge and insight as well as incomparable moral example.

This does not mean, however, that their task would be one of pure description. Rather, the theoretical task of economics was intrinsically tied to the practical task of building a concrete economic order:

> The authors consider that the most urgent task for the representatives of law and political economy is to work together in an effort to ensure that both disciplines regain their proper place in the life of the nation. This is not only for the sake of science but, more important, in the interests of the economic life of the German nation. (Böhm et al. 2017, 28)

It should be noted, however, that in the context of early twentieth-century German academia, the idea of science as a value-neutral domain was not as dominant as today. On the contrary, one of the defining questions of this era was how to reconcile between facts and values, the descriptive and normative aspects of scientific reasoning. In the works of scholars such as Max Weber and Ferdinand Tönnies, there emerged a new need for analytic distinctions regarding the normative and "value-free" aspects of science. Although Weber's own distinctions influenced substantially the post-WWII idea of value-free social science, his own account was actually much more nuanced (Bruun 2007). Weber used the concepts of "Wertfreiheit" and "wertfrei" in brackets, and he was primarily concerned of accounting for the emotional or impulsive character of our human choices. Although scientists should strive for ethical-normative neutrality, human intentions play a key part in social-scientific explanations.

Another crucial point to note is that for the German academics of the early twentieth-century, the idea of value-free science was often linked to the Marxist tradition. For it, science had become an important instrument in dissecting what they took as the fetishistic character of capitalist social relations, a fundamentally negative tool in uncovering the un-naturalness and untruth of these relations. Science played a key role also in the Marxist conception of historical and societal laws, which were seen as operating strictly according to logical principles. As the German sociologist Wernert Sombart put it, the entire Marxian system "contains not a single grain of ethics" (quoted in Proctor 1991, 124). The dominance of planned economies in the 1930s and 1940s was by no means a result of purely political decisions, but resulted from a creative combination of science and central planning.

Accordingly, the ordoliberal conception of scientific neutrality emerged in a context that was considerably more complex and nuanced than what is usually accepted. Eucken, for one, repeatedly warned against the kind of historical fatalism represented by Marxism, and argued that science should not have any particular role in the concrete economic decisions of market participants. Instead, science was to discover its new role as the "order-establishing power" (Eucken 1990, 338) of the modern state—a state that was constantly in danger of losing its source of legitimacy or falling into pure despotism. This presupposed, however, that science focuses itself solely to the question of "interdependence of orders" and restricts itself only to the formal conditions of the market (Eucken 1990, 340).

Despite this criticism of Marxism and planned economies, it should be emphasized that a significant part of the ordoliberal critique was actually directed against classical liberalism. Particularly in the works of Rüstow and Röpke, the doctrine of *laissez-faire* characteristic of classical liberalism was under constant critical scrutiny, and this for at least two reasons. First, even though this central doctrine of liberalism had contributed to the freeing of market economy from the control of the state, it offered a limited vision for a positive role of the state. Instead, it had created what Eucken called an "unbearable vacuum" that was replaced by a "belief in the total, all-powerful state" (Eucken 2017, 58). By neglecting the indispensable role of the state, *laissez-faire* had opened the door for both centralized authoritarianism and social democracy.

Second, the doctrine of *laissez-faire* seemed to imply a sort of metaphysical attitude towards market mechanisms. It implied that markets would be something that are born naturally, without human intervention. Röpke called it a "deistic philosophy" (Röpke 2009, 51). There was a need for a critical rethinking of the theological-metaphysical presuppositions arguing for the self-justificatory character of market economy. As Rüstow put it:

> This position of economics in relation to the whole system of liberalism arose to a large degree from the developments in the field of thought and, more particularly, in that of science. This was so because liberalism as a science had made its epoch-making discovery in the sphere of economic theory. This discovery was that of the automatism of the market economy, of the self-adjustment which takes place in the competitive system by means of the mechanism of supply and demand, and of the harmony which is established and maintained by means of this subconscious adjustment between the egoism of the individual and the greatest welfare of all. (Rüstow 2017, 152)

Rüstow did not deny the scientific character of classical liberalism as such. As is well known, liberals such as Adam Smith were inspired by Newton and the modern sciences and they aimed at articulating a vision of economy based on discoverable principles. Nevertheless, the language of classical liberalism contained within itself a belief in the automatism and self-adjusting character of markets, expressed most vividly in Smith's metaphor of the "invisible hand". As Lisa Hill has argued, this automatism was not based solely on experience but on a set of theological and metaphysical commitments. Although Smith was a typical Enlightenment era Christian with an anti-dogmatic twist, his thinking combined elements from the natural teleology of Aristotelianism, Stoic theodicy, and Newton's deism (Hill 2001, 4). There is a divine purpose in nature and the world—a sense of Providence—that goes beyond the will of the individual. And it was exactly these metaphysical connotations that Rüstow was so critical of:

> This theologico-metaphysical origin gave liberalism and liberal economics, at a time when the world was still dominated by theology, a tremendous missionary force and a formidable impetus. Its apostles felt themselves carried by the conviction: *Dieu le veult*! But it contained a fateful defect, and finally contributed to the breakdown of liberalism and to our present world catastrophe. (Rüstow 2017, 154)

In Rüstow's view, classical liberalism—despite its epistemological differences with German idealism—was likewise committed to the modern idea of universal history defined by divine providence. In his analysis, the key defect of classical liberalism was exactly the belief that history itself would have been on the side of science and reason. This meant that its central doctrine—*laissez-faire*—was nothing more than "a summons to honour God and an adjuration not to allow short-sighted human anxieties to interfere with the eternal wisdom of the natural laws" (Rüstow 2017, 153).

In Rüstow's own view, however, science had actually very little to do with natural or universal history. As a human construct based on the critical capacities of the mind, science was actually to be seen as an interruptive force within human history fighting all forms of superstition. What the ordoliberals criticized was the kind of fatalism that still left its mark on some of the representatives of both classical liberalism and Marxism. This fatalism was evident also among those theorists such as Immanuel Kant who aimed at articulating the liberal project at the level of interstate institutions (Kant 2007, 109). To construct liberalism as a science was to take it outside of all deterministic forces: nature, God, or even human spontaneity.[5]

[5] As already Michel Foucault already noted in his *Collège de France* lectures on biopolitics, the ordoliberal idea of science was based on a radical critique of classical liberalism. This critique, he argued, was founded on the refutation of a particular "naturalistic

3 Ordoliberal Idea of Science

The quest for a radically new, scientific foundation for liberalism reached its most analytic formulation in the work of Walter Eucken. Eucken, one of the authors of the aforementioned ORDO manifesto, began his academic career as a theorist of rather conventional topics such as maritime transport and monetary policy. Already in the 1920s, however, Eucken was an active societal commentator of issues such as welfare policies, religion, and the role of the state. Following the work of his father, Nobel-prize winning philosopher Rudolf Eucken, Walter Eucken wrote a series of short essays emphasizing the need to rebuild the social order based on humanistic, idealistic and Christian values. The rise of socialism and the political revolutions of the nineteenth century had coincided with the rise of a materialistic outlook of the world, which had produced a permanent "restlessness" into the life of the modern man. What the progressives called a "turn to realism" (*Wendung zum Realismus*) was in its core a destruction of the idea of spiritual "self-formation" (*Bildung*) as a cultural principle (Eucken 1930, 34).

Eucken did not become a philosopher or a theorist of education. His economic interest, however, started to move from more traditional problems such as trade or monetary policy to broader issues of political economy including the historical genealogy of capitalism, the problem of the state, and the role of science in shaping the economy (see Goldschmidt 2013). In one of his more philosophical lecture courses from 1936, titled "Battle of the Sciences" (Eucken 1936, manuscript), Eucken interpreted the task of science in two regards. First, it is an internal battle of the sciences in their quest to attain "objective truth" and the particular ideas that express it. But it is equally a struggle with the outside world on the legitimacy and validity of these ideas. As for Galileo, the key question was not only how to discover ideas but how to stand up for them in the eyes of the general public. Science is not only a battle for truth but for authority, legitimacy, and power.

naivety" (Foucault 2008, 172) of liberal thinkers on the basis of which they treated the market economy as a spontaneous order. For the ordoliberals, however, the very idea of market order was to be treated as fundamentally *un-natural*, as something that arises only on the basis of voluntary decisions to construct it. Science plays a key role in delineating the conditions for a functioning economic constitution.

Thus, it is possible to claim that for Eucken, the idea of science was not to be equated with a kind of neutral disinteredness. Instead, science played a key role in the reformation of market economy:

> The problem [of national economy] will not solve itself simply by our letting economic systems grow up spontaneously. The history of the century has shown this plainly enough. The economic system has to be consciously shaped. The detailed problems of economic policy, trade policy, credit, monopoly, or tax policy, or of company or bankruptcy law, are part of the great problem of how the whole economy, national and international, and its rules, are to be shaped. (Eucken 1950, 314)

This entailed, however, a fundamental reconfiguration of the science of economics. First, it needed to articulate itself in the form of a strictly *universalistic* science that founds itself on theoretical insights and ideal concepts. Without this element of universality, economics remains purely an accumulation of empirical facts without any general relevance. Secondly, it must be able to say something meaningful of the concrete economic world that we live in. Instead of being a science of individual transactions or a pure fantasy of the free individual, it must recognize and analyze the concrete political, legal and institutional constrains relating to the constitution of economy as a social phenomenon.

Eucken's argument was based on his interpretation on the more general methodological dispute known as the "Great Antinomy" (Eucken 1950, 47ff.). This confrontation took place between two competing interpretations of scientific economics in the late nineteenth century, historicism on the one hand, and apriorism on the other. In the works of the so-called Historical School of Gustav von Schmoller, economics had become a field of investigation that focuses on historical forms and institutions of production and exchange. More than mathematics, economics took advantage of ethnological, anthropological and sociological findings. Instead of general rules, historicism was interested in unique historical settings and types such as medieval feudalism or modern capitalism. In the works of apriorists such as Ludwig von Mises, the opposite was the case. Economics should formulate clear, universal principles that can work as a theoretical foundation for the analysis of economic decisions. As Mises argued, the key principles of his approach "are not derived from experience [...]"

> They are, like those of logic and mathematics, a priori. They are not subject to verification or falsification on the ground of experience and facts. They are both logically and temporally antecedent to any comprehension of historical facts. They are a necessary requirement of any intellectual grasp of historical events. (von Mises 1966, 32)

For Eucken's need, however, this was clearly not enough. In his view, the science of economics was in danger of collapsing into two completely distinct fields, historical and theoretical economics (Eucken 1950, 56). One would study into the actual history of different forms of production, but without any universal interest. The other would simply be interested in theoretical results, yet say nothing about concrete economic institutions. Thus Schmoller and historicism ended up in relativism, the Austrian School, Mises in particular, in dualism (Eucken 1950, 324).

While it is evident that a genuinely theoretical economics cannot rely solely on the accumulation of empirical facts, there is very little that an economic science of pure, a priori principles can achieve. Instead, there is a real danger that economists end up constructing "a chaos of concepts supplementary to the facts" (Eucken 1950, 54). If theoretical economics is unable to say anything relevant with regard to concrete economic relations, it ends up relying on the help of "practical experts" (Eucken 1950, 304). For liberal theory, this is of course not enough: it needs to be scientific but also relevant for concrete shaping of economic reality.

In Eucken's view, the only way to overcome this rift is to return to the origin of these concepts in *experience* (Eucken 1950, 28). To be more exact, it was the task of ordoliberal science to conceive itself with regard to two parallel domains, "everyday experience" and "scientific experience". As Eucken argued, everyday experience is the starting point of all serious questioning, something without which all research is in danger of falling into pure speculation. At the same time, everyday experience does not amount to science as such. Following the German philosopher and logician Hermann Lotze, Eucken claimed that scientific experience is about transforming "what is given to us as *happening* together into what is *connected* together" (Eucken 1950, 40). Economist must start from history, from actual forms of production, but work towards an analytic framework for their theoretical analysis (Eucken 1950, 37).

In the context of early twentieth-century German academia, it was Max Weber's theory of "ideal types" that had become the central point of reference for objectivity in social sciences (Weber 1949). With the help of this concept, Weber aimed at analyzing the type of ideality characteristic of social sciences in distinction from natural sciences. Unlike in natural occurences, in social phenomena there is always involved an element of subjective interpretation and historicity that cannot be fundamentally eliminated without trivializing the whole issue. The Protestant ethic, for instance, is this kind of ideal type that goes beyond mere empirical discussion—it can be understood apart from all particular individuals—however, not without a reference to history and culture.

In Eucken's view, however, this was not enough. In his view, what Weber failed to recognize was the "fundamental difference between real types and ideal types and their logical character, as well as the differences in the process of abstraction in constructing the two kinds of types" (Eucken 1950, 348, see Kolev 2018). In other words, the mere detachment from empirical events or particulars was not enough in order for economics to rise on the level of objective, theoretical science. What was needed was a more comprehensive and radical concept of ideality that could provide the foundation for universal analysis.

In this attempt to articulate a more radical concept of ideality Eucken was particularly influenced by the phenomenological philosophy of Edmund Husserl. This connection was not purely theoretical but biographical: Eucken and Husserl became family friends as Eucken began his professorship at the University of Freiburg in 1927. Husserl, who retired from his professorship at the same year, became the godfather of Eucken's daughter and stayed in contact with the Eucken family despite Husserl's difficult position as a Jew in Nazi Germany. At the heart of Husserl's phenomenological project, was the demand to return to the "things themselves" (Husserl 2001, 168). Instead of scholastic speculations, philosophy was to return to the origin of our concepts and ideas in experience, to investigate things in regard to their "givenness". It was only with the help of experience, Husserl argued, that the modern sciences could overcome their state of dispersion and work together in the pursuit for truth.

This did not mean, however, that science would amount to a mere description of everyday experience. Science is about gaining theoretical insights and ideas for the purpose of constructing an axiomatic system of knowledge. But ideas do not come from nowhere: they must be firmly anchored in experience. What Husserl called "eidetic reduction" was an intellectual process in which we vary our possible experience in order to gain insight into the essential structures of experience and the world. The key question was what can we remove from a particular phenomenon in order for it to remain its essence. Eucken himself called this "isolating abstraction" (Eucken 1950, 107).

It should be noted, however, that Husserl himself operated with a rather broad concept of ideality. He did not assume that all types of generalities from "chairs" to "political institutions". from "colors" to "numbers" could be analyzed with the help of a single concept of ideality such as exact mathematical ideality. Instead, Husserl developed a rather broad taxonomy of generality from "bound" to "free" idealities, from inexact to exact ideas. The kind of geometrical idealization characteristic of the modern natural sciences was only one type of idealization that was not to be confused with the kind of abstraction characteristic of, for instance, types of observational shapes ("treelike", "shiny" etc.). What was crucial was to avoid the kind of Kantian interpretation according to which ideas would function as unattainable "limit-values" for possible experience. Ideas should not be hypostatized into transcendent principles, but they must be firmly anchored in concrete experience.

4 Towards Liberalism as a Science: Theory of Orders

For Eucken and the ordoliberal tradition, it was the concept of order (*Ordnung*) that became the most important theoretical concept for the analysis of economic forms. "As the course of everyday economic life proceeds differently according to the form of the economic system", Eucken argued, "the knowledge of the different kinds of orders is the first step towards understanding of economic reality" (Eucken 1989, 58). To put it simply, order is that web of economic relations, institutions and technologies that forms the basis of our economic activity. What defines an economic order are not just economic classes or technologies of production, but all sorts of norms, rules and relations of influence.

Although Eucken occasionally spoke of historical "economic orders" (*Wirtschaftsordnungen*) such as the Roman or the Medieval ones (Eucken 1950, 76ff.), the key question was how to overcome the historicist idea according to which all economic forms are simply historical notions tied to a particular situation. Unlike "stages" and "styles" of economic development characteristic of the historicist approach, the concept of order was to be understood in terms of a "universal problem" (Eucken 1950, 30) leading to a theory of the essential features of all possible economic systems. By way of isolating abstraction and eidetic variation, the economist looks at historical orders and tries to isolate their ideal features. It is not for the love of abstraction, however, that the economist performs this variation. The key purpose is to understand the world of facts and their connectedness (Eucken 1954, 19).

In his attempt to arrive at a general scientific theory of economic orders, Eucken played central attention to the concept of the "rules of the game" (*Spielregeln*) (Eucken 1950, 186ff.). In order to recognize a particular economic order, one must ask what are the structural norms and principles that regulate the decisions of particular economic agents. It is not so much the question of division of labour that matters as it is the question of who makes the relevant economic decisions concerning *production and exchange*. Who makes the decisions on what to produce, how to do it, and how to exchange the products? Are these decisions made by a single person (or institution) or by the economic agents themselves?

In Eucken's view, this question could only be answered in two ways. Either the decisions concerning production and distribution are made by a central authority, or, these decisions are made by the indidivuals who take part in economy. In the first case, we are dealing with an ideal type of "centrally directed economy". In the latter, it is the case of an "exchange economy" (Eucken 1950, 117ff.). These two constitute the basic answer to the problem of ideality in economic forms: "No other types of economic system, or even traces of others – besides these two – are to be found in economic reality past or present" (Eucken 1950, 118). It is crucial to note, however, that these ideal concepts were not to be conceived as a typology of national economies. A simple household, a medieval village or a modern nation-state can all be analyzed with the help of these two ideal forms.

This is not to say, however, that all particular examples would fall strictly into either camp. In most cases, we are actually dealing with a combination of centralized and decentralized economic decisions (Eucken 1950, 232). Modern market economies are based on the decisions of invididual producers and consumers on what to produce or how to sell it; still, modern nations exercise considerable fiscal power regarding all sorts of centralized investments. They are, as we would put it, mixed economies. The ideal types are not to be taken as exclusionary categories, but as theoretical abstractions describing the logic of economic decisions and arrangements: How does the coordination of individual plans and economic decisions come about? (Eucken 1950, 130). Instead of being labels for economic systems, ideal forms describe how things are *connected* in the event of a particular institutional or other setting.

A closer look into Eucken's theory of ideal forms reveals that his typology was, at the end, rich and multifaceted. Exchange economies, for instance, can be divided into a number of sub-types from barter and monetary economies and further into simple (exchange-money) and more complex (credit-money) forms (Eucken 1950, 129ff.). Thus, the choice between exchange vs. centrally directed economies is not one of total presence vs. total absence of the state. Even in exchange economies, state plays a central role as the guardian of price stability and the whole system of prices.

The focus on ideas also means that one should not view economic phenomena primarily from the persepective of particular historical settings. The problems of monopolies and credit bubbles, for instance, appear only in market economies with developed central institutions and a banking system. They are not, however, problems that would characterize merely seventeenth-century mercantilism or contemporary financial capitalism. They are universal problems that have significance beyond individual events.

In this regard, science does not solve primarily the problems of individual historical epochs. Rather, it is only through the rigorous ideal-scientific analysis that economics can help us to solve the problems of national economy.

5 Normative Science

The central challenge of Eucken's approach—economics should be primarily a descriptive science—was how to comprehend the normative dimension of liberalism. How could market economy hold on to its moral superiority after it had been firmly based on scientific approach?

Here, Eucken resorted to two parallel approaches. First, the superiority of "exchange economy" with regard to all centrally directed forms rested on moral-philosophical arguments in line with the Kantian understanding of liberty and ethics. Exchange economy was morally superior because it corresponded with a view of human being as being responsible for one's actions. For Kant, freedom and accountability were the key conditions for any understanding of ourselves as moral actors. Centrally directed economy where decisions are made by some central authority destroys these conditions, or it makes impossible to adhere to them. Particularly in his *Grundsätze der Wirtschaftspolitik*, Eucken treated the state and different interest groups such as private companies as threats not only to the market but to the principle of liberty. This is because they violate another Kantian principle that every human being ought to be treated as an end in itself. In a centrally directed economy, where decisions are made by a central authority, the human being becomes a mere cog in the "anonymous political-economic machine" (Eucken 1990, 177). Thus, centrally directed economy destroys the very possibility of ethical behaviour.

The other line of argumentation is slightly more complex but equally crucial. It relates to Eucken's theory of ideal forms as carrying a ***normative significance*** on its own. As already indicated, the central thesis of the authors of the ORDO manifesto (including Eucken) was that the contemporary strains of historicism and marginalism had failed to provide a normative theory of state and market that could have served as an instrument of policy design. Instead, they remained primarity a theoretical analysis of market transactions or a historical description of particular forms of production. For the ordoliberals and Eucken in particular, this was not enough. Science was to be brought together with a more ambitious vision of political transformation with a focus on institutional design and social reform.

It was by no means a coincidence that ordoliberalism focused so heavily on law and rule-based instruments. If the "rules of the game" are constitutive for any form of economic activity, then it is only natural that the key political battles concern how these rules are actually shaped. A rule-based order is central for the limitation of the power of interest groups or ad hoc political decisions. The key question was, however, how to legitimize these rules without falling into yet another type of authoritarianism?

Here, Eucken seemed to follow a very specific line of thought stemming from two philosophical schools of his time, Neo-Kantianism and phenomenology. For the Neo-Kantian tradition—represented by philosophers such as Wilhelm Windelband (1848–1915), Heinrich Rickert (1863–1936) and Emil Lask (1875–1915)—the growing division between the descriptive and normative tasks of science had become one of the key intellectual problems. It reflected two parallel developments: first, the identity crisis of philosophy in the light of advancing natural sciences, and second, the growing division between the natural and the human sciences. It seemed that philosophy had lost its role as the driving force of modernity and the Enlightenment, and the rapidly advancing natural sciences held the monopoly for progress in the world of ideas. The natural sciences were able to make new discoveries and formulate empirically testable hypotheses. Philosophy and the human sciences could only speak of history or values without any claim for true objectivity, thus potentially plunging into relativism.

Neo-Kantianism sought to change this. By returning to Kant, they aimed at a radical reconfiguration of philosophy as a normative discipline capable of answering questions of validity and justification. Whereas sciences deal with the world as it is, philosophy should be interested in the causes and justifications of our knowledge, how knowledge arises from consciousness and what are the grounds of its justification. As Windelband put it, philosophy was to be reconfigured as a "system of norms": what are those conditions on the basis of which we take something to be true and valid? In Windelband's own work, however, this question did not receive a sufficient answer. According to many of his followers, he could not defend the strict separation between the natural and the normative, but had to resort to psychologistic language in explaining the genesis of norms.

Husserl's phenomenology provided one solution to Windelband's dilemma. Husserl followed the Neo-Kantian idea of philosophy as a normative discipline, however, with important amendments. For him, ideal and a priori structures of cognition were not just a collection of Platonic ideas but a set of ideal laws, generalities and principles. The normative validity of these laws, however, is not dependent on psychological processes. Rather, their normativity can only be assessed on the basis of a strict transcendental-phenomenological investigation. "There is undeniably a subjective, experiential distinction that corresponds to the fundamental objective-ideal distinction between law and fact", Husserl argued:

> If we never had experienced the consciousness of rationality, of apodeicticity in its characteristic distinction from the consciousness of facticity, we should not have possessed the concept of law. We should not have been able to distinguish generic (ideal, law-determined) generality

> from universal (factual, contingent) generality, nor necessary (i.e., law-determined, generic) implication from factual (i.e., contingently universal) implication. (Husserl 2001, 90)[6]

In other words, our ability to distinguish between fact and law depends on our ability to do conceive a particular idea in its universality. Although a factual generality can be expressed in the form of a general principles (e.g. "All swans are white"), they can never amount to the full sense of lawfulness characteristic of ideal, law-determined generality (e.g. Law of non-contradiction). A priori laws are thus defined by a strictly ideal content. Their normative validity, however, can only be understood with regard to a judging consciousness. It is only through a reflextive process on behalf of the subject that these laws can undergo what Husserl calls a "normative turn" and function as genuine norms for thinking and acting.

It is impossible to go into more details, but it should be noted that Eucken explicitly referred to Husserl on this point. Scientists start from the everyday experience and tried to proceed to ideas by abstracting from the empirical and factual contents. The goal of this investigation is to reach such ideal laws that are not bound to any particular instance. Accordingly, reality itself does not affect the truth of theory (Eucken 1954, 30). Eucken's so-called constitutive principles such as a "functioning price system", "freedom of contract" or the "principle of liability" were not simple theoretical generalizations. They were to be conceived as normatively binding principles derived from the ideal form of exchange economy. What concepts such as Max Weber's "ideal type" or Schumpeter's analysis of capitalism lacked was exactly this understanding of ideality as governed by a set of general laws, principles and ideal (not empirical) regularities (Eucken 1950, 330).

So, why law as a political instrument? First, because laws and rules themselves carry out an important constitutive principle of exchange economy: *principle of continuity* of economic policy. In Eucken's view, one of the central conditions of a functioning exchange economy was a stable environment for decisions on investment. Without some kind of reliability and predictability, economic decisions driving the market are left undone. Second, and more importantly, these constitutive principles that concern the market and the state are not just historical virtues derived

[6] See also Eucken's reference to Husserl's *Philosophy as Rigorous Science* in Eucken (1950, 321).

from experience. They are theoretical conditions of the ideal itself. Their normative primacy depends not on their historical success but on their logical necessity as ideal laws.

A stable and permanent rule-based framework is not only for the restriction of democracy. It is necessary because it complies with the ideal form of exchange economy. Eucken was well aware that the relation of theoretical ideals and concrete policies is often complex, and that one should not apply these principles blindly. Particularly in the case of so-called regulative principles such as antitrust policy, income policy (taxation), and correction of externalities, policy-maker cannot simply apply an a priori principle. They require constant vigilance and adjustment in the light of changing circumstances.

6 Conclusion

This article has been about the intellectual foundations of a particular variation of neoliberalism that is central to the post-WWII European economic constitution: German ordoliberalism. I have tried to accomplish two things. First, I have tried to emphasize that despite the tumultuous conditions that characterized the historical origins of ordoliberal movement, it was not a mere political or economic doctrine. Ordoliberalism as a philosophically motivated theory that emerged as a response to the crisis of economics and of scientific reason in general, that is, to the growing dispersion of individual sciences and the loss of their common foundation. Ordoliberalism was in fact a philosophical and moral programme that aimed at a fundamental revision of the ontological and epistemological foundations of liberal theory. It employed theoretical and conceptual resources from a variety of philosophical and intellectual traditions such as Neo-Kantianism, antipositivism, and phenomenology.

Second, the birth of ordoliberalism should be understood in regard to a long history of European neoliberalism as the rearticulation of liberal rationality from the early twentieth century onwards. This rearticulation, I claim, was not only about traditional concepts of liberalism such as freedom, autonomy, and the state. It relied on a new understanding of the role of normativity in science and a new philosophy of history.

To put it succinctly, ordoliberalism was an attempt to respond to the crisis of liberalism by inventing a new rational foundation for liberalism. It did this by reinterpreting some of the key concepts and ideas of the political domain and articulating a new philosophy of history that was critical of the progressive narrative of classical liberalism. It presented an all-encompassing vision of a functioning institutional order supported by a moral philosophy of an autonomous individual. At the heart of this undertaking, was a radical reversal of the traditional relation between economics and moral philosophy: Rather than being a part of moral philosophy, political economy was to produce a moral philosophy of its own.

The state and future of liberalism is one of the central questions of today's Europe. Yet I argue we have not understood the most significant revolution of liberal theory in the past hundred years. This is because we have focused primarily in political and economic ideas, or strategies of governance. What politically seems like a shock doctrine was intellectually a result of a long struggle for a new philosophical rationality for liberalism—a fundamental cultural and intellectual transformation. Understanding this transformation is vital for a more critical and nuanced understanding of European political economy.

Acknowledgement This article has been written under the Academy of Finland Centre of Excellence Law, Identity and the European Narrative, funding decision number 312430.

References

Allen, Christopher S. 2005. "Ordo-Liberalism Trumps Keynesianism: Economic Policy in the Federal Republic of Germany." In *Monetary Union in Crisis: The European Union as a Neo-Liberal Construction*, edited by Bernard Moss, 199–221. London: Palgrave.

Biebricher, Thomas. 2013. "Europe and the Political Philosophy of Neoliberalism." *Contemporary Political Theory* 12 (4): 338–75.

Blum, Reinhard. 1969. *Soziale Marktwirtschaft: Wirtschaftspolitik zwischen Neoliberalismus und Ordoliberalismus*. Tübingen: Mohr Siebeck.

Blyth, Mark. 2013. *Austerity: The History of a Dangerous Idea*. Oxford: Oxford University Press.

Böhm, Franz. 1937. "Die Ordnung der Wirtschaft als geschichtliche Aufgabe und rechtsschöpferische Leitung." In *Ordnung der Wirtschaft*, edited by Franz Böhm, Walter Eucken, and Hans Großmann-Doerth. Stuttgart and Berlin: W. Kohlhammer.

Böhm, Franz, Walter Eucken, and Hans Großmann-Doerth. 2017. "The Ordo-Manifesto of 1936." In *The Birth of Austerity: German Ordoliberalism and Contemporary Neoliberalism*, edited by Thomas Biebricher and Frieder Vogelmann, 27–39. London: Rowman & Littlefield.

Bonefeld, Werner. 2017. *The Strong State and the Free Economy*. London: Rowman & Littlefield.

Brunnermeier, Markus K., Harold James, and Jean-Pierre Landau. 2016. *The Euro and the Battle of Ideas*. Princeton, NJ: Princeton University Press.

Bruun, Hans H. 2007. *Science, Values and Politics in Max Weber's Methodology*. 2nd ed. Aldershot: Ashgate.

Dekker, Erwin. 2016. *The Viennese Students of Civilization: The Meaning and Context of Austrian Economics Reconsidered*. New York, NY: Cambridge University Press.

Demetriades, Panicos. 2015. "German Macroeconomics: Channels of Influence." In *German Macro: How It's Different and Why That Matters*, edited by George Bratsiotis and David Cobham, 36–41. Brussels: European Policy Centre.

Dullien, Sebastian, and Ulrike Guérot. 2012. *The Long Shadow of Ordoliberalism: Germany's Approach to the Euro Crisis*. London: European Council on Foreign Relations.

Eucken, Walter. 1930. "Wirtschaftsentwicklung contra Kulturentwicklung." *Die Tatwelt* 6, no. 1/3 (January–March): 33–7.

———. 1936, Kampf der Wissenschaft, Unpublished Lecture Manuscript, Available at Walter-Eucken-Archiv, Jena.

———. 1948. "On the Theory of the Centrally Administered Economy: An Analysis of the German Experiment." Translated by Terence W. Huchinson. *Economica* 15 (58): 79–100.

———. 1950. *The Foundations of Economics: History and Theory of Economic Reality*. Translated by Terence W. Huchinson. London: William Hodge and Company.

———. 1954. *Kapitaltheoretische Untersuchungen*. Tübingen: J.C.B. Mohr.

———. 1989. *Die Grundlagen der Nationalökonomie*. 9th ed. Berlin: Springer-Verlag.

———. 1990. *Die Grunsätze der Wirtschaftspolitik*. 6th ed. Tübingen: J.C.B. Mohr.

———. 2017. "Structural Transformations of the State and the Crisis of Capitalism." In *The Birth of Austerity: German Ordoliberalism and Contemporary Neoliberalism*, edited by Thomas Biebricher and Frieder Vogelmann, 51–72. London: Rowman and Littlefield International.

Foucault, Michel. 2008. *The Birth of Biopolitics: Lectures at the Collège de France 1978–1979*. Edited by Michel Sennelart. Translated by Graham Burchell. Basingstoke: Palgrave.

Fourcade, Marion. 2013. "The Economy as Morality Play, and Implications for the Eurozone Crisis." *Socio-Economic Review* 11 (3): 620–27.

Goldschmidt, Nils. 1998. "Christlicher Glaube, Wirtschaftstheorie und Praxisbezug: Walter Eucken und die Anlage 4 der Denkschrift des Bonhoeffer-Kreises." *Historisch-Politische Mitteilungen* 5 (1): 33–48.

———. 2013. "Walter Eucken's Place in the History of Ideas." *Review of Austrian Economics* 26 (3): 127–47.

Goldschmidt, Nils, and Michael Wohlgemuth. 2008. "Social Market Economy: Origins, Meanings and Interpretations." *Constitutional Political Economy* 19 (3): 261–76.

Habermas, Jürgen. 2012. *The Crisis of the European Union: A Response.* Cambridge: Polity Press.

Hall, Peter A. 2012. "The Economics and Politics of the Euro Crisis." *German Politics* 21 (4): 355–71.

Haselbach, Dieter. 1991. *Autoritärer Liberalismus und Soziale Marktwirtschaft: Gesellschaft und Politik im Ordoliberalismus.* Baden-Baden: Nomos.

Hien, Josef, and Christian Joerges. 2017. *Ordoliberalism, Law and the Rule of Economics.* Oxford and Portland: Hart Publishing.

———. 2018. "Dead Man Walking? Current European Interest in Germany's Ordoliberal Tradition." *European Law Journal* 24 (2–3): 142–62.

Hien, Josef. 2013. "The Ordoliberalism that Never Was." *Contemporary Political Theory* 12 (4): 349–58.

———. 2017. "The Religious Roots of the European Crisis." *Journal of Common Market Studies* 57 (2): 185–204.

Hill, Lisa. 2001. "The Hidden Theology of Adam Smith." *The European Journal of the History of Economic Thought* 8 (1): 1–29.

Husserl, Edmund. 2001. *Logical Investigations.* Edited by Dermot Moran. 2nd ed. London: Routledge.

Hutchison, Terence W. 1979. "Notes on the Effects of Economic Ideas on Policy: The Example of the German Social Market Economy." *Journal of Institutional and Theoretical Economics* 135 (3): 426–41.

Johnson, Daniel. 1989. "Exiles and Half-Exiles: Wilhelm Röpke, Alexander Rüstow and Walter Eucken." In *German Neo-Liberals and the Social Market Economy*, edited by Alan Peacock and Hans Willgerodt, 40–68. London: Palgrave Macmillan.

Kant, Immanuel. 2007. "Idea for a Universal History with a Cosmopolitan Aim." In *Anthropology, History and Education*, edited and translated by Robert B. Louden, and Günter Zöller, 107–20. Cambridge: Cambridge University Press.

Katzenstein, Peter J. 1997. *Tamed Power: Germany in Europe.* Ithaca, NY: Cornell University Press.

Kolev, Stefan. 2015. "Ordoliberalism and the Austrian School". In *The Oxford Handbook of Austrian Economics*, edited by P. J. Boettke and C. J. Coyne, 419–44. New York: Oxford University Press.

———. 2018. "The abandoned übervater: Max Weber and the neoliberals." Working Paper No. 2018–21, Center for the History of Political Economy. Duke University.

Langewiesche, Dieter N. 2000. *Liberalism in Germany*. London: Macmillan Press.

Manow, Philip. 2001. "Ordoliberalismus als ökonomische Ordnungstheologie." *Leviathan* 29 (2): 179–98.

Meiers, Franz-Joseph. 2015. *Germany's Role in the Euro Crisis*. Heidelberg: Springer.

Miksch, Leonhard. 1947. *Wettbewerb als Aufgabe: Grundsätze einer Wettbewerbsordnung*. Godesberg: H. Küpper.

Mirowski, Philip, and Dieter Plehwe, eds. 2009. *The Road from Mont Pèlerin: The Making of the Neoliberal Thought Collective*. Cambridge, MA: Harvard University Press.

Mises, Ludwig von. 1966. *Human Action*. 3rd rev. ed. Chicago: Henry Regnery Company.

Plickert, Philip. 2008. *Wandlungen des Neoliberalismus. Eine Studie zur Entwicklung und Ausstrahlung der "Mont Pèlerin Society."* Stuttgart: Lucius & Lucius.

Proctor, Robert N. 1991. *Value-Free Science? Purity and Power in Modern Knowledge*. Cambridge, MA: Harvard University Press.

Ptak, Ralf. 2009. "Neoliberalism in Germany: Revisiting the Ordoliberal Foundations of the Social Market Economy." In *The Road From Mont Pèlerin: The Making of The Neoliberal Thought Collective*, edited by Philip Mirowski and Dieter Plehwe, 98–138. Cambridge, MA: Harvard University Press.

Röpke, Wilhelm. 1998. *A Human Economy*. Wilmington, DE: ISI Books.

———. 2009. *The Social Crisis of Our Time*. New Brunswick, NJ: Transaction Publishers.

Rüstow, Alexander. 2017. "General Sociological Causes of the Economic Disintegration and Possibilities of Reconstruction." In *The Birth of Austerity: German Ordoliberalism and Contemporary Neoliberalism*, edited by Thomas Biebricher and Frieder Vogelmann, 151–61. London and New York: Rowman & Littlefield International.

Ryner, Magnus. 2015. "Europe's Ordoliberal Iron Cage: Critical Political Economy, the Euro Area Crisis and Its Management." *Journal of European Public Policy* 22 (2): 275–94.

Sally, Razeen. 1996. "Ordoliberalism and the Social Market: Classical Political Economy from Germany." *New Political Economy* 1 (2): 233–57.

Slobodian, Quinn. 2018. *Globalists: The End of Empire and the Birth of Neoliberalism*. Cambridge: Harvard University Press.

Streit, Manfred, and Werner Mussler. 1994. "The Economic Constitution of the European Community: From Rome to Maastricht." *Constitutional Political Economy* 5 (3): 319–53.

Tribe, Keith. 2009. "Liberalism and Neoliberalism in Britain, 1930–1980." In *The Road From Mont Pèlerin: The Making of The Neoliberal Thought Collective*, edited by Philip Mirowski and Dieter Plehwe, 68–97. Cambridge, MA: Harvard University Press.

Tuori, Kaarlo, and Klaus Tuori. 2014. *The Eurozone Crisis: A Constitutional Analysis*. Cambridge: Cambridge University Press.

Vanberg, Viktor. 2001. *The Constitution of Markets: Essays in Political Economy*. London: Routledge.

Weber, Max. 1949. "Objectivity in Social Science and Social Policy." In *The Methodology of the Social Sciences*, edited and translated by Edward. A. Shils, and Henry A. Finch, 50–120. New York: Free Press.

Wegmann, Milène. 2000. *Früher Neoliberalismus und europäische Integration: Interdependenz der nationalen, supranationalen und internationalen Ordnung von Wirtschaft und Gesellschaft (1932–1965)*. Baden-Baden: Nomos-Verlags-Gesellschaft.

Young, Brigitte. 2014. "The Power of Ordoliberalism in the Eurozone Crisis Management." In *The Eurozone* Crisis *and the Future of Europe*, edited by Daniel Dăianu, Carlo D'Adda, Giorgio Basevi, and Rajeesh Kumar, 126–37. Basingstoke: Palgrave Macmillan.

PART III

The Power of Ideas

CHAPTER 11

Classical Liberalism, Non-interventionism and the Origins of European Integration: Luigi Einaudi, Friedrich A. von Hayek, Wilhelm Röpke

Antonio Masala and Alberto Mingardi

1 Introduction

Recent literature has drawn attention to the international affairs dimension of so-called neoliberalism (see, inter alia, Slobodian 2018). In particular, the idea of the European Union is seen as an offspring of "neoliberalism," in the guise of a by-product of German Ordoliberalism. Such view goes particularly well with contemporary critics of "austerity,"

A. Masala (✉)
University of Pisa, Pisa, Italy

A. Mingardi
IULM University, Milan, Italy

© The Author(s) 2021

A. M. Cunha and C. E. Suprinyak (eds.), *Political Economy and International Order in Interwar Europe*, Palgrave Studies in the History of Economic Thought,
https://doi.org/10.1007/978-3-030-47102-6_11

who tend to see the euro as a neoliberal conceit and a cudgel to impose lower public spending on otherwise recalcitrant member states.[1]

Besides disparities in the ideological outlook, with this paper we aim at something different: that is, to investigate in what degree—if any—the strain of nineteenth-century liberal pacifism influenced the classical liberalism of the twentieth (or, "neoliberalism") and how Luigi Einaudi, Friedrich A. von Hayek, Wilhelm Röpke understood the problems of international order, particularly insofar as Europe as a political and economic area was concerned.

Dreams of European unification are often dated back to Kant (1795). Certainly ideas concerning a possible European federation have been discussed for quite a while, including those based on a clear democratic model, like in the case of Augustin Thierry (see Valverde 1994, 43–44). Their fate was, however, rather uneasy in nineteenth century Europe, which was living through nationalist uprisings and where federalism, including the American one, was seldom properly appreciated.[2]

The specific aspect of the classical liberal project upon which we will try to call attention, however, is the idea that free trade and economic cooperation brings by the easing of international controversies. This is a theme of paramount importance in the history of nineteenth-century liberalism.

Such emphasis on trade as a device for fostering mutual understanding and stronger economic interdependence is not, per se, mutually exclusive with the idea of an international legal framework.

This paper is an attempt to investigate how the lessons of nineteenth-century liberalism was in fact digested by twentieth-century thinkers such as Luigi Einaudi, Friedrich A. con Hayek and Wilhelm Röpke. These authors were "neo-liberal," so to say, in the proper sense: i.e., they envisioned the enterprise of a "new" liberalism which, though not unfriendly to the free market, featured a stronger role for government in order to be more cogent in the face of twentieth-century challenges. These thinkers were among the intellectual architects of post-WWII order: Einaudi as a

[1] Examples of this literature abounds. See, among many, Blyth (2013). Mazzucato (2013, 2018) builds on similar assumptions, to propose a different narrative aiming at glorifying government intervention.

[2] An exception was Jacques Necker who, forty years before Tocqueville, wrote a complex comparative treatise on executive power in which he showed to fully appreciate the advantages of the American model. See Craiutu (2018).

protagonist in his own right, Hayek as the founder of the Mont Pèlerin Society and probably the most influential classical liberal thinker of his century, Röpke because of his influence over the Ordoliberals and thus as the inspiration for Ludwig Erhard and a certain set of German policies. Were they thinking of revisiting twentieth-century "liberal pacifism"? Were they indifferent? Were they subscribing to an alternative approach to the international order?

We will endeavour to investigate this topic, at first providing a glance of classical liberal pacifism and later searching for its offsprings in authors such as Einaudi, Hayek and Röpke.

2 Free Markets in a Peaceful World. The Legacy of Richard Cobden

Plural as it is, liberalism (and, particular, classical liberalism) can be described as a theory aiming to stem and limit government's powers. These limits are necessary to allow for a sphere for economic action independent from politics but are all the more important when it comes to those activities in which the government can resort to its monopoly of violence: meaning administrating justice and waging war. Historical contingencies that brought classical liberals to side with contemporary conservatives have often made us forget how crucial the classical liberal approach to limit the resort to violence and war was, within the boundaries of the liberal doctrine.

We may distinguish classical liberal approaches to the issue of international peace in two camps: on the one hand, a focus on the need for procedures that somehow hold in check the destructive capacity of nation states. On the other hand, the idea that commerce will in itself strengthen and multiply the interests that, in different nation states, may oppose war. The problem is similar: how to increase the costs of war, how to make it less likely.

The growing costs of waging war are seen in terms of destruction of industrial capacity, loss of needed imports or disruption of international supply chains. Such considerations are, however, typically framed within the theme of the civilising effects of commerce: by trading, different people not only may mutually enrich one another but they learn of different cultures, thereby becoming more tolerant.

Hirschman (1977) produced a classic treatment of the so-called approach of doux commerce. Perhaps the most effective statement of such position is Benjamin Constant's 1819 speech on "The Liberty of the Ancients Compared with that of the Moderns" (Constant 1819, now in Constant 1988, 308–28). One of Constant's points, to prove the difference between the ancient liberty of the polis, focused on active involvement for keeping the city's independence, and the modern liberty of securing private independence under the rule of law and the peaceful enjoyment of commercial affluence, is that, unlike the ancients, the moderns are involved in commerce instead of war. "Ancient" republican liberty was associated with popular militias, whereas, "modern" liberty was built on standing armies, allowing the private individual to indulge in occupations other than war. The point was vividly made by H.T. Buckle, in the 1860s, as he stressed that the invention of gunpowder was one of the drivers of civilisation and peace:

> Before this time [of the introduction of gunpowder], it was considered the duty of nearly every citizen to be prepared to enter the military service, for the purpose either of defending his own country, or of attacking others. Standing armies were entirely unknown; and in their place there existed a rude and barbarous militia, always ready for battle, and always unwilling to engage in those peaceful pursuits which were then universally despised. Nearly every man being a soldier, the military profession, as such, had no separate existence; or, to speak more properly, the whole of Europe composed one great, army, in which all other professions were merged. (Buckle 1857, now in Buckle 1904, 117)

The tradition of doux commerce is often dismissed as unrealistic and naive, as it does not take into account the specificities of politics and the use of force by government.[3] This is easier when the theory is interpreted as being unidirectional: that, implying that by participating in trade people will sweeten and develop better manners and tolerance one with the other.

This is a bit of caricature. Most liberal pacifists indeed shared a theory that aim at a complex understanding of social reality in which, as in the case of Buckle, the unintended consequences of non-political facts (in this case, technological innovation) have political reverberations. In a sense, we need to recognise that these liberal authors were not only supporting

[3] A different criticism is the one provided by Gartzke (2005), which aims to complete the theory with considerations built on more recent empirical evidence of the benefits of economic freedom.

what they considered to be the road to peace but also seeing the international order as a complex reality which nonetheless was not independent of common individuals' behaviours and actions.

Classical liberal theories of international order are micro-founded: they stress how changes in the behaviour of individuals could have an impact on a realm as apparently divorced from the individual sphere as foreign policy.[4]

The normative assumptions of this view may be perplexing for us. Those holding such view estimated that, as war becomes more tangibly expensive for individuals qua economic actors, they would endeavour to oppose it. This requires a strong belief in the seeming omnipotence of "public opinion" in a liberal society and an equally strong belief in the fact that public opinion may allow dispersed interests in society (all those who will be affected and put in danger by war) to overcome strong pressure by concentrated interests, that are instead favourable to war.

Whatever the problems with classical liberal, market-based pacifism, what we want to stress in this paper is how central this commitment to peace was for nineteenth-century liberals—and how it was intertwined with their preference for a free market economy. Both the arguments—for peace and for markets—built on the same arsenal of arguments, including a particular attention towards unintended, unplanned consequences and, more general, an understanding of bottom up "solutions" as potentially more viable than top down ones.

Liberalism, as always, comes in shades and such an approach is by no means a matter of general agreement among liberals, even in the nineteenth century. One of the foremost British liberal thinkers, Herbert

[4] Panebianco (2018) is an ambitious attempt to read foreign policy in the light of individuals' interactions in the social and political spheres. While the actions and systems of beliefs of particular individuals can appear to be far away from the determinations of ministers and diplomats, they indeed contribute to shape and influence them. Panebianco's, contemporary understanding of the interaction between the micro and the macro sphere is not grounded in a rejection of the specific nature of politics, as he stresses that political obligation has a distinctively different nature from contract obligation. Yet he stresses that "if power needs, as it does, the intention of those who exercise it to exercise it, i.e. the intention of imposing their own will to somebody else, this does not mean that all consequences of the exercise of power are rightly foreseen, projected, willed" (Panebianco 2018, 131). It is in the realm of the (often unintended) consequences of such exertions of power, that common individuals, their ideas, their wishes, their sentiments, end up with having a say. Taking into account this fact is, for Panebianco, the rationale for a theory of international order which is micro-founded.

Spencer, profoundly subscribed to the views we have outlined above, that he integrated in his own philosophy of history. Spencer, as it is well known, saw political history as unfolding from "military societies" to "industrial societies."[5]

But this was hardly an ex post systematisation by a brilliant philosopher. We consider it important to examine, however briefly, the thought of the paramount champion of liberalism in foreign policy: Richard Cobden.

Cobden was the great hero of free trade, being the driving force behind the abolition of Corn Laws in 1846, but also an "international man," so Emile de Girardin called him and J.A. Hobson immortalised him in the title of his biography. As Hobson remarked, Cobden's perspective was such that

> protective tariffs and other trade impediments were condemned, not merely or mainly because they made food dear and otherwise impaired the production of national wealth, but because they interfered with the free and friendly intercourse of different nations, bred hostility of interests, stimulated hostile preparations and swallowed up those energies and resources of each nation that were needed for the cultivation of the arts of peaceful progress (Hobson 1918, now in Hobson 1968, 9).

While Cobden was destined, after the abolition of the Corn Laws, to be a fringe politician, his call for a more restrained foreign policy became distinctive of liberalism. Think about the call for Peace, Retrenchment and Reform which was made famous by William Gladstone. "Retrenchment" in a world in which public spending was almost entirely allocated to military spending means reduction of military and naval expenditure.

It was thus precisely military spending, using people's money to wage war, the source of liberal indignation against the "class legislation" fostered by the landed classes. The critique of special interest and corruption as inimical to unfettered, market competition prospered in that environment: in a much simpler political scene, it was easier to detect those very special interests manoeuvring Naval and imperial policies to their own benefits.

If Cobden always used a humanitarian language in his battles for free trade, he also used an economic language in his battles for peace. As John Morley remarked, "he opposed war, because war and the preparation for it consumed the resources which were required for the improvement

[5] On Spencer, see, among others, Mingardi (2011).

of the temporal condition of the population" (Morley 1903, 535). Any attempt to disentangle a humanitarian argument, based upon the need for global fraternity, from an economic argument, based upon some prospects of maximising opportunities and wealth, is destined to fail, in case of Cobden.

Indeed, he thought that

Men of war to conquer colonies, to yield us a monopoly of their trade, must now be dismissed, like many other equally glittering but false adages of our forefathers, and in its place we must substitute the more homely, but enduring maxim—Cheapness, which will command commerce; and whatever else is needful will follow in its train (Cobden 1835, now in Cobden 1903, 222).

In this perspective, monopolies and protection are decried for allowing for corruption and war is seen as a waste, as opposed to the cornucopia that could spring out of a stable peace. Retrenchment, doing away from wasteful military spending, is both morally and economically justified.

Practically, retrenchment implied leaving Europe to its own devices, renouncing Britain's pretences of fostering some sort of equilibrium in European politics.

Even Cobden, however, pronounced himself once in favour of a (limited) international infrastructure. In particular, he was convinced countries should bound themselves to arbitration, allowing for umpires to step into solve their own controversies before they degenerated.

In a letter to his friend George Combe, better known today as a leader of the phrenological movement than as a free trader, he observed:

> You seem to be puzzled about my motion in favour of international arbitration. Perhaps you have mixed it up with other theories to which I am no party. My plan does not embrace the scheme of a congress of nations, or imply the belief in the millennium, or demand your homage to the principles of non-resistance. I simply propose that England should offer to enter into an agreement with other countries, France, for instance, binding them to refer any dispute that may arise to arbitration. I do not mean to refer the matter to another sovereign power, but that each party should appoint plenipotentiaries in the form of commissioners, with a proviso for calling in arbitrators in case they cannot agree. (Morley 1881, now in Morley 1903, 508)

The idea of supranational arbitration was then interpreted by Cobden without seeking any real coordination or mutual agreement of sovereign powers. It was, indeed, envisioned as an attempt to have sovereigns submitting to rule of law institutions similar to those mediating disputes among firms.

We have referred before to the micro foundations of the theory of "liberal peace". This is true, in Cobden's case, on a variety of levels. John Morley so described Cobden's attitude:

> In other words he would have relied upon opinion. He was too practical to dream that regard for purely moral opinion could be trusted to check the overbearing impulse of powerful selfish interests. Wars, however, constantly arise not from the irreconcilable clashing of great interests of this kind, but from mismanaged trifles. This was what he had maintained in his argument for arbitration. The grave and unavoidable occasions for war, he said, are few. In the ordinary dealings of nations with one another, where a difference arises, it is about something where external opinion might easily be made to carry decisive weight. (Morley 1881, now in Morley 1903, 531)

In the overlapping registers of Cobden's rhetoric, one can find the shrewdness of the capable politician, who never strikes one chord at once. Yet if we assume (as overwhelmingly contemporary observers assumed too) that Cobden was essentially a believer in its own doctrine, before being its preacher, we may highlight some features of his liberal pacifism:

1. It is predicated upon the idea that actions and systems of beliefs of single individuals (the micro level) are both influencing and influenced by foreign policy;
2. War is considered wasteful not only because of the destruction it brings about, but because it diverts resources from other, more profitable uses: in modern jargon, war worsens the allocation of resources in society;
3. As such, war is considered as being in the interest of small groups favouring it (the aristocrats) at the expense of society at large;
4. Sovereigns are not considered as trustworthy, by and large because they are captured by landed classes;
5. Cobdenism is international in its goals (order, peace, international fraternity) but national in its means. At the very end it calls for retrenchment and spending cuts at the national level, assuming its consequence to be beneficial internationally.

While this fifth point is going to be disregarded by subsequent liberal thinkers, including the so-called "neoliberals," we consider the preceding four to inform even later classical liberal understanding of the international order.

3 Luigi Einaudi, the Division of Labour and the End of Sovereignty

On this background, we shall examine, albeit succinctly, some of Luigi Einaudi's contributions on the international order.

Einaudi wrote extensively on international matters, first between the beginning of WWI and 1925, then after 1943, after the Fascist government in Italy fell. These twenty years of silence coincide not only with the fascist era—but, broadly speaking, with the apparent triumph of nationalism throughout Europe.

The Piedmontese economist's reflections on international matters found their first, consistent exposition in a series of letters published in Corriere della sera (Italy's most prominent newspaper) between 1917 and 1919: later republished as Lettere politiche di Junius (1920), they represent formidable evidence of Einaudi's views on the unfolding of the post WWI world, in particular with a reference to the Wilsonian reshaping of Europe upon the principle of self-determination. In WWI, Einaudi was neither a neutralist (like the statesman Giovanni Giolitti, Piedmontese as well) nor a pacifist, but saw the clash of arms as a confrontation between an "English" and a "German" hegemony, supporting openly the first.

In a few instances Einaudi changed his mind. He opposed the Society of Nations as insufficiently forward-looking, and then hoped it may do some good. He called for a "functionalist" approach towards European integration, through a set of agreements on different issues, and later argued that European integration should be led politically, without technocratic subterfuges. At times Einaudi did favour inter-governmental restraints or cooperation but, for the most part, he supported the notion of nation-states foregoing sovereignty in favour of a "super-state" endowed with full financial autonomy.

Einaudi can certainly be seen as a protagonist, in the process of the making of the core institutions of the future European Community.[6] One of the most notable figure in this tradition[7] in the Italian public debate, Ernesto Rossi, was openly considered by Einaudi as one of his best students.[8] In his work, Einaudi maintained that the "absolute and exclusive sovereignty of each national State, embodied in the veto rule at the international diplomatic level, makes it impossible to pursue any collective action and provide a collective public good such as international peace" (Masini 2014, 121). This viewpoint has its foundations in Einaudi's economics and classical liberalism.

For one thing, Einaudi thinks that the nation state is out of touch with the features of modern economic growth.

It is a problem both of scale and of the nature of such an institution—i.e., the nature of sovereignty.

Insofar as their scale is concerned, Einaudi thought that "the modern European states are – economically – pygmies. Their surface is too small for a genuine division of labor to establish within their borders" (Einaudi 1952). His understanding of international issues was deeply depended upon his reading of modern economic development. For him, Smith's seminal insight that "the division of labour is limited by the extent of the market" is the truth that may help us in seeing how modern capitalism unfolds beyond the national dimension. In a complex economy, in which people demand and supply goods and services whose production involves a broad range of factors of production, which may be not be all available within national boundaries.

Why does a greater international division of labour entail the need to overcome nation states? Einaudi writes that "men living within a sovereign state must, from the necessities of living, be forced to secure the means of existence, the raw materials for their industries and the outlets for the products of their labor out of that state" (Einaudi 1945b). This

[6] Einaudi's support for European unification was shared by prime minister Alcide De Gasperi. De Gasperi's understanding of economic matter was indebted to Luigi Sturzo, an Italian Catholic priest and a champion of the market economy (Felice and Sandonà 2017).

[7] So, it is not surprising that Einaudi has been called "the father of the fathers of Europe" (Santagostino 2017).

[8] For an overview of the friendly and affectionate relationship between the two, see Omiccioli (2018, 87–90).

is perhaps the standard argument for the division of labour: in a complex economy, in which people demand and supply goods and services whose production involved a variety of factors of production, national boundaries are not enough to secure all those needed factors of production. But from this Einaudi moves on, arguing that this very need to expand the division of labour, if interpreted within the framework of national sovereignty, is likely the feed the quest for expansion and conquest. Sovereign nation-states are seen by Einaudi as "closed" states that strive to maintain that "closeness" and thus are forced to expand their boundaries: they "are forced to conquer the living space. The idea of living space is not the result of murky Germanic or Hitlerian imaginations; it is a fatal logic consequence of the principle of the sovereign state."

Such a process was self-feeding. "The more a state grows, the more its industries grow larger and become voracious absorbers of raw materials and in need of ever larger markets." Sovereign states seem to be inherently protectionist as, without constant conquests, they must "resign themselves to a miserable life economically and spiritually obscure, unworthy of human society" (Einaudi 1945b).

It should thus come as no surprise that, for Einaudi, the demise of the nation state is a matter of historical necessity. The very force of the capitalist system, its need for bigger and wider markets, is such that it changes the mindset and the habits of peoples, it equalises opportunities in different jurisdictions and calls for the "internalisation," so to say, of government. Einaudi openly contrasted this view with the idea of class struggle: the latter being a superficial phenomenon, whereas international, capitalistic cooperation is the beef of the modern economy (Einaudi 1915).

This was a matter that Einaudi, a first-hand witness of two world wars, saw as a requirement of the very survival for civilization. He held that the nation state was "the number one enemy of human civilization." Einaudi identifies sovereignty as the key feature of the modern, European nation state. "The sovereign state is synonymous with one authority, in the name of which laws, regulations, ordinances and provisions are issued by the center" (Einaudi 1945c). Indeed, the key point is that, by definition, "sovereignty is not limited." Sovereignty is the ability to say the last word. By the way, you may have noticed that I was supposed to be chairing this lunch, I was later recruited to be giving this talk, and I have no discussant. I can have the last word!

The concept "of the sovereign state, of the state which, within its territorial limits, can make laws regardless of what happens outside those limits" was for Einaudi "an idol of the formalistic legal mind and does not match any reality." And further:

A thousand and a thousand bonds tie men of a given nation to men of every other state. The claim to absolute sovereignty cannot be carried out within the limits of the so-called sovereign state. Men, in modern life dominated by the division of labour, by the great mechanised workshops, by rapid international communications, by the tendency to a high standard of living, cannot live, if their life is reduced to the limits of the state (Einaudi 1945b).

An important caveat: Einaudi considers the nation state as much an enemy of freedom to trade—so to say "on the top," or "on the outside"—as an enemy of local identities—"on the bottom," or "on the inside." The future President of Italy considered the country's tendency to centralise political matters quite critically. In one of his best known essays, "Via il prefetto!," he argues for doing away with prefects (the State's representatives in a province, enjoying wide administrative powers) and states that "Napoleonic centralisation has been put to the test and the outcome has proven to be negative" (Einaudi 1944). Indeed, Einaudi maintained that the idea of a federation was in itself "the opposite of subjugating the various states and the various regions to a single center" (Einaudi 1945a).

When it comes to the path towards a European federation, Einaudi often referred to the making of the United States, with the Articles of Confederation being superseded by the Constitution of Philadelphia. Einaudi did not see the Constitution of Philadelphia as the beginning of a process of increasing centralisation that ultimately led American institutions to resemble more and more European, nation states.[9] In a sense, Einaudi continued to see, regardless of contemporary developments such as the New Deal, American federalism as a set of institutions and ideas totally alternative to the European nation state. As for this latter, Einaudi saw it as "the number one enemy of human civilization:"

> … the dangerous agitator for nationalism and conquest. The concept of the sovereign state, of the state which, within its territorial limits, can make laws regardless of what happens outside those limits, is today anachronistic and false. That concept is an idol of the formalistic legal mind and does

[9] On this matter, see Bassani (2009).

> not match any reality. In a world crossed by railways, by rapid ships, by airplanes, in which the distances were cancelled by telegraphs and telephones with or without wires, the states, which once upon a time seemed big, like Italy, France, Germany, England, let alone the smaller ones, now look small as in the fifteenth century the free medieval towns.... To think that a state, only because it is called sovereign, can make laws to its own will is an absurdities. A thousand and a thousand bonds tie men of a given nation to men of every other state. The claim to absolute sovereignty cannot be carried out within the limits of the so-called sovereign state. Men, in modern life dominated by the division of labor, by the great mechanised workshops, by rapid international communications, by the tendency to a high standard of living, cannot live, if their life is reduced to the limits of the state. (Einaudi 1945b)

Hence, the economic argument is thus also an argument for peace, and in this an example of micro-founded foreign policy approach. The Piedmontese economist cares a great deal about increasing the cost of war via stronger economic cooperation engendering a healthier growth. He does so because he maintains that "autarky means misery; and necessarily pushes men to conquer." In a sense, this sentence simply means that the poorer they are, the more people will resort to all means to escape poverty. But it actually entails a stronger critique of nationalism, based upon a certain understanding of the inner tendency of modern sovereignty.

In other words, the idea of sovereign, independent states trading one with each other in peace is seen by Einaudi as an unstable equilibrium, that can't but end up in war, because the very idea of national sovereignty calls for it. Whatever the merits of his proposed therapy (the European federation), the Piedmontese economist highlights clearly two features, respectively of sovereignty and nationalism. Of sovereignty, he understands the tendency towards monopolisation: the idea of a decision-maker of last resort, the ultimate power in a giving territory that can legislate regardless of what happens all around it. Of nationalism, he sees the inner aggressive ethos, which is in a way a consequence of it being an ideology for the sovereign state. His opposition to such an aggressive ethos is reminiscent of Cobden's humanitarian liberalism.

In a sense, Einaudi's call for a federative process in Europe is an individualist call. He prefaces a rather important 1945 essay on the matter with a quote by Turgot, from a letter to Richard Price, included in the latter's Observations on the Importance of the American Revolution, and the Means of Making it a Benefit to the World:

> On that sacred principle, "liberty of commerce considered as a natural right flowing from the possession of property," all the pretended interests of commerce must vanish. – The supposed interest in possessing more or less territory disappear on this principle, "that a territory does not belong to nations, but to the individuals who are proprietors of the lands." The question, whether such a canton or such a village belongs to such a Province or such a State, ought not to be determined by the interest in it pretended by that Province or that State; but by the interest the inhabitants of the canton or village have in assembling for transacting their affairs in the place most convenient for them. (Turgot 1785, 118–19)

Here Turgot was criticising the pretence of the newly-independent American colonies to regulate commerce, a pretence to which he opposed the idea that, once trade is free, the dimension and extent of administrative units becomes not a matter of identity or national pride: but should simply depend on the interests of the people living within it. Such a view implies a completely desacralised approach to national sovereignty, which is seen as a matter of practical reasoning. Similar arguments have been put forward, in more recent years, to allow a variable geometry of jurisdictions or secessionism of a liberal bent.

Einaudi makes use of this argument, on the contrary, in his plea for European federalism. He did not favour inter-governmental restraints or cooperation but rather, right from the outset, supported "nation-states foregoing sovereignty in favour of a 'super-state' endowed with full financial autonomy" (Sarcinelli 2004, 112). Such a federalism clearly aims not to reproduce, on larger scale, the features of national sovereign states. European federalism, for him "from an economic point of view means assigning to the federal authority certain economic tasks strictly defined in the constitutional document of the federation … it is necessary to reduce to a minimum absolutely necessary the number of tasks assigned to the federation from the beginning" (Einaudi 1945a). These tasks include the regulation of transport, commerce with foreign states and the freeing up of trade within the boundaries of the federation. They thus aim basically at reducing at transaction costs: for this reason, he also foresaw a common currency. It is worth remembering that he also thought that "the abolition of the sovereignty of individual states in monetary matters" is a good in itself.

> Whoever remembers the bad use that many states had made and make the right to coin money cannot doubt the urgency of removing them

from such a right. It was essentially reduced to the right to falsify the currency ... The devaluation of the Italian lira and the Deutsche Mark, which ruined the middle classes and fed the malaise of workers, produced the gangs of unemployed intellectuals and troublemakers who gave power to dictators. If the European federation takes away from the individual federated states the possibility of coping with public works by making the ticket press groan, and will force them to provide for them only with taxes and voluntary loans, it will have, for this only, accomplished something great. (Einaudi 1945a)

Einaudi clarifies that he does not think that by definition a European currency will be properly managed, but thinks that its supranational nature may free it from undue political influence. Therefore, European subsidiarity, to use a more recent word, may limit rent-seeking.

The Italian economist was not a full fledged pacifist, and he actually hoped that the outcome of WWI was to be some sort of benevolent Anglo-Saxon hegemony. This view would have dismayed Cobden and Bright. Yet he was certainly an admirer of the two of them.

As early as in 1901, he told the story of the League in an almost epical tone, "the enterprise [Cobden and Bright's] was not easy. Parliament, the Church, the state, the great landlords, the industrialists enjoying protection and the monopolists: all of them were their enemies. In a country where everything which is ancient enjoys an almost superstitious respect, their enterprise seemed impossible. Yet apostles do not lose heart" (Einaudi 1900–1901).

4 Federalism, Pacifism and International Order: Friedrich A. von Hayek and Wilhelm Röpke

Friedrich A. von Hayek dedicated few yet important pages to the problem of peace and international non-interventionism. While some traces of his ideas can be found in some previous works (Masini 2005, 52ff.), the article where he openly addresses this issue is "The Economic Conditions of Interstate Federalism," published in September 1939.

In those years, there was much discussion about how federalism could be the way to avoid wars between states. Hayek was well acquainted with the ideas of his friend and companion Lionel Robbins (Robbins 1937, 1939) and with the work of Clarence K. Streit (Streit 1939), who advocated the federalist solution from a liberal perspective. The Austrian thinker was also a member of the Federal Union, the British federalist association created in 1938 that set up the Federal Union Research Institute, where classical liberal ideas on federalism were discussed, even if they suddenly became less relevant (Rosenboim 2014; Milani 2016).

In his essay, Hayek immediately stresses with extreme clarity the positive relationship between federalism and peace, and he also points out the conditions for an interstate federation able to guarantee peace. These conditions are free economy and trade, on one hand, and, on the other hand, an effective international order of law and the abolition of national sovereignties. The first condition would want such an interstate federation "to do away with the impediments as to the movement of men, goods, and capital between the states and render possible the creation of common rules of law, a uniform monetary system, and common control of communications" (Hayek 1939, 255).

According to Hayek, a mere political union would not be sufficient to achieve the goal of peace, economic unity would be a prerequisite for peace, and such unity could only be achieved by free market principles. Firstly, Hayek develops a robust criticism of the nationalism, interventionism and protectionism that were prevalent in his age and that had been blamed for the war. His criticism is summarised in the idea that, because of the economic frontiers, "all conflicts of interests tend to become conflicts between the same groups of people, instead of conflicts between groups of constantly varying composition. The peoples are projected in conflicts between states, which hide the reality that the interests of inhabitants are not always the interests of the nation" (Hayek 1939, 257).

In the concluding chapter of The Road to Serfdom—in some way, a follow-up to the 1939 article—he develops the same concept. Nationalist ideologies convince their citizens that their national industries should be defended, which can be achieved by appealing to the sense of community, to national pride, but certainly not to a proper economic interest, which, if duly understood, would cut across the national one.

In an interstate federation, all this could not happen, and the deception would be revealed: interventionism and protectionism are impossible in a federation, precisely because of the non-homogeneous composition of its peoples. When different peoples cohabit, the myth of nationality disappears and makes strongly interventionist economic policies, which always benefit social groups or economic sectors to the disadvantage of others, unacceptable.[10] Customs tariffs protecting an economic sector, or helping it grow faster, would no longer be accepted by citizens. "Is it likely that the French peasant will be willing to pay more for his fertiliser to help the British chemical industry? Will the Swedish workman be ready to pay more for his oranges to assist the Californian grower?" (Hayek 1939, 262; see also Hayek 1944, 228).

A similar argument was suggested for social legislation: "even such legislation as the limitation of working hours or compulsory unemployment insurance, or the protection of amenities, will be viewed in a different light in poor and in rich regions and may in the former actually harm and rouse violent opposition from the kind of people who in the richer regions demand it and profit from it" (Hayek 1939, 263). Then, Hayek makes some almost prophetic reflections on what the course of European integration will be, on how such a federation should also achieve a common foreign and defence policy, as well as a monetary union.

However, Hayek is also aware of how it is always possible for the states of a federation (he quotes the historical cases of Switzerland and the USA) to circumvent the rules that prohibit customs tariffs, maybe by making use of administrative controls and health rules. Because of that, the federation should be given "the negative power of preventing individual states from interfering with economic activity in certain ways, although it may not have the positive power of acting in their stead" (Hayek 1939, 267), as is established, for instance, by some clauses of the US Constitution.

In this course of action, many of the activities currently carried out by the national states can be very likely carried out by smaller territorial entities, and the "local level" could be more efficient than the national states. Forms of economic policy will remain (Hayek himself says that "extreme laissez-faire" is not necessary in economic matters), but

> planning in a federation cannot assume the forms which today are pre-eminently known under this term; that there must be no substitution of day-to-day interference and regulation for the impersonal forces of the market; [...] In a federation economic policy will have to take the form of providing a rational permanent framework within which individual initiative

[10] A similar argument is proposed when States, instead of being grouped into very large federations, are very small. Also, in this case, interventionism and protectionism would be impracticable, and political fragmentation would favour peace (Hayek 1939, 264).

> will have the largest possible scope and will be made to work as beneficently as possible; and it will have to supplement the working of the competitive mechanism where, in the nature of the case, certain services cannot be brought forth and be regulated by the price system». (Hayek 1939, 268–69)

What seems more interesting for our purposes is how he judges a federal interstate project that abolishes national sovereignties and creates an "effective international order of law" as "a necessary complement and the logical consummation of the liberal program." In fact, he shares the idea expressed by both Robbins and Streit that "the main deficiencies of nineteenth-century liberalism that its advocates did not sufficiently realize that the achievement of the recognized harmony of interests between the inhabitants of the different states was only possible within the framework of international security" (Hayek 1939, 270). A point to which he will return strongly in The Road to Serfdom, where he writes: "An international authority which effectively limits the powers of the state over the individual will be one of the best safeguards of peace. The International Rule of Law must become a safeguard as much against the tyranny of the state over the individual as against the tyranny of the new super-state over the national communities. Neither an omnipotent super-state, nor a loose association of 'free nations', but a community of nations of free men must be our goal" (Hayek 1944, 243).

In his 1939 essay, as in The Road to Serfdom, Hayek does not mention Cobden, but the echo of his ideas, as noted by Jorg Spieker, is noticeable in many ways: free trade is seen as an essential condition for peace, in the analysis of international economic relations we should focus not on states but on interests and relationships, and the whole case against limitation of free trade is very similar to the Cobdenite non-interventionist argument. However, "Hayek rejected Cobden's assumption of the existence of a natural harmony of interests" and, while "for Cobden the liberalization of international trade would be sufficient for the realization of an international harmony of interests, Hayek emphasized the need for international government" (Spieker 2014, 936).[11]

[11] Spieker also underline how Lionel Robbins, in the book quoted by Hayek (Robbins 1937), was firmly persuaded, probably much more than Hayek, of the need for an international authority with coercive powers. Two years later (Robbins 1939), he also «explicitly attacked Cobdenite liberalism for its inconsistency» and «emphasised the failure

Hayek is firmly convinced that the limit of nineteenth-century liberalism was the illusion that free trade, and the peace process between nations, would be spontaneously established. It is not enough to implement liberal policies at the national level and wait for them to have positive effects in the international arena. Instead, international order must be built through a federation that must have the same characteristics as those of the limited state of classical liberalism, that is, taking on minimal tasks such as making free trade and the rule of law adhered to in the international arena. To his mind, thinking about these aspects and working towards this goal must be the new task of liberalism.

Hayek would never systematically to back to such issues. He would not reject what he wrote in 1939, but he would not even reiterate the need for an interstate federation with coercive powers, even if he was still convinced that the vast dimensions and the diversity of culture and interests of a federal structure could be a very suitable instrument to promote the anti-collectivist positions (Hayek 1960, 379). One could well believe that he was still convinced of the usefulness of federalism as a tool to avoid centralisation and nationalism, and therefore to promote peace.

It has also been argued that the most liberal phase of the European integration process did confirm Hayek's prediction "that the integration of previously sovereign nation-states in Europe would reduce the capacity of states to regulate the capitalist economy and to burden it with the costs of an expensive welfare state" (Scharpf 2010, 239), although this result comes more from the legal spur of the European Court of Justice than from the pressure of competition, and it is constantly threatened by governmental negotiation as much as by the regulatory activism of the European authorities (Reho 2016, 32–40).

Hayek does not address the problem of how to build intra-state federation, what kind of steps and players would be required, and this is certainly a limit of his analysis. What seems certain is that, in Hayek's view, a federation that could promote peace would be impossible without a common agreement on the minimal values of the liberal tradition, and his scientific life, like many of his organisational activities, including the Mont Pèlerin Society, was intended to promote those values.

of nineteenth-century liberalism to recognise the need for "a framework of international security" and "a super-national authority»" (Spieker 2014, 924). On Hayek and Robbins, see also Felice (2016, 104–20).

Concern for common agreement on liberal values as well as a commitment to promoting them also featured in Wilhelm Röpke's reflection.[12] Throughout his life, Röpke focused his attention on how to achieve a liberal interstate federation. In the following pages, we will outline his ideas on international politics as they emerged in the Thirties and Forties, and we will attempt to see how they are rooted in a classic liberal vision of international relations.

Using the terminology we relied upon before, Röpke's reflection entails an attempt at a micro foundation of international order. He thought that, to promote economic international integration, conferences and "bargaining" between countries were essentially useless. One should look, instead, at the domestic politics and at the "spirit" and economic convictions that underlie a nation: the individual beliefs that are at the centre of international order too. Consistently with such view, he indicates the cause of the "disintegration of the international order" in the domestic social and political crisis of many, or almost all, countries. He sees the political crisis of his time as closely linked to the change in economic ideas, which have become favourable to protectionism, and exemplified the trade between states with the language of conflict and economic war.

In German Commercial Politics, he shows how dangerous autarkic tendencies and "wrong" economic ideas can be. He starts by recalling how one hundred years earlier Europe lived in an era of "economic liberty and worldwide solidarity," which seemed to have totally collapsed in 1934. The source of such change is a mistrust of the benefits of free trade having spread across all nations. That mistrust has conquered public opinion, and today "People are led to believe that in all matters of commercial policy the interests of the different nations are lined up against each other like two hostile armies, so much so that every concession made in commercial treaties appears as a sacrifice made by the whole nation to the foreign country" (Röpke 1934, 5).

The 1834 Zollverein is a symbolic date of an era in which the ideas of the "free trade pure and simple," were dominant. Together with the abolition of the Corn Laws in 1846, the establishment of the Zollverein is a recurring theme for Röpke: he deliberately refers to the world of

[12] Hayek and Röpke already knew each other fairly well in the 1930s, and in the post-war years they worked together at the Mont Pèlerin Society project. In this sense, it is rather surprising that, in his vast production, Röpke disregards Hayek's essays.

free trade as a situation worth returning to. We can therefore find a Cobdenian echo here. However, the theme of trade as fostering peace between nations and the idea that free trade is functional to peace are given as implied, but are not systematically and extensively developed.

Röpke maintains that the era of free trade—which would gradually begin to collapse in the 1890s—emerged on the basis of moral and legal principles, shared by people and politicians, the most important of which were the right to private property, compliance with contractual obligations and the non-discrimination of foreigners. They led to the international division of labour, which was fundamental for economic growth across the world, and the result was prosperity and (relative) peace between nations.

The end of that era, and the crisis of the interwar period, is the consequence of the spreading of protectionist nationalism. An essential part of Röpke's reflection, influenced by Alexander Rüstow as well as by Ortega y Gasset, is focussed on the dangers of mass society, and on a kind of capitalism that increasingly takes on "giant" and inhuman forms. And he proposed to go back to an economy that puts widespread ownership, small businesses, the retail trade and agriculture at the centre; an economy that puts man at the centre and overcomes the problems of alienation (Röpke 1942b, 1944). But it is interesting to note then that the whole argument about free trade is not affected by such criticism of mass economy, and Röpke believes that there is no risk of "massification" from the development of international free trade (Röpke 1946, 108–10). And it is also interesting to observe how, in Röpke, the reference to the need for an active state that provides a functioning competitive market, something that does not happen naturally, seems to be strictly put on a domestic level, and not scaled up to the level of a supranational institution.

Many of Röpke's concerns were already evident in some of his 1930s writings. In his opinion, the only way out to find "peace, prosperity, civilization" in Europe is to "adapt the degree of political co-operation among nations to the degree of their economic co-operation and thus to supplement economic integration by political integration" (Röpke 1933, 76). It is, therefore, the nations that must return to support free trade and the free market, and this is the solution to attain peace and economic integration. Over the years, Röpke would elaborate on these thoughts, maintaining that any form of agreement between nations is bound to fail, unless the conditions for success are met on a national level, and such conditions depend on the prevalent political and societal ideas.

These themes are developed in the two works International Economic Disintegration (Röpke 1942a) and International Order (Röpke 1945). The content of these essays would sometimes be replicated in a very similar manner in some works published in the Fifties and Sixties, demonstrating the consistency of Röpke's thought. In International Economic Disintegration, he claims that the states lost their role as impartial instruments to safeguard competition and free markets (which is the way to serve the common good of the whole country), and became complicit in sectional interests, and in the collapse of the set of moral codes that is a prerequisite of any national and international order.

In International Order,[13] Röpke addresses the problem of how to rebuild the economy, society and relations among states once the conflict was over. He restates that "the international crisis is only a part of the general social crisis" and for this reason all the international conferences, negotiations and plans for an international order will fail "as long as the conditions for success were not fulfilled on the national level," and as long as the delegates met at the conferences with wrong economic ideas. When the right economic ideas are shared within the nations, then the international order will be created autonomously, beyond any conference and specific agreement. It is what happened in the age of free trade, when a "truly international monetary system" was set up without conferences or conventions, on the basis of the gold standard, which seems a far better solution than any international monetary one (Röpke 1945, now in 1959, 15ss).

Röpke's is, therefore, a plea to overcome the great spiritual crisis of the time, a crisis that has weakened norms and values which are not only the basis of a proper functioning of the economy but also of all human coexistence. Unless the spirit and morality of society and individuals are re-established, an international order would be impossible too. As long as individual countries are driven by wrong economic ideas, any

[13] The contents of the Internationale Ordnung, published in 1945 and never translated into English, will merge, with changes and additions, into Internationale Ordnung—Heute, 1954, translated into English in 1959 as International Order and Economic Integration. In the literature, such English translation has sometimes been mixed up with the 1945 edition.

attempt to achieve an international order through agreements or negotiations will fail. No healthy international order or economic integration can result from international agreements alone, as they also need shared moral values, besides economic integration: free trade, freely convertible currencies and gold standards are the pillars of international order, which stems from nations that respect property rights and the non-discrimination of foreigners.

Then, the problem was to understand how the new international community could actually limit national sovereignty, and how the feeling of national belonging could be transformed. Röpke sees the solution in a federal structure, both at a national and international level. Such structure lets the burden of political powers be shared within and among the states, and "preserves the individual rights of each member unit, without endangering the necessary combination in the respective overall associations" (Röpke 1945, now in Röpke 1959, 45).

This solution poses serious challenges, because the nation state is never willing to reduce its power in favour of local communities or supranational organisations. The process would, therefore, be long and necessarily gradual, and it has to involve an increasing level of federalism within the states. This is of vital importance, because "The education in mutual respect for individual rights within the state which federalism effects would also have beneficent results in international relations and would further the same liberal outlook as we find today in the few really federal states such as Switzerland" (Röpke 1945, now in Röpke 1959, 46). Once again, micro factors are at play to produce a macro output: in this case, institutional reform at a much lower level of government.

In 1945, these considerations led him to see a project of a European federation as appropriate and necessary. Moreover, Röpke recalls how the problem of a fair national order is the necessary premise of the international one: if the states do not have a political, social and economic structure conforming to an international peaceable order, all efforts for a union of peoples will be in vain. This structure can only be liberal, or at least (in order to avoid lexical misunderstandings) "non-collectivist."

From what we have seen so far, it is clear that, on one hand, Röpke shares the Hayekian hope of an interstate federalism, and, on the other hand, he points to a great deal of problems in its accomplishment, problems that were never faced by Hayek. In Röpke, the Hayekian perspective seems to be overturned. While the Austrian thinker focussed all his attention on how a federation would, by its very nature, "automatically" lead to the development of a free market and free trade, Röpke argues that, without the nations coming to a preliminary agreement about the importance of economic freedom, a federation would not be possible or would have disastrous results. These concerns were widely developed in his further reflections and by carefully looking at the first steps in the process of community integration.

We saw how Hayek's perspective, which imagined an interstate and federal structure as capable by its nature of promoting the principles of the free market and therefore of peace, was different from that of Cobden. In some ways, Röpke's position is close, instead, to that of the British politician, both in his recurring references to nineteenth-century liberalism (and in particular to the Zollverein and the Corn Laws) as a sort of golden age and in his idea that a "healthy" international order can only be built on different nations sharing the same liberal values. Federalism is seen as a useful tool, but the starting point of it all must be the national states respecting individual rights and the principles of the free market. However, we will now see how the German thinker did not certainly intend to advocate a simple return to the past, and how he saw considerable difficulties in the process of European economic (and political) integration.

5 Wilhelm Röpke's Criticism of European Integration

Röpke paid great attention to the theme of a European federation, and not surprisingly he was quite soon disappointed with the way things went with European integration. The jumble of European economy was in his opinion not so much the consequence of the war, but the result of top-down economic policies "that created chaos in the name of planning." And the "treatment" for its sickness could be only a return to free trade and to a free market economy. (Röpke 1947, 123ff.). Since European states are stuck with a protectionist and dirigiste regime, what needs to be done is to remove collectivist positions at a national level and rebuild a European economic integration, starting with those national economic policies that support free trade and a free market.

In the article "The fight for economic sanity in Europe." regarding the possibility of a federation of European states, Röpke outlines three conclusions: (1) any form of federation is impossible if the member states remain on a national collectivist position, and in this sense "European integration begins at home" (how Cobdenian!). (2) The supposed liberalizations of intra-European trade "cannot be genuine unless there is a real dismantling of national collectivism." (3) Abolition of exchange control "is the cardinal problem," without which no form of European Currency Union is imaginable, apart from a "collectivist European superstate." The liberal policies of Federal Germany pursued by Erhard, are, according to Röpke, a successful model, which should be followed by other European countries, even in the crucial point of monetary policy (Röpke 1950, 28).

In the following years, Röpke was critical about the European unification process, which seemed to want to promote free trade only partially and only in some sectors, and was faultily restricted to the members of the Union. This process was considered dangerous because, in the absence of free market policies at a domestic level, it could lead to a European Government that aimed at unifying individual economies into a collectivist project: something impossible and bound to fail, and Röpke also criticised the danger of a new European bureaucracy, capable of slowing down or stopping any attempt at a free market process (Röpke 1951, 43ff.).

At a conference in 1957, Röpke went out to criticise the Treaty of Rome, accusing it to foster a project that would lead to a planned international economy. He came to argue that Germany would have to leave the EU if it kept going against free trade (Gregg 2010, 156) and maybe he played a part in turning the Swiss away from the Common Market (Audier (2013, 48–76).

In September 1958, in an article appeared in "The Banker" (eventually published as an epilogue to International Order and Economic Integration), Röpke harshly criticises the way in which the common market and the European Coal and Steel Community (ECSC) were designed, because they would lead to a "supra-national political order" to implement the integration process. If the common market "is not capped by the free trade area it will disintegrate Europe," and a correct process of European economic integration should be nothing but a return to the free trade system of the previous century (Röpke 1959, 259).

This is what Röpke defines as the "liberal method of integration," and other methods, i.e. such regional agreements as GATT, are wrong because they limit the principle of free trade.[14] In the integration process, any agreement should have an "open character," as an agreement rooted in a specific area that will naturally tend to extend to the rest of the world. This is not the case, and Röpke is outspokenly critical of those politicians (his main target is France) who think that one can benefit from the advantages of the free market without enforcing it to the full.

The final part of the essay reiterates the idea that a constant general reduction of tariffs would be a more coherent and effective course of action to bring about the unification of Europe than the attempt to create a common market with the "regional" method. Markets will meet distortions which "are likely to be much more enduring or harmful than those of the free trade area: for they will be aggravated by the effects of its supra-national economic planning."

Röpke develops his analysis in an article published by the American conservative journal "Modern Age" (Röpke 1958), where he claims that free trade is the only way to harmonise the European economy and to reduce the existing differences in labour and capital cost. All European countries should pursue the achievement of international free trade and work to convince their public opinion. Six years later, in the same journal (Röpke 1964), he clearly repeats his perplexities about the process of European integration but also develops the idea of Europe as a "cultural and spiritual union." A union that can rediscover its role as a world guide if only it could recognise the right role of economic freedom and free trade. Central to understanding how to achieve true integration is keeping in mind that Europe is "a genuine 'cultural system'", based on "the common patrimony of Humanism and Christianity" but also a "unity in diversity." Therefore, trying to standardize (economically and politically) the European nations in a political/bureaucratic project would be a serious mistake. To promote integration, a form of federalism is required that leaves the greatest degree of independence to the nations, but that is based on a deeply rooted liberal economic vision in every state of the union.

In order to understand the problems of European integration, Röpke recalls the difference with the Zollverein, established in a liberal era when all states were open to free trade, while the current era has liberal states

[14] Nonetheless, Röpke acknowledges that there is also a problem of strategy, in terms of how to achieve "economic liberation," because of the opposition of public opinion (Röpke 1959, 261).

and interventionist and protectionist states all clumped together. This difference leads the EEC to attempt a "harmonisation" between different policies and visions which are in reality incompatible, and to try to do so "through concessions which assured some vested interests a privileged position." This is a wrong approach, and the process of integration can instead be pursued only by creating the "most elementary conditions of economic integration," which are the "absence of quantitative trade controls" and "a moderate height of customs tariffs" with all other countries. These conditions existed in the "liberal century," and this is why European economic integration meant essentially a "reintegration." And while, "like charity, European economic integration had to begin at home it was not unimportant that this indispensable national action was assisted by international action on the regional scale of Europe" (Röpke 1964, 237).

Röpke's ideas were very influential on Ludwig Erhard, German Minister of Economic Affairs since 1948 and Chancellor from 1963 to 1966, and, while substantial differences can be glimpsed in their views (Mierzejewski 2006; Masala 2017, 102ff.), the commonality of ideas about Europe and international politics is always clear. Erhard was firmly in favour of open international markets, and, exactly like Röpke, he thought that European integration could be achieved through pan-European free trade and freely convertible currencies. Erhard, like Röpke, was worried about the growing role and dimension of European bureaucracies and about their tendency to economic dirigisme (Erhard 1953; Erhard 1957, 211ff.).

In the crucial years 1956 and 1957, Erhard expressed a strong opposition to the idea of harmonising welfare standards (shaped on the French model) and excluding non-member countries from the free trade agreements (Erhard 1958). This led him to engage in a tough fight with Chancellor Konrad Adenauer, who was mainly interested in fully reintegrating Germany into European diplomacy and who, for this reason, took positions that were gradually closer to France. Finally, Adenauer won and removed Erhard from any foreign policy assignment.

Röpke and Erhard's position was somehow unfair, and the process of European integration was an alternation of different positions. For example, a year after the Treaty of Rome, France (the main target of Röpke's polemics) had made significant changes in the plan worked out by another classical liberal thinker (also a member of the Mont Pèlerin Society), Jacques Rueff, the author of the "Rueff-Pinay economic Plan," which stabilised France's national budget and ensured the convertibility of the franc.

Anyway, despite Röpke and Erhard's fierce criticism, we cannot fail to notice that their position was anything but ideological and was open to exceptions and gradualness in its accomplishment. For example, some degree of protectionism and interventionism was considered appropriate in a developing country, on the proviso that they should be temporary measures, to be abandoned as soon as circumstances so allowed. And they were justified on technical grounds (capital formation and the need to provide infrastructure and services that an underdeveloped market was unable to produce) as well as on cultural grounds: for Röpke, the market alone is not capable of creating the mindset, the values it takes to make it work, in particular those pre-economic preconditions that allow market economies to grow and flourish.[15]

In any case, regardless of the success of Röpke and Erhard's ideas, it is undeniable that post-war Germany was in the position of being the most pro-free trade and pro-market European country ever, at the time of Keynesian consensus, when socialism and interventionism were very popular. Although Erhard and Röpke had often been in minority positions, their ideas and actions played an essential role in the building of the European Union.

Since the second half of the 60s, due to a multitude of concomitant causes, the EU has more firmly taken the route to free trade and a free market. Hayek's prediction that an interstate federation cannot coexist with a harmonised welfare state and a robust regulated economy has partly come true. It was indeed thanks to the impetus of the EU that many national states have undertaken, sometimes unwillingly, market-focussed liberalizations and policies. Unfortunately, there's no way of knowing what Röpke would have thought of the EU "liberal period," since he died in 1966. While, however, that phase of the integration process seems to have proven Hayek right, the last years of the process, and the current credibility crisis that the EU seems to be going through, seem to remind us of the admonition of Röpke (and Erhard) that "European integration begins at home."

The ideas of "union in diversity" and of having to start the integration process "at home" by adopting policies that favour the free market, as well

[15] In this respect, crucial is Röpke's experience in the "underdeveloped" Turkey, see Masala and Kama (2018).

as the admiration of the Zollverein and the Corn Laws, certainly show some closeness between Röpke's and Cobden's thoughts. The same can be said of the idea that the principle of free trade should be extended to those countries that were left out of the process of European integration and, in perspective, to the rest of the world. However, there was one significant exception to this, the Communist bloc, all trade relations with which had to be avoided in order to accelerate its collapse.

This point shows how far even Röpke, and not only Hayek, was in many ways from Cobden's vision, not least because of the changed historical circumstances. He was in fact persuaded, much more than other liberals,[16] that free trade would have been ineffective against communism, and suggested that, on the contrary, a more aggressive attitude was needed. Consequently, free trade could not be thought to be the right instrument for achieving peace among nations around the world.

But the distance from Cobden is also measured by other important aspects of his thinking, which have been mentioned before. Reference was made to the way Röpke (largely influenced by Alexander Rüstow, as well as by Ortega y Gasset) was convinced that the free market needed moral values in order to function, values which the market did not produce, and that "consume" itself. This led him to think of some necessary economic structures in which widespread private property is central, in which small trade and small businesses are predominant (his model, as it was for the federal structure, was Switzerland), while large companies (which always entail what he called proletarianisation) are very limited. In order to achieve this, one could certainly not rely on the simple dynamics of the free market; it takes a political programme, a programme that he called the "third way."

Such a program therefore calls for the state to give a specific shape to the economic system, so that the moral values required for the market to work, but above all for a full life and for a Civitas Humana to spread (Röpke 1944), could be preserved (Masala 2017, 70ff.).

[16] Here, the difference is not only with Hayek—with whom (also) on the subject of a much more aggressive anti-communist attitude there was a break-up that would later have repercussions on the Mont Pèlerin Society—but with other liberals as well. In particular, Milton Friedman was convinced that it was his duty (in order to contribute to improving the living conditions of the population) to give good economic advice also to those politicians who had nothing to do with liberalism; and in fact he did his best to give advice not only to Pinochet's Chile, but also to communist China (Masala 2017, 194ff.).

When we think of these aspects, central to Röpke's thought, it is clear that, although his convergences with Cobden and the principles of nineteenth-century free trade may seem fairly sound, a very different view underlies them. For the German thinker, liberalism (in its economic and moral dimensions) is something that must be built and preserved, and this is also true of the international and federal dimensions. It will emerge "spontaneously" (if one can use this term here) from individual states that adopt liberal policies, but in individual states liberalism must be "planned" and built in a way that Cobden would probably have never conceived.

6 Conclusion

In these pages, we have tried to highlight some characteristics of twentieth-century liberalism with respect to the problems of federalism and peace among nations, and to investigate the continuity between different approaches to international order, from nineteenth-century liberal pacifism to twentieth-century liberalism.

Although in different ways, Einaudi, Hayek and Röpke all placed some emphasis on the fact that they were breaking with the older classical liberal tradition.[17] In all three authors, there is a clear awareness that the old belief in liberal pacifism cannot be re-proposed on the same terms, and everyone is looking for new conditions, institutional, legal or moral, capable of accomplishing a new international order on a liberal basis.

However, in spite of these deep differences, the comparison with Cobden's view is interesting, and there also seems to be some continuity with a few of his ideas about international order. Looking at Cobdenite pacifism could therefore be a useful vantage point to put some developments that occurred in the second half of the twentieth century into perspective.

Critics of neoliberalism sometimes consider its allegiance to projects of European unification as a form of nostalgia for the Habsburg Empire (Hazony 2018, passim). Perhaps, such attitude was instead driven by a deep commitment to peace and trade, seen as an inseparable couple. How to achieve them was a matter of contention and debate, with serious differences in nuances: from Röpke's inward-looking foreign policy to

[17] In our understanding, the only author who claimed without compromises to be rejuvenating the classical liberal approach for the twentieth century was Ludwig von Mises.

Einaudi and Hayek's shared support of a form of a European project. These differences show a doctrinal pluralism, which is typical of classical liberalism as a set of political ideas, and perhaps also differences in the national political culture and setting. Anyway, as well as nineteenth-century liberals, all the three thinkers we have herewith discussed were aware that, to promote peace between nations, the free trade needed to gain consensus among the liberal ideas.

Whatever our opinion of the current progress of the European project, it has some liberal roots, and they can, in turn, be traced back to an older stream of classical liberalism, which always saw economic integration and international pacification as two sides of the same coin.

References

Audier, Serge. 2013. "Une voie allemande du libéralisme?" *L'Économie politique* 4 (60): 48–76.

Bassani, Luigi M. 2009. *Dalla rivoluzione alla guerra civile: Federalismo e Stato moderno in America 1776–1865*. Soveria Mannelli: Rubbettino.

Blyth, Mark. 2013. *Austerity: The History of a Dangerous Idea*. Oxford: Oxford University Press.

Buckle, Henry T. 1904 [1857]. *Introduction to the History of Civilisation in England*. Edited by J. Robertson. London: Routledge.

Craiutu, Aurelian. 2018. "A Voice of Moderation in the Age of Revolutions: Jacques Necker's Reflections on Executive Power in Modern Society." Paper Presented at the Conference "Resistance from the Inside: Institutional and Constitutional Dissent," Program on Constitutionalism and Democracy, University of Virginia, Charlottesville, March.

Cobden, Richard. 1903 [1835]. *The Political Writings of Richard Cobden*. 2 vols. London: Fisher Unwin.

Constant, Benjamin. 1988 [1919]. "The Liberty of the Ancients Compared with That of the Moderns." In *Political Writings*. Translated and edited by Biancamaria Fontana, 308–28. Cambridge: Cambridge University Press.

Einaudi, Luigi. 1900–1901. "Per la giustizia tributaria." Now: Accessed January 27, 2019. http://www.luigieinaudi.it/doc/per-la-giustizia-tributaria/?id=183.

———. 1915. "Di alcuni aspetti economici della guerra europea." Now: http://www.luigieinaudi.it/doc/di-alcuni-aspetti-economici-della-guerra-europea-2/?id=909.

———. 1944. "Via il prefetto!" Now: Accessed January 31, 2019. http://www.luigieinaudi.it/doc/via-il-prefetto/?id=434.

———. 1945a. "I problemi economici della federazione europea." Now: Accessed January 31, 2019. http://www.luigieinaudi.it/doc/i-problemi-economici-della-federazione-europea-2/?id=282.
———. 1945b. "Il mito dello Stato sovrano." Now: Accessed January 31, 2019. http://www.luigieinaudi.it/doc/il-mito-dello-stato-sovrano/?id=531.
———. 1945c. "La sovranità è indivisibile?" Now: http://www.luigieinaudi.it/doc/la-sovranita-e-indivisibile/?id=2550.
———. 1952. "Tipi e connotati della federazione discorrendo di comunità europea di difesa." Now: http://www.luigieinaudi.it/doc/tipi-e-connotati-della-federazione-discorrendo-di-comunita-europea-di-difesa/?id=2029.
Erhard, Ludwig. 1953. Deutschlands Rückkehr zum Weltmarkt. Edited by Herbert Gross, Econ Verlag, Düsseldorf; English Translation Germany's Comeback in the World Market. London: Routledge, 2006.
———. 1957. Wohlstand für Alle, Econ Verlag, Dusseldorf; English Translation *Prosperity Through Competition*. New York: Praeger, 1958.
———. 1958. "Germany's Economic Goals." *Foreign Affairs* 36 (4): 611–17.
Felice, Flavio. 2016. "Postfazione." In *Le condizioni economiche del federalismo tra stati*. Edited by F. A. von Hayek. Soveria Mannelli: Rubbettino.
Felice, Flavio, and Luca Sandonà. 2017. "Italian Values-Grounded Liberalism and the German Social Market Economy: A Transnational Convergence Behind the Treaty of Rome of 1957." *The Journal of Economic History* 3: 95–117.
Gartzke, Erik. 2005. "Economic Freedom and Peace." In *Economic Freedom of the World*. 2005 Annual Report, edited by James Gwartney, Robert Lawson, and Erik Gartzke, 29–44. Vancouver: Fraser Institute.
Gregg, Samuel. 2010. *Wilhelm Röpke's Political Economy*. Northampton, MA: Edward Elgar.
Hayek, Friedrich A. 1948 [1939]. "The Economic Conditions of Interstate Federalism." In *Individualism and Economic Order*, edited by F. A. Hayek, 255–72. Chicago: University of Chicago Press.
———. 2001 [1944]. *The Road to Serfdom*. London: Routledge.
———. 2011 [1960]. *The Constitution of Liberty*. Chicago: The University of Chicago Press.
Hazony, Yoram. 2018. *The Virtue of Nationalism*. New York: Basic Books.
Hirschman, Albert. 2013 [1977]. *The Passions and the Interests: Political Arguments for Capitalism Before Its Triumph*. Princeton: Princeton University Press.
Hobson, John A. 1968 [1918]. *Richard Cobden: The International Man*. London: Benn.

Kant, Immanuel. 1917 [1795]. Zum ewigen Frieden: Ein philosophischer Entwurf; English Translation *Perpetual Peace: A Philosophical Essay*, Translated with Introduction and Notes by M. Campbell Smith. London: George Allen and Unwin.
Masala, Antonio. 2017. *Stato, libertà e società. Dal liberalismo al neoliberalismo*. Soveria Mannelli: Rubbettino.
Masala, Antonio, and Özge Kama. 2018. "Between Two Continents: Röpke's Years in Istanbul." In *Wilhelm Röpke (1899–1966): A Liberal Political Economist and Conservative Social Philosopher*, edited by Patricia Commun and Stefan Kolev. London-Berlin: Springer.
Masini, Fabio. 2005. "Designing the Institutions of International Liberalism: Some Contributions from the Interwar Period." *Constitutional Political Economy* 23 (1): 45–65.
———. 2014. "Luigi Einaudi and Italian Liberalism, 1940–1960." In *Re-Inventing Western Civilisation: Transnational Reconstructions of Liberalism in Europe in the Twentieth Century*, edited by Hagen Schulz-Forberg and Niklas Olsen, 117–36. Newcastle: Cambridge Scholars.
Mazzucato, Mariana. 2013. *The Entrepreneurial State: Debunking Public vs. Private Sector Myths*. London: Anthem Press.
———. 2018. *The Value of Everything: Making and Taking in the Global Economy*. London: Allen Lane, Public Affairs.
Milani, Tommaso. 2016. "From Laissez-Faire to Supranational Planning: The Economic Debate Within Federal Union (1938–1945)." *European Review of History: Revue européenne d'histoire* 23 (4): 664–85.
Mierzejewski, Alfred C. 2006. "Water in the Desert? The Influence of Wilhelm Röpke on Ludwig Erhard and the Social Market Economy." *Review of Austrian Economics* 19 (4): 275–87.
Mingardi, Alberto. 2011. *Herbert Spencer*. New York: Continuum.
Morley, John. 1903 [1881]. *The Life of Richard Cobden*. London: Fisher Unwin.
Omiccioli, Massimo. 2018. *La «strana» biblioteca di uno «strano» economista*. Roma: Banca d'Italia.
Panebianco, Angelo. 2018. *Persone e mondi: Azioni individuali e ordine internazionale*. Bologna: Il Mulino.
Reho, Federico O. 2016. "Federalismo hayekiano e integrazione europea." In *Le condizioni economiche del federalismo tra stati*, edited by F. A. von Hayek. Soveria Mannelli: Rubbettino.
Robbins, Lionel. 1937. *Economic Planning and International Order*. London: Macmillan.
———. 1939. *The Economic Causes of War*. London: Jonathan Cape.
Röpke, Wilhelm. 1969 [1933]. "The Secular Significance of the World Crisis." In *Against the Tide*, edited by Wilhelm Rôpke. Chicago, IL: Regnery.
———. 1934. *German Commercial Policy*. London: Longmans, Green & Co.

———. 1942a. *International Economic Disintegration*. London: William Hodge.
———. 1942b. Gesellschaftskrisis der Gegenwart. Zurich: Reutsch; English Translation *The Social Crisis of Our Time*. New Brunswick, NJ: Transaction, 1992.
———. 1944. Civitas Humana: Grundfragen der Gesellschafts. Zurich: Reutsch; English Translation *Civitas Humana: A Humane Order of Society*. London: William Hodge & Company, 1948.
———. 1945. *Internationale Ordnung*. Zurich: Reutsch.
———. 1969 [1946]. "The Centenary of British Free Trade." In *Against the Tide*, edited by Wilhelm Rôpke. Chicago, IL: Regnery.
———. 1969 [1947]. "Marshall Plan and Economic Policy." In *Against the Tide*, edited by Wilhelm Rôpke. Chicago, IL: Regnery.
———. 1950. "The Fight for Economic Sanity in Europe." *Commercial and Financial Review*, March 16.
———. 1987 [1951]. "The Problem of Economic Order." In *Two Essays by Wilhelm Röpke: The Problem of Economic Order; Welfare, Freedom and Inflation*, edited by Wilhelm Röpke. Lanhan, MD: University Press of America.
———. 1954. *Internationale Ordnung – Heute*. Zurich: Reutsch (revised edition of Röpke 1945).
———. 1958. "Political Enthusiasm and Common Sense: Some Comments on European Economic Integration." *Modern Age* 2 (2): 170–76.
———. 1959. International Order and Economic Integration. Dordrecht: Reidel; English Translation of Röpke (1954), with the "Epilogue" "European Free Trade: The Great Divide." Originally Published in «The Banker», September 1958, 10–20.
———. 1964. "European Economic Integration and Its Problems." *Modern Age* 8(3): 231–44.
Rosenboim, Or. 2014. "Barbara Wootton, Friedrich Hayek and the Debate on Democratic Federalism in the 1940s." *The International History Review* 36 (5): 894–918.
Sarcinelli, Mario. 2004. "European Federation and Currency: The Contributions of Luigi Einaudi." *BNL Quarterly Review*, 229: 109–30.
Santagostino, Angelo. 2017. *Luigi Einaudi: The Father of the 'Fathers of Europe'*. Cambridge: Cambridge Scholars.
Scharpf, Fritz W. 2010. "The Asymmetry of European Integration, or Why the EU Cannot Be a 'Social Market Economy'." *Socio-Economic Review* 8 (2): 211–50.
Slobodian, Quinn. 2018. *Globalists: The End of Empire and the Birth of Neoliberalism*. Boston: Harvard University Press.
Spieker, Jorg. 2014. "F.A. Hayek and the Reinvention of Liberal Internationalism." *The International History Review* 36 (5): 919–42.

Streit, Clarence K. 1939. *Union Now*. London: Jonathan Cape.
Turgot, Anne. R. J. 1785. Letter in Richard Price, Observations on the Importance of the American Revolution, and the Means of Making It a Benefit to the World. To Which Is Added, a Letter from M. Turgot, Late Comptroller-General of the Finances of France. London: Cadell.
Valverde, José L. 1994. *Europa. Una idea en marcha*. Granada: Edicciones del Parlamento europeo.

CHAPTER 12

Staving off the Protectionist Slide: Snowden and the Struggle to Keep Britain Open

Oksana Levkovych

The introduction of the Import Duties Act and the Ottawa Agreements by the National Government in 1932 marked a decisive break with Britain's historic fiscal policy of free trade, in place since the repeal of the Corn Laws in 1846. Systemic-level theories explain this shift as a response to Britain's long-lasting relative economic decline, to rising protectionism in Europe exacerbated by the onset of the Great Depression (Gilpin 1975; Keohane 1984; Kindleberger 1986; Krasner 1976, 1978), and emphasize macroeconomic disturbances brought by crises, financial instability, and unemployment (Eichengreen 1981, 1992a; Gourevitch 1986; Irwin 2011, 2012), which gradually pushed free trade into retreat (Trentmann 2007; Howe 1998; Irwin 2005, 189–205). Domestic-level explanations focus on government policy capture by interest groups (businesses, the City, the Dominions) (Capie 1983; Chase 2004; Drummond 1972, 1974; Marrison 1996; Rooth 1992), the fall of the Labour Government,

O. Levkovych (✉)
London School of Economics and Political Science, London, UK
e-mail: O.Levkovych@lse.ac.uk

© The Author(s) 2021

A. M. Cunha and C. E. Suprinyak (eds.), *Political Economy and International Order in Interwar Europe*, Palgrave Studies in the History of Economic Thought,
https://doi.org/10.1007/978-3-030-47102-6_12

and the overwhelming Conservative majority in Parliament following the 1931 election (Williamson 1992; Self 1986). By excluding individual actors as causally significant, these accounts miss out on a crucial factor: the resilience of free trade liberalism at the highest ranks of the British political establishment, which shaped the trajectory of Britain's long slide towards protectionism. Focusing on individual agency and the role of economic policy ideas (Morrison 2012; Irwin 1989), this chapter aims to change the way in which we regard systemic assumptions about the transformation of international trade regimes.

During the interwar period, economic protectionism rapidly became a global trend (Krasner 1976, 325–26; Gowa and Hicks 2013, 443–46; Irwin 2011, 174–76; Kindleberger 1986, 123–27) and was accompanied by significant domestic political overhauls (Simmons 1994, 219). Although protection had always been desired in the UK (Williamson 1992, 504; Cain and Hopkins 2001, 186; Young 1928, 221, 234; Lobell 1999, 677–78; Capie 1980, 431; Eichengreen 1992b), during the 1929 election, the Conservative Party, bruised by their previous defeats, renewed their pledge against food taxes and general tariffs (Thorpe 1991, 32; Craig 1970, 45; Boyce 1987, 185). Such a moderated approach had been challenged by Conservative die-hards for whom their leadership's commitment to limited safeguarding and imperial preferences was out of step with the urgent need to create employment and foster the economic development of the Empire (Marrison 1996, 390–92; Craig 1970, 44–45). Labour's victory and formation of the minority Government, with support from Liberal Members of Parliament (MPs), signalled an unequivocal pledge to the "internationalist" policy of free trade (Boyce 1987, 197, 217–19; Clavin 2013, 39–45). Both parties would split internally over the growing demands for protection from 1929 to 1931. The problem of unemployment proved especially challenging to the Labour Government (Capie 1998, 258; Marrison 1996, 393; Rooth 1992, 48). Even John Maynard Keynes, a long-time free trade liberal, urged the introduction of tariffs to tackle unemployment under the gold standard constraint (Eichengreen 1984, 364), at first expressing his views in private consultation (Williamson 1992, 65–66, 73–75; Howson and Winch 1977, 24–29; Keynes and G. D. H. Cole 1930, 175; E.A.C. 1930, 202, 209–10), and then making his support for a revenue tariff public in spring of 1931 (Keynes 1931a, b, c, d; Robbins 1931).

In 1930, the movement for protection in Britain significantly strengthened calls to bring trade policy up for reconsideration. The Tariff Truce convention—initiated by William Graham, the President of the Board of Trade, at the League of Nations on behalf of the British government as a strategy to cope with declining exports through reduction of protection in Europe—was about to expire, lacking signing countries' ratifications (Boyce 1987, 235–40, 275–76). The United States triggered a global tariff retaliation spiral by passing the Smoot-Hawley Tariff Act in June 1930 (Irwin 2011, 4–5), which raised American tariffs against 20,000 imported goods by as much as 50%. The steep rise in unemployment (Capie 1998, 258) (from 1.66 million in April to 2.2 million, almost 20% of the insured workforce, by October [Williamson 1992, 60]) combined with the retreat of free trade (Trentmann 2007, 20), added momentum to calls for protection in preparation for the Imperial Conference.

Against this protectionist tide stood Philip Snowden, Labour's Chancellor of the Exchequer, whose unwavering faith in economic liberalism remained intact throughout his career, making him the most orthodox interwar Chancellor wedded to economy, free trade and gold with "fanatic tenacity" (Laybourn 1987, 65, 67–68, 72; Jovitt 1987, 55). Snowden had maintained categorical opposition to protection in all forms since the introduction of the McKenna duties in 1915 because of his Cobdenite beliefs in free trade for economic and peace reasons (Jovitt 1987, 50). His first Chancellorship (1923–1924) had revealed that "both he and the Treasury were thoroughly Gladstonian" (Cross 1966, 198). Snowden ran fiscal policy independently, without interference from Prime Minister Ramsay MacDonald (199). Snowden appears to have "abolished the McKenna duties in 1924 without any discussion in the Cabinet" (204), acting according to his free trade principles and entirely on his own initiative (Hirst 1925, 86; Cross 1966, 204).[1] His foremost critic, Winston Churchill, himself a liberal free trader turned pragmatic protectionist, described Snowden's "rigidity of doctrine" as "impenetrable" (Churchill, n.d., 224–25). According to Colin Cross, Snowden's biographer, Snowden saw "sound" money "as the bedrock

[1] The McKenna import duties (on cars, cycles, musical instruments, clocks and cinema films) were introduced by the Coalition Government in 1915 as a temporary wartime measure during the First World War, but continued after the war's end. In 1924, they were yielding £3 million a year, under their shelter car-production industry that emerged in the Midlands. See Cross (1966, 204).

of social progress" (Cross 1966, 202) and "made his adherence to the Gold Standard absolutely definite from the moment of taking office" in 1929 (242). As Chancellor by general consensus, leader of House of Commons in MacDonald's absence and de facto deputy prime minister (234), he occupied the key position in the Cabinet. When the Opposition called for extending safeguarding duties and preferences in July 1929, Snowden reaffirmed the Government's plans for the reversal of protection: "It was known that if we were returned these duties would be repealed...the country at the recent General Election had given an emphatic verdict against Protection" (HC Deb. 9 July 1929, vol. 229 c747; Snowden 1934, 773–74).[2] Regarding Imperial Preference, he did not believe that this "would be mutually advantageous to both countries by a system of preferential tariffs" (HC Deb. 9 July 1929, vol. 229 c754). Throughout his term in office (until resignation from the National Government in September 1932), Snowden thwarted numerous internal attempts to introduce protectionist measures and firmly resisted mounting external pressure for the abandonment of free trade.

1 Narrative

1.1 1930: The Rise of the Protectionist Tide

1930 became an essential year in the history of British public opinion on the tariff question. At the beginning of June, the Manchester Chamber of Commerce members voted "overwhelmingly ... against Free Trade" (HC Deb. 17 June 1930, vol. 240 c7; Marrison 1996, 398). Such a fall in the citadel of free trade served a truly devastating blow to the Liberal case for universal free trade. The Trades Union Congress followed suit by "calling for the empire to be turned into an economic bloc" (Gallagher 1982, 115–16; *Times of India*, 28 June 1930, 12). The British Preparatory Committee for the Imperial Conference representing the British Chambers of Commerce, the Federation of British Industries and the Chamber of Shipping of the UK were unanimous in recommending "not only to increase the volume of trade within the Empire but, by organizing the Empire upon sound economic lines to enable it [to] contribute as a unit, in a larger degree than at present, to the total volume of

[2] UK Parliamentary Papers, House of Commons Debate (hereafter HC Deb.) 9 July 1929, vol. 229 c747.

world trade" (*Times*, 14 July 1930, 13). Another shocking "national turning point" (*Morning Post*, 5 July 1930) and a crushing verdict on the Tariff Truce was delivered by a group of twenty-three formally pro-Free Trade City Bankers who urged "reciprocal trade agreements between the nations constituting the British Empire" while "being prepared to impose duties on all imports from all other countries" (*Times*, 5 July 1930, 14). According to the *Daily Telegraph* (July 5, 1930), "[T]he water has got in among the foundations of Cobdenite Free Trade at last, and the walls are visibly crumbling".

J. H. Thomas, Secretary of State for Dominion Affairs, responded to the calls for protection by announcing that the Government would go into Imperial Conference excluding "nothing from our consideration" and "...with a single-minded desire to do all that is possible...in the interests of the Empire as a whole" (HC Deb. 26 June 1930, vol. 240 c1397). Informally, Thomas let it be known that Cabinet had discussed tariff plans and everyone was in favour except for Snowden and Graham. It appeared that Labour had been presented with a good chance of exploiting the rising tide of protectionist sentiment in the country and negotiating an ambitious scheme of trade preferences with the Dominions, thereby winning pro-imperialist press support and leaving Tories high and dry (Boyce 1987, 263–64): "Snowden was the only serious obstacle, 'and if he won't come in he may have to be thrown overboard'" (as quoted in Boyce 1987, 263).

While others within the Labour and Liberal Parties were changing their minds about free trade, Snowden kept railing against protection and Imperial Preference throughout 1930. Shielding free trade from attack, he made his (and by default, the Government's) position known to his opponents. In March, Snowden denounced "economic unity" aspirations as an "Empire Protectionist stunt" and pledged "we [Labour Government] shall not place that subject on the agenda [at the 1930 Imperial Conference]" (HC Deb. 27 March 1930, vol. 237 c597). "[S]peaking for the Government" on 16 July, he swore to "be no party to the imposition of food taxes, of taxes upon raw materials or of protective duties", and at the Imperial Conference to "approve no final conclusion which involves this country in a food taxation policy or a general Protectionist policy" (HC Deb. 16 July 1930, vol. 241 c1318). For Snowden, his beliefs in free trade were sacrosanct. Any interference in the market for foodstuffs, such as registration fees, quotas, import boards, or tariffs meant restriction on supply that would burden consumers with increased prices and inflation, and incentivise other industries to seek protection. According to Boyce (1987, 259), "So far as he [Snowden] was concerned the debate had ended in 1846 and there was nothing more to be said".

Neville Chamberlain, the Shadow Chancellor of the Exchequer and future British Prime Minister, warned that Snowden's "intense and fanatical dislike of Protection" tied his party "absolutely to the rejection of any system of Protective duties" without pragmatic regard to "what benefits and advantages...may contribute to the reduction...of unemployment" (HC Deb. 16 July 1930, vol. 241 c1416). He expressed the concern of many that as a result of the Labour Government being in office during the Imperial Conference, "the greatest opportunity for laying the foundations of a united Empire that has ever been presented" would be "lost and thrown away" (c1421). The Dominions' absence from the Tariff Truce conference already had been considered a warning about the potential failure of the upcoming Imperial Conference in October 1930. The influential trade-related bodies were opposed to Tariff Truce. The Federation of British Industries made representations to the Government not to adopt it because "...it would be against the interest of this country" (HC Deb. 4 March 1930, vol. 236 c291). The main point of criticism was that Tariff Truce participation would damage every prospect of establishing economic cooperation based on imperial preferences.

Under mounting pressure for protection and preferences, the British government postponed the Ratification of Convention for Tariff Truce twice: in June (CAB 23/64/10, 24 June 1930, 201)[3] and in August 1930 (CAB 23/64/26, 6 August 1930, 433–35). MacDonald summed up the view of "the majority" of the Cabinet that "it would be inadvisable to ratify the Convention... until the probable result of the negotiations could be forecast" (435). On September 2, the ratification of the Tariff Truce Convention was brought up again, and the Cabinet split over its clash with Imperial Preference. Graham urged his colleagues' approval insisting "[i]t was impossible to postpone question of ratification until after the Imperial Conference" (CAB 23/65, 2 September 1930, 6–7). "Failure to ratify", Graham argued, would lead "foreign Powers to infer that Great Britain was about to revise her whole fiscal policy" (6). (That was precisely why MacDonald was postponing ratification. He was pragmatically considering a 10% revenue tariff since the summer of 1930

[3]The National Archives of the United Kingdom (TNA), Records of the Cabinet Office (hereafter CAB), Cabinet Meeting Minutes. CAB 23/64/10, 24 June 1930, 201.

[Rooth 1992, 54; Snowden 1934, 923–24; Williamson 1992, 97; Boyce 1987, 258; Cross 1966, 254], which would be impossible if the UK ratified the Tariff Truce.) Thomas objected, pointing out that "practically every British trade and commercial interest" had expressed views "hostile to ratification". In Thomas's opinion, "the damage had therefore been done before ratification" because, since the signing of the Convention, "many European Powers had increased their tariffs" (CAB 23/65, 2 September 1930, 5). Snowden "could not see how ratification could hamper the proceedings of the Imperial Conference" (8), arguing that he had made "perfectly clear, in Parliament" that while the Government was "prepared to discuss any proposals at the Conference, they could not agree to any taxation on food or any general Protectionist policy" (8). As for the idea that "the Government should keep their hands free ...to impose import duties in the next Budget", Snowden "wished to make it quite clear that whatever the position might be, such a proposal, so far as he was concerned, was out of the question" (8). Using MacDonald's absence to his advantage, Snowden firmly supported Graham's request despite Thomas's vehement objections. The divided Cabinet agreed to approve ratification of the Tariff Truce Convention by a majority of eight to two (CAB 23/65, 2 September 1930, 9; Boyce 1987, 267). Without Snowden, Graham would not have been able to affirm Britain's commitment to delay any protectionist measures until 1 April 1931, at a time when the prospects of all-round ratification of the Tariff Truce convention had been greatly diminished by the onset of the Great Depression and "since all Europe" was "following [a] protectionist trend" (Streit 1930, 2).

1.2 *Imperial Conference 1930: "Critical Juncture"*[4]

The 1930 Imperial Conference was arranged to complete the implementation of the 1926 Balfour Report, which had launched the Dominions' legal and political independence. With the creation of the Commonwealth, the concept of the imperial economic unity became the central issue for the preservation of the self-governing Empire (Williamson 1992, 80–82). It was evident that the desire for common imperial foreign policy was underpinned by anxiety about the loss of British power. By October

[4] Capoccia and Kelemen (2007, 341) emphasize the enduring impact of choices made by actors during critical junctures in history which close off alternative options.

1930, when Imperial Conference participants met, the British economy had deteriorated significantly with no signs of recovery in sight (60). According to Philip Williamson (1992, 522–23), the problems related to the Empire, the economy, and public finance generated a climate of "national crisis", which confronted all-party leaders with politically challenging decisions. At the start of the Conference, Canadian Prime Minister, R. B. Bennett, a Conservative, speaking on behalf of all delegates, issued a forceful call for approval or rejection of Imperial Preference as a principle: "There is here no room for compromise ... [T]he day is now at hand when the peoples of the Empire must decide, once and for all, whether our welfare lies in a closer economic union or whether it does not. ...The time for action has come" (Imperial Conference 1930, 651). Bennett suggested 10% ad valorem duties on non-Empire food as a minimum that Canada would accept, which was delivered as "an ultimatum" (Jones Jr. 1934, 198; Snowden 1934, 868–69, 872). Everyone understood that Bennett's demand implied "the break-up of the Empire should Britain refuse" (Jones Jr. 1934, 226).

Bennett "surprised" Snowden "by his apparent ignorance of the attitude of the Labour Government to Tariff policy" (Snowden 1934, 868). The Dominions' request for the introduction of tariffs on foreign goods in exchange for tweaking—not removing—their own tariffs was incomprehensible to Snowden (Snowden 1930, 13). Despite Thomas's pleas with his Cabinet colleagues to make some decisions and make some concessions "other than preferential tariffs" (CAB 24/216/16, 27 October 1930, 101), Bennett's offer was rejected due to Snowden's unwavering opposition (Williamson 1992, 83–84; Boyce 1987, 272–75). He had no plans for emergency tariffs, least for permanent fiscal reform that would make Britain abandon free trade. Snowden reiterated that although "anxious ... to foster inter-Imperial trade," the Government "would not support ...the taxation of food, raw material, or a general Protectionist policy" (Snowden 1930, 13). He was sure that if Thomas "could have his own way...he would have conceded [to] the demands of the Dominions for a larger measure of Imperial Preference" (Snowden 1934, 871). Snowden threatened resignation in October 1930 when the idea of a revenue tariff seemed to be gaining a majority support in the Cabinet (Boyce 1987, 274) and only conceded to allowing existing preferences remain until their expiry in three years (CAB 24/216/28, 11 November 1931, 171). The Government tried to cushion the blow by moving to discuss quotas (*Economist*, 22 November 1930), but its refusal to make any concessions regarding Imperial Preference caused "great offence to Canadian and Australian delegates" (Williamson 1992, 83).

The Conference was deemed unsuccessful, with Snowden admitting as much himself: "After six weeks of this time-wasting procedure, the Conference ended with practically nothing accomplished" (Snowden 1934, 870). All that could be saved was the agreement to examine "various methods by which each country could make the greatest possible contribution to economic cooperation within the Empire" (CAB 24/216/28, 11 November 1931, 171) at the economic conference in Ottawa planned to take place in August 1931. There was not much enthusiasm, however, if the Labour government were to remain in power (Williamson 1992, 84). Baldwin, the leader of the opposition, accused Snowden of making the conference a failure even before it started: "...the 9th July of last year [1929] ... he made it quite clear that there could be no change in fiscal policy to meet any request from the Dominions; and we all know that without any change in fiscal policy it is perfectly impossible to advance ... economic Imperial unity" (HC Deb. 27 November 1930, vol. 245 c1547). Bennett's offer and the principle of Empire preference were accepted on behalf of the Conservative Party (*Times*, 3 December 1930, 8). In December 1930, the Conservative Research Department's Tariff Committee chaired by Philip Cunliffe-Lister, a former president of the Board of Trade, started building permanent tariff structures with scope for imperial preferences capitalizing on the growing erosion of support for free trade (Rooth 1992, 58–59). Considering the circumstances, Snowden's principled objection to imperial protectionism is significant. He effectively deferred the introduction of preferences until the ratification of the Ottawa agreements in autumn of 1932.

To show just how important free trade was to him, Snowden took the fight to Manchester, which after having been a bastion of free trade for nearly a century, was now slipping into protectionism. For the second time since 1888, the Manchester Chamber of Commerce passed a resolution for protection urging the Government to postpone any decision with respect to the signing of the Tariff Truce (HC Deb. 27 November 1930, vol. 245 c229) until additional European countries signed. Snowden argued that crisis was no reason to abandon a principled approach to trade:

> I do not underestimate the magnitude of the task in which we are engaged, but it would be disastrous not only to this country but for the world if at this time this country, in a state of panic, were to change its well-tried fiscal policy. We have a great heritage to maintain …not only for ourselves but for the world. Free trade has withstood many assaults in the past, and I am confident that, if we will do our duty in this crisis, if we will bring home to people the full, solid facts of the case, we shall add one more success to the great victories we have achieved in the past. (Snowden 1930, 13)

1.3 Snowden: Liberalism's Last Gasp

By the end of 1930, Snowden felt unwell and depressed. His Budget was unbalanced—the forecast in 1930–1931 was for a £37 million deficit—mainly because the revenue failed to meet Treasury estimates (Snowden 1934, 901–2). Exports fell by 30% during 1930 while rising unemployment unsettled the Insurance Fund due to weekly borrowing of up to £1 million (Cross 1966, 259). Despite his poor health and declared intention of moving on, Snowden declined the offer of a peerage in March 1931. He feared that his job would go to J. H. Thomas, a supporter of tariffs and that only he could ensure that the principles of "sound finance" in dealing with the fiscal policy were safeguarded (Cross 1966, 269; Snowden 1934, 924).

While he was away, Snowden kept blocking key protectionist proposals. On 4 March, MacDonald conveyed to the Cabinet that Snowden "was opposed to the majority recommendation" for the urgent wheat quota, which was crucial for the Ottawa Imperial Conference in August 1931 to go ahead (CAB 23/66/17, 4 March 1931, 248–49). The Conference was postponed due to the political situation in the UK. It was recognized abroad that "while Snowden is Chancellor of the Exchequer in Britain there can be no progress towards greater imperial preference" (*New York Times*, 7 June 1931, 12). Snowden's 1930–31 Budget, which he had prepared alone in his sickbed, was considered "within the limitations imposed on him by his Free Trade principles, an eminently sensible piece of work" (HC Deb. 28 April 1931, vol. 251 c1563). During the discussion of the Budget in the House of Commons on 27 April 1931, Snowden made it known that formalizing the financial arrangements for the year had to wait for the recommendations of the May all-party report on the National Expenditure. He warned "any gap…in the finance of the year should be met by economy" (HC Deb. 27 April 1931, vol. 251

c1408). He also made clear that "[A] revenue tariff, apart from its Protectionist object, is a means of relieving the well-to-do at the expense of the poor, and is an indirect method of reducing wages. I shall *never* be a party to any such imposition" (c1403; emphasis added). This prompted Neville Chamberlain to reply: "…here is the last Chancellor of the Exchequer who will *ever* again introduce a Free Trade Budget in this House" (HC Deb. 28 April 1931, vol. 251 c1479; emphasis added).

Although the collapse of the Tariff Truce was always anticipated, it was still a serious blow to the Government's economic strategy when it happened (Boyce 1987, 310–11; *Manchester Guardian*, 20 June 1931, 16). Graham tried to negotiate a 25% tariff reduction on selected tariffs bilaterally with existing most-favoured-nation partners (Germany, France, Belgium, Poland, Italy, and Austria) to keep the Tariff Truce proposal alive, but failed (CAB 23/66/4, 20 May 1931, 92–93; Boyce 1987, 276, 310). In 1931, sixty-one countries raised import duties and introduced stricter types of import restriction, including eighteen British Dominions or possessions. Churchill, Ernest Bevin, and Walter Citrine of the Trades Union Congress (TUC), John Simon a senior Liberal MP, and many other principled free traders came to embrace protective tariffs (Cross 1966, 274). Keynes issued a public call for "a restriction of imports to support our balance of trade and to provide employment" in the absence of "a concrete, practical proposal for stimulating our export trades" (Keynes 1931a, 176). He stated unequivocally that "Free Traders may, consistently with their faith, regard a revenue tariff as our iron ration, which can be used once only in emergency. The emergency has arrived" (Keynes 1931d, 54). According to Cross (1966, 274), Snowden's reaction to such "desertions from free trade" was that "tabernacle now needed to be defended more vigorously than ever".

When the Macmillan Committee report, published on 14 July 1931, justified the abandonment of Britain's free trade policies because of the country's chronic economic disequilibrium and as a means to obtain additional revenue for the National Exchequer, Snowden ensured that it warranted no immediate discussion or response (Boyce 1987, 331–32). Any serious consideration of the proposal for a comprehensive average tariff of 10% could have compromised the Government's principles of internationalism (Eichengreen 1984, 366; Boyce 1987, 283, 331).

Snowden's handling of the May Report on the National Expenditure published on 31 July produced a much more dramatic effect with far-reaching consequences for the Labour Government. The report revealed budget expenditures and deficits of about £120 million (later to be revised up to £170 million) that needed to be addressed by making economies and finding additional revenue (CAB 24/222, 27 July 1931; Snowden 1934, 933–34). The Treasury had provided the figures for the report (so he could not have been surprised), and Snowden later admitted that he withheld it for at least two days so it would not be debated. Snowden did not even consult with MacDonald, who together with their Cabinet colleagues, dispersed for the holidays without fully grasping its implications. Snowden planned to use the recess to prepare an economy programme for unconditional approval, first at the Labour Party conference and then by the House of Commons. If all went well, the financial crisis would be surmounted with Labour in office and Snowden's policy of "sound finance" vindicated (Snowden and MacDonald both agreed that reduction of the unemployment insurance expenditure was needed [Cross 1966, 280; Snowden 1934, 932–33]). But Snowden miscalculated when he assumed that the Labour Party, having accepted the appointment of the May committee and his Budget, had already committed itself in principle to his policy (Cross 1966, 280).

With the May Report triggering a confidence crisis and a run on the pound sterling, the Bank of England began pressuring the Government to balance the Budget in order to obtain American and French loans (Williamson 1992, 308; Morrison 2016, 192–96). On 7 August, Snowden called MacDonald back to London (PRO 30/69/260, Snowden to MacDonald, 7 August 1931; Boyce, 1987, 348). Snowden was "convinced of the terrible gravity" of the situation: the prospect of four million unemployed in 1932 made burden of financial support unsustainable. "I have given up all hope of a revival of trade. I am sure it will get worse", he wrote to MacDonald while urging him to get the Cabinet Economy Committee (consisting of himself, MacDonald, Thomas, Graham, and Secretary of State for Foreign Affairs Arthur Henderson) together without delay: "The collapse is almost certain to come before then [25 August] if we delay" …"We cannot allow matters to drift into utter chaos, and we are perilously that. I am having a full statement prepared of the outlook for the Budget which will be a very appalling one. Under existing trade conditions the limits of taxation have been reached" (PRO 30/69/260, Snowden to MacDonald, 7 August 1931).

MacDonald called the meeting of the Cabinet Economy Committee immediately after arriving in London on 11 August, planning to work out a compromise between what the May Report had demanded and what Labour would accept (Cross 1966, 281). Pressured by the Bank of England and the Opposition to correct the budget by retrenchment (Williamson 1992, 308), the Committee prepared a proposal for social spending cuts and additional taxation based on the principle of "common sacrifice and effort" (CAB 23/67/16, 19 August 1931, 310). The main controversy was over Snowden's proposal to cut unemployment benefits and his principled refusal to include revenue tariff (wanted by Henderson, Graham, the TUC, and bankers), which could help reduce the expenditure costs and address the balance of trade deficit. On 18 August, MacDonald wrote in his diary: "I am disappointed with the scheme & disheartened. Discussed a revenue tax, 4 in favour and the Chancellor against" (PRO 30/69/1753, MacDonald Diaries, 18 August 1931)[5]; and on 19 of August: "All except Snowden recommend revenue tariff (Henderson even on food) to help the unemployed from having too great a cut". When the Committee presented its proposal on 19 August, MacDonald "[A]sked [Cabinet] opinion on revenue tax 15 [ministers voted] for 10 [ministers] on manufactured goods only, 5 [ministers] on everything" (PRO 30/69/1753, MacDonald Diaries, 19 August 1931). But the Cabinet agreed "to defer further consideration of...Revenue Tariff" to 21 August (CAB 23/67/16, 19 August 1931, 314) as it was decided that the opposing minority, including Snowden, was too large for the tariff to be adopted (Cross 1966, 288). It has been speculated that "[F]irm leadership by MacDonald, and willingness to drop Snowden, might at this stage have turned the tariff into definite Government policy and so changed the character of future events" (Cross 1966, 290). Although there is no proof that anyone could remove Snowden or seriously ignore his position on tariffs at this stage, it is easy to imagine such a counterfactual considering the high stakes involved and that MacDonald had a Cabinet majority supporting him. The TUC was willing to accept tariffs with members' approval (CAB 23/67/18, 21 August 1931, 326). Crucially, a revenue tariff offered "badly needed flexibility" in bargaining with the Conservatives, and "given the Bank of England support, even with the Liberals" (Williamson 1992, 308; CAB 23/67/17, 20 August

[5] TNA, Records of the Public Record Office (hereafter PRO), James Ramsey MacDonald Papers. PRO 30/69/1753, MacDonald Diaries, 18 August 1931.

1931, 318). Against all these odds, Snowden's principles had a real effect on policy. Even under the threat of imminent political demise, the divided Labour Cabinet "thanks to a mixture of gut reaction and Snowden's obduracy…remained committed to the free-trade cause" (Thorpe 1991, 236).

On 21 August "the situation had completely altered" due to "the rejection by the Liberal party of any such expedient [revenue tariff]". In the Cabinet, there was "considerable support for the view that the Revenue Tariff should be excluded from proposals if, and only if, no further economies were made in regard to Unemployment Insurance". When Snowden, "expressed the strongest possible objection to the Government being committed in any way to the principle of a Revenue Tariff", MacDonald assured him that in the discussions with the Opposition leaders and the representatives of the Bank of England, "it would be clearly understood that no decision of any kind had been reached on a subject of a Revenue Tariff" and "[T]here would not, however, be included in the proposals any reference…to a Revenue Tariff in view of the failure to reach agreement" (CAB 23/67/18, 21 August 1931, 335). On 23 August, after an American loan had been secured based on Snowden's and MacDonald's commitment to a 10% cut in unemployment benefits, Henderson's (and six other Cabinet Ministers') refusal to accept it combined with a "too strong" opposition from TUC led to Cabinet resignation (PRO 30/69/1753, MacDonald Diaries, 23 August 1931). After being invited by the King to stay as Prime Minister and form an all-party National government, MacDonald concluded: "It was plain that I would be left almost alone with Snowden…" (PRO/30/69/1753, MacDonald Diaries, 24 August 193). The Labour Government, the Labour Party, and the Labour Movement were all overtly sacrificed for the sake of free trade.

Even the gold standard was effectively gambled because Snowden was so unwilling to bend on free trade. Snowden's most austere Budget in Britain's history—"a considerable rise in taxation…accompanied by very large economies" (CAB 23/68/6, 3 September 1931, 103)—was voted through Parliament, but it did not manage to prevent its suspension in September (Morrison 2016, 197–98; Cross 1966, 309; CAB 23/68/13, 20 September 1931, 229). Balancing trade became ever more implicit in the stability of sterling (Williamson 1992, 389). Estimates for the deficit "varied from/£50 millions to £100 millions a year, but there was great uncertainty" (CAB 23/68/12, 17 September 1931, 211). MacDonald established a committee consisting of Snowden, Neville Chamberlain and Reading, Henderson's successor as Foreign Secretary so that the existing Cabinet could deal with the trade deficit as a continuing emergency (HL Deb 17 September 1931, vol. 82 cc64–93).[6] They were expected to produce a policy addressing the trade deficit through a modified Conservative tariff package that would be acceptable to ministerial free traders. Despite working hard, the committee antagonized the key players over the choice between an emergency or a general tariff (Williamson 1992, 400–401).

Against prominent bankers' advice (CAB 23/68/12, 17 September 1931, 212) and on the Conservatives' instigation (which received support from Thomas and Snowden), the Cabinet agreed to call a general election (Williamson 1992, 401; Thorpe 1991, 125) to break the deadlock over the trade deficit and "[t]ariffs obstacle" (PRO 30/69/1753, MacDonald Diaries, 16 September 1931). The Cabinet now had to reconcile incompatible protectionist and liberal positions on trade policy to approach the election on one "National" platform (CAB 23/68/22, 2 October 1931, 334–37). After a week of intense negotiations over the election formula,[7] it was agreed for MacDonald to lead the Government into the election on a pledge "to take all measures for the stabilization of the £ sterling, with nothing excluded" (CAB 23/68/23, 5 October 1931, 342) and requesting a "free hand to deal with the question of the balance of trade" (Snowden 1934, 991). Although Snowden accepted the offer of the peerage and was going to be a new member of the House of Lords (Williamson 1992, 399; PRO 30/69/1314, MacDonald to Baldwin, 5 September 1931),[8] he had high stakes in the election because he was determined to safeguard free trade (Thorpe 1991, 233, 238). During the Cabinet discussions, Snowden "worked with the two Liberal members [Samuel and Reading] and entirely shared their views" "prepared to…ask

[6] UK Parliamentary Papers, House of Lords Debate (hereafter HL Deb.) 17 September 1931 Vol. 82 cc64–94.

[7] See TNA, Cabinet Minutes. CAB 23/68/21, 1 October 1931, 326–27; CAB 23/68/22, 2 October 1931, 334–37; CAB 23/68/23, 5 October 1931, 341–43.

[8] MacDonald wrote to Baldwin, "As to ourselves – Snowden, as you know, is going out. He had warned me of that three or four months ago, and before we thought of anything like this happening I had been discussing with him whether or not he would like to go to the House of Lords". PRO 30/69/1314, Ramsey MacDonald to Stanley Baldwin, 5 September 1931.

for mandate to complete our work" but not prepared to go to the country on a tariff issue" (Snowden 1934, 991; Cross 1966, 311). Subsequently, Snowden and Liberal free trade ministers formed one free trade opposition group within the National Government (Snowden 1934, 1003–5). His other objective was to keep Labour out of power (Cross 1966, 311–16; Snowden 1934, 995). Snowden's visceral attack on his former colleagues through a series of high-profile public statements made "a great and unexpected impact on the campaign" (Thorpe 1991, 231–32).

The general election on 27 October 1931 resulted in an overwhelming Conservative majority (Williamson 1992, 455; Craig 1970, 63). However, MacDonald remained Prime Minister as head of a National Government, a coalition formed between the Conservatives, National Labour, and multiple Liberal factions. Winning as a coalition had its advantages in providing unity for restoring Britain's economic position, but at some cost to the Government's freedom to carry out tariff reform quickly and without compromise (Wrench 1984, 148). According to Snowden (1934, 997), "[T]he Labour Party were not merely defeated, but decimated". As Cross (1966, 325–26) put it, Snowden "more than any other single individual had constructed the National Government's overwhelming victory. Now the Government he had made was doing things he hated". In the Cabinet reshuffle, Snowden accepted the position of Lord Privy Seal hoping that only by staying in office he might still be able to forestall the adoption of full protection (Cross 1966, 322; Thorpe 1991, 233, 238; Snowden 1934, 998, 1000). To strengthen opposition to protectionists in the Cabinet, he lobbied MacDonald to appoint Walter Runciman, a well-known Liberal free trader, to the key position of President of the Board of Trade (Snowden 1934, 999).[9]

Snowden and free trade ministers came to accept the need for temporary emergency revenue tariffs to correct the trade deficit and decrease feared immediate pressure on a floated sterling (CAB 23/69/5, 12 November 1931, 55; CAB 23/69/6, 13 November 1931, 65). However, they did so only under the promise of "*an impartial enquiry*" into the balance of trade deficit and after distinguishing them from protection (Snowden 1934, 1005; Williamson 1992, 509). According to Snowden

[9] Snowden (1934, 999): "I had suggested Mr. Runciman for this position because of his pronounced of Free Trade. He had been regarded as one of the strongest free traders in the country, holding his views with unshakeable tenacity. How tragically mistaken I was later events proved"!

(1934, 1004–5), "[F]ree Traders could not take responsibility of breaking up the National Government at that stage" and although they had not opposed the Abnormal Importations Act they "were very much concerned about the immediate future of fiscal policy". It seems they worried not without good reason. On 2 December, Snowden sent a letter to MacDonald raising concern about the apparent move into full "permanent" protection with the introduction of significant food tariffs by the Horticultural Products (Emergency Customs Duties) Bill (Wrench 2000, 70). The new Lord Privy Seal wrote: "I feel that by making concessions in one direction and another to the Protectionists we are getting into a compromised position…I cannot go on sacrificing beliefs and principles bit by bit until there are none left" (as quoted in Snowden 1934, 1006). MacDonald himself was "getting unhappy" that "recent discussions on duties have been put forward quite openly as protection, not as a means of balancing trade…" (as quoted in Wrench 1984, 150). It was clear that after relinquishing the Exchequer and staying in the Cabinet dominated by protectionists, Snowden's ability to block protection disappeared. Still, his reputation demanded that his views had to be accommodated and everyone knew that introducing tariffs with Snowden in the Government was not going to be an easy task (Williamson 1992, 393). As future events demonstrated, even in his limited capacity, Snowden would staunchly defend free trade.

In December, MacDonald appointed the Cabinet Balance of Trade Committee, which included Snowden and Home Secretary Herbert Samuel, to find out if there was an adverse balance of trade and advise how it should be addressed (CAB 23/69/17, 11 December 1931, 228–29). The National Government's future was hanging in the balance pending the acceptance of the Committee's proposal by the Cabinet free traders. Runciman pleaded with Snowden to accept a general 10% revenue tariff, which would enable reduction on income tax, a precedent established by the Netherlands. Having worked closely on the proposal with Neville Chamberlain, now Chancellor of the Exchequer, Runciman expected that protectionist members of the Balance of Trade Committee would accept it, and thus more extreme tariff proposals could be avoided. Snowden replied: "…he could not expect me to commit myself to such proposal, but I would think it over. I gave him no encouragement to believe that I should support it" (1934, 1007–8). At the final Committee meeting on 18 January 1932, Snowden announced he could not subscribe to the majority report and would submit a note of dissent. He argued that the adverse balance of trade was exaggerated, it was going "far beyond the programme upon which the National Government went to the country", and could not warrant "a complete and permanent reversal of fiscal policy" (CAB 24/227, 21 January 1931, 340). On 21 January, when the Committee proposed immediate introduction of permanent general tariff reform with provisions for the Imperial Preference (CAB 23/70/5, 21 January 1931, 85–116) "the agreement on the report could not be secured" (Snowden 1934, 1010), and Snowden and the Liberal Free Traders threatened to resign. "Hopeless deadlock", according to MacDonald, "Snowden just as stiff necked and unaccommodating as ever he has been. What a situation". Suspending the practice of Cabinet responsibility averted resignations. MacDonald managed to persuade Snowden and others not to quit by offering them "agreement to differ": "Solution found. Let them vote and speak against Tariffs" (PRO 30/69/1753, MacDonald Diaries, 22 January 1932).

Snowden and the others accepted the offer on condition that "[t]his freedom [to speak and vote against any tariff proposals] was to extend to Members of Parliament...The Party Whips were not to exert any influence to get votes for tariff proposals and Liberals could run Free Trade candidates at the election". Again, Snowden knew that "...if we did not accept it we should be open to the charge that we had rejected an unprecedented offer of personal freedom, and that we were determined to break-up the Government and were indifferent to the consequences of such action" (Snowden 1934, 1011). But the introduction of the Import Duties Bill in February was too much for them (Williamson 1992, 509–10). The Bill was designed to address the adverse balance of trade, reduce unemployment, reunite with the Empire to ward off foreign competition and enhance self-sufficiency. Additionally, it was meant to bring in revenue, force foreigners to lower their tariffs, restore the efficiency of industry, and support sterling. It introduced a general ad valorem duty of 10% upon all British imports, with exceptions for the goods, mainly food and raw materials, on the "free" list. The Bill established an Import Duty Advisory Committee that was empowered to apply adjustable surtax as "an instrument to obtain rationalization of domestic industries and reductions of foreign tariffs" (Williamson 1992, 506). The British Empire goods were exempted from tariffs until the Imperial Conference at Ottawa (HC Deb. 04 February 1932, vol. 261 cc279–96). Snowden mounted fierce opposition to the Import Duties Bill, now as a member of the House of Lords:

> "This is the most important measure dealing with trade and commerce which has been before Parliament for nearly a century. The measure is revolutionary in its character."[...]"It is criminal to gamble with the vital interests of the country by adopting a policy while staring us in the face are the facts of the disastrous failure of that policy elsewhere."[...]"This Bill will pass. As Mr. Chamberlain said, arguments will then pass into facts, and that, my Lords, is our satisfaction in this our temporary defeat. Facts and experience will finally settle this question. Free Trade is not dead." (HL Deb. 29 February 1932, vol. 83 cc684–97)

When Snowden's "last-ditch attempt to prevent ratification of Ottawa" (Cross 1966, 329) agreements failed ("a piece of colossal hambug" according to Snowden [1934, 1027]), he finally abandoned MacDonald and the Government, but not his faith in free trade (1018–30)[10]:

> I can no longer without loss of all self-respect, remain a member of a Government which is pursuing a policy which I believe is disastrous to the welfare of this country, which will lead to the disruption of the Empire, and which is fraught with great danger in our international relations. ...So I go now. (as quoted in Cross 1966, 329–30; Snowden's resignation letter, September 1932)

2 Conclusion

Traditional narratives of the interwar collapse of European and international integration emphasize causal structural explanations of policy changes as outcomes. This chapter shifts analytical focus to agency and showcases how individuals can shape policy transitions towards specific outcomes as a result of their economic beliefs and political decisions. Snowden worked assiduously to stave off the protectionist slide because of his principled beliefs in free trade. As a veto player in the Government's decision making over commercial policy, Snowden effectively tempered a shift towards protection in 1930–31. His near-autonomous control over fiscal policy is well documented. Being "the most autocratic Chancellor the twentieth century had ever seen" (Cross 1966, 207) he effectively contributed more than any other actor to the deferral of introduction

[10] MacDonald noted, "Snowden looked unusually unkempt & unshaven as though growing moustache or beard, cold, repelling, vindictive. I am disheartened". PRO 30/69/1753, MacDonald Diaries, 28 September 1932.

of general protection until 1932. Crucially, absent Snowden, the policy outcomes could have been different.

Snowden's case is exemplary of pivotal actors' relevance to the analysis of policy change as it can be traced through the "critical junctures" determined by "structural fluidity and heightened contingency" (Capoccia and Kelemen 2007, 352) when "decisions by influential actors…steer outcomes towards a new equilibrium" (354). "But for the presence of Snowden", as Rooth argues, the Labour Government "would almost certainly have introduced protectionist measures in 1930" (Rooth 1992, 54; Fearon 1991, 180–82). Snowden was instrumental to Britain's ratification of the Tariff Truce Convention in MacDonald's absence and his zealous adherence to free trade had a direct influence on the rejection of the Imperial Preference policy in autumn 1930, and of the revenue tariff during the August-September crisis in 1931. The Agreement on Imperial Preference could have taken place during the Imperial Conference. By that time, it was clear that foreign governments would not complete ratification of the Tariff Truce Convention. The key players within the Cabinet were in support, and they actively promoted some form of protection. As the most orthodox liberal Chancellor, Snowden, however, was resolved that Britain's fiscal policy based on free trade should be defended and rejected the proposals (Rooth 1992, 54). His threats to resign were effective for achieving his goals and reveal the significant leverage that he had over his opponents. Although Snowden's opposition was not the sole reason for the Imperial Preference talks to collapse, the failure was clearly associated with his name, and it could be traced back to his handling of fiscal policy and his attitude at the Conference.

Snowden's resilience and unwillingness to compromise on protection are especially significant in the presence of policy alternatives and structural dictates. Under new economic conditions, Keynes's tariff proposals offered practical solutions to unemployment, whereas, Snowden failed to recognize immense social and economic upheavals that the First World War had created which warranted novel approaches to fiscal policy (Jovitt 1987, 41, 56). Furthermore, although the Imperial Preference implied the irreversible break with a traditional *laissez-faire* policy, at the same time, it also provided the opportunity for Britain to be actively engaged in halting the rise of protectionism within the Empire, which many believed could be a step towards a global trade revival. During the August-September crisis, acceptance of a revenue tariff could have alleviated expenditure cuts and pressure on sterling. It could perhaps even prevent the Labour Government's dissolution if MacDonald who "considered several possible choices at certain junctures" (Fearon 1991, 193) did not bend to Snowden's intransigence and had him resigned. Such arguments "can be judged more credible or less credible, depending on our use of historical detail and theories about the way people behave" (195). Although despite Snowden's vehement opposition (to the point of breaking the National Government) protection was introduced by pragmatic liberal free traders, thanks to Snowden, it was done in a much-attenuated form.

The example of Britain's interwar "exit" from the liberal trading regime offers some new insight into its recent "Brexit" from the European Union. Specifically, we see the critical role that individual policymakers play in defining the terms, timing, and trajectory of such shifts. In 1931, the British electorate, faced with economic stagnation and financial calamity, voted for change. Implicitly, they voted for the abandonment of free trade and pursuit of closer economic integration with the British Empire. The crossroads had preceded that historic policy shift in 1930 when politicians were confronted with a tangible choice between two options: to trade on with Europe ("remain" free trade) or to trade with the Empire ("leave" for protection). For a free trading nation with imperial commitments, the political choice between economic internationalism (Tariff Truce) or economic nationalism (Imperial Preference) during the early 1930s was as important and divisive as the choice between "leave" or "remain" in the single European market and customs union during the Brexit political crisis from 2016 to 2020. Snowden's case serves as an example of how "the balance of [trade-creating and trade-diverting] effects depended on the motivations of policymakers and hence on the structure of their policies" (Eichengreen and Irwin 1993, 4). Hopefully, this insight can improve our understanding of trade policy decisions in a world that is increasingly dominated by the mercantilist rivalry between the United States and China and divided by the politics of Brexit and US President Donald Trump, especially considering potential long-term systemic effects of individual actions involved and how much is at stake.

References

Boyce, Robert W. D. 1987. *British Capitalism at the Crossroads 1919–1932: A Study in Politics, Economics, and International Relations*. New York: Cambridge University Press.

Cain, Peter. J., and Antony G. Hopkins. 2001. *British Imperialism, 1688–2000.* 2nd ed. New York: Longman.

Capie, Forrest. 1980. "The Pressure for Tariff Protection in Britain, 1917–31." *Journal of European Economic History* 9 (2): 431–47.

———. 1983. *Depression and Protectionism: Britain Between the Wars.* Boston: Allen & Unwin.

———. 1998. "The Sources and Origins of Britain's Return to Protection, 1931–2." In *Free Trade and Its Reception 1815–1960. Freedom and Trade: Volume I*, edited by Andrew Marrison, 246–77. London: Routledge.

Capoccia, Giovanni, and R. Daniel Kelemen. 2007. "The Study of Critical Junctures: Theory, Narrative, and Counterfactuals in Historical Institutionalism." *World Politics* 59 (3): 341–69.

Chase, Kerry. 2004. "Imperial Protection and Strategic Trade Policy in the Interwar Period." *Review of International Political Economy* 11 (1): 177–203. https://doi.org/10.1080/0969229042000179802.

Churchill, Winston S. n.d. "Literary: 'Short Biographies': Proofs 2." In *Winston S. Churchill Papers*, CHAR 8/591. Churchill Archives Centre, Cambridge, UK.

Clavin, Patricia. 2013. *Securing the World Economy: The Reinvention of the League of Nations, 1920–1946.* New York: Oxford University Press. https://doi.org/10.1093/acprof:oso/9780199577934.001.0001.

Craig, F. W. S., ed. 1970. *British General Election Manifestos 1918–1966.* Chichester, UK: Political Reference Publications.

Cross, Colin. 1966. *Philip Snowden.* London: Barrie and Rockliff.

The Daily Telegraph. 1930. "Bankers and Fiscal Policy: A Recognition of Changed World Condition." July 5. Bank of England ADM10/44, Bank of England Archives.

Drummond, Ian M. 1972. *British Economic Policy and the Empire 1919–1939.* London: George Allen & Unwin Ltd.

———. 1974. *Imperial Economic Policy 1917–1939: Studies in Expansion and Protection.* London: George Allen & Unwin Ltd.

E.A.C. [1930] 1977. "The Economists' Report. Report Committee of Economists. P.R.O., Cab. 58/151, E.A.C. (H.)127, 24 October 1930." In *The Economic Advisory Council*, edited by Susan Howson and Donald Winch, 180–243. New York: Cambridge University Press.

The Economist. 1930. "The Imperial Conference." *The Economist.* November 22. Historical Archive.

Eichengreen, Barry. 1981. *Sterling and the Tariff, 1929–32, Princeton Studies in International Finance.* Princeton, NJ: Princeton Studies in International Finance, Department of Economics, Princeton University.

———. 1984. "Keynes and Protection." *The Journal of Economic History* 44 (2): 363–73.

———. 1992a. *Golden Fetters: The Gold Standard and the Great Depression, 1919–1939*. New York: Oxford University Press.

———. 1992b. "The Eternal Fiscal Question: Free Trade and Protection in Britain, 1860–1929." In *Protectionism in the World Economy*, edited by Forrest Capie, 162–90. Aldershot: E. Elgar.

Eichengreen, Barry, and Douglas A. Irwin. 1993. "Trade Blocs, Currency Blocs and the Reorientation of World Trade in the 1930s." NBER Working Paper Series, No. 4445. Cambridge, MA.

Fearon, James D. 1991. "Counterfactuals and Hypothesis Testing in Political Science." *World Politics* 43 (2): 169–95.

Gallagher, John. 1982. *The Decline, Revival and Fall of the British Empire: The Ford Lectures and Other Essays*. Edited by Anil Seal, 73–154. Cambridge: Cambridge University Press. https://doi-org.gate3.library.lse.ac.uk/10.1017/CBO9780511523847.

Gilpin, Robert. 1975. *U.S. Power and the Multinational Corporation: The Political Economy of Foreign Direct Investment*. New York: Basic Books.

Gourevitch, Peter A. 1986. *Politics in Hard Times: Comparative Responses to International Economic Crises*. Ithaca, NY: Cornell University Press.

Gowa, Joanne, and Raymond Hicks. 2013. "Politics, Institutions, and Trade: Lessons of the Interwar Era." *International Organization* 67 (3): 439–67. https://doi.org/10.1017/S0020818313000118.

Hirst, Francis W. 1925. *From Adam Smith to Philip Snowden: A History of Free Trade*. London: T. Fisher Unwin Ltd.

Howe, Anthony. 1998. *Free Trade and Liberal England 1846–1946*. New York: Oxford University Press. https://doi.org/10.1093/acprof:oso/9780198201465.001.0001.

Howson, Susan, and Donald Winch. 1977. *The Economic Advisory Council 1930–1939. A Study in Economic Advice during Depression and Recovery*. New York: Cambridge University Press.

Imperial Conference, 1930: Summary of Proceedings. 1930. London: His Majesty's Stationary Office.

Irwin, Douglas A. 1989. "Political Economy and Peel's Repeal of the Corn Laws." *Economics and Politics* I (1): 41–59.

———. 2005. Keynes and the Macroeconomics of Protection. In *Against the Tide: An Intellectual History of Free Trade*, 189–205. Princeton, NJ: Princeton University Press.

———. 2011. *Peddling Protectionism: Smoot-Hawley and the Great Depression*. Princeton, NJ: Princeton University Press.

———. 2012. *Trade Policy Disaster: Lessons from the 1930s*. Cambridge, Mass.: MIT Press.

Jones Jr., Joseph M. 1934. *Tariff Retaliation: Repercussions of the Hawley-Smoot Bill*. Philadelphia: University of Pennsylvania Press.

Jovitt, Tony. 1987. "Philip Snowden and the First World War." In *Philip Snowden: The First Labour Chancellor of the Exchequer*, edited by Keith Laybourn and David James, 39–57. Bradford: Bradford Libraries and Information Service.

Keohane, Robert O. 1984. *After Hegemony: Cooperation and Discord in the World Political Economy*. Princeton, NJ: Princeton University Press.

Keynes, John Maynard. 1931a. "Economic Notes on Free Trade. I—'The Export Industries'." *The New Statesman and Nation*, March 28, 175–76. London School of Economics (LSE) Library: Main Collection Journals.

———. 1931b. "Economic Notes on Free Trade. II—'A Revenue Tariff and the Cost of Living'." *The New Statesman and Nation*, April 4, 211.

———. 1931c. "Economic Notes on Free Trade. III—'The Reaction of Imports and Export'." *The New Statesman and Nation*, April 11, 242–43.

———. 1931d. "Proposal for a Revenue Tariff. By J. M. Keynes." *The New Statesman and Nation*, March 7, 53–54.

Keynes, John Maynard, and G. D. H. Cole. [1930] 1977. "The Economic Outlook. Report by Chairman (Mr. J. M. Keynes) and Mr. G. D. H. Cole. E. A. C. (H.) 85, 2 May 1930." In *The Economic Advisory Council*, edited by Susan Howson and Donald Winch, 174–77. New York: Cambridge University Press.

Kindleberger, Charles P. 1986. *The World in Depression, 1929–1939*. Berkeley: University of California Press.

Krasner, Stephen D. 1976. "State Power and the Structure of International Trade." *World Politics* 28 (3): 317–47.

———. 1978. *Defending the National Interest: Raw Materials Investments and US Foreign Policy*. Princeton, NJ: Princeton University Press.

Laybourn, Keith. 1987. "Philip Snowden: The Road from Leeds to the Lords." In *Philip Snowden: The First Labour Chancellor of the Exchequer*, edited by Keith Laybourn and David James, 59–80. Bradford Libraries and Information Service.

Lobell, Steven E. 1999. "Second Image Reversed Politics: Britain's Choice of Freer Trade or Imperial Preferences, 1903–1906, 1917–1923, 1930–1932." *International Studies Quarterly* 43 (4): 671–93. https://doi.org/10.1111/0020-8833.00141.

The Manchester Guardian. 1931. "Tariff Truce Shelved: Time Not Ripe for Application Geneva Decision a Moral Obligation on Governments." June 20. ProQuest Historical Newspapers.

Marrison, Andrew. 1996. *British Business and Protection, 1903–1932*. Oxford: Clarendon Press.

Morning Post. 1930. "The Bankers' Blow to Free Trade: An Epoch-making Event in National Life. Political Situation: Strong Industrial Support for the Manifesto." July 5. Bank of England ADM10/44, Bank of England Archives.

Morrison, James Ashley. 2012. "Before Hegemony: Adam Smith, American Independence, and the Origins of the First Era of Globalization." *International Organization* 66 (3): 395–428. https://doi.org/10.1017/S0020818312000148.

———. 2016. "Shocking Intellectual Austerity: The Role of Ideas in the Demise of the Gold Standard in Britain." *International Organization* 70 (1): 175–207. https://doi.org/10.1017/S0020818315000314.

The New York Times. 1931. "Empire Conference for 1931 Postponed: Parley Is Deferred Because of Elections in Australia and New Zealand. Britain Opposed Agenda Greater Tariff Preferences Seen as Impossible as Long as Snowden Is in Office." June 7. ProQuest Historical Newspapers.

Robbins, Lionel. 1931. "A Reply to Mr. Keynes by Lionel Robbins." *The New Statesman and Nation*, March 14, 98–99. London School of Economics (LSE) Library: Main Collection Journals.

Rooth, Tim. 1992. *British Protectionism and the International Economy: Overseas Commercial Policy in the 1930s*. New York: Cambridge University Press.

Self, Robert C. 1986. *Tories and Tariffs: The Conservative Party and the Politics of Tariff Reform, 1922–1932*. New York: Garland Publishing.

Simmons, Beth A. 1994. *Who Adjusts? Domestic Sources of Foreign Economic Policy During the Interwar Years*. Princeton, NJ: Princeton University Press.

Snowden, Philip. 1930. *The Menace of Protection: Speech Delivered at Free Trade Hall, Manchester, October 20, 1930*. London: The Labour Party.

———. 1934. *An Autobiography: Volume Two 1919–1934*. London: Ivor Nicholson and Watson Limited.

Streit, Clarence K. 1930. "Britain May Abandon Tariff Truce Pact, Geneva Is Warned." *The New York Times*, September 14. ProQuest Historical Newspapers.

The Times (London). 1930. "Empire Trade. The Bankers' Statement. Effect on Party Policy." *The Times*, July 5. Digital Archive.

———. 1930. "Work for the Conference." *The Times*, July 14. Digital Archive.

———. 1930. "Dominions and Preference. Lords Vote Against Government." *The Times*, December 3. Digital Archive.

The Times of India. 1930. "Commonwealth Trade: Empire Unity T.U.C. Committee's Suggestions." June 28. ProQuest Historical Newspapers.

Thorpe, Andrew. 1991. *The British General Election of 1931*. New York: Oxford University Press. https://doi.org/10.1093/acprof:oso/9780198202189.001.0001.

Trentmann, Frank. 2007. *Free Trade Nation: Commerce, Consumption, and Civil Society in Modern Britain*. New York: Oxford University Press.

Williamson, Philip. 1992. *National Crisis and National Government: British Politics, the Economy and Empire, 1926–1932*. New York: Cambridge University Press.

Wrench, David J. 1984. "'Cashing in': The Parties and the National Government, August 1931-September 1932." *Journal of British Studies* 23 (2): 135–53.
———. 2000. "'Very Peculiar Circumstances': Walter Runciman and the National Government, 1931–3." *Twentieth Century British History*, 11 (1): 61–82 https://doi.org/10.1093/tcbh/11.1.61.
Young, Ralph A. 1928. "Great Britain's Recent Trend toward Protection." *The Annals of the American Academy of Political and Social Science* 135: 189–250.

Government Documents

The National Archives of the United Kingdom (TNA), Kew, United Kingdom.
Records of the Cabinet Office
CAB 23, War Cabinet and Cabinet: Minutes.
CAB 24, War Cabinet and Cabinet: Memoranda (GT, CP and G War Series).
Records of the Public Record Office
PRO 30/69, James Ramsey MacDonald Papers.
UK Parliamentary Papers, ProQuest.
House of Commons Debates, 5th series.
House of Lords Debates, 5th series.

CHAPTER 13

The Formation of Research Institutes on Business Cycles in Europe in the Interwar Period: The "Kiel School" and (In)Voluntary Internationalization

Harald Hagemann

1 Introduction

Theoretical and empirical research on business cycles became the dominant theme in economics in the interwar period. The foundation of the Harvard Committee on Economic Research in 1917 and the National Bureau of Economic Research NBER in 1920 in the United States stimulated the foundation of similar research institutions in many European countries, often co-financed by the Rockefeller Foundation. The Harvard Committee under its director Charles J. Bullock (1869–1941) soon hired Warren M. Persons (1878–1937) as its leading statistician who in 1919 was also appointed Professor of Economics at Harvard University and the

H. Hagemann (✉)
University of Hohenheim, Stuttgart, Germany
e-mail: Harald.Hagemann@uni-hohenheim.de

© The Author(s) 2021

A. M. Cunha and C. E. Suprinyak (eds.), *Political Economy and International Order in Interwar Europe*, Palgrave Studies in the History of Economic Thought,
https://doi.org/10.1007/978-3-030-47102-6_13

first editor of the committee's journal, *The Review of Economic Statistics*. Persons was instrumental in the creation of the famous Harvard Index of General Business Conditions, a three-curve barometer designed to forecast future outcomes by generalizing past experiences and as an indicator of turning points in the business cycle. Persons's pioneering methods to eliminate seasonal and trend influences from time series data temporarily gave academic respectability to business cycle barometers in the 1920s during which the Harvard barometer disseminated quickly internationally.[1]

Wesley C. Mitchell (1874–1948), who became the founding director of the NBER from 1920 to 1945, was already considered as the preeminent economist in business cycle research in the USA at the time of his appointment. Whereas in his earlier *Business Cycles* Mitchell (1913) had surveyed existing theories of economic fluctuations as well as the state of empirical knowledge about business cycles, and in contrast to later unfair attacks as "measurement without theory" acknowledged that theories determined which empirical facts should be examined more closely, in his subsequent *Business Cycles: The Problem and Its Setting* Mitchell (1927, 2) emphasized: "We must find out more about the facts before we can choose among the old explanations or improve upon them." Although he pointed out that statistical data are of little use without illumination by theory, his priority to extensive description and measurement of real cycles, together with the empirical work at the NBER in his period to trace the timing of movements and of the amplitude of hundreds of variables within a cycle, across cycles and countries, without fully returning to address the question of causation, evoked some critique by more theoretically-minded economists.

From the mid-1920s onwards more systematic empirical research on business cycles became a major issue also in the German language area[2] where new institutes were founded in Berlin and Vienna in 1925 and 1927, respectively. The *Deutsches Institut für Konjunkturforschung*, today's DIW,[3] benefitted from the strong institutional cooperation with

[1] For greater details on the importance of Persons's methods to decompose economic time series for the development of applied econometrics and on the rapid international dissemination of the Harvard Index see Morgan (1990) and Lenel (2018).

[2] For an informative study on the beginnings of systematic empirical research on business cycles in Germany in the critical phase between 1925 and 1933 see Kulla (1996).

[3] On the history of the Berlin Institute see Krengel (1986).

the *Statistisches Reichsamt*. Ernst Wagemann (1884–1956), the director in the first two decades was also the president of the Statistical Office of the Weimar Republic until he was dismissed from that position by the new Nazi-led government in March 1933. Ludwig von Mises was instrumental in the foundation of the *Österreichisches Institut für Konjunkturforschung*, today's WIFO. Friedrich August Hayek (1899–1992) became the first director, succeeded in 1931, after his move to the London School of Economics, by Oskar Morgenstern (1902–1977) who stayed in that position until March 1938 when the Vienna Institute lost its independence after the "Anschluss" and became a branch office of the German Institute in Berlin.

In their empirical work both institutes were heavily influenced by the new methods of business cycle research, as they had been developed by Mitchell and the NBER and particularly by the Harvard University Committee on Economic Research. This was also noticed in the USA as, for example indicated by the two well-informed reports on the Austrian and German Institutes written by Carl Theodore Schmidt (1931a, b). The author gave particular attention to the extended elaboration of a series of "barometers" by Wagemann and his team, which took care of structural differences between the German and the US economies in their approach to the problem of economic forecasting.[4] This system of indices consisted of eight sectoral barometers covering production, employment, storage, foreign trade, business transactions, credit, comparative prices in security, money and commodity markets, and commodity prices.

Earlier on the Harvard index had also a stronger influence on the London and Cambridge Economic Service LCES which since its foundation in 1932 had a stronger cooperation with the Harvard Economic Service from which it also received substantial financial support until 1935.[5]

In 1928 the *Verein für Sozialpolitik*, the Society for German-speaking economists, focused on the explanation of business cycles as the core topic for its annual meeting in Zurich. In his contribution on 'Tasks and

[4] The business-cycle barometer constructed by Arthur Spiethoff (1873–1957) in the mid-1920s, on the other hand, almost exclusively concentrated on the consumption of pig iron. Most leading international researchers contributed to the Festschrift for Spiethoff on *The State and the Near Future of Business Cycle Research* (Clausing 1933).

[5] For a detailed analysis of the history and contributions of the LCES, in whose activities leading economists on both sides were involved, see Cord (2017).

limits of the institutes for research on business cycles' the young Morgenstern (1928a) distinguished two types of institutes, namely those with pronounced research intentions and those providing regular information services and forecasts for the subscribers of their publications. Whereas he classified the Kiel Institute of World Economics like the NBER in the former category, Morgenstern counted the institutes in Berlin and Vienna like the Harvard Economic Service to the latter. However, the separation between the two types was not an absolute one. This is demonstrated by the fact that Hayek as the first director of the Vienna institute exactly in those years made significant contributions to the (Austrian) theory of business cycles. In his keynote address to the 50th anniversary of the Austrian Institute Hayek (1977) confessed explicitly that business cycle *theory* always had interested him far more than regular reporting on the state of the economy and forecasting but that the latter was necessary to raise the money from business. Hayek had already the opportunity to study the new methods at Harvard and the NBER during his fourteen months stay in the USA in 1923–1924. However, in *Monetary Theory and the Trade Cycle* Hayek ([1929] 1933, 27–28) entirely agreed with Löwe's view that "empirical studies…cannot, in themselves, provide new insights into the causes or necessity of the Trade Cycle…and that to expect an immediate furtherance of *theory* from an increase in *empirical* insight is to misunderstand the logical relationship between theory and empirical research."

Something similar can be said of the Berlin institute. Wagemann's statistical approach is characterized by historical description and the construction of a series of indices, carefully avoiding (in contrast to Spiethoff) any simple general index of business conditions and a commitment to a clear formula of forecasting. No wonder that he is not even mentioned in Haberler's great survey *Prosperity and Depression* (1937) which puts emphasis on the *theoretical* analysis of cyclical movements. But despite Wagemann's aversion against theory it should not be overlooked that important theoretical contributions were made by members of the Berlin institute as, e.g. Arthur Hanau's famous study on the cyclical fluctuations of supply and prices of pigs whose causes were explained in the form of the cobweb theorem (Hanau 1927), and thus contributed to the surmounting of the static by a more dynamic analysis of the cycle.

The Berlin "institute was perhaps the most important single influence in spreading knowledge of modern statistical methods (as then understood). Its methodological work is therefore of historical importance" (Schumpeter 1954, 1155). Wagemann, no doubt, was a capable organizer of economic research as was Bernhard Harms (1876–1939), "one of the most efficient organizers of research who ever lived" (ibid.), who had founded the Institute of World Economics at the University of Kiel in February 1914.[6] Until the mid-1920s the institute had collected masses of statistical material on international trade and sea traffic and was engaged in building up an impressive library but did not enter into deeper theoretical analysis. This changed completely when in April 1926 Harms hired Adolf Löwe (1893–1995, since September 1939 Adolph Lowe) to build up a new department for research in statistical economics and trade cycles (*Abteilung für Statistische Weltwirtschaftskunde und Internationale Konjunkturforschung* ASTWIK) which soon acquired international reputation.

Although Löwe had closely cooperated with Wagemann since he had been appointed head of the international department in the Statistical Office in 1924, and in particular in the foundation process of the Berlin Institute,[7] the research work at Kiel was remarkably different from the work in Berlin. It transcended beyond statistical economics and trade cycle analysis, addressing also long-run growth, structural change and employment consequences of technological change, and had a much stronger theoretical flavour. Like Morgenstern (1928b) Löwe was skeptical about economic forecasting. These differences contributed to an increasing alienation between Löwe and Wagemann who had established a new department on the statistics of business cycles at the Statistisches Reichsamt in 1924 which gave enormous support to the empirical work at the Berlin institute. Nevertheless Wagemann, who admired Mitchell's synthesis of theoretical, statistical and historical work on business cycles,[8] defended himself against the reduction of the efforts of the institutes to pure empirical-statistical work. Löwe, on the other hand, recognized that the Berlin institute with its much greater man power had comparative advantages on the empirical side and concentrated his own efforts more on the theoretical side, as best reflected in his methodologically oriented Kiel habilitation thesis with the Kantian-inspired question "How is business-cycle theory possible at all?" (Löwe 1926), in which he

[6] The original name was *Institut für Seeverkehr und Weltwirtschaft*.

[7] See also Lowe's reflections on business cycles research in Weimar Germany (Löwe 1989).

[8] Mitchell wrote a Preface to the English translation of Wagemann's *Konjunkturlehre* (1928).

placed the problem of (in)compatibility of the analysis of cyclical fluctuations within the dominant equilibrium approach in economics into the centre. He also criticized Wagemann when he pointed out: "To expect an immediate furtherance of theory from an increase in empirical insights is to misunderstand the logical relationship between theory and empirical research" (Löwe [1926, 166] 1997, 246). Löwe's criticism was shared by the Austrians Mises, Morgenstern and Hayek who "recognized that the use of statistics can never consist in a deepening of our theoretical insights" (Hayek [1929] 1933, 32). The controversy, which sometimes contained elements of a new *Methodenstreit* (dispute on method), reflected a still existing gap between theoretical and empirical work among many contemporary researchers on business cycles in the interwar period.

In the following I will focus on the Kiel group which spread out internationally after the Nazis' rise to power in 1933. An important role in the process was played by the Rockefeller Foundation giving financial support which became particularly important during the years of the Great Depression.

2 The Role of the Rockefeller Foundation

"The Kiel Institute constitutes one of the bright spots in German economics," John Van Sickle, the assistant director of the social science division of the Rockefeller Foundation RF wrote to the director Edmund Day in his European office in Paris on August 2, 1932.[9] A year before he had already noticed in his diary that Harms "had gathered around him some of the best young economists in Germany" (Craver 1986, 216). Tracy Kittredge, Van Sickle's successor considered the Kiel Institute even as "a Mecca for research workers interested in international economic problems".[10] Beardsley Ruml, who had been appointed director of the Laura Spelman Rockefeller Memorial in 1922, was already very much impressed with the facilities, particularly the library, when he first visited the Kiel Institute in 1925. In the same year the University of Kiel, at the initiative of Harms, awarded an honorary doctoral degree to John

[9] RF Archive Center RAC, Record Group 1.1, series 7175, box 20, folder 180.

[10] RAC, ibid., folder 186.

Maynard Keynes and Herbert Hoover, then Minister of Trade and later US President, on 10 June.

"[T]he work being done in Kiel was the kind of work done by the kind of economists, that directors of the [RF] foundation most wished to support and encourage," Earlene Craver (1986, 216) notes in her excellent survey of the activities of the RF in Europe in the interwar period. This holds in particular for the ASTWIK whose members had acquired a high national and international scientific reputation in the last years of the Weimar Republic. However, it was not before spring 1931 that the RF decided to support the scientific programme with an annual amount of $10,000 over a period of three years.[11] Before the Kiel Institute had only received library grants of $1600 for 1925 and $10,000 for 1926–1927 to buy foreign books and journals which was a great help for the building up of its impressive library. Until today the library is a great worldwide attractor for economists to spend research periods at the Kiel Institute. The long-time director Wilhelm Gülich (1926–1960), who had established the famous Kiel catalogue, himself had visited the USA with a RF fellowship, and in 1926 had been considered a serious candidate for directorship of the library of the League of Nations in Geneva which also was financially supported by the RF.

Although $10,000 in 1926 amounted to almost 10% of the overall budget of the Kiel Institute, it was only a small sum compared to the $1,245,000 which the LSE alone received between 1924 and 1928. In that period emphasis of the RF was on institutional grants to foster strong centres of interdisciplinary research, preferably applying modern methods of empirical research such as the NBER. Major beneficiaries in Europe were also three institutions in Geneva, Stockholm and Copenhagen (Craver 1986, 208). German and Austrian economists mainly benefitted from the fellowship programme of the RF as, for example Gottfried Haberler, Ludwig Mises and Oskar Morgenstern. During his stay in the US the latter also developed a closer personal friendship with Andreas Predöhl (1893–1974) who later became director of the Kiel Institute in the Nazi period from 1934 to 1945. Predöhl, whose main area was

[11] See Take (2018, 258) who has carefully documented the support of the Kiel Institute by the RF in the period 1925–1950.

location theory,[12] was one of the two from Kiel out of thirteen German fellows in economics until 1928.

As well explained by Craver (1986, 210ff.), after the outbreak of the Great Depression with the crash on Wall Street in October 1929 and under the new directorship of Edmund E. Day in the social sciences, the RF changed its funding policy in favour of institutes and projects aiming to find causes of cyclical fluctuations. "Economic stabilization became one of the three principal topics of interest of the social science division during Day's administration" (212). A major beneficiary *was* the *Institut scientifique de recherches économiques et sociales* IRES founded by Charles Rist (1874–1955) in Paris in October 1933 with a seven years grant of $350,000. From today's perspective the list of recipients documents an excellent knowledge and assessment of the quality of the research work being done at the various European institutes for research on business cycles. Besides the institutes in Paris, Vienna, Berlin, Kiel and the LSE also the one at the University of Oslo (Ragnar Frisch), the Dutch in Rotterdam (Peter Lieftinck and Jan Tinbergen), the Belgian in Louvain (Léon Dupriez), the Swedish in Stockholm (Bertil Ohlin) the Bulgarian in Sofia (Oskar Anderson), the Hungarian in Budapest (Stephan Varga), the Polish in Cracow (Adam Heydel) and the Roumanian in Bucharest (Dimitrie Gusti).[13] Anderson, Dupriez, Morgenstern, Ohlin, Rist and Tinbergen also attended the meetings of the Committee of Experts in Geneva from 29 June to 2 July 1936 to discuss Part II "Synthetic exposition relating to the nature and causes of business cycles" of Haberler's investigation *Prosperity and Depression,* carried out on behalf of the League of Nations and financed by a grant from the RF.[14] The RF was also a key driving force and sponsor of the network of international cooperation between the national institutes which developed in the 1930s but collapsed with the outbreak of WWII. In Germany other recipients were also Arthur Spiethoff in Bonn and the Institute for Social and State Sciences at the University of Heidelberg with the two directors Alfred Weber (the younger brother of Max) and Emil Lederer, who moved to Berlin in 1931, and after his emigration in 1933 became the first Dean of

[12] See, for example, Predöhl (1928) as a main publication from this period.

[13] The Russian Konjuncture institute in Moscow which had been founded in 1920 was already closed down in 1928 and its director Nikolay Kondratieff was sent to Siberia where he was murdered in 1938 at the order of Stalin.

[14] See Boianovsky and Trautwein (2006, 62–76) for further details.

the "University in Exile" at the New School for Social Research in New York. The Kiel Institute, however, was favoured by the RF since due to the broad team composition and high quality of its research staff it was least likely to succumb to the tendency of German institutes that with the death, retirement or moving away of the director the Institute vegetates or disappears, as Kittredge reflected in his report.[15]

3 The Kiel Institute of World Economics: Excellence for Seven Years

The years of high theory started at the Kiel Institute in April 1926 and lasted exactly for only seven years. Within a short period of time Löwe was able to hire a top-calibre crew of young and innovative researchers who developed a great team spirit and soon won (inter)national reputation. The group of highly qualified researchers included Gerhard Colm (1897–1968), an expert on public finance,[16] who in April 1927 was recruited by Lowe from the Statistical Office in Berlin where he had developed an internationally comparative financial statistics which was important for the reparation problem. Colm was a pioneer in national income and wealth accounting. After Löwe was appointed Full Professor at the University, Colm succeeded him in March 1930 as head of the business cycle research department with Neisser as his deputy. Hans Neisser (1895–1975) also came in 1927 from Berlin, where he had worked as a researcher in the Enquête Aussschuss (State Committee of Industrial Investigations), to Kiel. He established himself as a leading monetary theorist with his habilitation thesis *The Purchasing Power of Money* but also contributed to general equilibrium theory, the machinery problem and other theoretically difficult and practically relevant topics. Neisser was highly appreciated by Keynes and Hayek alike and described by Schumpeter (2000, 247) "as a brilliant scientist". Löwe, Colm and Neisser formed the core of the Astwik group that later came to be known as the "Kiel School".[17] The team included other excellent young economists

[15] See T.B. Kittredge, Social Sciences in Germany, August 9, 1932, RFA, R61.1, Series 717, box 20, folder 181. See also Craver (1986, 215) and Take (2017).

[16] See his Kiel habilitation thesis *Economic Theory of Government Expenditures* (Colm 1927).

[17] See Hagemann (1997).

such as Fritz Burchardt (1902–1958) or Alfred Kähler (1900–1981). The outstanding quality of the Kiel group is also indicated by the fact that two young émigrés from Russia, who later became world-famous economists joined the team for some years: Wassily Leontief (1905–1999) from April 1927 to April 1931, only interrupted by a twelve-months stay in China, and Jacob Marschak (1898–1977), "probably the most gifted scientific economist of the exact quantitative type now in Germany" (Schumpeter 2000, 247), from 1928 to 1930.

Löwe had already examined the existing body of theoretical and empirical work on business cycles in his survey "The present state of research on business cycles in Germany" (Löwe 1925) before he wrote his methodologically oriented Kiel habilitation thesis with the Kantian-inspired question "How is business-cycle theory possible at all?" (Löwe [1926] 1997), in which he raised the problem of incompatibility of business cycle theory within the dominant equilibrium approach in economics. Löwe clearly was inspired by the fundamental distinction between statics and dynamics in Schumpeter's theoretical system and Schumpeter's view that a Walrasian system of general economic equilibrium was inappropriate for the analysis of business cycles, when he made his claim for a new dynamic theory "in which the polarity of upswing and crisis arises analytically from the conditions of the system just as the undisturbed adjustment derives from the conditions of the static system. Those who wish to solve the business cycle problem must sacrifice the static system. Those who adhere to the static system must abandon the business cycle problem" (Löwe [1926] 1997, 267).

Löwe's influential role in the subsequent debate can best be seen by looking into Hayek's *Monetary Theory and the Trade Cycle* ([1929] 1933) which is characterized by the challenge arising from Löwe's attack which poses a major issue for Hayek. Whereas he agrees with Löwe's identification of cyclical fluctuations in equilibrium theory as the crucial problem of business cycle theory; however, Hayek seriously disagrees in the conclusion drawn. Hayek's writings on monetary theory and business cycle theory in the interwar period are firmly based on an equilibrium approach. He therefore also considered it essential to start the explanation of cyclical fluctuations from an assumption of an economy in equilibrium with full utilization of resources.

The contemporary theoretical debate in the German language area was dominated by the economists from Kiel and Vienna. This is also indicated by a second controversy which extends into modern times.

Whereas Hayek and Löwe agreed that business cycle theory must present an endogenous factor causing fluctuations, they differed in the decisive dynamic impulse identified. In contrast to Löwe, who in line with Wicksell and Schumpeter emphasized technical progress as the fundamental causal factor, Hayek, in agreement with Mises, considered cyclical fluctuations to be caused by monetary factors. He later had a life-long controversy with Hicks who, as Löwe, considered technological changes as more fundamental. Löwe's main intention in his contribution "On the Influence of Monetary Factors on the Business Cycle" to the 1928 Zurich meeting of the Verein für Sozialpolitik, which he had already presented earlier to the Austrian Economics Society (Nationalökonomische Gesellschaft) in Vienna, was to show that monetary factors are neither necessary nor sufficient for the explanation of business cycles. Löwe's analysis was supported by the parallel study on the evolution of monetary theory by his closest research collaborator Burchardt (1928), which was distributed to the participants of the Zurich meeting, where the issue of monetary versus non-monetary business cycle theories had been chosen as a special theme. Recognizing that monetary influences manifested themselves primarily through changes in the price level, Burchardt concluded that monetary factors alone could not explain cyclical fluctuations. Non-monetary factors, in particular technical progress, play a central role. Thus Burchardt pointed out that in Wicksell's theory the equilibrium of an economy is disturbed by technical progress which causes the natural rate to rise above the market rate of interest.

Hayek appreciated Burchardt's essay as "very valuable in its historical part" (Hayek 1929, 57), but he criticized Löwe and Burchardt for resting their essential point "exclusively on the idea that only general price changes can be recognized as monetary effects" (Hayek [1929] 1933, 123). Therefore, in his *Monetary Theory and the Trade Cycle*, which is an expanded version of his own contribution to the Zurich meeting, he emphasizes that monetary theory has by no means accomplished its task when it has explained the absolute level of prices. Hayek argues against simplified monetary theories of the business cycle which focus exclusively on the relation between changes in the quantity of money and changes in the general level of prices. A far more important task is to explain changes in the structure of relative prices caused by monetary injections and the consequential disproportionalities in the structure of production which arise because the price system communicates false information about consumer preferences and resource availabilities. Misallocation of resources due to credit expansion could even occur despite price level stability.

While in *Monetary Theory and the Trade Cycle* Hayek's focus is on the monetary factors causing the cycle, in his subsequent *Prices and Production* based on his LSE lectures (Hayek 1931), emphasis is on the real structure of production. Here we come to a third important point of agreement and disagreement between Hayek and the members of the Kiel School.[18] Both identified changes in the structure of production as a key characteristic of cyclical fluctuations which has to be addressed by business cycle theory. In the famous triangles of *Prices and Production* Hayek applies Böhm-Bawerk's Austrian representation of the structure of production in which a sequence of original inputs of labour is transformed into a single output of consumption goods. In this unidirectional way of representing the production process only intermediate capital goods but not fixed capital goods or circularity exist as in a sectoral input–output system of a Leontief-Sraffa type. Burchardt and Löwe, on the contrary, preferred a horizontal or sectoral approach as in Marx's schemes of reproduction. In two important essays Burchardt (1931–1932) provided the first synthesis of the schemes of the stationary circular flow in Böhm-Bawerk and Marx, i.e. of the vertical and the horizontal approach.[19]

With the beginning of the new academic year in October 1931 Burchardt moved with Löwe to Frankfurt where the Goethe University had developed into a leading reform university in the social sciences during the Weimar Republic. Fifteen months later he submitted his habilitation thesis on Quesnay's *Tableau Économique* as a foundation of business cycle theory. However, due to the Nazis' rise to power shortly afterwards the habilitation process remained unfinished. Whereas at Frankfurt Löwe succeeded the Austrian Carl Grünberg (1861–1940) who became a victim of the Gestapo, the Christian Albrechts University in Kiel offered Löwe's former chair to Hans Mayer (1879–1955) who had succeeded Friedrich von Wieser at the University of Vienna in 1923 on the chair formerly held by Carl Menger from 1879 to 1903. Mayer who also edited the Vienna-based *Zeitschrift für Nationalökonomie* had

[18] For a more detailed discussion see Hagemann (1994).

[19] For its significance for modern theories of structural change see the contributions in Baranzini and Scazzieri (1990).

substituted Löwe's professorship since the Winter semester 1931/32 and already accepted a full professorship beginning with the Summer semester in April 1933. However, after some Nazi raids in the Institute of World Economics he revoked on April 21 anticipating his dismissal and returned to Vienna (Take 2019, 73–74), where he behaved in a more opportunistic way after the "Anschluss" in March 1938 and remained in all his positions during the Nazi period.

4 (In)Voluntary Internationalization

On October 22, 1932, shortly after his move from Bonn to Harvard, Schumpeter wrote in a letter to Keynes: "Harms...has built up the finest economic institute in the world" (Schumpeter 2000, 224). Less than six months later, on 7 April 1933, the Nazi government launched the Restoration of Civil Service Act which enabled them to dismiss civil servants either for racial and/or political reasons. Within a short time, almost 3000 scholars were removed from their academic positions, about 85% for their "non-Aryan" descent and 15% as political enemies. Starting on April 1, the day of organized boycott against Jewish shops, five brutal raids took place in the Kiel Institute. At the end of the month six Astwik members, with Colm and Neisser on top, and four from a related department were kicked out of the Institute.[20] Over the summer the director Harms (neither Jewish nor a social democrat but for having promoted too many of them) was attacked, thrown out and replaced by a young Nazi economist Jens Jessen who came from Göttingen. When in summer 1933 the RF sent Alva and Gunnar Myrdal to Kiel for assessing the situation, they delivered a precise and well-informed Report[21] on the new situation. They pointed out that all talented economists were thrown out, that there remained only "a somewhat unimportant rump faculty," and considered Jessen as a fanatic Nazi who "is not a very prominent scholar".[22] It took until 1936 that the RF under its new president Raymond Fosdick finally stopped the (in) direct financial support of the Kiel institute.

[20] For greater details see Take (2017, 2019).

[21] Alva and Gunnar Myrdal, Report to Dr. John Van Sickle in Paris, 20 July 1933, Stockholm, RFA, RG 1.1, series 717S, box 20, folder 1933.

[22] Jessen was replaced as the director by Predöhl in the following year and executed in November 1944.

On the other hand, the RF was a most important source of financial support for the émigré scholars from the beginning. For example, they co-financed the salary of Hans Neisser over several years during his time as professor at the Wharton School of Finance of the University of Pennsylvania in Philadelphia.[23]

On April 19, only twelve days after the Restoration of Civil Service Act, Schumpeter wrote a letter from Harvard to Wesley C. Mitchell asking for support of outstanding Hebrew colleagues in Germany (Schumpeter 2000, 246–48). "The men listed may all of them be described as more than competent." The ranking list of Schumpeter contained Gustav Stolper (his friend from Vienna whose son Wolfgang had moved with him as a PhD student from Bonn to Harvard in September 1932), Jacob Marschak, Hans Neisser, the sociologist Karl Mannheim, Emil Lederer, Adolph Löwe, Gerhard Colm, Karl Pribram and Eugen Altschul, i.e. four economists who had spent some years at the Kiel Institute between 1926 and 1933. Leontief was appointed Assistant Professor at Harvard at the same time when Schumpeter arrived. He had moved from Kiel to the U.S. already in the preceding year and spent the time at the NBER in New York. Eugen Altschul, the director of the Frankfurt Society for Research on Business Cycles (Frankfurter Gesellschaft für Konjunkturforschung) from its foundation in June 1926 to April 1933, who had edited the German translation of Mitchell's *Business Cycles*, also got a position at the NBER from December 1933 to 1939. The important publication series which he had initiated at Frankfurt started with Oskar Anderson's (1929) critical evaluation of the Harvard methods to decompose statistical time series. Anderson, an excellent statistician maintained closer contacts with the Vienna Institute in the 1930s, as, for example indicated by Morgenstern's lecture "Organisation, achievements and further tasks of business cycle research" delivered in Sofia on 2 April 1935 (Morgenstern 1935). Due to Predöhl's initiative Oskar Anderson (1887–1960) came to Kiel in May 1942 as the director of a new department on Eastern research at the Institute of World Economics (Take 2019). In 1947 Anderson was appointed Professor at the University of Munich.

Jacob Marschak was thrown out of his position in Heidelberg in April 1933. Immediately afterwards he suggested to the RF that the dismissed scholars from Kiel and Heidelberg should form a kind of "University in

[23] On Neisser see also Trautwein (2017).

Exile" in Geneva with the redirected funds which the RF had donated to the German institutes (Take 2017, 284–86). After his proposal was rejected Marschak emigrated to Great Britain where he became Chichele Lecturer in economics at All Souls in Oxford in fall 1933. In 1935 Marschak was appointed Reader in Statistics and the founding Director of the Oxford Institute of Statistics OIS which received substantial financial support from the RF. In September 1936 the OIS hosted the famous conference of the Econometric Society at which John Hicks presented his "Mr. Keynes and the 'Classics'" formalizing Keynes' *General Theory*, which marked the beginning of the IS-LM model and the birth of the neoclassical synthesis. During the few years of Marschak's directorship the OIS established itself as a leading international centre for empirical research in economics, advancing modern statistical and econometric techniques.

During the Nazi period the OIS hosted many refuge scholars from Central Europe. Among them was (since his emigration to England in 1935 Frank) Burchardt who built up the Institute's *Bulletin*. In 1944 he edited the famous *The Economics of Full Employment*, a collection of six studies in applied economics (Burchardt 1944). With Burchardt, Michal Kalecki, E. F. Schumacher, Thomas Balogh and Kurt Mandelbaum five of the six authors were émigrés. In 1949 Burchardt became director of the OIS.

Due to their high academic qualification and their open-mindedness the former Astwik members were much better connected with the international community than most other contemporary German economists and social scientists. Particularly former RF fellows or RF-funded researchers had easier access to financial support from the Deposed Scholars Program. Marschak is an outstanding case. In December 1938 he embarked for the USA with a one-year fellowship from the RF. After the outbreak of WWII he remained in America, succeeding Gerhard Colm on his chair at the New School after the latter's joining the Roosevelt administration.[24] Colm like Alfred Kähler, who, while at Kiel, had written an important study *The theory of the displacement of workers by machinery* (Kähler 1933) in which he analyzes the problem of technological unemployment on the basis of an early static input–output model, had been a

[24] On the 'University in Exile'see most recently Friedlander (2019). For greater details on the emigration of German-speaking economists to Britain and the USA see Hagemann (2007, 2011).

member of the "Mayflower" generation of professors of the "University in Exile" in 1933.[25] In January 1943 Marschak was appointed Professor of Economics at the University of Chicago and Director of the Cowles Commission for Research in Economics. Under Marschak's directorship (1943–1948) the Cowles Commission soon became the world centre of the econometric revolution in economics.

At the New School Marschak had met again his lifelong friend Adolph Lowe who came over from Manchester to New York in summer 1940. Lowe and Marschak were highly appreciated by the RF as "A-1, both scientifically and from the point of view of character",[26] and regularly consulted by the Academic Assistance Council/Society for the Protection of Science and Learning to assess the qualification of persecuted social scientists who were looking for help.[27] The most prominent PhD student of Marschak and Lowe was Franco Modigliani (1918–2003),[28] himself an émigré economist from fascist Italy who had arrived in New York four days before the outbreak of WWII, and later received the Bank of Sweden Prize in Economic Sciences in Memory of Alfred Nobel in 1985 for his work in macroeconomic theory. On the Modigliani homepage of the Nobel Prize Committee we read:

> I had the great luck of being awarded a free tuition fellowship by the Graduate Faculty of Political and Social Science of the New School for Social Research...as I was discovering my passion for economics, thanks also to excellent teachers, including Adolph Lowe and above all Jacob Marschak to whom I owe a debt of gratitude beyond words. (Modigliani Homepage Nobel Prize Committee 1985, 1–2)

As a lecturer in econometrics and research associate of the Institute of World Affairs at the New School Modigliani cooperated closely with Neisser (who had come from Philadelphia to New York in 1943) in the

[25] On Colm see also Milberg (2017).

[26] John van Sickle, Paris, to the headquarter in New York, 10 May 1933; RAC, RG1.1, 200/109/539.

[27] The AAC was founded in May 1933 (renamed into SPSL in 1936) at the initiative of William Beveridge to help "University teachers and investigators of whatever country who, on grounds of religion, political opinion or race, are unable to carry their work in their own country".

[28] See Hagemann (2017).

years 1944–1948 which amounted in their joint publication *National Incomes and International Trade: A Quantitative Analysis* (Neisser and Modigliani 1953). The book contained the most comprehensive econometric investigation of its era, elaborating and extending earlier work on foreign trade, business cycles and structural change in the global economy. Neisser had already started similar work in Kiel and continued in Philadelphia (Trautwein 2017, 942–45). The *Institute of World Affairs* which officially was opened in November 1943 with enormous financial support from Doris Duke but was already engaged in major research projects since America's entering the war in 1941, many of them financed by RF, was the research arm of the New School (Friedlander 2019, 149–51). At its creation the role model was the Kiel Institute of World Economics, an impression strengthened by the fact that Lowe was appointed its Director of Research who played a similar role as in Kiel 1926–1930.

Some of the scholars dismissed in Kiel temporarily or permanently remained in Europe. Rudolf Freund (1901–1955) who worked at the Kiel Institute from 1926–1929 and from 1931–1933 as the expert for international trade and cyclical fluctuations in the agricultural sector stayed as researcher at the Stockholm School of Economics until 1939 when he was appointed professor at the University of Virginia. He was strongly supported by Gunnar Myrdal as was the sociologist Svend Riemer (1905–1977) who moved further to the U.S. in 1938 where he ended up as professor at UCLA. The employment of Freund and Riemer was financed by the RF and the Swedish Academic Assistance Council. Konrad Zweig (1904–1980) who had worked in the Astwik as a specialist for the statistics of international capital movements was among the many émigré scholars who could not pursue an academic career, despite high appreciation by Hayek, Löwe and Colm alike. He earned his living by working for Lyons, a food manufacturer in London. On the other side, the high quality of the work at Kiel is illuminated also by the career of Hal C. (Hermann Christian) Hillmann (1910–1990), who was the student assistant of Colm and chairman of the socialdemocratic student group at the University of Kiel. After several months in a concentration camp he could escape to Britain in January 1934. During the war he worked as a research officer and expert on the German war economy in the Royal Institute of International Affairs at Balliol College in Oxford.[29]

[29] For greater details on Freund, Hillmann, Zweig, Herberts et al. see the contributions in Hagemann and Krohn (1999).

An interesting case is John H. (Jean) Herberts who was born in Bremen in 1905 and whose traces got lost in Paris at the beginning of WWII. He was dismissed in Kiel in August 1933 for his "non-Aryan" descent. In the same month he emigrated to France where he got a position at the IRES in Paris in the following May. Interestingly, Herberts who, for example represented the Institute at the fifth international conference of the research institutes on business cycles, which was organized by Oskar Morgenstern in Vienna in July 1936,[30] was able to publish an informative article on the Paris institute in the *Weltwirtschaftliches Archiv* (45, 1937), the journal of the Kiel Institute which had thrown him out four years before. In those years enormous efforts were made to establish a permanent secretariat for the international network of the business cycles research institutes. The chairman Rist and the majority favoured Geneva as the location, which made sense because of the League of Nations, ILO and a lot of statistical material available there, and Morgenstern as the half-time Secretary. Both proposals were heavily opposed by Dupriez who considered Geneva as a place too much dominated by Protestants and was against Morgenstern due to his double role and burden as the president of the Vienna institute. In May 1937 Dupriez also visited the Institute of World Economics in Kiel and the Berlin Institute directed by Wagemann, who two years earlier had opposed Van Sickle's proposal to appoint Loveday as the coordinator of the conference of the business cycles research institutes. In his report to the RF of 9 July Dupriez, like so many before and after him, praised the excellent library of the Kiel Institute but understandably was critical of the overall intellectual climate in Germany. No doubt, in the years 1933–1938 the Vienna Institute under Morgenstern's direction had the pole position in the German language area. Nevertheless it was shortly before the Anschluss in March 1938 that the coordinating secretariat was located at the Rist institute in Paris and Robert Marjolin, himself a former RF fellow, was appointed Secretary. Shortly afterwards the political events caused an end to the promising international cooperation of the leading research institutes on business cycles.

[30] Among other participants were Alvin Hansen, Haberler, Tinbergen, Ohlin, Anderson, Mises, Schwartz (LCES), Dupriez, Pedersen (Copenhagen), Lipinski, Varga, Kittredge (RF) and also some Japanese.

The spirit of international cooperation among the participating economists, however, was not dead. A characteristic example is Marschak's article "Peace Economics," written within the New School's Peace Studies Project in summer 1940 when Nazism after the defeat of France was at its peak. Here the author attributes the rise of National Socialism in Germany, and the success of radical political parties in other countries, to the failure of the existing democracies to solve the mass unemployment problem. "No peace will be a lasting one with the economic problem unsolved" (Marschak 1940, 283). Marschak points out three postulates for peace economics, namely that there should be no idle resources, resources should be allocated in an optimal way and developed in the best possible proportions. "The first postulate is [...] equivalent to a requirement that booms and depressions be mitigated" (286). The first postulate is the most important one where "the necessity to remove depression, comes in: idle resources must be put to work" (287). Time and again the author emphasizes that depression "has produced more unrest, and has been responsible for more dangers to the peace of the world than any difficulties in reconstructing equipment damaged by war or any delay in the development of new resources" (289).

Against superprotectionism, *sauve qui peut* or "beggar my neighbor" policies which would cause retaliation and thereby a downward spiral, Marschak favours policies that will safeguard internal equilibrium and external equilibrium simultaneously which "is the real problem of economic policy in a world where idle resources are possible" (292). Unilateral policies of austerity or devaluation are doomed to fail. However, internationally coordinated public works programmes between the major countries eliminating fears of balance of payments problems are a precondition for a successful antidepression policy and thereby a major contribution to peace. Such a "*pari passu* policy against booms and depressions" should also include "a joint development of the so-called backward countries" (291). Marschak's position as a genuine internationalist is also reflected in his final plea for a setting up of institutions as instruments for a peaceful economic order such as the International Equalization Fund, an International Public Works Board or a Bank for International Credit, preshadowing the creation of institutions for international economic cooperation at Bretton Woods four years later.

References

Anderson, Oskar. 1929. *Zur Problematik der empirisch-statistischen Konjunkturforschung*. Bonn: Verlag Kurt Schroeder.

Baranzini, Mauro, and Roberto Scazzieri, eds. 1990. *The Economic Theory of Structure and Change*. Cambridge: Cambridge University Press.

Boianovsky, Mauro, and Hans-Michael Trautwein. 2006. "Haberler, the League of Nations, and the Quest for Consensus in Business Cycle Theory in the 1930s." *History of Political Economy* 38 (1): 45–89.

Burchardt, Fritz A. 1928. "Entwicklungsgeschichte der monetären Konjunkturtheorie." *Weltwirtschaftliches Archiv* 28: 78–143.

———. 1931–32. "Die Schemata des stationären Kreislaufs bei Böhm-Bawerk und Marx." *Weltwirtschaftliches Archiv* 34: 525–564 and 35: 116–176.

———, ed. 1944. *The Economics of Full Employment*. Oxford: Basil Blackwell.

Clausing, Gustav, ed. 1933. *Der Stand und die nächste Zukunft der Konjunkturforschung. Festschrift für Arthur Spiethoff*. Munich: Duncker & Humblot.

Colm, Gerhard. 1927. *Volkswirtschaftliche Theorie der Staatsausgaben*. Tübingen: Mohr.

Cord, Robert A. 2017. "The London and Cambridge Economic Service: history and contributions." *Cambridge Journal of Economics* 41: 307–26.

Craver, Earlene. 1986. "Patronage and the Directions of Research in Economics: The Rockefeller Foundation in Europe, 1924–1938." *Minerva* 24: 205–22.

Friedlander, Judith. 2019. *A Light in Dark Times: The New School for Social Research and Its University in Exile*. New York: Columbia University Press.

Haberler, Gottfried. 1937. *Prosperity and Depression: A Theoretical Analysis of Cyclical Movements*. Geneva: League of Nations.

Hagemann, Harald. 1994. "Hayek and the Kiel School: Some Reflections on the German Debate on Business Cycles in the Late 1920s and Early 1930s." In *Money and Business Cycles: The Economics of F. A. Hayek*, Vol. 1, edited by Marina Colonna and Harald Hagemann, 101–20. Aldershot: Edward Elgar.

———. 1997. "Zerstörung eines innovativen Forschungszentrums und Emigrationsgewinn. Zur Rolle der 'Kieler Schule' 1926–1933 und ihrer Wirkung im Exil." In *Zur deutschsprachigen wirtschaftswissenschaftlichen Emigration nach 1933*, edited by Harald Hagemann, 293–341. Marburg: Metropolis.

———. 2007. "German-Speaking Economists in British Exile." *Banca Nazionale del Lavoro Quarterly Review* LX (242): 323–63.

———. 2011. "European Émigrés and the 'Americanization' of Economics." The European Journal of the History of Economic Thought 18 (5): 643–71.

———. 2017. "Franco Modigliani as 'American' Keynesian: How the University in Exile Economists Influenced Economics." *Social Research* 84 (4): 955–85.

Hagemann, Harald, and Claus-Dieter Krohn, eds. 1999. *Biographisches Handbuch der deutschsprachigen wirtschaftswissenschaftlichen Emigration nach 1933*. Munich: K.G. Saur.

Hanau, Arthur. 1927. *Die Prognose der Schweinepreise*. Berlin: Duncker & Humblot.

Hayek, Friedrich A. [1929] 1933. *Monetary Theory and the Trade Cycle*. London: J. Cape.

———. [1931] 1935. *Prices and Production*. London: Routledge & Kegan Paul.

———. 1977. "Zur Gründung des Instituts." In *Österreichisches Institut für Wirtschaftsforschung*, 50 Jahre, 13–19. Vienna: WIFO.

Kähler, Alfred. 1933. *Die Theorie der Arbeiterfreisetzung durch die Maschine. Eine gesamtwirtschaftliche Abhandlung des modernen Technisierungsprozesses*. Greifwald: Julius Abel.

Krengel, Rolf. 1986. *Das deutsche Institut für Wirtschaftsforschung (Institut für Konjunkturforschung), 1925–1979*. Berlin: Duncker & Humblot.

Kulla, Bernd. 1996. *Die Anfänge der empirischen Konjunkturforschung in Deutschland 1925–1933*. Berlin: Duncker & Humblot.

Lenel, Laetitia. 2018. "Futurama. Business Forecasting and the Dynamics of Capitalism in the Interwar Period." Working Paper No. 3 of the DFG Priority Programme 1859 Experience and Expectations, Historical Foundations of Economic Behaviour. Berlin: Humboldt University.

Löwe, Adolph. 1925. "Der gegenwärtige Stand der Konjunkturforschung in Deutschland" In Die Wirtschaftswissenschaft nach dem Kriege. Festschrift für Lujo Brentano zum 80. Geburtstag, edited by Julius Bonn and Melchior Palyi, Vol. 2, 329–77. Munich and Leipzig: Duncker & Humblot.

———. 1926. "Wie ist Konjunkturtheorie überhaupt möglich?" Weltwirtschaftliches Archiv 24: 165–97; English translation as "How Is Business-Cycle Theory Possible at All?" *Structural Change and Economic Dynamics* 8: 245–76, 1997.

———. 1928. "Über den Einfluß monetärer Faktoren auf den Konjunkturzyklus." English translation "On the Influence of Monetary Factors on the Business Cycle." In *Business Cycle Theory. Selected Texts 1860–1939, Vol. III: Monetary Theories of the Business Cycle*, edited by Harald Hagemann, 199–211. London: Pickering & Chatto, 2002.

———. 1989. "Konjunkturtheorie in Deutschland in den Zwanziger Jahren." In *Studien zur Entwicklung der ökonomischen Theorie*, edited by Bertram Schefold, VIII, 75–86. Berlin: Duncker & Humblot.

Marschak, Jacob. 1940. "Peace Economics." *Social Research* 7 (3): 280–98.

Milberg, William. 2017. "Gerhard Colm and the Americanization of Weimar Economic Thought." *Social Research* 84 (4): 989–1019.

Mitchell, Wesley C. 1913. *Business Cycles*. Berkeley: University of California Press.

———. 1927. *Business Cycles: The Problem and Its Setting*. New York: NBER.

Morgan, Mary S. 1990. *The History of Econometric Ideas*. Cambridge: Cambridge University Press.

Morgenstern, Oskar. 1928a. "Aufgaben und Grenzen der Institute für Konjunkturforschung." In *Beiträge zur Wirtschaftstheorie. Part II: Konjunkturforschung und Konjunkturtheorie, Schriften des Vereins für Sozialpolitik*, Vol. 173/II, edited by Karl Diehl, 337–53. Munich and Leipzig: Duncker & Humblot.

———. 1928b. *Wirtschaftsprognose. Eine Untersuchung ihrer Voraussetzungen und Möglichkeiten*. Berlin and Heidelberg: Springer.

———. 1935. "Organisation, Leistungen und weitere Aufgaben der Konjunkturforschung." Publications of the Statistical Institute for Economic Research No. 1. Sofia: State University.

Neisser, Hans. 1928. *Der Tauschwert des Geldes*. Jena: Gustav Fischer.

Neisser, Hans, and Franco Modigliani. 1953. *National Incomes and International Trade: A Quantitative Analysis*. Urbana: University of Illinois Press.

Predöhl, Andreas. 1928. "The Theory of Location in Its Relation to General Economics." *Journal of Political Economy* 36: 371–390.

Schmidt, Carl T. 1931a. "The Austrian Institute for Business Cycle Research." *The Journal of Political Economy* 39 (1): 101–3.

———. 1931b. "The German Institute for Business Cycle Research." *The American Economic Review* 21 (1): 63–66.

Schumpeter, Joseph A. 1954. *History of Economic Analysis*. London: George Allen & Unwin.

Schumpeter, Joseph A. 2000. *Briefe/Letters, edited by Ulrich Hedtke and Richard Swedberg*. Tübingen: Mohr Siebeck.

Take, Gunnar. 2017. "American Support for German Economists after 1933: The Kiel Institute and the Kiel School in Exile." *Social Research* 84 (4): 809–30.

———. 2018. "One of the Bright Spots in German Economics." *Jahrbuch für Wirtschaftsgeschichte* 59 (1): 251–328.

———. 2019. *Forschen für den Wirtschaftskrieg. Das Kieler Institut für Weltwirtschaft im Nationalsozialismus*. Berlin and Boston: De Gruyter.

Trautwein, Hans-Michael. 2017. "Hans Neisser: The 'Guardian of Good Theory'." *Social Research* 84 (4): 929–54.

Wagemann, Ernst. 1928. Konjunkturlehre. Eine Grundlegung zur Lehre vom Rhythmus der Wirtschaft. Berlin; English translation as *Economic Rhythm*. New York: McGraw-Hill, 1930.

CHAPTER 14

Divided by an Uncommon Language? The Oxford Institute of Statistics and British Academia (1935–1944)

Roberto Lampa

1 Introduction

From October 1935 to 1944, due to the rise of Nazism, the Oxford Institute of Statistics (OIS) turned into a "sanctuary" for anti-nazi economists. Since its foundation, with J. Marschak as the director, émigré economists from central Europe—such as F. Burchardt, K. Mandelbaum, E.F. Schumacher, T. Balogh and M. Kalecki[1]—dominated the research staff of the OIS (Hagemann 2005, 2007, 2011).

[1] Actually, T. Balogh had moved to England in 1932, the anti-Jewish laws introduced in Hungary by the regime of Miklós Horthy essentially motivated his emigration.

R. Lampa (✉)
CONICET (National Scientific and Technical Research Council), Buenos Aires, Argentina

Universidad Nacional de San Martin, Buenos Aires, Argentina

© The Author(s) 2021

A. M. Cunha and C. E. Suprinyak (eds.), *Political Economy and International Order in Interwar Europe*, Palgrave Studies in the History of Economic Thought,
https://doi.org/10.1007/978-3-030-47102-6_14

Such emigration inescapably led to fertile discussions about the research agenda to be implemented, since the economists grouped in the OIS did not share the same background as the British colleagues. Rather than following the Marshallian tradition (which was hegemonic, in its different versions, both in Cambridge and in Oxford) the OIS staff assumed a different scheme of thought. In line with the continental tradition, they were influenced by Marx, Walras and the Austrians and also by the German "Kiel School," a research centre funded by the Rockefeller Foundation focused on empirical investigation and trade cycles. Accordingly, they promoted the use of statistics in social studies, assuming that business cycles and economic fluctuations were the most relevant research topics to be investigated, especially after 1929 breakdown.

In a short lapse of time, the non-aligned features of OIS's economic staff (when compared to the British tradition) became evident both from a methodological and a theoretical point of view. In a sense, one may legitimately state that between 1935 and 1944 the economists' circle was divided between a (mostly) Continental Oxford and a Marshallian—that eventually turned into "Keynesian"—Cambridge.

From this perspective, the Oxford Institute of Statistics certainly became an atypical research centre within the English academia.

Furthermore, such a different background influenced the political stances of several members of the OIS. Because of the shock represented by the rise of Nazism, economic cooperation and European integration became two prior issues. In particular, a reform of the international institutions in the post-war world was considered inescapable in order to moderate trade imbalances, fierce competition and antagonism between countries, which had led to the tragedies of Nazism and WWII in the OIS members' eyes.

Given this premise, the aim of the chapter is to re-read some of the works published by the OIS's leading economists (Marschak and Burchardt, who acted as directors) in the examined period, interpreting them as a challenge to the pre-existing paradigms, especially Cambridge's tradition. In this sense, we are going to put particular emphasis on the role of the economists and their economic and political ideas, also with regard to European integration and economic cooperation.

Accordingly, this chapter aims first to re-examine the early period of the OIS (1935–1939) from our specific angle, recovering Marschak's article on "Peace Economics" (Sect. 2). In light of this premise, in Sect. 3 we emphasize the crucial role played by F. Burchardt, as director of both the

Oxford Bulletin and the 1944 collective book on "The Economics of Full Employment." Finally, in Sect. 4, we draw some conclusions about the relationship between the OIS and the pre-existing Schools of economics in the United Kingdom, particularly Keynesian theory.

2 Beginnings: The Birth of OIS Under Marschak's Direction (1935–1939)

The birth of OIS is strictly connected to the strong financial support provided by the Rockefeller Foundation. However, such a support depended also on the German background of the economists grouped around the OIS.

In fact, since the mid-1920s, the Foundation had financed several European institutions, whose research was interdisciplinary and focused on the development of empirical methods of investigation. For instance, between 1924 and the early 1930s, London School of Economics became a major beneficiary due to its commitment for the "collection and examination of facts" (Craver 1986, 208). On the other hand, the faculty of economics of Cambridge received no funds at all, since it looked "satisfied with being an isolated university (...) little interested in social side but only in financial analysis" (*Ibidem*) to the foundation's officials eyes.

Along these lines, after 1929 breakdown, the Rockefeller Foundation showed an increasing interest in finding the ultimate causes of cyclical fluctuations, in order to foster a rapid recovery of capitalist economies. Accordingly, they shifted their attention to the German academia, particularly the Kiel *Institut für Weltwirtschaft*, whose specialism was the collection and study of empirical data in order to provide a thorough interpretation of the business cycle. From this perspective, the research done in Kiel was certainly "the kind of work, done by the kind of economists, that directors of the foundation most wished to support and encourage" in those days (Craver 1986, 216), as evidenced by the generous 106,000 USD donations, between 1931 and 1933.

Unfortunately, the rise of Nazism forced almost all the economists in Kiel to flee abroad, since they were mostly socialist and Jewish. Such event triggered the reaction of several outstanding economists who appealed the Rockefeller Foundation for help. The letters of Sir William Beveridge, Josef Schumpeter, Wesley Clair Mitchell, Alva and Gunnar Myrdal eventually convinced the Foundation's officials to interrupt their funding to the Kiel Institute. At the same time, the existing funding was redirected to the OIS in Oxford (Craver 1986), which subsequently became a sanctuary for émigrés economists.

It is important to stress, however, that the foundation's grant was not subject to conditionalities, since the only request was that the studies to be developed in Oxford should have been related to the problems of modern society (Young and Lee 1993). Accordingly, in October 1935, Marschak was free to organize the Institute with his German background in mind. For instance, already on September 26, 1936, the OIS hosted the meeting of the Econometric Society (Hagemann 2005). Rather than a convergence with the other lines of research pre-existing in Oxford, such academic freedom, together with the different background, inescapably determined an increasing detachment from the rest of the economic research groups, particularly about methodological assumptions and political implications of economic theorizing.

2.1 *Marschak's View About the Scope and Method of Economics and the Oxford Milieu*

On September, 1939 Marschak left the OIS. Soon after, he was appointed Professor of Economics at the New School in New York. A few months later, in a short article, he explained his methodological assumptions together with his broader beliefs about the scope and method of economics. Such a work becomes a crucial source in order to retrospectively interpret his differences with the Oxford milieu.

In Marschak's view, it is pointless to interpret induction and deduction as alternative methods in economics. Economists should simply assume that both induction and deduction are necessary and, therefore, statistics must complement economic analysis:

> Methodology may talk of induction and deduction; but it should itself work as an inductive science, should build on experience. For example: to state a priori that economics can never become quantitative is as invalid as the older statement a priori that men will never fly because flying is against man's nature. (Marschak 1941, 441)

A great part of the controversy between the economists may be labelled instead as "causal vs. stochastic". According to Marschak, two competing visions characterize economics: one strictly based on the existence of mechanical relationships and another focused around the concept of probability. However, a synthesis becomes possible once we assume that "*systematic relationships are, in any case, overlaid by random disturbances and can be observed only as statistical averages*" (Marschak 1941, 443). The solution is therefore represented by "modern" business cycle theories, like Tinbergen's, since they are able to explain observed regularities of more complex phenomena (e.g. prices, output) in terms of elementary relationships (446). In other words, only abandoning static equilibrium analysis economists can become genuine "social engineers" rather than false "prophets" (448).

If, vice versa, economics had stuck to the traditional equilibrium theories it would have rapidly turned into the "*pseudo-science of inevitable*" (Marschak 1940, 280), studied by "*not trade cycle minded*" men, who can conceive fluctuations, recessions or unemployment only as outliers.

From this perspective, Marschak certainly brought the continental tradition with him while directing the OIS (Cherrier 2010), using both economic theory and statistics to characterize regularities in the data (Mehrling 2010).

In light of this premise, it is possible to understand Marschak tortuous relationship with the Oxford milieu.

Besides the OIS *émigrés*, in those days several important economists (such as Meade, Phelps Brown and, above all, Roy Harrod) were grouped around the Oxford Economic Research Group (OERG).

In H.D. Henderson's intention, the OIS should have complemented and supported the OERG agenda providing statistical evidences, since this latter area should have investigated capital market in connection with trade fluctuations (Young and Lee 1993). However, the collaboration between the research groups was definitely scarce.

No work published by the OERG dealt with economic fluctuations during the period examined (Besomi 1998). In change, OERG was committed to the study of the role played by entrepreneurial expectations. Drawing on Keynes's *General Theory*, OERG researchers aimed at providing an empirical verification of the factors determining the trend of economic activity. Therefore, their main activity was recollecting interviews of businessmen, in order to try to test Keynes' hypothesis about the irrelevance of the variations of the rate of interest for the investment decisions.

Roy Harrod repeatedly manifested a genuine interest in business cycle theories. However, his methodological assumptions deeply diverged from

Marschak's, being a generalization of the Marshallian and Keynesian approach (Besomi 1998).

Marschak was aware of such discrepancies; however, he was optimistic about the possibility of deepening the intellectual exchange with Harrod:

> Harrod..., although not seriously engaged himself in empirical research (except as a member of the 'Economists Research Group' which interprets the 'behaviour of entre-preneurs') [holds] methodological views... such as to favour the type of work pursued hitherto by the Institute. (Marschak 1939, cited in Besomi 1998, 560)

Unfortunately, Marschak's optimism had already proved to be unjustified. During August and September 1938, Harrod discussed a first draft of his "Essay in Dynamic Theory" with Marschak.

As evidenced by Sember (2010), Harrod deliberately ignored Marschak's remarks on his draft because he was unable to fully understand them. In light of their conflicting approaches to business cycle theory, on the one hand, Marschak interpreted Harrod's work as a dynamic model, in which oscillations were around equilibrium. Such interpretation was in line with the continental tradition in business cycle theory, represented, in those days, by Frisch, Tinbergen and Kalecki. On the other hand, Harrod thought at dynamics in terms of different as well as consequential stages, since he was deeply influenced by the Keynesian theory rather than the continental debates. As a result, Harrod overlooked Marskak's remarks as if an uncommon language divided them.

From our perspective, such dialogue of the deaf denotes a broader lack of interplay between the OIS and the other research bodies in Oxford. On the other hand, the astonishing and non-concluding conclusion of the correspondence between Harrod and Marschak reinforces the idea that the OIS economists belonged to a continental tradition, relatively obscure within the British academia.

2.2 *Marschak's Political Stances: A Restricted Minimalist Integration for the Post-war World*

Marshak's emphasis on business cycle is well reflected also by his political stances, expressed in a 1940 article on "Peace Economics."

Broadly speaking, the paper puts in perspective (and goes beyond) Keynes well-known book on the economic consequences of peace. It also reflects Marschak's different political background, when compared to both Oxford's and Cambridge's intellectual milieu.

Marschak was a social democrat who had been the Minister of Labour of the short-lived Menshevik Republic of Terek. After the defeat of the Anti-Bolshevik movement in the Russian Civil War, he fled abroad; however, he still manifested a strong interest in politics, which brought him to study the rise of Fascism in Italy. In his analysis, dated 1923, the only reasonable way of avoiding similar aberrations was represented by dampening the international business cycle by means of active policies. Since Fascism was the result of economic uncertainty and unemployment resulting from the post WWI scenario, only improving human organization and international cooperation a similar catastrophe might have been prevented (Cherrier 2010).

Along these lines, Marschak 1940 article explicitly assumed that the rise of Nazism relied upon economic crisis and mass unemployment. In his view, German people exchanged freedom for economic security, considering that regimentation was the only viable solution to their severe economic problems.

Differently from Keynes, however, Marschak puts in perspective the role played by the Versailles treaty. If it is undeniable that such international agreement negatively affected German economy, it is also true that during the years of growth Germans did not manifest any sympathy for Hitler and the Nazis and seemed not to care at all about the "dishonour" of Versailles treaty:

> I inquired recently among my German colleagues (in exile, but capable, I think, of unbiased recollection). They all confirmed my own impressions of 1926-28: in those years of prosperity few Germans really worried about Versailles. The curve of the electoral successes of the National Socialists closely coincided with the fluctuations of unemployment. Of the items of Versailles, the reparations clause was the only one which prevailed in the public mindfar above all others: not disarmament, not the paragraphs concerning "honor," not even the change of frontiers, apart only from the regions on the country's periphery economically hurt by the painful dislocations of markets and the necessity of adjustment which the new frontiers involved in a protectionist Europe. (Marschak 1940, 282–83)

Rather than blaming Versailles, Marschak emphasizes the disastrous role played by U.S. and British economic policies on the German balance of payments between 1930 and 1932. It is exactly because of such policies that the German government had to implement a brutal fiscal adjustment, which eventually led to deflation and, therefore, the Nazi success:

> How differently would the economics of Brüning's Germany (1930-32) have developed if Germany could have embarked on a public works program without fearing for her balance of payments! That would have been the case if the United States or England had shown signs of a similar policy. Instead, the European balances of payment collapsed because of the withdrawal of American credits, and England devalued the pound. This induced Brüning's deflation (…). (Marschak 1940, 297)

In other words, yet in 1940 Marschak's biggest concern became how to mitigate the effects of international business cycle on the balance of payments, in order to guarantee economic prosperity and good level of employment to all the countries.

From this perspective, he was persuaded that the most effective antidote to Nazi regimentation was cooperation between nations, meant as a tool of avoiding *beggar thy neighbour* policies resulting from fierce economic competition.

Stated succinctly, peace depended on the right economic policies. In turn, in order to be "right", economic policies had to guarantee three results: the disappearance of idle resources; the optimal allocation of such resources and the development of the resources through time. However, in order to satisfy these conditions, several obstacles had to be removed.

In the first place, Marschak blamed protectionism, which he defined as the measure calculated to help one country at the expense of others. Protectionism was an outstanding example of *"sauve qui peut"* policy, which triggered trade wars and eventually affected also the country that originally implemented it.

In place of protectionism, Marschak proposes a mix of policies aimed at guaranteeing what he defines "collective security"; however, he emphasizes that such policies should not be implemented in the name of an alleged collective interest. Quite the contrary, they should be accepted for considerations of coldest "*sacro egoismo*" that is for utilitarian and selfish reasons.

Secondly, Marschak emphasizes that the German case shows that wage deflation is one of the most pernicious policies in political terms. This notwithstanding, a country may be forced to cut wage rates if the other countries do not implement similar policies for reasons of competitiveness. Therefore, the solution is represented by the concerted implementation of anti-cyclical policies: deflationary policies in times of boom and expansionary policies in times of slump.

Thirdly, Marschak points the finger at currency speculation, suggesting the creation of an international equalization fund which acts resolutely in order to prevent devaluations in response to unemployment. He stresses that this is not a plea for fixed exchange rates or a single currency regime, since in his mind national currencies should be revised by international agreements from time to time in order to correct external imbalances.

Finally, Marschak deals with the institutional framework necessary to guarantee a durable economic prosperity, which in his view necessarily implies a durable peace.

He seems to be sceptical about multilateralism and a comprehensive European integration. In particular, Marschak explicitly states not only that a world conference would be an unnecessary complication, but also that it would be better if the most important economies set the new rules of the game, implicitly imposing them to the rest of the countries. In a similar way, he suggests to create a limited number of international institutions since, in a strict sense, only an International Equalization Fund would be necessary for the tasks of peace and prosperity:

> For the international handling of booms, depressions and money, no comprehensive "world economic conferences" are really needed. If three or four economically leading countries make the necessary agreements and keep them, if, in addition, they set up institutions (such as the International Equalization Fund and, less important, an International Public Works Board or a Bank for International Credits), and if they give the other countries the right to join, half of the task is done, even if the other countries do not join. (Marschak 1940, 296–97)

Marschak's "minimalist proposal" is a further indication of his detachment from the British political and intellectual milieu.

3 1940–1945 Burchardt's Nouvelle Vague and the Bulletin

On August 1938, Marschak left the OIS to join the New School of Social Research in New York. He was shortly replaced by H. E. Caustin. However, already in February 1940 Caustin left the direction to join the Civil Service: A. L. Bowley was appointed director until December 1944. The change in the direction of the Institute also implied a reassessment of the research agenda to be implemented. From this perspective, Bowley faced a major issue since, because of the war, almost all the English members of the Institute had moved to Civil Service. Accordingly, the *émigré* economists nearly represented the whole research staff of the department. The mission then became observing the impact of the war on the economies of the countries involved.

3.1 Burchardt Remarks to Keynesian Theory

Notwithstanding the aforementioned appointment of Bowley as director of the OIS, in 1940 two important facts took place, changing the orientation of the Institute's research focus. The University authorities had decided to establish a diary of statistical information in November 1939. Such publication expanded in October 1940, becoming the well-known *Bulletin of the Oxford University Institute of Economics and Statistics*.[2] On June 1940, Burchardt, who was formerly hired as a librarian, was appointed editor of the Bulletin. At first sight, this fact may seem as a normal bureaucratic procedure of no particular importance. However, it played a pivotal influence on the Institute's agenda. Notwithstanding Bowley was no mere figurehead, as he showed a remarkable interest in the work of the younger colleagues coming from central Europe, he was only able to be in Oxford part-time because of personal reasons. Accordingly, the effective day-to-day running of the institute was carried out by Burchardt, who acted as a *de facto* director (Worswick 1959).

Under the guidance of Burchardt the mission of the Institute became to study the transition period, that is the risks and the implications of the transition from war economies to peace. Such a topic reflected Burchardt's background, since he was trained in the Kiel School. As we explained in the previous section, the Kiel School was a centre in political economy with equal emphasis on theoretical and empirical research. During his training as a young researcher, Burchardt studied in-depth philosophy and sociology, in addition to economics. His dissertation dealt with Joseph Schumpeter: Burchardt tried to merge a historical concept of the stationary state with a formal model of fluctuations. Such a choice

[2] The bulletin is still published under the name of *Oxford Bulletin of Economics and Statistics*.

reflected Burchardt's belief that economic processes have to incorporate both the *value* and the *physical* dimension. Along these lines, Burchardt was unsatisfied with both Cambridge and Lausanne schools (Lowe 1959), since the task of political economy should have been providing a non-monetary theory of business cycle, able to grasp the unstable and anarchic dynamics of capitalism, as well as the constraining role played by technical progress and institutions (Hagemann 1997). From this angle Burchardt was influenced by the works of Quesnay, Marx and Bohm-Bawerk. In particular, a synthesis between the two latter was at the origin of his theory of production, which represented a pioneer work in the tradition of the vertical integration approach (Hagemann 1997). In other words, Burchardt adhered to a continental tradition that assumed that market forces alone couldn't ensure human and progressive social outcomes, and, therefore he manifested a strong confidence in State intervention. He was also conscious of the limitations of orthodox theory; nevertheless he focused on extending the limitations of neoclassical economics, particularly in light of Marxian theory, rather than embracing the Keynesian revolution. While acknowledging the importance of the *General Theory*, Burchardt and the economists coming from the Kiel School assumed a different methodology, in which historical and institutional enquiry still represented the inescapable point of departure of economic analysis (Mongiovi 2005).

After Burchardt guidance, the different lines of research existing in the institute merged into a book dated 1944 and edited by him: *The Economics of Full Employment* (Burchardt 1944), which intended to identify the strategic factors of a policy of permanent full employment in industrial nations. Besides Burchardt himself, the contributors were Germany's Kurt Mandelbaum (later Martin), and Ernst F. Schumacher, the Hungarian Thomas Balogh, the Polish Michael Kalecki[3] and David Worswick.

Since the foreword of the book, Burchardt puts the accent on the limitations of the British debate around full employment. On the one hand, there was a widespread consensus about the necessity of implementing active policies in the labour market (well exemplified by the *White Paper on Employment Policy*). On the other hand, the institutional constraint

[3] Kalecki's contribution to the OIS research agenda is the object of a parallel work, see Lampa (2017).

over full employment played by capitalist institutions was completely overlooked. Therefore, the book aimed at filling this gap focusing not only on the technical tools necessary to reach full employment but also on the institutional and governance reforms necessary to maintain a stable full employment in a market economy.

Burchardt emphasizes one missing element of the British debate (triggered by the publication of Keynes book), i.e. that there are several ways to reach full employment, and to each one of them corresponds a "different distribution of incomes, a different standard of welfare and a different structure of industry and foreign trade" (Burchardt 1944, iii).

> Digging holes in the ground and filling them up again will, as Lord Keynes has put it, produce full employment, and so will the pyramiding of armaments or of industrial equipment. (…) But by choosing useful public works, by subsidizing mass consumption, or by redistributing incomes, employment can be pushed to the same level and, at the same time, the standard of living of the community as a whole be raised higher than by digging useless holes. (Burchardt 1944, iii–iv)

Subsequently in the first chapter of the book, Burchardt deals with the different theoretical explanations of unemployment.

Burchardt asks himself why the belief that there is always a wage level which provides full employment dies so hard. This belief implies that wage reductions can achieve the goal of eliminating excess labour supply. However, contemporary contributions (such as Keynes' book) had shown the fallacy of such a theoretical assumption. Nevertheless, most of economic theorists and businessmen enthusiastically adhere to such a view. In order to outline an explanation, Burchardt rejects the traditional arguments raised by critical or non-orthodox economists. In his view, the real issue has nothing to do with economic analysis; rather it can be explained studying the social background and the ideological stances behind the price flexibility mechanism.

In Burchardt's view there are three ideological stances that stand behind the traditional theory of unemployment. Firstly, business men usually share the fallacious belief that what is good for the individual enterprise is good for the whole community. Accordingly, they assume that if they impose a reduction of wages in their own firm they are going to get a competitive advantage by means of which they will expand their market share at lower prices. Burchardt stresses that as soon as the other entrepreneurs stick to the same pattern, not only the initial advantage disappears, but the whole market contracts due to the sharp fall in aggregate demand. Therefore, the economic welfare of the whole community is affected by the decisions of a single entrepreneur pursuing his own interest at the expense of the other employers. Second, there is the argument relying on the traditional theory of international trade and exchange. In this case, in a system of fixed exchange rates, when a country tries to adjust its external imbalances by means of deflationary policies, in order to restore competitiveness, it does so at the expense of foreign producers. Like in the previous case, the selfish bias of a country will lead to a reaction of the other countries, which will also shrink their wages. Also in this case, the overall effect will be a generalization of deflation and unemployment across countries. Flexible exchange rates, on the contrary, together with trade controls, provide instruments to regulate the foreign balance by appropriate currency and trade policies. Third, a deeper and underlying ideological bias against state intervention relies on the belief in the beneficial nature of the automatism of the market process. Along the years, such a prejudice had survived several adverse empirical evidences, being modified accordingly. In turn, such ideological stance reflected a widespread fear among the businessmen: the fear of State interventionism. More precisely, entrepreneurs feared that the State will use its powers to favour certain social groups, that the State will not adhere to the traditional codes of conduct of the private business community or that State power will be used for political purposes.

In other words, Burchardt states that traditional theory is a rationalization of political prejudices and ancestral fears. Therefore, the critique of orthodox theory cannot merely rely on logical and analytical arguments.

Not coincidentally, Burchardt puts forward a reproach also to the contemporary theories of business cycle. On the one hand, he does not deny that trade cycle theory represented an important critique to traditional economic equilibrium theories, since they explicitly assumed the existence of instability and fluctuations in capitalist economies. On the other hand, these theorists shared also an ideological bias with traditional theory, since they assumed that instability and fluctuations are "natural" and therefore that they represent the price that a country has to pay in order to grow. In some cases they even emphasized that slumps and "destruction" of branches of the economy are good for the task of developing. In Burchardt's view such a posture is rather unjustified, since it assumes institutions as an exogenous variable:

> The pattern of the cycle was partly conceived as something unavoidable, imposed by natural, uncontrollable conditions, which could not and should not be interfered with. (…) The resulting business cycle is beyond human control and (…) there is nothing to do but submit to it. (…) Adherents to this view –and there are many among economists, administrators and business men –point out that depressions are necessary to eliminate the excesses of the boom. (Burchardt 1944, 22)

In our view, Burchardt's distance from both orthodox traditional and business cycle theories is a further example of the singularity of the OIS within the British academia. While recognizing the important advancement contained in Keynes' book as well as the new trade cycle theories, Burchardt is clearly drawing on a different intellectual tradition.

3.2 *Balogh and the International Post-war Integration*

A similar stance characterizes also a chapter of the book edited by Burchardt written by Thomas Balogh on the international aspects of full employment. Thomas Balogh was a Budapest-born economist who studied in the Universities of Budapest and Berlin. Before immigrating to England, he worked in the Reichsbank, in the Banque the France and in the Federal Reserve. He had been in England since 1932, first working (thanks to J.M. Keynes) for O.T. Falk & Co in the City of London, then as a lecturer at University College London 1934–1940, before becoming a lecturer at Balliol College Oxford; he was naturalized as a British subject in 1938.

His contribution to Burchardt's book dealt in particular with the problem of economic and political integration. Broadly speaking Balogh shared Burchardt's view on Keynesian theory, since his contribution can be interpreted as a development of Keynes' Bretton Woods proposals motivated by the latter's deficiencies.

Balogh's point of departure is the functioning of international monetary system. Given the unequal level of development of different countries, an uneven distribution of international reserves becomes a structural element of capitalism. Such issue has got important implications. If we assume an even distribution of international reserves, the mere appearance of external imbalances does not necessarily lead to deflation and fiscal adjustment. In fact, a country running an external deficit may legitimately choose to use part of its international reserves in order to implement expansionary policies. However, such assumption would be definitely unrealistic given the features of the international monetary system. Consequently, a deflationary bias is imparted to the whole world economy. In case of external imbalances, any country will immediately aim at reducing the level of imports and increasing exports. Therefore, depreciation of currency and domestic deflationary policies become the tools that any country uses in event of external imbalances. In other words, beggar thy neighbour policies become the ordinary instruments to address the problem of international trade.

In light of this premise, a reform of international institutions becomes inescapable. In Balogh's eyes, multilateralism is the only reasonable answer to the permanent tensions produced by international transactions. According to Balogh, the aforementioned problem can be solved, by international agreements, in two alternative ways. The first way is the implementation of a scheme that would allow any of the participating countries to apply expansionary policies irrespectively of their consequences on the balance of payments. This approach, which Balogh calls the liquidity approach, implies the creation of some kind of international means of payment to restore the liquidity of the country in question. The other possible solution, which Balogh calls the equilibrium approach, consists in creating additional effective demand and divert them from the surplus countries, or to impose to the surplus countries measure oriented to eliminate such a surplus (for example, devaluation of the currency).

It should be noticed, however, that Balogh shifts away from Keynes' contemporary proposals. He compares the liquidity approach with Keynes' proposal for an International Clearing Union concluding that this latter relies on an automatism that cannot be taken for granted, i.e. that an increased volume of money will automatically transform into additional effective demand. Quite the contrary, Balogh stresses that it is necessary to introduce an international body, which acts resolutely in order to ensure that the newly created liquidity turns into additional effective demand.

> Lord Keynes' high hopes for his multilateral clearing scheme seem to be based on a (…) misapprehension (…). This misapprehension amounts to equating the volume of money with demand. (…) On the international plane there must exist an 'outside' (supernational) body which creates new international cash whenever international effective demand flags, and this

> body must induce a country or a group of countries to use this newly created cash and thus convert it into effective demand. *The automatism postulated by Lord Keynes is non-existent*. (Balogh 1944, 159–60 fn. 1, emphasis added)

Finally, Balogh addresses the question of regional integration. In his view, worldwide multilateralism would be the best choice in order to guarantee a sustainable and prolonged economic growth. However, he is also aware of the difficulties arising from the attempts to implement such a worldwide reform. An alternative solution would be the constitution of regional blocks whose functioning must mimic the rules of a worldwide-integrated system. More precisely, any regional block should possess its own Monetary Fund and Investment Board. Members of the full employment block must commit to a common economic policy that cannot be changed without agreement of the other members. Special emphasis is put on the control of capital movements, be it intra-block movements or movements between the full employment block and outside unstable areas. The theoretical defence of free capital movements is based on the fallacious belief that capitalists will choose to invest in areas were returns are the highest, finally determining the convergence of the economies. Quite the contrary, returns on capital largely depend on other factors such as the degree of monopoly of a country which determines a permanent imbalance in the international capital flows.

In short, we can affirm that also with regard to the political aspects of economic integration, Balogh's chapter is a further example of the non-aligned features of the OIS, particularly in light of his critique to Keynes proposal which embodied the official posture of the British government to be discussed at Bretton Woods.

4 Concluding Remarks

The discourse developed in this chapter highlights the non-aligned features of the Oxford Institute of Statistics economic staff when compared to the contemporary British tradition. Such a difference is evident from both a methodological and a theoretical point of view.

Since the Institute's foundation in October 1935, the high degree of academic freedom, resulting from the external funding provided by the Rockefeller Foundation, which aimed at promoting the analysis of business cycles, inescapably determined an increasing detachment from the rest of the economic research groups in Oxford. In this early period, Marschak's correspondence with Roy Harrod probably represents the most outstanding example of such a dialogue of the deaf, reinforcing the idea of a scarce interplay between the OIS and the other research bodies in Oxford.

On the other hand, when Burchardt substituted Marschak as a *de facto* director in 1940, the Institute's critique to both orthodox and business cycle theories represented another example of the singularity of the OIS within the British academia. In addition, while recognizing the advancement contained in Keynes's book, Burchardt and the OIS staff moved important critiques to Keynesian theory. Given Burchardt's belief that economic analysis had to incorporate both a value and a physical dimension, the task of political economy should have been capturing the unstable and anarchic dynamics of capitalism as well as the constraining role played by its institutions. From this particular angle, Burchardt's critique to Keynes seems to be motivated by this latter's oversimplified description of the economic role played by capitalist institutions over the economic process.

Stated succinctly, in Burchardt's view, Keynesian theory could become a consistent alternative paradigm only on condition to amend it with the continental and Marxian tradition.

Also on a political plan, we can affirm that the OIS had an autonomous research agenda. As evidenced by Balogh's work, contained in Burchardt's 1944 book, a reform of international institutions becomes inescapable in order to sustain full employment policies. However, he stressed that multilateralism should be preferred to regionalism since it allowed to develop the international division of labour to its maximum possible degree. Accordingly, Keynes' proposal for an International Clearing Union grasped an important element of the discussion on the post-war world. Nevertheless, such proposal was also criticized by Balogh for his naïve idea that international balance of payments adjustments could be solved merely by increasing international liquidity, which implied the belief of an automatic relationship between volume of cash and effective demand.

In a sketch, we can affirm that between 1935 and 1944 the Oxford Institute of Statistics certainly represented an atypical research centre within the academia of the United Kingdom. No relevant collaboration can be observed between the Institute's researchers and their British colleagues, even when their research agenda had strong similarities. In a sense, one may even conclude that an uncommon language inescapably divided them.

References

Balogh, Thomas. 1944. "The International Aspects of Full Employment." In *The Economics of Full Employment*, edited by Frank Burchardt, 126–80. Oxford: Basil Blackwell.

Besomi, Daniele. 1998. "Roy Harrod and the Oxford Economists' Research Group's Inquiry on Prices and Interest, 1936–39." *Oxford Economic Papers* 50 (4): 534–62.

Burchardt, Frank, ed. 1944. *The Economics of Full Employment*. Oxford: Basil Blackwell.

Cherrier, Beatrice. 2010. "Rationalizing Human Organization in an Uncertain World: Jacob Marschak, from Ukrainian Prisons to Behavioral Science Laboratories." *History of Political Economy* 42 (3): 443–68.

Craver, Earlene. 1986. "Patronage and the Directions of Research in Economics: The Rockefeller Foundation in Europe, 1924–1938." *Minerva* 24 (2–3): 205–22.

Hagemann, Harald. 1997. "Burchardt, Fritz (Frank) Adolph (1902–1958)." In *Business Cycles and Depressions. An Encyclopedia*, edited by David Glasner, 59–60. New York & London: Garland Publishing.

———. 2005. "Dismissal, Expulsion, and Emigration of German Speaking Economists After 1933." *Journal of the History of Economic Thought* 27 (4): 405–20.

———. 2007. "German-Speaking Economists in British Exile 1933–1945." *BNL Quarterly Review* 60 (242): 323–63.

———. 2011. "European émigrés and the 'Americanization' of Economics." *European Journal of the History of Economic Thought* 18 (5): 643–71.

Lampa, Roberto. 2017. "Full Employment as a Condition of Crisis: Kalecki's Critique to Keynes and the Fabians (1942–1945)." HES Annual Meeting, Toronto, 22–25 June, 2017.

Lowe, Adolph. 1959. "F. A. Burchardt. Part I." *Bulletin of the Oxford University Institute of Economics and Statistics* 21 (2): 59–65.

Marschak, Jacob. 1940. "Peace Economics." *Social Research* 7 (3): 280–98.

———. 1941. "Methods in Economics: A Discussion." *Journal of Political Economy* 49 (3): 441–48.

Mehrling, Perry. 2010. "A Tale of Two Cities." *History of Political Economy* 42 (2): 201–20.

Minister of Reconstruction. 1944. *White Paper on Employment Policy*, Cmd. 6527.

Mongiovi, Gary. 2005. "Emigré Economists and American Neoclassical Economics, 1933–1945." *Journal of the History of Economic Thought* 27 (4): 427–37.

Sember, Florencia. 2010. "Closing the Model? The Harrod–Marschak Correspondence on the Draft of the 'Essay in Dynamic Theory'. *Journal of the History of Economic Thought* 32 (4): 583–608.

Worswick, George David Norman. 1959. "F. A. Burchardt. Part II." *Bulletin of the Oxford University Institute of Economics and Statistics* 21 (2): 66–71.

Young, Warren and Frederic Lee. 1993. *Oxford Economics & Oxford Economists*. London: Macmillan.

CHAPTER 15

Postscript: The Intellectual Origins of European Integration

James Ashley Morrison and José Luís Cardoso

1 Introductory

It is hard to overstate the degree to which the First World War disordered the international system. It materially, irreversibly altered the principal structures that had defined the nineteenth century global order: the distribution of power within and between the rival empires; the relations between classes within and across societies; and the relationship between states and markets more generally. This alone was a cataclysm virtually without precedent in human history. And, yet, it was only the beginning of the end of the First Era of Globalisation. Among those structures that did manage to survive the Great War, most were hollowed by the Great Depression and laid waste by the Second World War.

J. A. Morrison (✉)
London School of Economics and Political Science, London, UK

J. L. Cardoso
Instituto de Ciências Sociais, Universidade de Lisboa, Lisboa, Portugal

© The Author(s) 2021

A. M. Cunha and C. E. Suprinyak (eds.), *Political Economy and International Order in Interwar Europe*, Palgrave Studies in the History of Economic Thought,
https://doi.org/10.1007/978-3-030-47102-6_15

Yet, at the same time, the shattered order created space for new actors and new ideas to come to the fore. Women, working people and others from the "peripheries" within and across Europe's imperial orders pressed themselves upon the global stage, exerting more influence than ever before. In that sense the twentieth century's Great Destabilisation was not merely destructive but also generative. It generated new models, new sensibilities and new approaches advanced by new people from unconventional perspectives and backgrounds. Seldom was there better cause for collective soul-searching; and seldom has there been richer, and more diverse, inquiry into the nature and causes of global order.

The interwar period was thus one of the most challenging, but also one of the most innovative, periods in modern history. To be sure, some of the "new" forms and ideas, like fascism, were abhorrent—exceeded in their intellectual bankruptcy only by their practical brutality. But others, like the many varieties of socialism, were varied in their design and execution. Some such experiments, like those in Bolshevik Russia, proved immensely disappointing—all the more so because others, like those in Labour's Britain, had demonstrated such great promise. And, of course, the stalwart liberal orthodoxy was itself wholly reinvented and given new births in a wide range of forms, from John Dewey's "new liberalism" to the Germans' ordoliberalism (Dewey 1935, 12).

The chapters in this volume sample the range of responses to these destabilising forces and show some of the boldest endeavours to re-form a reformed international order. But they can only be but a sample. And the scope conditions for the enterprise have led to an emphasis on (principally) intra-European discussions, leaving extra-European perspectives as promising avenues for future enquiry.

Similarly, the main topics to which the title of the book refers—political economy and international order—by no means correspond to a comprehensive coverage of the wide range of analytical contents encompassed in the various chapters. Therefore, it is important to recognise that the generic designation of "political economy" here has a twofold meaning: on the one hand, it refers to a variety of contending theoretical approaches that reveal this period's importance for the formation of contemporary economics; on the other hand, it considers a variety of doctrinal perspectives within the political and economic fields that challenge the strength of the conventional models and solutions (liberalism and socialism) that dominated the European ideological scene after the First World War. With regard to the "international order," we understand the intention of the editors of this book to find a short and neutral designation, which, however, should not overlook the diverse set of processes fostering the creation of new institutions of national and transnational scope (political, economic and scientific research institutions, in the areas of labour and employment, cooperation and collective security) and, above all, initiatives, plans and projects aimed at building European integration. The international order, therefore, refers to a comprehensive view of political and economic relations between nations that seek the implementation of common strategies.

In undertaking such inquiries, it quickly becomes obvious that it is impossible to maintain a strict separation between positive and normative questions. That is, one cannot deal with "pure" theoretical axioms without taking care to explicate their doctrinal, philosophical and ideological foundations—and their consequences. The Wars, the failures to restore the pre-war order and the Great Depression all underscored the enormous stakes at issue. In the pre-war days of growth and plenty, it may have been (relatively) easy to defer the questions of fairness about how the many gains should be distributed between economies and between classes. But, in the hard times of contraction and scarcity, there was no putting off what became questions of whom should suffer and whom should perish. In this sense, the place of political-economic theory is better defined when we look at the way in which the articulation between individual interest and general well-being is conceived, on the possible compromise between a model of society based on the will of the individual and on the virtues of free competition in the market, and a model based on the advantages of a strong and authoritarian state that imposes its control on an economy subject to planning rules and programmes.

At the workshop that took place in Lisbon in February 2019, the origin of the chapters now gathered in this book, these inquiries were brought to bear on the key questions surrounding the intellectual origins and construction of European integration. The essays in this volume acknowledge (at least implicitly) that a new agenda for Europe was in the making, i.e. the emergence and development in interwar Europe of consistent lines of reflection on the challenges of an international order that, without dispensing with the autonomy of national states, could frame institutional solutions with a higher level of cooperation and integration. Clearly, the most stable solutions were only achieved in the post-war reconstruction process fuelled by the Marshall Plan, mainly through the monetary integration mechanisms put in place by the European Payments Union.

However, there were signs of some uniformity in decision-making within the scope of the definition of employment policies framed by international organisations, among which the International Labour Organization stands out. The role played by research institutes dedicated to the production of economic knowledge with an impact on public policies must also be highlighted.

These questions, and others, are reconsidered in this postscript under several headings. First, we consider the attempts to "rethink the state," particularly in the wake of the many experiments—natural and contrived—that followed during and after the First World War. At the heart of these inquires lay broader philosophical questions over the concepts of law and order. The revisiting of those axioms gave rise to some of the most interesting and productive discussions of this period: namely, the debate between "new liberals" like Keynes and the "ordoliberals" like Hayek. While certain figures loomed large in those interchanges, none could escape those questions, and, as this volume shows, virtually every thinker and doer took them up at one point or another. This leads naturally into a discussion of the many new methods and approaches that were brought into the field at this point—and that met with equal measures of great fanfare and considerable chagrin. We reflect on both in turn. Taken all together, this grants the opportunity to reflect on the place of Europe within these debates and in the world. Of course, all of the new circumstances and new thinking directly shaped the post-war crafting of "Europe," as we discuss. But we also reflect some on how European centrality itself—both intellectual centrality and material, geographic centrality—shaped this post-war order.[1]

2 Reconceiving the State

However true the myth of "nineteenth century *laissez-faire*," the twentieth century cataclysms wiped out whatever remained of the pre-war, "classical liberal" order. Beyond the growth of the state and attendant government borrowing, the First World War brought unprecedented controls over prices, wages and the movement of people, capital and goods and services. The putative "returns" to pre-war liberalism with the "new gold standard" and Europe's "tarrif truce" in the 1920s were

[1] In this chapter, we borrow some of the useful concepts and formulations developed earlier in this volume. We cite all external references throughout.

attenuated and proved short-lived. When the crisis of liberal political regimes was plunged into an economic depression, a growing number of critics questioned the ability of Western economies to restore social and economic equilibria without strong state intervention. This triggered an intense wave of reflection on alternative economic systems, particularly "third way" solutions that promised the benefits of the pre-war system while avoiding the excesses of both capitalism and socialism.

Politically, the story was mixed. In *extremis*, the "total war" wrought between 1914 and 1918 brought conscription across Europe and its empires and unrestricted warfare waged upon civilians—both enemy alien and neutral, alike. Broadly speaking, individual freedom had never been restricted so deeply in so many ways for so many people. At the same time, those very actors most put upon—most formally marginalised—became increasingly conscious of their inherent centrality to the global order. To borrow from Marx and Engels, these groups' "strength [grew], and they [felt] that strength more" (Marx and Engels 1977, 252). In Dublin, the French trenches and Saint Petersburg, there was wartime rebellion and mutiny. With the War's dusk came a rapid wave of enfranchisement to working men and (progressively) to women in several dozen countries. These were only the first hints of the anti-colonial, democratic and working class movements now coalescing. The figures discussed in this book recognised these transformations; and they sought to understand, harness and shape the forces at work. Indeed, this volume shows that the story of interwar political–economic thought can be told partly as a story of the clash of those ideas—and, at points, those figures proffering them.

For the advocates of corporatism and tripartism, the apparent success of wartime government economic management pointed the way towards potential future models that advanced beyond the simple state-market binary. At the same time, these models emphasised the importance of local traditions and extolled the non-economic facets of human experience, not least religious identities. Among the plurality and diversity of recommended alternative solutions, one can also find perspectives based on the traditions of Christian social thought, personalism and spiritual humanism, organicism, solidarism and guild socialism—that is, a set of doctrinal streams that converge in their applause of social and political models based on the ideas of order and social harmony. For many, this was a potent alternative to the steamroller that had been pre-war liberalism, variously flattening cross-country distinctiveness, essentialising "the individual," and totalising "the market." These new approaches similarly served the purposes of social balance in market economies regulated by sovereign states in democratic regimes (Schmitter 1979).

Cole, in particular, emphasised the cosmopolitan nature of individuals themselves. After all, every person is a unique conglomeration of numerous overlapping, and often conflicting, identities. Recognising this, Cole baulked at the old, simplistic labels based on occupation, class, race or religion. At points, this line of heterodoxy propelled him to bold thinking that brought him close to libertarianism. Ultimately, however, the questions of practical governance remained. Cole settled on the ideal as economic planning run by democratically organised, self-governing guilds.

Perroux was similarly concerned with the "freedom of the person," but he manifestly resisted the individualisation of rights. Instead, he viewed freedom through the lens of corporatism, communitarianism and other "non-conformist" ideas. In contrast with Cole and some others, Perroux proved less willing to settle on a precise model of the best "third way." His thought remained "confusing and unstable"—befitting the times, it seems. Yet, Perroux's explicit recognition of the dissonance, contradiction and plasticity of individuals' numerous identities was itself a productive contrast from the reductionism imposed by the totalising alternatives: communism's class membership; fascism's race identity; and capitalism's essentialisation of *homo economicus*.

For some, however, confusion spelt opportunity. Regrettably, autocrats like Salazar, Franco and Mussolini effectively mobilised the old institutions and invoked the social fabric as bulwarks against reform and democratisation. The defence of corporatist or neo-corporatist solutions, the call for convergence of interests, the belief in the advantages of tripartism (that is, the negotiation and reconciliation of positions involving employers, employees and government agencies), the declaration of the end of the class struggle as a driving element for the advancement of societies—all these were ideologies put into the service of authoritarian and dictatorial regimes. Indeed, many of the corporatist parliaments went beyond just legitimising these co-options. Despite their good intentions, some became the very "locus of that process." On the other extreme, even international regimes with reformist ambitions, such as the ILO, broadly neutered the radical movements following the Russian Revolution. Rather than emerging from the international labour movement itself, it seems that the ILO may have been deliberately created to "depotentiat[e] socialist-revolutionary impulses" and to preserve the capitalist order.

In the end, the claim that the twentieth century would be the "century of corporatism" (Manoilescu 1934) proved premature. Of course, the interwar atmosphere fostered such proclamations—and such aspirations. But that is not to say that these movements went nowhere. In fact, the perceived failure of any of these many "third way" approaches to emerge as a singular, robust alternative to the old ways led theorists back to the timeless debates about the old rules.

3 Revisiting "The Rules of the Game"

Perhaps no theorists recoiled more from the dangers of totalitarianism than did the ordoliberals.[2] Determined to support—to leave free—the "autonomous individual," the ordoliberals saw fascism, communism and even the many "third way" alternatives as anathema to individual liberty. Dreading the tyranny of the majority, they were deeply suspicious of every attempt to prioritise social demands or collective objectives.

But this was far from a mere defence of the "classical liberal" order. Indeed, they squarely challenged that tradition's founding trope: the free market.[3] They did not go quite as far as did, say, Karl Polanyi, who famously proclaimed that "*laissez-faire* was planned" (Polanyi 1957, 141). But Miksch, at the Freiburg School, led the charge to denaturalise "the market." Rather than a default, "natural" state of human existence, the emergence of "free markets" followed from choices actively made through political processes.

This new starting point had profound philosophical implications. Liberals like Smith had argued that liberty could be attained by restoring the natural state of things—by, as Rousseau had instructed, peeling back the corrupting artifices of political society. But if, as the ordoliberals argued, the "free market" were not itself "natural," what could be said

[2] This is not to suggest that their attacks exceeded those levied by, say, Orwell (1950) and Arendt (1958).

[3] It is useful to remember that "the market" was indeed a figure of speech, the generalisation of a particular locus of economic interchange used as a metaphor for the broader economy. Watson (2018).

for its normative priority over alternative arrangements of state-market relations?

Keynes, too, learned the import of this challenge as the Second World War approached. In his 1938 essay on his "Early Beliefs," he grappled with what he called his pre-war, "flimsily based" "immoral[ism]." He maintained that he "remain[ed], and always will remain, an immoralist." But the great disorder of these decades had taught him to "respect the extraordinary accomplishment of our predecessors in the ordering of life…[and] the elaborate framework which they had devised to protect this order" (Keynes 1938). This was a Burkean defence of tradition, justified on consequentialist grounds.

The ordoliberals took an altogether different approach to the same challenge. Drawing on a range of deontological continental philosophers—Kant, in particular—the ordoliberals offered a new—"neoliberal"—political economy based on adherence to established rules. Hayek and Eucken repeatedly stressed this point. A common set of standards—and shared expectations about the enforcement of those standards—would offer vital reliability and predictability. Certainly, history appeared to confirm the advantages conveyed by such pre-war incarnations of this principle: price stability, enforcement of contracts, and clear delineations of liability. But Eucken praised these institutions not merely because they worked well. They also had an independent normative basis. This approach was justifiable on the grounds of fairness, as all actors could play to the same rules and expect the same results. Crucially, a rules-based order would limit the caprice and arbitrariness that follows inevitably from ad hoc decision-making.

Keynes shared the ordoliberals' abiding concern with the rise of totalitarianism. He famously praised Hayek's *Road to Serfdom*, writing that he was "deeply moved" by the "grand book." Not for nothing, he read it as he steamed across the water to the Bretton Woods conference in 1944. One can only wonder how often it sprung to his mind in the weeks that followed, as he crafted the very "international authorit[ies]" to govern what Hayek hoped would become "a community of nations of free men…" (Hayek 1994, 259).

Yet, Keynes and the ordoliberals remained at an impasse over the old tension between rules and discretion. Indeed, as Hayek rendered it, they carried on in this debate right until Keynes's untimely, tragic end. Hayek feared what he saw as Keynes's reckless guile, Keynes's belief that great intellectuals could and should pilot considered opinion and public policy through every tempest (Hayek 1983a, 360). But it would not be fair to suggest that Keynes did not appreciate the power of dangerous ideas. Quite the contrary: his closing words in the *General Theory* were a meditation on the devastating consequences of having adhered to the pre-war orthodoxy across the new conditions of the 1920s and 1930s. Rather, Keynes's axiom was that there was no Archimedean point from which to formulate timeless, unbiased policy levers. Today's rules were always just the dictates laid out by "some academic scribbler of a few years back" (Keynes 1936, 7:383). Just as important, time does not stand still. The rules crafted in one context will often have unpredictable—perhaps even directly contrary—effects as the context changes unexpectedly. The gold standard, the principal purpose of which was to provide "a stable measuring-rod" of value, was the quintessential example of this.[4] This insight was among Keynes's most profound contributions: at many points, the state can only provide stable conditions—so wisely appreciated by the ordoliberals—by suspending the formal rules. In those instances, discretionary authority is not an alternative to caprice, but the necessary counter to it.[5]

Here, the difficult normative questions reappear. How much ought we to allow the "bloody and invisible hand" of history push us along and pull our strings?[6] To advocate, as Justice Scalia put it, that "the Rule of Law, the law of rules, be extended as far as the nature of the question allows," is to bracket the many injustices that often become enshrined as law (Scalia 1989, 1187). Must the rules of serfdom remain in perpetuity? Yet, to say otherwise is to assault private "property." Should the sanctity of contract bind generations of Germans to pay the Kaiser's bond? Yet, to say otherwise is to absolve sovereign debt and destabilise financial markets. And what of the ancient rules of citizenship that determine where people can (must) live, work, and die? Yet, to say otherwise is to invite massively

[4] Keynes (1923b) Preface. See also Hayek (1943, 176).

[5] Of course, it is possible to craft rules—such as with the "non-accelerating inflation rate of unemployment," the Taylor rule, etc.—that define monetary policy in relation to the inflation rate itself. Such rules aim to stabilise the real purchasing power of a currency while still limiting the monetary authorities' room for discretion. But this might just shift "the politics of money" onto the measures of inflation, the time-frames considered, and the construction of the price indices: do we include the costs of housing? Do we include the cost of imported consumables? et cettera.

[6] Shakespeare, William. *The Tragedy of Macbeth*.

destabilising labour migration. In each of these cases, liberals—of all varieties—might agree today that the laws in question never ought to have been instituted. But if the same reasoning has been used—successfully, for long periods—to defend bad rules, does that not raise difficult questions about the normative basis of a rules-over-discretion order, as such? It would be nice if every person subject to the law had that (ancient) liberty to help write and rewrite those laws. But that has never been true anywhere. Even today, citizens service the odious debts of their forebears, consent (although only tacitly) to participate in un-free, unequal markets not of their making, and face ever-higher walls to exercise the right of "exit" if not also their rights of "voice" (Hirschman 1970).

Yet, without rules, we can have no order. Certainly, we should have no liberty without law and legislation (Hayek 1983b). But these discussions from the interwar period remind us that the "law of rules" is not always the same as the rule of justice. And even if it were so, Portia reminds us, the strictest enforcement of justice is assuredly not the path to our salvation.[7] This is, perhaps, the clearest lesson taught by the merciless measures of justice meted out by the Treaty of Versailles.

4 New Methods and Approaches

One of the main features of the interwar period is the theoretical pluralism and methodological diversity within the scientific territory of political economy. For the hasty reader of any textbook on the history of economic thought, there is the risk of reaching the false conclusion that the interwar period is characterised by the exclusive or dominant presence of John Maynard Keynes (Williamson 2003, 13). It is also tempting to simply draw the conclusion that Keynes was right—that he was right in his indictment of 1919 and right in his prescriptions for the world after 1945. Certainly, he did receive a much better hearing the second time around; and who would argue that he was wrong at either point?

But such a perspective, while true, is also thin. It overstates the singularity of Keynes's clairvoyance and understates the importance of Europe's shifting position in the world and the evolving threats it faced. After all, Keynes was not the only one to recognise the failings of the pre-war order or the several attempts to restore it. He was a decade

[7] Shakespeare, William. *The Merchant of Venice*.

ahead of his peers when, in early 1922, he warned about the movement that powered fascism; but, in the same breath, he contemptuously, vulgarly, and prematurely dismissed the "besotted idealism and intellectual error" of "Bolshevism."[8] Also, Keynes's own views and approach evolved remarkably across this period. There were his evolving—Hayek might have said, mercurial—views on the gold standard and free trade. More broadly, the polemicist behind the incomparable *Economic Consequences of the Peace* and *Tract on Monetary Reform* was not (yet) the draughtsman who crafted *The General Theory of Employment, Interest and Money* and forged the Bretton Woods institutions (Keynes 1919, 1923b, 1936). Without questioning Keynes's extraordinary influence on economic thought and policy, the contributions gathered in this book highlight several additional currents of economic theory, based on different assumptions, methods and approaches. They answer the calls issued long ago (by, for example Shackle 1967; Hall 1989; Laidler 1999) to remember that Keynes was not preaching alone, that his message was received and appropriated in many different ways, and that this period is fecund with under-utilised insights and promising roads yet to be explored.

The debates on the (ir)rational behaviour of economic agents, or on causal relations in the explanation of economic phenomena, also demonstrate that the diversity of theoretical and methodological points of view was not a factor of fragility, but rather a sign of vitality of economics in the interwar period. In addition to both the developments in neoclassical theory of general equilibrium, and the new contributions within the scope

[8] In part, Keynes was misled by his own prejudice. The full remark ran, "Bolshevism is such a delirium, bred by besotted idealism and intellectual error out of the sufferings and peculiar temperaments of Slavs and Jews. But we can no more regard this culminating delirium as a lasting fact or influence than the rule of Robespierre or the Jacobins" (Keynes 1922, 372–73). He had forgotten that Robespierre was followed by Bonaparte; and, so, too, was Lenin followed by Stalin. Yet, Keynes was uncanny in his warnings about the German ultranationalists. As France prepared to occupy the Ruhr (in January 1923), he predicted, "There exist already over a large part of Europe situations worse than the gloomiest prophets foresaw...A sensational denouement can only come about through a political event—a strike in the Ruhr, a fall of government in France or a reactionary Putsch in Germany...The combination of economic distress with patriotic rage might at last drive Germany desperate. A movement of violence from reactionary Bavaria, aided perhaps by the Communist left, would face us with a German government of an entirely different complexion and ideas of policy from those we have dealt with hitherto." (Keynes 1923a, 105). Hitler's Beer Hall Putsch–in Munich, Bavaria–transpired ten months later.

of the traditions of the German historical school and American institutionalism, the emergence of new theoretical constructions that critically dialogue with Keynes's work stands out. This is the case for the rise of the concept of social market economy associated with German ordoliberalism, or of the Hayekian vision focused on an analysis of solutions to problems of economic imbalance based on the real structure of production and non-monetary factors. Throughout this period, further to these distinct theoretical contributions, there are relevant developments on the theory of business cycles and economic fluctuations and on the analysis of the dynamics of international trade, which owe little to the Keynesian legacy. And even in applied fields in which Keynes' work proved to be unavoidable, namely in what concerns the design of the international monetary system and the short-term budgetary and monetary macroeconomic policies, other authors disputed the alleged Keynesian primacy.

It was during this period that the bases for a sophisticated statistical and econometric analysis of macroeconomic variables were created. Keynes was somehow responsible for introducing and spreading a new macroeconomic jargon, despite that he was relatively less concerned with the measurement of quantitative data (and even questioned their use in economic forecasting).

The interwar period witnessed the rise of a new agenda for research institutions interested in the development of statistical methods and measuring, which proved to be decisive to accommodate a new type of economic inquiry: time-series data and empirical testing as toolboxes at the service of economic forecasting. The main issue at stake was the need to control the uncertainty and unpredictability associated with economic fluctuations and business cycles.

Under the influence of American institutions, such as the NBER (National Bureau of Economic Research), economic research institutes flourished in Berlin, Frankfurt and Vienna, enrolling some of the most prestigious and promising German-speaking economists. The creation of such institutions was made possible through financial sponsorship by the Rockefeller Foundation, which was particularly effective in the case of the Kiel Institute for the World Economy, between 1926 and 1933. Among the researchers at Kiel one can name Adolphe Löwe, Gerhard Colm, Hans Neisser and Fritz Burchardt, as well as two émigrés from Soviet Union, whose contributions to scientific development in economics would be in the future greatly acclaimed: Wassily Leontief and Jacob Marschak.

The rise of Nazism in Germany after 1933 and the "Anschluss" in March 1938 dictated the forced emigration of these outstanding scholars to the US and to different countries in Europe, especially to the UK, thus contributing to the renewal of economic research in the universities and research institutes that welcomed them. Notwithstanding the well-known cases of Schumpeter, von Mises, Hayek, Morgenstern and other Austrian economists (Craver 1986), the careers developed by the members of the Kiel Institute in American and British Universities are particularly worth noting—as stressed in two of the essays in this book.

In this context, the role played by the émigrés Marshack and Burchardt at the Oxford Institute of Statistics was of a particular relevance. In addition to their strong commitment to promote the use of statistical data and empirical tests in economics and social sciences, they also recognised the need for a global, European response to redraught the blueprints of economic progress and prosperity. They knew that this could only be possible through cooperation between nations. Thus, if the United Kingdom's victory at Waterloo were "won on the playing fields of Eton," Europe's post-war unification was forged in these academic fields.[9] The post-war European project built upon the work done by these figures in journals, at conferences and in research centres to transcend the interwar period's deepening divides between traditions, cultures and countries.

Realising this potential, however, required formal institutions capable of advancing this progress and fostering further evolution in the organisation of society. It also required the exaltation of cooperation over conquest. But more than just the peace of this region was at stake. By thus binding up the wounds of Europe, it might also show the way to mind the European wounds that now wound around the world.

5 Europe at the Centre

It is hardly surprising that "Europe"—broadly construed—loomed immensely large in these discussions. Of course, the major figures considered in this book were themselves all essentially Europeans. But it went well beyond that. Europe had been at the centre of the pre-war First Era of Globalisation. Certainly, it was the epicentre of the global war that brought that order's demise. Yet, so much had changed and, many

[9] The (apocraphyl) remark is associated with the Duke of Wellington.

thought, so much ought to be learned, that it would prove folly to attempt to simply roll back the clock and to restore things the way they had been.

But what might be the alternative? What lessons could Europe learn from these great cataclysms? What would be the place of Europe in the new world order?

For many, European integration was a middle ground between the old imperialist nationalism and the neophyte, abstract internationalism. The former was increasingly unsustainable—the First World War having both revealed the dangers it fostered and sapped the capacity of the European states to foist it upon the world in any case. The latter, however, was still nascent. The moral imperative of cooperation had been clear since Kant at least; but, in terms of practical politics, global cosmopolitanism remained a political non-starter. As the essays in this volume show, Europe's leading states were still deeply rooted in their varied traditions, bitter enmities and persistent structural imbalances. Overcoming these obstacles would be no mean feat.

Yet, there was a serious question about the relationship between the political and economic "liberalism" at the core of the European project. It was well and good where integration of the one fostered the integration of the other. But what of those who sought the benefits of economic cooperation but wanted to retain political sovereignty?[10] Or what of those who believed in the political project but baulked at exposing their domestic economies to international market forces? All of these questions were particularly pressing for Europe's smaller countries, which enjoyed little bargaining power and only unappealing exit options.

Also, what of the effects beyond Europe's core? The commercial liberal premise, crystallised in the ECSC, might render impossible conflict among its members; but might it not align their interests against those of non-members? Might it not divert trade from its natural channels, attenuate Europe's traditional connections with the world and become an effective substitute for the global cosmopolitan project? Might not the new Europe, Röpke asked, just become another *Zollverein*?

Tinbergen was particularly sensitive to these questions. Born in the Hague at the turn of the century, he inherited the distinctive Dutch

[10] This question is alive and well in the haggling over Brexit.

international legal tradition and came of age just as the pre-war pacifist movement reached its crescendo. But this was not all. There was another Dutch practice that pre-dated even Grotius: colonialism. And this "history" was far from over, even after the Second World War.

Tinbergen grappled with these tensions throughout his storied career, from his time at the League of Nations to his Wicksell lectures in Sweden in the 1960s. At his most idealistic, Tinbergen resisted the efforts of European integration in the progressive spirit of global internationalism. In particular, he feared that unifying Europe could undermine the advantages of the former colonies' independence. Rather than being ruled individually within separate empires, they might be dominated *en masse* via international regimes run collectively by a European superstate. This view was remarkably prescient. Even today, the world's liberated colonies enjoy formal sovereign equality and, in the case of the WTO, even veto power. But they are nevertheless dominated by the powerful countries, not least the EC/EU (Barton et al. 2006, Ch. 3).

Yet, what is the alternative? Tinbergen's interchanges with Frisch in the 1960s clarified the disappointing, but abiding, reality that empires had been replaced by superpowers. Forming a European superstate was thus the only hope for "a third way" between East and West and for some rebalancing between rich and poor. It was thus incumbent upon Europe's own "small" states—the Dutch and the like-minded Scandinavian powers—to pull the rest of Europe in a positive direction. At the same time, Tinbergen identified organisations like the G77 as a potential counter to the radical inequality in bargaining power at the global level.

Triffin arrived at similar conclusions by an analogous path. He, too, hailed from one of Europe's smaller powers; and, like Tinbergen, he came to appreciate the importance of smaller powers pooling their strength. His experience studying and advising "peripheral" Latin American economies in the interwar period became unexpectedly relevant in the post-war European context. As Europe became peripheral to the centres in the West and the East, the old great powers began to experience the global order as their own colonies had done. This was a humbling turn of events; and it drove home the importance of designing international regimes that moderated these imbalances, broadly construed.

In his eponymous "dilemma," Triffin put his finger on the perilous global imbalances among (even) the western, developed countries. Just as Smith had done in the case of early modern Spain and Portugal, Triffin explained how the USA's provision of international liquidity (under the

Bretton Woods arrangements) undermined its balance of trade (Smith 1976, Book IV, Ch. 5). But, as Triffin well knew, this was just the latest incarnation of a transcendent, timeless problem of perennial global imbalances. Whereas the "classical school" fixated on the final equilibrium, Triffin followed Keynes in thinking through the periods and the mechanisms of adjustment.

Simply put, different economic growth rates, asynchronous macroeconomic cycles and shocks—among other things—generate pressures towards "surplus" and "deficit" among the world's many economies. There are numerous mechanisms by which these imbalances can be resolved, which Friedman succinctly summarised in his landmark 1953 "essay" on flexible exchange rates (Friedman 1953). But each of these tools has different distributive and thus political implications. There is quite a difference, after all, between commercial policy (that "protects" some producers at the expense of consumers) and contracting the money supply (that is deflationary). For decades, the gold standard orthodoxy eschewed the most democratically appealing options. It forbade capital controls and exchange rate manipulation; and it deprecated commercial policy (such as tariffs). Of course, surplus countries could amass reserves indefinitely. Deficit countries, however, were limited by their pre-existing stock of reserves, plus whatever they could borrow internationally. This left only domestic macroeconomic adjustment—or, rather, surrendering domestic macroeconomic policy to the dictates of global market forces. For deficit countries, that often meant austerity. Despite the overtures to the orthodoxy in the 1920s, the experiments of the 1930s saw all of these mechanisms employed variously even in the central gold standard countries. Gone was the old trump card that austerity was necessary to preserve the sacred gold standard. At the same time, the advance of democratic political reforms and social-democratic norms and demands only heightened this proclivity and raised the stakes. Triffin learned a crucial lesson: the reality is that politics, as much as economic ideology, would determine how countries faced their imbalances.

This was true at the international level as well. After all, the balance of payments constraint only requires that balance is restored—that *an* equilibrium is achieved, rather than that any particular equilibrium is reached. Knowing that adjustment is seldom painless, clear-eyed policymakers prefer that the adjustments happen abroad rather than at home. So, rather than inflating their price levels, surplus countries press deficit countries to swallow deflation. Triffin recognised that these impositions are not distributed equally or even in proportion to the level of imbalance. Here again, power comes into play: larger, more diverse economies, often with security linkages on the table, are able to drive hard bargains.

For Triffin, this unpleasant reality was the starting point for post-war Europe. As a collection of medium-sized economies with no reserves dependent on the USA and the USSR for vital inputs and security, Europe must not only be split but also dominated by the two superpowers. Instead, Triffin re-deployed the lessons learned in interwar Latin America—many of them taught by Raúl Prebisch—in this European context. In particular, the European Payments Union and his proposed European reserve fund were the culmination of this thinking about the problems of global imbalances. In the first instance, a robust monetary union would pool Europe's reserves, reducing intra-European competition for scarce gold and dollars and deepening the well of resources available in a crisis. More broadly, such a union would align the member countries' interests and pool their bargaining power, evening the power disparity between Europe and the US. So far from undermining the global level regime—the Bretton Woods System—such regional-level integration was crucial to ameliorating the imbalances—economic *and* political—that imperilled it. At his most ambitious, Triffin hoped that such efforts could be multiplied elsewhere, rebalancing the global order more generally.

Few efforts have been more ambitious than those to build a new Europe and, with it, a model for regional cooperation more broadly. At the same time, the magnificence of the achievement owed less to the boldness of the vision than to the adroit—and tireless—industry with which it was effected. After all, the post-war order built directly upon the intellectual, if not the political and economic, foundations laid in the pre-war era. Cobdenism remained the guiding star for many of the interwar liberals, and the progress achieved in the nineteenth century offered evidence that such a world was possible. From Hayek to Einaudi, this history inspired the confidence necessary to carry on this tradition, even as it also provided the clues to the limitations inherent in its prior incarnation.

But there was more than just the memory and promise of bonny days gone by. While it might strain belief, the reality is that the damage to the old order could have been yet worse. Indeed, much was done, even in the darkest hours, to preserve the pre-war globalising norms and institutions. Of course, we rightly remember the heroic (if not sometimes also tragic) efforts of Conservatives like Churchill and liberals like Keynes. But we too often forget the pivotal part played by labour, particularly the British

Labour Party's Prime Minister and Chancellor of the Exchequer: Ramsay McDonald and Philip Snowden, respectively. Distrusted by the right and (now) reviled by the left, that these figures are so often deprecated is a testament to the enormity of the sacrifices they made in the name of these ideals. At the same time that Churchill was castigating the British Labour movement as "Bolshevism" and that Keynes was making (reasonable but dangerous) allowances for protectionism, McDonald and Snowden were doing everything in their power to save the gold standard and, particularly in the case of Snowden, to maintain free trade. They did this—imposing austerity rather than a revenue tariff at the height of the Great Depression—even as it meant sacrificing the Labour Government, the Labour Party and, perhaps, the interwar Labour Movement. In hindsight, we know better how they might have proceeded. Keynes, and then Friedman, prescribed the solution: embrace flexible exchange rates to obviate tariffs. But the Labour leaders' lack of clairvoyance in 1931 should not overshadow the valour of the sacrifices they made—quite knowingly—in their best efforts to preserve international cooperation.

It is truly remarkable to see that the ordoliberals' political home in interwar Britain might well have been among the ranks of the "socialists." It is only by doing the hard work of serious historical investigation, as the authors in this volume have done, that such wholly unexpected connections are uncovered. And this is much more than a mere historical curiosity. It upends our understanding of the relationship between class and ideology, and it reminds us of the crucial role that pivotal, principled actors play at critical junctures. As we ourselves face one crisis after another, there was never a better time for such a heartening lesson—and such laudable examples of public-spirited, globally-minded leadership.

6 Conclusion

As we progress deeper into our current century, the distinctiveness of the interwar period increasingly fades from view. It is tempting to simply cast the first half of the prior century as horrifying and its second half, as hopeful. Certainly, that rendering would not be wrong. But such a simple bifurcation would obscure much of what proved essential on both sides of 1945.

The First World War and its aftermath materially changed the world. But it did not dictate the responses to those changed circumstances. That, instead, depended on the ideas and choices made by the men and women who made "[their] own history" (Marx 1977). The figures considered here were some of those who did so. They were also some of the most dynamic, creative and influential thinkers and doers in their time. Returning to them is vital to understanding both the generally disappointing dynamics of the interwar period and the promising successes in the years after the Second World War.

These figures also teach us in a broader way. They illustrate the richness of human experience, sample the variety of perspectives we can hold, and prove humanity's mettle in even the most challenging of times. But they also leave many questions unanswered, many insights undeveloped and much work incomplete. Let us then follow their example, continue where they left off, and, in Churchill's favourite phrase, "go forward together" (Langworth 2017).

References

Arendt, Hannah. 1958. *The Origins of Totalitarianism*. 2nd ed. New York: World Publishing Company.

Barton, John H., Judith L. Goldstein, Timothy E. Josling, and Richard H. Steinberg. 2006. *The Evolution of the Trade Regime: Politics, Law and Economics of the GATT and WTO*. Princeton and London: Princeton University Press.

Craver, Earlene. 1986. "The Emigration of the Austrian Economists." *History of Political Economy* 18 (1): 1–32.

Dewey, John. 1935. *Liberalism and Social Action*. New York: G. P. Putnam's Sons.

Friedman, Milton. 1953. "The Case for Flexible Exchange Rates." In *Essays in Positive Economics*, 157–203. Chicago: University of Chicago Press.

Hall, Peter A., ed. 1989. *The Political Power of Economic Ideas: Keynesianism across Nations*. Princeton and London: Princeton University Press.

Hayek, Friedrich A. 1943. "A Commodity Reserve Currency." *The Economic Journal* 53 (210/211): 176–84.

———. 1983a. "Interview with Tom Hazlett, November 12, 1978." In *Nobel Prize-Winning Economist: Friedrich A. Von Hayke*. Oral History Program, University of California, Los Angeles.

———. 1983b. *Law, Legislation, and Liberty: Volume I, Rules and Order*. Chicago: University of Chicago Press.

———. 1994. *The Road to Serfdom*. Chicago: University of Chicago Press.

Hirschman, Albert O. 1970. *Exit, Voice, and Loyalty: Responses to Decline in Firms, Organizations, and States*. Cambridge, MA: Harvard University Press.

Keynes, John Maynard. 1919. *The Economic Consequences of the Peace*. In *Collected Writings*. Vol. 2.

———. 1922. "On the Way to Genoa—What Can the Conference Discuss?" In *Collected Writings*. Vol. 17.
———. 1923a. "Suppose the Conference Breaks Down?" In *Collected Writings*. Vol. 18.
———. 1923b. *A Tract on Monetary Reform*. Vol. 4.
———. 1936. *The General Theory of Employment, Interest, and Money*. Vol. 7.
———. 1938. "My Early Beliefs." In *Essays in Biography*, vol. 10, 433–50. London: Macmillan.
Laidler, David. 1999. *Fabricating the Keynesian Revolution: Studies of the Inter-War Literature on Money, the Cycle, and Unemployment*. Cambridge and New York: Cambridge University Press.
Langworth, Richard M. 2017. "How Many Times Did Churchill Say, 'Let Us Go Forward Together'?" The Churchill Project, Hillsdale College. https://winstonchurchill.hillsdale.edu/forward-together/.
Manoilescu, Mihail. 1934. *Le siècle du corporatisme*. Paris: Félix Alcan.
Marx, Karl. 1977. "The Eighteenth Brumaire of Louis Bonaparte." In *Karl Marx: Selected Writings*, edited by David McLellan, 2nd ed. Oxford: Oxford University Press.
Marx, Karl, and Friedrich Engels. 1977. "The Communist Manifesto." In *Karl Marx: Selected Writings*, edited by David McLellan, 2nd ed. Oxford: Oxford University Press.
Orwell, George. 1950. *Nineteen Eighty-Four*. New York: New American Library.
Polanyi, Karl. 1957. *The Great Transformation*. Boston: Beacon Press.
Scalia, Antonin. 1989. "The Rule of Law as a Law of Rules." *The University of Chicago Law Review* 56 (4): 1175–88.
Schmitter, Philippe. 1979. "Still the Century of Corporatism?" In *Trends Towards Corporatist Intermediation: Contemporary Political Sociology*, edited by Philippe Schmitter and Gerhard Lehmbruch, Vol. 1, 17–52. London: Sage.
Shackle, George L. S. 1967. *The Years of High Theory: Invention and Tradition in Economic Thought, 1929–1936*. Cambridge and New York: Cambridge University Press.
Smith, Adam. 1976. *An Inquiry into the Nature and Causes of the Wealth of Nations*. Edited by AS Skinner and RH Campbell. Oxford: Clarendon Press.
Watson, Matthew. 2018. *The Market*. New York: Columbia University Press.
Williamson, Philip. 2003. *National Crisis and National Government: British Politics, the Economy and Empire, 1926–1932*. Cambridge and New York: Cambridge University Press.

Index

© The Editor(s) (if applicable) and The Author(s), under exclusive license to Springer Nature Switzerland AG 2021
A. M. Cunha and C. E. Suprinyak (eds.), *Political Economy and International Order in Interwar Europe*, Palgrave Studies in the History of Economic Thought,
https://doi.org/10.1007/978-3-030-47102-6

FSC
www.fsc.org
MIX
Papier | Fördert gute Waldnutzung
FSC® C083411

Kolibri 360 GmbH
Ferdinand-Jühlke-Straße 7
99095 Erfurt, Deutschland
produktsicherheit@kolibri360.de